Beyond the Terror

Beyond the Terror

Essays in French Regional and Social History, 1794–1815

❖◇❖

Edited by

GWYNNE LEWIS
Reader in History, University of Warwick

COLIN LUCAS
Fellow of Balliol College, Oxford

CAMBRIDGE UNIVERSITY PRESS

Cambridge

London   New York   New Rochelle

Melbourne   Sydney

Published by the Press Syndicate of the University of Cambridge
The Pitt Building, Trumpington Street, Cambridge CB2 1RP
32 East 57th Street, New York, NY 10022, USA
296 Beaconsfield Parade, Middle Park, Melbourne 3206, Australia

First published 1983

Printed in Great Britain by the University Press, Cambridge

Library of Congress catalogue card number: 82-25508

British Library Cataloguing in Publication Data

Beyond the Terror.
1. France—Social conditions
I. Lewis, Gwynne   II. Lucas, Colin
944.05   HN425

ISBN 0 521 25114 1

Essays for
RICHARD COBB

Contents

Preface	page	iv
1 Cobb and the historians MARTYN LYONS		1
2 The reconstruction of a church 1796–1801 OLWEN HUFTON		21
3 Picking up the pieces: the politics and the personnel of social welfare from the Convention to the Consulate COLIN JONES		53
4 Conscription and crime in rural France during the Directory and Consulate ALAN FORREST		92
5 Common rights and agrarian individualism in the southern Massif Central 1750–1880 PETER JONES		121
6 Themes in southern violence after 9 thermidor COLIN LUCAS		152
7 Political brigandage and popular disaffection in the south-east of France 1795–1804 GWYNNE LEWIS		195
8 Rhine and Loire: Napoleonic elites and social order GEOFFREY ELLIS		232
Index		269

Contributors

Geoffrey Ellis
Fellow of Hertford College, Oxford

Alan Forrest
Senior Lecturer, University of Manchester

Olwen Hufton
Professor, University of Reading

Colin Jones
Lecturer, University of Exeter

Peter Jones
Lecturer, University of Birmingham

Gwynne Lewis
Reader, University of Warwick

Colin Lucas
Fellow of Balliol College, Oxford

Martyn Lyons
Senior Lecturer, University of New South Wales

Preface

It is perhaps significant that friends of Richard Cobb should have been anarchical enough to fail to publish these essays on the occasion either of his sixty-fifth birthday (already passed) or of his retirement from the Chair of Modern History at Oxford (still to come). However, it is also appropriate that this publication does not encounter any of the festivals connected with a *festschrift*. This is not a *festschrift* in the ordinary practice of that institution. There hangs about such publications a suspicious odour of the *notice nécro-logique* with its pious sanctification. Richard Cobb is a busy and productive historian to whose scholarly activity and influence the passing of birthdays and the occupancy of a professorial chair are irrelevant. These essays do not seek formally to celebrate a career, or to perfume the passage of time. Rather they are an attempt to make a coherent and significant contribution to the understanding of a period of French revolutionary history.

One of the most important conclusions to be drawn from this collection of essays is the importance of the Thermidorean and Directorial period, still, despite much valuable recent research, a relatively under-developed region of French Revolutionary studies. It has long been established that it was during this period that the foundations were laid for some of the policies – in education and monetary reform for example – which were to be pursued more vigorously under Napoleon. Not so much emphasis has been placed on the importance of popular resistance during the later 1790s against those policies initiated by the revolutionary bourgeoisie long before 1794: the Civil Constitution of the Clergy, the war with Europe, a more individualist economic programme. For it was only after 1794 that the wealthy elite (that social alloy refined in the crucible of the Terror) began to articulate a much more positive and self-confident philosophy of individualism. During the Directory, the holy revolutionary trinity of *liberté*, *égalité*, *fraternité* would continue to be worshipped, but the greatest of these three was henceforth to be *liberté*. Almost every contribution in this collection posits, with differing degrees of emphasis, the existence of a 'Thermidorean Reaction', leading, in certain regions, to widespread popular resistance. The objective of this resistance was not so much the fear of a revived jacobinism (although many a *représentant en mission* in the south-east of France was anxious to load the responsibility for the failures of the Revolution onto the backs of the village Robespierres), but the impact of the state, in its military, religious and economic guise, upon the lives of ordinary French men and women. The year 1795 may well have represented the 'year of the loss of illusions', but it was to be the loss of illusions with far more than jacobinism: it marked the increasing hostility of those who had hoped for so much but who had gained so little from the Revolution since 1789.

It is hardly surprising that the impact of the state should have been resisted most fiercely in the regions of the west and the south-east of France where separatism and 'localism' – a second major theme of this collection – were founded upon differences of geography and culture, as well as centuries of opposition to central authority. Unlike those regimes which immediately preceded and followed it, the Directory was determined to 'roll back the frontiers of state interference' by allowing each department, indeed, each individual, to interpret the significance of the changes wrought by revolution and war in whatever way he or she deemed appropriate, so long, of course, as the necessary tribute to the state in the form of money and men was forth-coming. The ambitious, embryonic programme for a 'welfare state' was to be abandoned after Thermidor enabling future social policy to be conducted within a local framework: 'philanthropy had its virtues, but not the least of them was making the world safe for entrepreneurs'. Antagonism towards the gendarmerie saddled with the unenviable task of entering hostile villages to round up young men for the army was not always motivated by hatred of conscription; it could also reflect the determination of villagers to defend local practices, like the illegal exploitation of forests, from the prying eyes of policemen and soldiers. Constitutional priests were frequently dismissed as 'les intrus'. Even the bloodshed and violence which characterised so much of the resistance to the Revolution in the south-east frequently operated accord-ing to traditional rules and hierarchical values and could therefore be inter-preted as part of a more general reassertion of localism. In a wider context, although Roman law theoretically governed property relations in many parts of the south of France, in practice, 'jurisprudence yielded to usage and usage to social and ecological environment'. Once again, local communities tended to shape their own destinies, rough-hew them as the Romans and the Revolution might.

Finally, this collection of essays stresses the 'popular' nature of the resist-ance to the Revolution. It was, after all, the poorer members of society who had been most adversely affected by the social and economic consequences of revolution and war. No doubt, for those *propriétaires* wealthy enough to exploit the abolition of feudal dues and the *dîme*, for those *laboureurs* or *ménagers* who had enough hard currency in their stockings to purchase *biens nationaux*, the Revolution brought substantial benefits. The lists of *notables* and of the 600 *plus imposés* under the Consulate and the Empire testified to the victorious emergence of post-revolutionary local elites firmly rooted in landownership. But these were the minority; for the majority, the victory of the few meant increasing antagonisms and jealousies within the local community and the alienation of many of the poorer peasantry from the Revolutionary land settlement, *particularly* after 1795 when a far more determined effort was made to deny such peasants free access to the fields and the forests. We need many more detailed studies on the evolution of peasant societies between 1794 and the end of the Napoleonic period. However, it is fairly clear that the scale of popular resistance in the west and the south-east was not unrelated to the economic policies pursued by the government after 1794. It is also clear that popular resistance to the Revolution was not a male preserve under the Directory. The rejection of the religious settlement of the Revolution was largely the work of women, of 'les femmes crapuleuses et séditieuses' whose devotion to 'les bons prêtres' laid the basis for the spread of a more popular form of catholicism during the late 1790s. Again, in order to evaluate the true significance of forms of popular protest under the Directory, it would be useful to study, comparatively, the resistance to Napoleon towards the end of the Empire, together with the nature of the White Terror of 1815.

This collection is focused on the period of the Revolution to which Richard Cobb's own interest has increasingly moved since the publication of *Les Armées révolutionnaires*. The contributors are scholars who either are or who have been actively engaged in research into that particular period. They dedicate the collection to Richard Cobb as an expression of affection and as an acknowledgement of the influence that he has had at some point in their development as historians. However, the collection also shows how diverse are the interests, approaches and perceptions of those who have been influenced by him. No one should read this collection as somehow the homage of a school to its master, the burning of candles in some historical chapel. As Martyn Lyons' introduction demonstrates, there is a strong Cobb influence but there can be no Cobb school. These are essays by friends of Richard Cobb. Not all the contributors were his pupils; not all his pupils are contributors; and certainly the contributors do not constitute all his friends. The composition of the group of authors is entirely determined by the desire to produce a volume that makes coherent sense as a piece of history-writing about the French Revolution. We hope that this itself is the best illustration of what the historiography of the Revolution owes to Richard Cobb.

G.L.
C.L.

I

$\diamond$

Cobb and the historians

MARTYN LYONS

'Mr Cobb's real subject is anarchy.'
(Norman Hampson, *English Historical Review*, 80 (1965), 363)

Present-day scholars who approach the history of France, and especially the history of the French Revolution, must negotiate three main ideological currents: first, the Anglo-Saxon tradition of empiricism, of which Richard Cobb provides an eccentric example; secondly, the French Marxist tradition of historiography; and thirdly, the influence (some would now say the imperialistic influence) of the *Annales* school. This triangular definition of the forces in play is, of course, a crude one, which shelters many exceptions. Anglo-Saxon Marxist historians do exist, but George Rudé seems in this respect a lonely example of a very rare species, occasionally sighted by careful readers of *History Workshop* or *Social History*. French historians are not necessarily Marxists or Annalists: Professor Jacques Godechot of Toulouse is one who has successfully managed to dodge the cross-fire. When, however, the student surveys the historiography of the French Revolution to consider general interpretations and approaches to research, these three influences appear to dominate the field.

Most British historians of the Revolution would be horrified to be told that they belonged to a school of thought. This might suggest to them that their individuality had been infringed, their personal integrity somehow compromised, their intellectual privacy violated. In recognition of these prickly susceptibilities, I refer not to an English or an Anglo-Saxon school, but to an Anglo-Saxon tradition. It is a tradition which envisages historical writing as a literary pursuit, and which abhors theoretical discussions and analytical systems. In one reviewer's phrase, it has exhibited the 'native passion for unadulterated facts'.[1] It has specialised in dismantling hypotheses and criticising general interpretations. Professor Alfred Cobban turned this

---

[1] J. Harris in *Social History*, 5, no. 3 (1980), 487.

'revisionist' technique against the Marxist school in his short and controver-
sial book that is well-remembered in France for its polemic against the theory
of the bourgeois nature of the French Revolution.[2] The Cobban tradition is
currently being regenerated by William Doyle, who approaches the history
of the Revolution from the traditional and conservative perspective of the
Parlement of Bordeaux.[3]

Theodore Zeldin's recent history of modern France belongs, despite some
appearances, to the same tradition.[4] For all its innovative attempts at a history
of social psychology, it remains a rather disconnected mass of detail and
insights, challenging accepted views, sometimes arranging material in an
exciting way, but declining to offer a general synthesis or argument to give
coherence to the 2,000-page text. It is a long, invertebrate sort of animal, and
the publishers have had little difficulty in cutting it into segments to form
separate volumes under the alluring general title of the *Histoire des passions
françaises*.[5]

The French Marxist school, by contrast, has a greater unity and a more
readily recognisable historiographical tradition. Closely associated with the
Société des études robespierristes, and its journal, the *Annales historiques de la
Révolution française*, French Marxist historians of the Revolution recognise
Georges Lefebvre and Albert Mathiez as their intellectual ancestors. The
Marxist tradition, however, goes back further, to Jean Jaurès and his pioneering attempt to write the first socialist history of the French Revolution.[6] The
works of Jaurès and Mathiez, of Soboul and Rudé illustrate the fertility and
vigour of the Marxist inspiration, which has produced a greater awareness
of the historical importance of social class, and profitably explored the nature
of popular radicalism in the French Revolution.[7] Yet the Marxist school is
accused of narrow sectarianism, of intellectual rigidity, of a lack of imagination, and a disheartening tendency to repeat worn-out slogans – in short,
the entire critical arsenal used against the 'old left' by hostile caricaturists
since at least 1968.

The Annalists are not chiefly interested either in dissolving theoretical
constraints, or in examining the social bases of revolutionary political
struggles. They are more concerned with 'la longue durée', with the under-
lying social and mental structures of French society before and after the
Revolution. The Annalists have exploited the enormous gap in socio-

[2] *The Social Interpretation of the French Revolution* (Cambridge, 1964).
[3] Notably in 'Was there an aristocratic reaction in pre-revolutionary France?', *Past and Present*,
57 (1972), 97–122; and *Origins of the French Revolution* (Oxford, 1980).
[4] *France, 1848–1945* (2 vols., Oxford, 1973–7).
[5] Published in 5 vols. by Recherches (1978–9), and subsequently by Seuil (1980), under this title.
[6] J. Jaurès, *Histoire socialiste de la Révolution française* (8 vols., Paris, 1922–4).
[7] E.g. A. Mathiez, *La vie chère et le mouvement social sous la Terreur* (Paris, 1927); A. Soboul,
Les sans-culottes parisiens en l'An II (Paris, 1959); G. Rudé, *The Crowd in the French Revolution*
Oxford, 1959).

cultural history left by the more politically orientated Marxists. They have preferred the history of crime and poverty, the history of education and literacy, of birth control and abandoned children, to the more traditional concerns, like the policies of the Girondins or the strategies of Robespierre. Studying social and cultural change over a long period, however, has tended to undermine the political significance of the revolutionary events themselves, and historians like François Furet have repeatedly fallen foul of Marxist critics for underplaying the historical significance of jacobinism.

The three currents outlined above have innumerable points of contact. Furet's attacks on the Marxist 'catechism' distantly echo Cobban's anti-Marxist approach.[8] The triangular situation has produced some strange alliances and some blistering polemic. The Marxist spokesman Claude Mazauric accused Furet of being unpatriotic and anti-French in his interpretation of the Revolution.[9] Olwen Hufton found Cobb's *Police and the People* was a manifesto against the quantifiers and systematisers, 'those who would squeeze men into the restricting corset of sociological categories, would prod them into a convenient group philosophy, would pinch them when they forgot to act out their ineluctable social role of opposition to the bourgeoisie and would minimize their brutality in order to make them more intrinsically worthy to inherit the earth, their political destiny'.[10] If Richard Cobb's personal contribution to the history of France is to be assessed objectively, he must be placed not only in the context of this short-sighted rhetoric, but also in relation to the main trends in the historiography of France already outlined. Cobb's history remains unique – inspiring, exhilarating and infuriating all at once – but his main concerns do have something in common with Marxists, Annalists and Cobbanites. What follows is an attempt to define this uniqueness, and to situate Cobb in relation to the work of past and present professional historians at a time when he has acquired a wide general readership, when he is eulogised as the Breughel or the Goya of the historical profession,[11] and when every Cobb publication seems to acquire the status of a literary event. This is a disconcerting development, for it is occurring just as these publications are becoming slimmer and slimmer, and the proportion of footnotes within them correspondingly larger. How does he do it? Loved by publishers, praised by the lay public, where does Cobb stand with the historians?

Cobb would probably deny that he offers any significant innovations in historical methodology. He is, on the contrary, suspicious of all methodologies, inclined to denounce historians who attempt a 'scientific' analysis of

---

[8] F. Furet, 'Le catéchisme révolutionnaire', *Annales E.S.C.* (1971).
[9] C. Mazauric, *Sur la Révolution française* (Paris, 1970), p. 60.
[10] Review in *English Historical Review*, 86 (1971), 802–4.
[11] Breughel according to Hufton, ibid.; (10), Goya according to Gwyn Williams; and see *Times Higher Education Supplement* (1.8.80), 7.

general historical problems, the quantifiers, the social scientists, anyone who dares to propose 'models' instead of 'suggesting hypotheses' in the traditional phraseology. General problems do not concern Cobb; he has never and will never participate in the grand debate on The Causes of the French Revolution. 'For myself,' he has written, 'history has never been an intellectual debate.'[12] In Cobb's historical anti-method, what matters is the individual, and he or she is best understood, not by graphs and models, but through historical imagination and intuition.

In a sense, Cobb has something in common with the late Professor Cobban. Intentionally or not, both helped to undermine existing orthodoxies, challenge previous assumptions, to confound simple explanations and blur easy distinctions. In *The Police and the People*, Cobb provided a picture of the *sans-culotte* movement, including its attitudes to violence and to the crucial problem of food shortages.[13] In contrast to the more schematic social analysis of popular movements of Rudé and Soboul, Cobb's version gives us well-rounded historical personages, placed precisely in an authentic setting. Cobb's writings on the *sans-culotterie* do not lead to any abstract, generalised conclusions; but they beat with the authentic rhythm of popular life. The *sans-culotte* movement is portrayed as a frail and above all fragmented phenomenon. Soboul's overall scheme is dissolved by Cobb's profusion of detail and the geographical complexities he gives to *sans-culotte* militancy. Seeking a synthesis, Cobb felt, would produce bad history: 'my subject is chaotic, and I may well have written about it chaotically'.[14]

It is more rewarding, then, for Cobb to explore variety rather than to establish patterns, and to emphasise accidental factors rather than to expose the determinism of structures (in the *Annales* fashion). Chaos is more interesting than order, even if it is less digestible. But Cobb's claim to work in an 'impressionistic', or 'pointillistic' way should deceive no one. Cobb's *sans-culotte* is the product of a powerful historical imagination; he is nevertheless the outcome of very close and precise observation of the details of his private life, his social habits, the rhythm of his work and leisure. Detailed information on the regular itineraries and daily routine of the urban poor is not just provided by guesswork; it is plundered from the records of policemen, judges and administrators in the rich archival resources of provincial France. Fundamentally this is what distinguishes Cobb from Cobban and what constitutes his greatest contribution to the study of French history today. For what Cobb writes is based on a wealth of documentary erudition. This is why French scholars may vilify Cobban *ad nauseam*, and yet retain a profound respect for Cobb's early books, for his knowledge of the French archives of the revolutionary period is without parallel. Furthermore, if

[12] *A Second Identity: Essays on France and French History* (London, 1969), p. 17.
[13] *The Police and the People: French Popular Protest, 1789–1820* (Oxford, 1970).
[14] Ibid., p. xvii.

English-speaking historians are now to be encountered in the archives not only of Bordeaux, Lyon, Toulouse and Marseille, but also in St Flour and Vannes, Privas and Epinal, this is in no small way attributable to the lasting influence of Cobb on the study of French history. Cobb's anti-method may claim to be impressionistic, but paradoxically it is based on exhaustive research.

If one searches in Cobb's work for a positive contribution to historical method, one must first cross the barrier imposed by his insistent denial of systems, models, and World-Views (I borrow the derisive capital letters often used by Cobb). Once one has passed this rhetorical minefield, one begins to discern a distinctively Cobbian technique, an approach to historical investigation which almost amounts to a method and, beyond that, something which the barrage of abuse has camouflaged in vain: a very personal philosophy of history.

Cobb, for example, has shown how to extract the most from the rich resources of police records, used as a source for the history of popular protest. The first section of *The Police and the People* is devoted to a discussion of a methodological problem – how to interpret police evidence.[15] The historian must beware of police informers who have a vested professional interest in inventing conspiracies, with a multitude of suspects and infinite ramifications. This was especially true in the Terror of prison stooges, who bartered information in return for their release (or so they hoped). Yet the police provide a privileged historical source. Just as Inspector Maigret could penetrate and predict the assumptions and ambitions of the Parisian *petite bourgeoisie*, so the police of eighteenth-century France had a close acquaintance with the popular milieu in which they worked. They knew in detail the social topography of their 'beat', they knew the local meeting-place and who they were likely to find there, they knew which categories of workers were most likely to commit what crimes, and they were immediately suspicious if their routine surroundings were disturbed by some one or some thing new. The police, of course, had certain deep-rooted prejudices or convictions: that river-workers were habitually violent, for instance, or that anyone in a nomadic occupation, from bargee to *colporteur*, was always a prime suspect. Time and time again, they would repeat the order of the policeman at the end of the film *Casablanca*: 'round up all the usual suspects'. The police were creatures of habit, but Cobb has used their dossiers to great effect as a source for the social history of the urban poor.

Simenon's Inspector Maigret is an example to which Cobb often refers to illustrate the possibilities which the police offer a social historian. Simenon describes Cobb's Paris, the Paris of the 1930s and 1940s, before La Défense and the Autoroute du Nord, the Tour Montparnasse and the gentrification

---

[15] Ibid., pt I, 'The sources of French popular history and their interpretation'.

of the Marais. He describes a social stratum of ordinary people with whom Cobb is also familiar. Maigret's world is principally a *petit bourgeois* world of *petits patrons*, concierges, widows, salesmen, office workers and garage mechanics, a world of people like the artisan-jeweller Célérin, making elegant brooches in his little workshop high up in the Rue de Sévigné, a *sans-culotte* surviving into the 1970s.[16] Simenon, like Cobb, is a close observer of the social habits of these characters. Called to the scene of the crime, Maigret instinctively tries to assemble a mental picture of the surroundings and acquaintances of the victim. Cobb attempted a similar exercise, for Parisian suicides in the 1790s, in *Death in Paris*.[17] When Maigret, however, is summoned to the Hotel Georges V, he feels like a fish out of water amongst Italian countesses and English playboys. He is uneasy because he cannot apply his instinctive knowledge of his own familiar universe.[18] So Cobb too prefers to leave to other historians the analysis of the mentality of Louis XVI's court, or the nobility of the Bourbon Restoration, for this is not his 'beat'. Maigret, like the eighteenth-century police, was an observer of the predictable, 'a historian', as Cobb called him, 'of the déjà vu'.[19]

Simenon's books are perhaps not quite as reassuring as Cobb would have them be. His stories expose the personal secrets behind the façade of normality, respectability, the steady job and the apparently happy marriage. Behind reassuring appearances are individuals liable to commit violent acts; suicide, blackmail and even murder, in the defence of wounded pride, family ambition, revenge or out of sexual jealousy. The predictable social round is sometimes a hypocritical pretence to hide some very nasty domestic skeletons. As a result, Simenon's books often leave a bitter and depressing after-taste, which seems quite alien to Cobb's effervescent optimism.

Two further elements of Cobb's approach must be discussed as distinctive features of his historiographical contribution. One is his use of the individual case-history; the other his sense of place and his insistence on the importance of the physical environment. The popular movements discussed by Cobb are firmly rooted in, and indeed conditioned by, their particular geographical surroundings. In *Reactions to the French Revolution*, for instance, Cobb evokes the townscape of revolutionary Lyon, with its many bridges for dumping corpses, its suburbs for hiding fugitives, and the underground cellars and ruins which protected clandestine bands of criminals and counter-revolutionary assassins.[20] Cobb is not alone in paying so much attention to the physical environment. In France, history and geography were for long considered closely allied disciplines, and the philosophy of the *Annales* school attributed

---

[16] G. Simenon, *Les Innocents* (Paris, 1972).   [17] *Death in Paris, 1795–1801* (Oxford, 1978).
[18] G. Simenon, *Maigret voyage* (Paris, 1958) and, e.g., *Maigret et l'affaire Nahour* (Paris, 1967).
[19] See 'Maigret's Paris' in *Tour de France* (London, 1976), p. 182.
[20] *Reactions to the French Revolution*, 'Counter-revolution and environment: the example of Lyon' (London, 1972).

great importance to placing societies in their geographical context. But Cobb's approach to place is not that of a Le Roy Ladurie, whose *Paysans de Languedoc* included a chapter on the history of its vegetation;[21] neither is it that of traditional French local studies, often introduced by massively detailed surveys of the pattern of landownership and population distribution.[22] For Cobb is not just situating the action in a certain socio-economic context; for him the place and its intimate geography are 'the ingredients of a collective mentality'.[23] The high buildings of Lyon overshadowed streets which were deep, dark and sinister-looking. The whole personality of the city was sinister and secretive. The steep hillside created a different *quartier* at every level, cut off from its neighbours by the gradient. It was thus a city penetrated only with difficulty by the outsider, in which individual districts and suburbs had a remarkably self-sufficient and closed character. Cobb is not just describing a place – he is illustrating a violent, secretive and xenophobic local mentality.

Cobb's emphasis on 'the sense of place' is therefore an element both in his analysis of popular attitudes and in his contribution to French provincial history. Cobb's insistence on the geographical fragmentation of the *sans-culotte* movement has already been mentioned. In fact, all national political movements, when examined by Cobb, tend to dissolve into inter-village rivalries, longstanding feuds at the level of province, town or suburb, or at the level of individual personalities. It is precisely on this world of small towns and villages that he concentrates. 'My history,' Cobb has written, 'is not French history, but French provincial history: Lyonnais history, Norman history, Lille history, Paris history.'[24] *Les armées révolutionnaires* teems with examples of small-town jealousies and prejudices.[25] The *armées* are described as instruments of provincial terror, sent on punitive forays to assure both the food supplies and political dominance of the local urban *sans-culottes*.[26] In the hands of unscrupulous local militants, they are used, too, to settle old scores against ancient enemies. For a few months, the *armées révolutionnaires* enjoyed almost unlimited powers, requisitioning supplies and carrying out political repression in their own local spheres. They were part of that revolutionary anarchy which is Cobb's perennial theme, and which he describes so anarchically.

One of Cobb's main contributions, then, is to have municipalised the history of the Revolution. French provincial historians generally prefer, as their frame of reference, an economic region, a department or an old regime province. Cobb's influence has been rather towards studies of cities such as

---

[21] E. Le Roy Ladurie, *Les paysans de Languedoc*, 'La civilisation végétale' (2 vols., Paris, 1966).

[22] One recent example is G. Frêche, *Toulouse et la région Midi-Pyrénées au siècle des lumières, vers 1670–1789* (Paris, 1974).

[23] *Reactions*, p. 56.

[24] *Second Identity*, p. 50.

[25] *Les armées révolutionnaires* (2 vols., Paris, 1961–3).

[26] Ibid., esp. vol. 2.

Bordeaux, Marseille, Lyon, Toulouse. His emphasis on place has usually meant concentration on an exclusively urban environment. The particularities of terrorism are discussed town by town in the *Armées révolutionnaires*: Bordeaux terrorism reflects the cosmopolitain, commercial population of a great sea-port, while in a garrison town like Lille, soldiers make a large contribution to terrorist militancy.[27] In an article typically entitled 'Quelques conséquences sociales de la Révolution dans un milieu urbain', the response of Lille artisans to the upheaval of the urban economy is analysed. Jewellers, and other artisans in luxury trades, sought refuge in the military administration, as did shoemakers and metal-workers, whose leather and iron was requisitioned by the army. *Petits commerçants* threatened by the effects of war (closure of traditional markets, shortage of raw materials, conscription of the labour force) looked to revolutionary institutions to provide an alternative source of livelihood. What counts for Cobb, here as elsewhere, is urban society and the urban landscape. The historian must learn to appreciate, then, the individual character of each town. 'A great deal of Paris eighteenth-century, of Lyon nineteenth-century, history,' wrote Cobb, 'can be walked, seen, and above all heard, in small restaurants ,on the platform at the back of a bus, in cafés, or on the park bench.'[28]

This municipalisation of French history is justified in a society like eighteenth-century France, where a substantial proportion of the population lived in small agglomerations. The Revolution was largely inspired by small-town lawyers and officials, whose traditional universe was no bigger than Robespierre's native town of Arras. The political structure of the Revolutionary Government in the Year II strengthened the administration of the large towns, or at least of the districts, at the expense of the more conservative or federalist-inclined departmental administrations. In addition, the whole problem of food supplies and shortages compels study at this local level. The vexed *problème des subsistences* was essentially one of communal egoism, with towns competing with each other and with the demands of the army for precious grain supplies. From all these points of view, the municipal perspective is a correct one.

But what about the peasantry? The countryside rarely appears in Cobb's history, except as either a stamping-ground for bandits, or else through the antagonistic eyes of the hungry urban *sans-culotterie*. Cobb once lamented that historians in general had been slow to follow the lead of Georges Lefebvre in studying peasant history. Only recently have the Marxists taken up the history of the peasantry once again,[29] while, in a series of articles, Peter Jones has adopted a Cobb-inspired approach in studying the villages of the

---

[27] Ibid., pp. 334–58.   [28] *Second Identity*, pp. 19–20.
[29] A. Soboul, *Problèmes paysans de la Révolution, 1789–1848* (Paris, 1976); F. Gauthier, 'Sur les problèmes paysans de la Révolution', *Annales historiques de la Révolution française*, 232 (1978), 305–14.

Massif Central.[30] In Cobb's own preoccupations, however, the peasant seems principally an object of prejudice and contempt in the mental universe of the urban classes. In *Les armées révolutionnaires*, the countryside is a hostile and suspicious world, in which the *sans-culotte* militia feels isolated and afraid. Its reaction (a mixture of hatred, panic and exasperation) is to shock the unco-operative peasant as brutally as possible. Hence the smashing of holy relics, the abusive mimicry of religious rituals, the blasphemy and iconoclasm, with which the impotent urban *sans-culottes* deliberately offended the peasantry's religious susceptibilities.

An even better example of the town/country conflict in Cobb may be found in *Paris and its Provinces*, a book foreshadowed, like so many of the others, by an earlier article in *Terreur et subsistances*.[31] Cobb's subject here is 'the geography of mistrust', the mutual hatred and suspicion which poisoned relations between Parisians and the inhabitants of the out-lying villages. Mistrust is an understatement, for Cobb analyses something stronger which he calls 'a permanent form of a *grande peur*', the Parisians' traditional and visceral fear of the surrounding communes, where enemies lurked, and innocent weekenders might be shot for infringing the country code. The surroundings of Paris, however, are seen chiefly through the eyes of govern-ment spies and the jacobin club of Belleville. From this perspective, Villejuif and Vaugirard, Gentilly, Fontenay-aux-Roses and Carrières-sous-Charenton formed a hostile jungle, inhabited by sullen, inbred and isolated communities, which were quick to identify outsiders from the capital. It is suggested that the attitudes of the Paris Commune of 1871 to the army of the Versaillais, as well as the political crisis of ventôse–germinal Year II, may be seen in the light of this recurrent fear of the dark, tribal lands on the periphery of Paris.

The sense of place is then strongest in an urban environment. With Cobb, one is tempted to go further. If one is to define Cobb's own 'territory of the historian',[32] it must be not just the French provincial town, but the *quartier*. It is at the micro-level of the street or neighbourhood that Cobb's gifts find their fullest expression. In *The Streets of Paris*, Cobb patrolled popular Paris on foot, like a modern-day Restif de la Bretonne, peering into courtyards and examining graffiti.[33] Unlike Restif, however, he was accompanied by a

---

[30] P. Jones, 'The rural bourgeoisie of the southern Massif Central: a contribution to the study of the social structure of *ancien régime* France', *Social History*, 4 (1979), 65–83; '*La République au village* in the southern Massif Central, 1789–1799', *Historical Journal*, 23 (1980), 793–812; and also 'Political commitment and rural society in the southern Massif Central', *European Studies Review*, 10 (1980), 337–56.

[31] *Paris and its Provinces, 1792–1802* (London, 1975), esp. ch. 4; *Terreur et subsistance* (Paris, 1965) 'Le complot militaire de ventôse an II'.

[32] The title of a collection of essays by E. Le Roy Ladurie, *Le territoire de l'historien* (2 vols., Paris 1973–8).

[33] *The Streets of Paris*, with photographs by Nicholas Breach (London, 1980).

perceptive photographer. In spite of its title, the book was a photographic study not of the whole capital, but of a few *quartiers* including, notably one in Belleville (20^e *arrondissement*), and another near the canal Saint Martin (10^e) Cobb was hunting for the remains of a nineteenth-century world of small workshops and *boutiques*, the traditional urban 'village', unspoilt by pizzeria, antique shops, expensive restaurants and, his constant *bête noire*, the fashionable intellectual. He and his companion were trying to record the intimate scale of the Parisian neighbourhood.

For Cobb, the successful French historian must mark out his own *quartier*, as a social, economic and political unity. Parisian sectional politics in the Revolution were managed at the level of the *quartier*, and through them, the local *juge de paix* and the occasional unneighbourly denunciation, one can reconstruct French social life at street level. If the historian knows who lives where, who is employed in which workshop, if he can penetrate the networks of kinship, professional ties and local loyalties, then he is better able to understand and predict social behaviour and political commitment. In Cobb's view, the successful historian of France must establish his *quartier*, know its *habitués*, discover its secret itineraries, and he must himself become a familiar figure in the landscape, if only as M. l'Anglais, Le Gallois (I will answer these days to L'Australien). In theory, it takes a knowledge of colloquial French, a friendly disposition and regular drinking habits. A bonus qualification would be an ability to handle avaricious, inquisitive and racialist concierges, from whom so much local information can be gleaned, as it no doubt was by the ancien regime police.

After the sense of place, the most striking aspect of Cobb's historical approach is the use of individual case-histories. Whereas George Rudé is concerned to elucidate the general characteristics of the revolutionary crowd, Cobb tries to atomise the crowd into a host of individual faces, with private biographies, which illuminate the history of the Revolution from unexpected angles.[34] In *Les armées révolutionnaires*, this approach is used to give us the details of the careers of leading and second-rank *sans-culotte* militants, like Ronsin, Momoro and Grammont.[35] Officers of the *armées*, according to Cobb, were typically sons of artisans, who had enrolled in a military career at the time of the Seven Years' War, bought themselves out in the 1780s, arrived in Paris as clerks or *petits commerçants*, and joined the National Guard before enlisting in the *armée révolutionnaire* of the capital. They were mature married men who, by 1793, had already participated in several revolutionary *journées*. The sources of their political commitment lay not only in class hatred or attachment to radical ideologies, but also in a wide range of different, and very personal, motives. They were after 'le bon temps', 'le pillage gastronomique', good wages and farm girls, or else the uniform

[34] Rudé, *The Crowd*.
[35] *Armées révolutionnaires*, vol. 1, 'L'Armée parisienne'.

simply flattered their vanity.[36] This approach makes it very difficult to generalise about the *sans-culotte* movement which, as we have seen, Cobb has already splintered into a myriad different geographical units. The *sans-culotterie* instead appears as

a mere *agglomérat* of negative attitudes and prejudices, of crude fears, of collective antipathies, of shared and accepted patterns of violence, and of violent solutions, of a range of personalities extending from the semi-literate Breton market porter or Aveyronnais water-carrier, to the sophisticated but embittered *clerc de procureur*, the self-satisfied, domineering building contractor, the successful grocer, and the much respected, wise doctor . . .[37]

The *sans-culotterie* is made to come alive but, at the same time, it loses its coherence.

In *Les armées révolutionnaires*, Cobb's personal biographies were constructive because they concerned men who played an important political role in the Revolution, and because he attempted to give a picture of the typical militant. In later works, he has turned to much more marginal personalities, abandoned attempts to describe general or typical characteristics, and indulged his taste for the bizarre and anarchic characters of the period. This tendency was quite clear in *Reactions to the French Revolution*, although this book did contain perhaps the finest example of Cobb's use of the individual case-history, in his account (based on a book review) of the obscure militant Guénot.[38]

The personal biography of Guénot begins on the river Yonne, where he worked in the very dangerous log-rolling trade in the violent company of the *flotteurs de bois*, who brought timber down-river to Paris. So far, Guénot can illustrate two general points. First, he was engaged in a trade which involved frequent contact with Paris, and this may have been an important factor in his radicalisation. Secondly, his resentment against his employers, the rich timber-merchants of the Yonne, may allow us to place his militancy against the background of a kind of class conflict. Cobb noted this, but he found Guénot interesting largely for other reasons: his tendency to violence, and the wild, desperate consequences of his revolutionary involvement. Guénot stayed in Paris, enlisted in the Gardes Françaises, where he was noted for bouts of insolence and brawling which often landed him in prison. He was employed by the police in the district of the Palais-Royal, where he mixed with an underworld of prostitutes, gamblers and counterfeiters. He was eventually employed by the Committee of General Security, which entrusted him with the arrest of the poet André Chénier, and several large timber-merchants (thus he was able to settle accounts with his old masters

36 Ibid., pp. 181–2, 194.
37 *Reactions*, p. 117.
38 Ibid., ch. 3, 'The biographical approach and the personal case history'.

and exploiters). He somehow survived the Thermidorean period but, in the Consulate, he was sent back to his home department, where he suffered the vengeful persecutions of his local acquaintances. Hounded by a vindictive local community, Guénot took to the woods where for years he lived like a hermit, finding whatever sustenance he could in the forests, which had once provided him with a very different sort of livelihood. Guénot, for Cobb, illustrates the whole history of the Revolution, not because he exemplifies a class conflict inherent in the emergence of the *sans-culotterie*, but because he used the Revolution to satisfy personal grudges, and because of the way in which his local community turned against him afterwards, evoking 'the everlasting memories of rural vengeance'.[39] 'Guénot', for Cobb, 'was the product of a society, of a place and of a trade.' Above all, his career was one in which private resentments merged indistinguishably with public policy.

Cobb's chapter on Guénot provides perhaps the most vivid justification for the individual biographical approach when handled by a historian of sensitivity and imagination. There are times, however, when the justification is not so obvious. *Death in Paris*, for instance, was a rather slight and indulgent book, which attracted a general consensus of applause. One critic, at any rate, was sober enough to find it 'overpraised'.[40] In it, Cobb attempts a post-mortem reconstruction of private lives from personal debris and minutiae. Cobb reassembles the evidence of violent death recorded in the Basse-Geôle of Paris under the Directory. The aim is to reconstruct the individual lives of the desperate Parisian poor from their corpses, bruised, deformed, or bandaged, from their few possessions, tattered clothes and the brief recollections of acquaintances. The result is a brilliant piece of historical detective work, leading apparently nowhere. The dangers of Cobb's very personal approach seem to be clearly exposed: the love of detail for its own sake, the deliberate refusal to place material in a general historical context and the tendency to reduce history to a string of anecdotes, whose significance escapes most readers.

Cobb has turned to a study of those obscure and often untraceable characters who lived on the margins of French society, just as they have lived in the margins of historical writing to date. The criminals, beggars, prostitutes and the insane are now brought onto the centre of the page, as it were, not so much to explore the workings of society as a whole, but because their private odysseys are regarded as valuable in their own right. With *Death in Paris*, this is carried to an extreme where few could, or would want to, follow. For Cobb has ceased to be a historian of the French Revolution. He has become, instead, a chronicler of the lives of the poor, who happened to be alive at the time of the Revolution. One chapter of *Reactions to the French Revolution* is

[39] Ibid., p. 91.
[40] *Death in Paris*, reviewed in *Social History*, 5 (1980), 449.

unequivocally entitled 'The irrelevance of the Revolution', echoing, although exceedingly distantly, Cobban's 'The myth of the French Revolution'.[41]

Cobb is attempting to establish the private calendars of the Parisian poor, and to show that their rhythms and landmarks in no way obeyed the calendar of the Revolution or of its political events. It is a calendar in which dates like 14 July 1789 have no importance, for the Revolution brought little fundamental change in the routine lives and preoccupations of all those silent individuals 'on the fringes' of society. Their lives, rather, were punctuated by festivals and religious holidays, by births, deaths and marriages, by rentdays, harvests and famines. They moved to a rhythm whose beat can be heard from time immemorial, with a continuity which Cobb finds reassuring. In *Death in Paris*, for example, he establishes a calendar of suicide, 'the Saturday night fall downstairs or over the bannisters, the Sunday-morning suicide favoured by girls; the Monday-morning suicide favoured by young men; the mid-week or any day suicide of the very old with time on their hands'.[42] Cobb's subjects die, as they have lived, according to habitual practices, and unmoved by the turmoil of public affairs.

Cobb's anti-method, anarchic though it seems, does imply a certain philosophy of history and of life. It cannot be associated with any political stance, beyond a very vague anarchic individualism. His subject, it has been suggested, is anarchy – the anarchy of the Terror, the anarchy of the counter-Terror – and he is eternally hostile to all those who exercise power. Amongst these enemies, the prime villains are Robespierre, the soulless puritan, and Napoleon's faceless bureaucrats. 'Napoleon, mon cul' (Napoleon my arse): at the conclusion of his Zaharoff lecture, Cobb endorsed this abusive comment by Queneau's *Zazie dans le métro*.[43] What matters in history is the individual, for the justification of history for Cobb 'is the exploration of the wealth and variety of human motivations, the myriad variations of individual lives, which will, I hope always defy the monolithism of parties and doctrines, the blind disciplines of collective fanaticisms, the orthodoxies of fashion, by emphasising the apartness and integrity of the individual',[44] just as he spectacularly emphasises his own apartness.

For individuals are reassuring, and he rejoices in those cases of individual survival, of the regularity of family and private life, which resist interruption by impersonal historical forces, and dramatic eruptions like the French Revolution. Cobb experienced at first hand a particularly violent period in French history – the 1930s and the immediate post-war years – and he writes

---

[41] A. Cobban, 'The myth of the French Revolution', reprinted in his *Aspects of the French Revolution* (London, 1968).
[42] *Death in Paris*, p. 47.
[43] *Raymond Queneau: the Zaharoff Lecture for 1976* (Oxford, 1976), p. 18. It would be a pity if this part of Zazie's anatomy were to have a permanently crushing effect on Napoleonic studies in Britain.
[44] *Tour de France*, p. 8.

by preference about violent periods, like the French Revolution or the German Occupation. All his books testify to his fascination for violence, its laws, vocabulary and those who habitually and casually practise it. Against a background of cruelty and vengeance, the continuities of personal survival emerge more starkly, and are discovered with greater relief and satisfaction. Cobb's outlook is perversely optimistic, for he finds studying the Revolution

a reassuring, even a hope-giving exercise, if one can take one's eyes off so much random killing and forget the cost, in personal and family terms, of murder and maiming. For it illustrates the limitless capacity of the individual to live out of reach of terrible and dangerous events and to shut the door on the shouting, the screams, the roars, the howls, the ugly surge of collective commitment and of vengeful lust.[45]

This is an eloquent, but still a very big IF, and this wave of sympathy for the individual behind closed doors seems to me very questionable in practical, let alone moral terms. For the great collective fanaticisms, the historical juggernauts which have thundered down the streets of Cobb's own lifetime, have shown little mercy to the innocent individuals sheltering in doorways along the route. And to say that much is to assume that innocence is even possible for those who try to shut out 'the shouting, the screams, the roars, the howls'.

In this outline of what I have called Cobb's 'anti-method', his sense of place and use of the individual case-history, I may be guilty in the eyes of his critics of attributing a kind of logic and consistency to his work where little exists. Consistency is not perhaps the most obvious of the qualities of such an anarchic temperament. We should talk instead, perhaps, of favourite methods, of recurrent themes. At any rate, it should now be possible to point out where the paths of Cobb, the Marxists and the Annalists separate and converge.

Cobb's path converged directly with the Marxists in the late 1940s, when party members (in Paris) extended him their much-needed hospitality.[46] Cobb was not merely a dinner-guest; what he has always had in common with Marxist historians like Albert Soboul is a burning interest in popular history. Cobb, like Soboul and Rudé, has made a leading contribution to the altered perspective of French Revolutionary history since the war, away from the debates in the Convention and revolutionary assemblies, away from the factional struggles of revolutionary politics, towards a new focus on popular protest and popular militancy. Cobb, Soboul and Rudé have all taught us to see the Revolution from the angle of the street or the Paris section, that is from below rather than from above.

In *Les armées révolutionnaires*, Cobb seemed to write about the *sans-culottes* with a sense of political commitment which might attract the sympathy of Marxist historians. This impression may be deceptive: I cannot tell. What did become clear, however, was that Cobb was much more interested than

[45] *Reactions*, p. 127.   [46] *Second Identity*, p. 37.

Soboul, for instance, in popular protest for its own sake, in counter-revolutionary as well as revolutionary militancy, and indeed in any manifestation of popular action, however spontaneous or disorganised.

With the *Police and the People*, then, Cobb had clearly distanced himself from his former *camarades*. The *Annales historiques de la Révolution française* found that his criticisms of Marxist historiography led him up the same *cul-de-sac* in which François Furet had already lost his way.[47] His treatment of local events and personalities failed to place them in a general context. The *enragés* were portrayed as isolated individuals, rather than spokesmen for a widespread popular response to the crisis and food shortage of the Year II. The journal objected to his description of the *sans-culotte* movement as an ephemeral and wholly unstructured phenomenon. Cobb, it seemed, had failed to understand the contradictions and class conflict inherent in the relations between the popular movement and the predominantly bourgeois revolutionary government. Cobb was accused of analysing political struggles at a superficial level, without taking enough account of the 'infrastructure'. He ought, furthermore, to have recognised that the memory of the popular struggles of 1793–5 inspired the democratic movement in France for decades to follow.

Albert Soboul hinted very discreetly at the distance which separates Cobb from the Marxists in a recent historiographical review, in which he remarked that Cobb cannot be considered a disciple of Georges Lefebvre.[48] There are several reasons for this, which Soboul did not enumerate, but in the light of Cobb's published appreciation of Lefebvre, his comment appears to be justified.[49] Cobb's comments, however, are very far from the polemical tone adopted by Cobban. Cobb appreciated Lefebvre's dynamic treatment of the structure of ancien regime rural society, even if such sociological analysis was not to his taste, and 'when one looks at the 200 pages of statistics at the end of his thesis, one can understand why he has no imitators'.[50] Cobb appreciated Lefebvre above all as a historian of food supplies and collective mentalities, as the author of *La Grande Peur*, a thorough cartographical analysis of the spread of panic through the French countryside in the summer of 1789.[51] The main difference between their outlooks was probably the fact that Lefebvre was a militant defender of the jacobin tradition of French republicanism, which is a nationalist, centralising, anti-clerical and very pro-Robespierrist tradition. Cobb found Lefebvre's dogmatism on these subjects, as well as his austere life-style, as antipathetic as Danton must have found Robespierre's.

[47] G. Lemarchand's review of the French translation of *The Police and the People* in *Annales historiques de la Révolution française*, 231 (1978), 135–8.

[48] A. Soboul, 'L'historiographie classique de la Révolution française: sur des controverses récentes', *Historical Reflections/Réflexions historiques*, 1 (1974), 143, n. 11.

[49] 'Georges Lefebvre' in *Second Identity*.

[50] Ibid., p. 95.

[51] G. Lefebvre, *La Grande Peur de 1789* (Paris, 1932).

Cobb diverged notably from the Marxists in his interpretation of the Babeuf conspiracy of the Year IV. While recognising the eighteenth-century and pre-industrial roots of Babeuf's communistic political philosophy, Marxist historians have seen his conspiracy as a forerunner of later revolutionary movements. His use of the secret conspiratorial cell made him an ancestor of Leninist revolutionary techniques, and his ideas on the production and distribution of agricultural produce in common secured Babeuf a place in the martyrology of the proletarian revolution.[52] Cobb finds this a distorted view, which fails to appreciate Babeuf's very limited role in the popular movement under the Directory. In place of the clandestine Leninist cell, Cobb sees a naïve organisation of incompetent amateurs, easily infiltrated by police informers. The ramifications of the conspiracy were grossly and indiscreetly exaggerated by Babeuf on paper, as they were by the political police which moved against him. Cobb thus accuses the Marxists of repeating the mistake of the revolutionary police. Babeuf was in his view not a milestone in revolutionary history, but a conspirator with no real following or great importance, and a bad revolutionary. The study of Babeuf has become a booming academic industry in France. In the latest published bibliography of the Directory, 20 per cent of the works on France are concerned with Babeuf and Babouvisme,[53] and this does not include the current edition of Babeuf's complete works.[54] In *The Police and the People*, in contrast, Babeuf is accorded barely two pages.[55]

In other works Cobb diverged even further from the Marxist tradition. For although he has always written history 'from below', he is decreasingly concerned with popular militants, whether revolutionary or counter-revolutionary. As we have seen, he has turned away from political activists to concentrate on the unwritten history of all those who played no political role: criminals, bandits, prostitutes, suicides. At a colloquium held in Paris to celebrate the centenary of the births of Albert Mathiez and Georges Lefebvre, English historians of the French Revolution were collectively accused of the crime of 'revisionism', and the chairman was provoked to remark that 'prostitutes do not make history'.[56] Cobb's emphasis on the 'marginal' characters of history has thus been clearly branded as heretical in the Marxist view, and his estrangement from Marxist historiography appears to be com-

---

[52] For a balanced and up-to-date account, see R. B. Rose, *Gracchus Babeuf: the First Revolutionary Communist* (Stanford, 1978).

[53] Compiled by J.-R. Suratteau in the complete re-edition of G. Lefebvre, *La France sous le Directoire (1795–1799)* (Paris, 1977).

[54] *Oeuvres de Babeuf*, vol. 1, ed. Daline, Saitta and Soboul (Paris, 1977, commission d'histoire économique et sociale de la Révolution française, mémoires et documents, XXXIII).

[55] *Police and the People*, pp. 71–2.

[56] Held in Paris in 1974. A selection of the proceedings, but not this part of them, was published in *Annales historiques de la Révolution française*, 219 (1975). The chairman was Albert Soboul.

plete. Cobb has not responded to demands that individual case-histories be placed within a wider context of group interests and class struggles.

Cobb has more in common with the *Annales* school of history, although appearances suggest the contrary. Cobb's evocation of local detail, his anecdotal approach and emphasis on the individual appear diametrically opposed to the aims of those aspiring to 'histoire globale', the history of long-term movements, of entire societies and continents, drawn from the systematic scrutiny and 'processing' of long series of mainly statistical data. Braudel, in complete contrast to Cobb, urged historians to 'go beyond' (*dépasser*) the individual, towards 'l'histoire anonyme, profonde, et souvent silencieuse' of the *longue durée*.[57] But Cobb will have little truck with the social sciences, and his history is anything but 'anonyme'. Cobb is a master of what some Annalists have too lightly dismissed as 'l'histoire événementi-elle', the history of the accidental, the contingent and the individual. Cobb is interested in a very personal reality, not in cycles and structures and models. He is writing the diaries of the silent poor, not charting the inexorable surge of the centuries.

But Braudel is not the *Annales*, whose direction has perhaps altered in recent years. Professor Lawrence Stone at least thought so, suggesting a new trend towards the rehabilitation of narrative history.[58] Cobb has more in common with another eminent *annaliste*, Emmanuel Le Roy Ladurie. As a determined exponent of quantitative methods in history, Ladurie may seem an unlikely point of contact between Cobb and the *Annales*. Ladurie, how-ever, is a prolific and many-sided historian. *Montaillou*, his reconstruction of life and custom in a fourteenth-century Pyrenean village, and *Le Carnaval de Romans*, which sees social conflict through the eyes of one particular local incident, are much closer to Cobb in their approach than most other works of the *Annales* school.[59]

One will not find Cobb quoting Lévi-Strauss or Durkheim, as Le Roy Ladurie does in *Le Carnaval de Romans*, but one will find him analysing urban society in terms of the sort of neighbourhood or family conflicts which determined social relationships in Le Roy Ladurie's Montaillou and Romans. *Montaillou*, in particular, turns on a typically Cobbian theme – the struggle for village power between two clans, the Clergues and the Azémas. In the French Revolution, village cliques would use the visiting *représentant en mission* to arrest their local enemies as counter-revolutionary agitators. In Montaillou, the game was similar, and the stakes were just as high. The outcome depended on Clergue's ability to manipulate the power of the

57 F. Braudel, *Ecrits sur l'histoire* (Paris, 1969), p. 21.
58 L. Stone, 'The revival of narrative: reflections on a new old history', *Past and Present*, 85 (1979), 3–24.
59 E. Le Roy Ladurie, *Montaillou: village occitan de 1294 à 1324* (Paris, 1978); and *Carnaval de Romans* (Paris, 1979).

Inquisition for his private and local ends, to protect his clients and trounce his rivals. *Montaillou* was perhaps untypical of the *Annales*: it was based on a traditional non-statistical source, it was narrowly focused in time and place and it was about real people rather than impersonal trends. Because it was untypical, it became a bestseller, and demonstrated at the same time possible points of contact between Cobb and Le Roy Ladurie.

Cobb has effectively disguised any affinities he may have with the pre-occupations of the *Annales* by reserving for them some of his most vitriolic broadsides.[60] He attacked, with justification, the pretentious and obscure jargon which often blights the pages of this illustrious journal. Secondly, in a vigorous and witty article, he attacked quantitative history altogether. Yet it is far too superficial to see Cobb as an outright and wilful Luddite, opposed to statistics, computers and all forms of depersonalised history by numbers. For Cobb himself has been known to count to good effect enumerating, for example, the victims of the murder gangs of the White Terror.[61] In *Terreur et subsistances*, he temporarily joined the ranks of the demographers in an article about dearth and mortality in revolutionary Rouen.[62] Cobb has never in fact denied the value of a statistical approach to the history of dearth and mortality, literacy, wills and marriages, crime and church attendance.[63] There are things, however, which are not measurable, and ideological commitment is one of them. What most provokes his formidable ire is the quantitative approach to stylistic analysis. Projects to put the *cahiers de doléances* through a computer, to record the incidence of words such as 'feodalité' or 'liberté' are meaningless and profitless exercises, in his view. The hardest things to quantify are what the *Annales* call *mentalités*, and it is no exaggeration to describe Cobb as a historian of *mentalités*, a historian of mental attitudes and assumptions. One will not find Cobb spending long on an analysis of the *mercuriales*, the ancien regime records of the fluctuating market price of grain, but one will find a discussion of popular attitudes to dearth. Cobb has a healthy respect for Georges Lefebvre, not because of his oft-quoted advice 'il faut compter', but because his *Great Fear*, a minute appraisal of popular reactions to famine in 1789, was a pioneering work in the history of *mentalités*.

Mentalités is one of the *Annales* keywords; *sociabilité* has become another, and it is an idea applicable to Cobb's work. The history of *sociabilité* is simply the history of social contact, of social institutions and their purpose, of how, why and when people meet. In Maurice Agulhon's work, it has covered the history of Provençal brotherhoods of Penitents, masonic lodges and literary circles from the point of view of social history, and it has become associated

---

[60] See 'Nous des Annales' in *Second Identity*; and 'Historians in white coats', *Times Literary Supplement* (3.12.71), reprinted in *Tour de France*.

[61] *Police and the People*, pp. 131–50.

[62] *Terreur et subsistances*, 'Disette et mortalité à Rouen'.   [63] *Tour de France*, p. 8

perhaps with a peculiarly Mediterranean style of social life, characterised by ostentatious piety, spectacular ceremony and public display.[64] Cobb, too, is a historian of *sociabilité*, that is of popular social life, popular leisure and popular habit. His world is not that of any of the social institutions analysed by Agulhon; it is rather the universe of rented furnished rooms and their tenants, a world of casual but habitual encounters in bars, on bridges, in inns or stage-coaches, leading to seduction, robbery or murder. Like the writers he so often refers to, Restif de la Bretonne and Georges Simenon, Cobb is a close observer of the habits of social intercourse, he knows who travels where, how wide is their network of acquaintances, where they will congregate to relax after work, what sort of amusement they prefer on a Sunday afternoon. This information may not be acquired or presented in a manner the *Annales* would class as 'scientific', but it forms a very rich part of the history of *sociabilité*.

Cobb's history touches the main trends in contemporary French histori-ography at various points, and clashes violently with them at others. But he remains a law unto himself, an idiosyncratic figure, admired by a wide public for his human approach to history, while his very personal preoccupations make his work harder and harder to absorb into the mainstream of histori-ography. There is a very old joke that if you ask who is the greatest figure in French literature, the answer will be Victor Hugo, *hélas*! Cobb, one might say, is our greatest historian of France *malgré lui*. Great for his human sym-pathy, his eloquence, his effervescent historical imagination, his unparalleled archival knowledge; *malgré lui* because of his adamant refusal to build structures, to make syntheses, to refer to historical problems others wrestle with, because for him the everyday details are all. Is Cobb a novelist *manqué*? Such a question could only be asked by someone who mistakenly assumes the novelist to be necessarily more creative than the historian. It is hard to see how the novel could offer Cobb a better medium for his incomparable talents.

In conclusion, I cannot resist the temptation to award the Lyons prize for the best work of history to Richard Cobb, for the opportunity to do so will certainly never arise again. In spite of the virtues of *The Police and the People*, my choice must be for *Les armées révolutionnaires*. This is perhaps the preference of a professional historian; it cannot be that of the general public, since it has unfortunately never been translated into English.[65] It is a book which, I believe, illustrates all Cobb's positive characteristics as a historian: the insistence on local variations, the individual case-histories, the wealth of evocative detail of violent popular protest, the vigour and colour of his writing. At the same time, it remains a mine of information on the popular movement in the Year II. Unlike its successors, it has another important

---

[64] M. Agulhon, *Pénitents et francs-maçons de l'ancienne Provence* (Paris, 1968); *Le Cercle dans la France bourgeoise* (Paris, 1977).

[65] Marianne Elliott is engaged in an English translation for Yale University Press.

quality: it has a clear structure, moving logically and, for the most part, chronologically, from the moves to create the *armées*, to their personnel, grade by grade, to their repressive work in the field. It is, in other words, the product of a fertile and erudite historical imagination, combined with the discipline and organisation imposed by the demands of a French doctoral thesis.

2

The reconstruction of a church 1796–1801

OLWEN HUFTON

'deux sortes de queues: queues à la messe, queues à la porte des boulangeries'.

(Paris, Lent, 1795)

'La Révolution aux yeux du peuple catholique est promotion bourgeoise et protestante.'

(A. J. Tudesq)

'Laissez une paroisse vingt ans sans prêtre, on y adorera les bêtes.' (Curé d'Ars)

In the history of catholicism in France the years 1789–1801 constitute a watershed. It was not merely that the church lost its landed wealth or its claim to a monopoly of truth, that 50 per cent or more of those responsible for the cure of souls in 1789 found themselves in flight or that images were broken and acts of orgiastic desecration were perpetrated. It was that the total experience had a profound and lasting effect upon the laity. Neither catholics nor the institution to which they lent adherence were ever quite the same again. The revolutionary decade emphatically severs a world of almost unquestioned obeissance to catholic teaching from one in which significant sectors of the populace slipped away into indifference.[1]

The eighteenth-century church was very much the product of the post-Tridentine reform movement. Its most outstanding characteristic was a seminary-trained priesthood whose education, periodically reinforced by conference and retreat, committed the parochial clergy to define their chief function as the elevation of the spiritual level of their flock by unproved catechetical instruction, a remorseless attack on lax morality and on the 'superstitious' aspects of popular religion, such as local cults of pagan or doubtful derivation, or customs, such as the ringing of the parish bell to avert hail. It has been argued that as a result of the church's efforts to put the people's religion onto a higher plane the relationship between priest and

[1] F. Le Brun (ed.), *Histoire des catholiques en France du XVe siècle à nos jours* (Paris, 1980), pp. 273–4, seeks to draw out many significant contrasts.

people became a more distant and sometimes alien one. The clergy encountered multiple defeats from rural intransigence in clinging to the religion
of their forebears. Notwithstanding, before 1750 they seem to have achieved
a near totality of observance relative to attendance at mass on Sundays,
Easter, days of obligation etc., and though complaints were frequent about
the perfunctory way in which confession was made, at least it would appear
to have taken place once a year in the course of Lent, and there were few
complaints relative to laxity over the last rites.

During the last three decades of the ancien regime, however, some
significant if nonetheless minority changes appear to be discernible amongst
certain sectors of the populace in certain areas. A growing literate male
bourgeoisie (professional rather than capitalist) requested, with diminishing
frequency in their testaments, masses for the repose of the soul in Purgatory
and, instead of filling their libraries with holy books, turned to the literature
of the impious enlightenment.[2] At the same time and with significant local
and regional variation have been detected signs of aberrance on the part of
certain sectors of the adult male working populace. These belonged to the
drink trades (*cabaretiers, brassiers, vignerons*) or were textile-workers, bargees
or others involved in river traffic, soldiers (but not sailors who had a very
pious record) or they were the progeny of unconvinced *nouveaux convertis*.
In addition, migrant labourers and vagrants, whose numbers were swelling
in the difficult economic circumstances of the closing decades of the ancien
regime, were irregular worshippers once they had left their native parishes
behind them.

From the evidence of visitation registers the aberrant rarely accounted for
more than 5 to 6 per cent of any rural parish. They were virtually non-
existent in the extreme west (the Vendée, Brittany, the Cotentin) and the
east (Alsace, Franche-Comté and Lorraine) and in Flanders, but they appeared
with greater frequency in a north-to-centre block (parts of the Île de France,
particularly contiguous to Paris, the Seine Valley, Champagne, western
Burgundy, the Auvergne and the Limousin) where enclaves are found with
a mixed commitment to regular practice, and a significant discrepancy was
discernible between the performance of adult men and women *vis-à-vis*
Lenten confession and Sunday observance. In 1780, for example, at Mennecy
near Gonesse (Seine-et-Oise), 91 out of 198 male householders, 149 out of
198 married women, 28 out of 66 bachelors over the age of 25 and a totality
of widows and spinsters performed their Easter duties. Finally, the Midi
seems to proffer the most marked contrasts, with pious mountains and

---

[2] J. Quéniart, *Les hommes, l'Eglise et Dieu dans la France du XVIIIe siècle* (Paris, 1978), pp. 240–73,
attempts to summarise M. Vovelle, *Piété baroque et déchristianisation en Provence au XVIIIe siècle*
(Paris, 1973), and J. Quéniart, *Culture et société urbaine dans la France de l'Ouest au XVIIIe siècle*
(Paris, 1978), on the secularisation of bourgeois elites in the eighteenth century.

garrigues contrasting with some of the villages of the plains and the foothills, which had a more variegated pietistical record.[3]

Observations based on practice alone, of course, tell us little of the quality of religious life, and there is much to suggest that even between areas of the same nominal conformity there were significant contrasts in degrees of religious fervour. Historians of the counter-Revolution in Brittany and the Vendée, for example, in demarcating *bleu* (patriot) and *blanc* (counter-revolutionary) villages are prepared to make of the former, in terms of religion, villages of nominal but perfunctory commitment; and of the latter, villages of fervent devotion to traditional catholic practice, and maintain that such distinctions prefigured the Revolution and evidently survived it.[4] Such considerations are obviously important, but, given that quality is far harder to determine than quantity, the criteria of determining a catholic by his or her preparedness to recognise the importance of the rules governing catholic behaviour remains crucial. After 1801 and the formal re-establishment of a Roman Catholic church with full state recognition in France, it was apparent that there was a considerable discrepancy in the degree of preparedness of communities and individuals to return to the church. In the long run, by the closing decades of the nineteenth century, the norm was for majoritative female conformity and minoritative male, though in some instances, particularly in the textile cities of the Nord, the exodus of female textile workers preceded that of the male peasantry of Flanders. This process of female commitment and male rejection seems to have received its first considerable expression in the course of the French Revolution. Women responded in much more hostile fashion than their menfolk to the dismantling of the established church and the process of dechristianisation. They were much more active in the maintenance of a clandestine church and absolutely decisive in the reconstitution of a church after Thermidor. Indeed, it was the determined boycott by women of the schismatic constitutional church between 1796 and 1801 which determined its ultimate demise. In the words of its leader, the Abbé Grégoire, that church was strangled by 'les femmes crapuleuses et séditieuses'.[5] Those same women, though we reject the Abbé's adjectives, were the basis on which the nineteenth-century church was to rest. They were the foundation of that women's church which represented the last phase of the Roman Catholic church in France, a church which produced nuns in superabundance and suffered no real crisis of vocations as long as pious mothers picked out the son they did not want to lose to another

[3] O. Hufton, 'The French Church', in W. J. Callahan and D. Higgs (eds.) *Church and Society in Catholic Europe of the Eighteenth Century* (Cambridge, 1979), pp. 13–33.

[4] On this continuity and indeed a dichotomy reflected in nineteenth-century political developments, J. Delumeau (ed.), *Histoire du diocèse de Rennes* (Paris, 1979) pp. 160–8; and C. Petitfrère, *Bleus et blancs d'Anjou (1789–1793)* (2 vols., Lille III, 1979).

[5] Bibliothèque de la Société de Port-Royal, Correspondance Grégoire: carton Calvados, 8 March 1797.

woman and directed his feet towards the priesthood. It was a church conspicuous for its lack of intellectualism, prepared to adopt the people's cults,
such as the Curé of Ars, the women's confessor of the century, Saint Berna-
dette and in due course the 'little' Saint Thérèse when the predilections of the
hierarchy lay with the cult of the Immaculate Conception and the Sacred
Heart. It concentrated on notions of family and parochial solidarity and
provided an alternative sociability to that of the tavern, the *fête civique* and
dangerous radical politics.[6]

The role of women in returning to catholic worship in 1796 has been
acknowledged and in some instances strenuously explained away. For
Aulard, Mathiez and a socialist male chauvinist tradition, women turned
from the *fanatisme de leurs clubs*, closed by the *Comité de Salut public*, to the
fanatisme des prêtres as an alternative source of emotional investment.[7] For
more recent historians, military conscription, the laicisation of male leisure
and the politicisation of working men within the focal point of the tavern
were lasting repellents for men from a church which resolutely turned its
back on radicalism, socialism and all the winning issues of the nineteenth
century and proclaimed itself for losers such as legitimate sovereignty, papal
infallibility and patronal responsibility.[8] Historians of sexual practice have
perceived as a growing obstacle to male commitment the increasing use after
1790 of contraceptive techniques (coitus interruptus and the condom) for
which the male partner carried the moral responsibility in the eyes of the
church.[9] Some recent historians of the church have proposed that the post-
revolutionary male was less disposed than his wife to admit in the con-

---

6 *Histoire des catholiques*, pp. 317–55.

7 J. Michelet, *Les femmes de la Révolution* (Paris, 1854); A. Aulard, *Le culte de la raison et de l'Etre
suprême, 1793–94* (Paris, 1892); *Paris pendant la réaction thermidorienne et sous le Directoire* (Paris,
1898–1902). Aulard drew his evidence from the vocabulary found in his *Recueil des Actes du
Comité de Salut Public avec la correspondance officielle des représentants en mission et le registre du
Conseil éxecutif provisoire* (Paris, 1881–1951). Much of what was written about women in
Revolution at the turn of the century was coloured by the great socialist debate of whether the
struggle for women's rights detracted from the issue of the workers' struggle and political and
social claims. It should be remembered that some of these socialists were afraid that women's
suffrage would only buttress a right-wing clerical representation in the Assembly. The debate
surrounding whether Mademoiselle Jaurès should receive her first communion (as her mother
wanted) or be obliged by her father to step forward without such indoctrination was both
lively and acrimonious. However, for Aulard, Jaurès and later Mathiez the record of women
in the Revolution of 1789–1801 was obviously a cautionary tale.
      R. Dupuy, 'Les femmes et la Contre-Révolution dans l'Ouest', *Bulletin d'histoire économique et
sociale de la Révolution française*. Année 1979 (Paris, 1980), pp. 61–70 is an excellent synthesis of
the historiography of women, religion and counter-Revolution which compares some old
assertions with the facts.

8 A comprehensive bibliography on practice in the post-revolutionary period is found in *Histoire
des catholiques*, pp. 366–8.

9 J. Flandrin, *L'Eglise et le contrôle des naissances* (Paris, 1970), summarised in J. Quéniart, *Les
hommes*, pp. 135–54.

fessional the error of his revolutionary ways, and certainly was not prepared to make good the absence of formal religious instruction during the Revolution by catechism classes, which in his view were the preserve of young children.[10] Others, concentrating upon what brought women back rather than what kept men out, have insisted upon *sociabilité* and *acculturation*.[11] What held women in the church was a nun-based education and when Napoleon put back female education into the hands of female religious orders he assured the perpetuation of the process. Others have argued that the association of the church with temperence movements was an attraction to women but a repellent to men. In short, the approaches to explaining the phenomena are legion, even without the common anthropological fallback of the quintessential religiosity of the sex condemned to all the physical risks involved in reproducing the species.

My aim at this juncture is not to proclaim the plausibility of any one or all of these explanations, but to identify what has been recognised to be a significant aspect of the religious history of modern France. Between 1790 and 1796 a church was dismantled: between 1796 and 1801 popular demand for whatever reason made its restoration a political necessity. Yet the religious history of the period 1796–1801 scarcely exists outside fragmentary local studies and rarely receives more than a few lines in diocesan histories. The ecclesiastics, who until recent times had a quasi-monopoly of religious historiography, placed their emphasis on the efforts of the hierarchy to resurrect a church from the ashes rather than upon the efforts of the laity to place a church (their church) in the hands of a priest. For the Marxist tradition this popular revival was something to be ignored or glossed over. It has also suffered too from the fact that it can only be assessed from fragmentary and scattered evidence. Many local officials only told the central government what it wanted them to know.

There are signs, however, that the significance of the work of religious reconstruction preceding the Concordat is finding greater recognition, and what follows is a contribution towards understanding the religious revival proferred in honour of the historian who added an entirely new dimension to our appreciation of the twilight zone between Thermidor and Napoleon. In the Directorial quartet and the essays on dearth Richard Cobb conveyed the emotional intensity, hatred, hunger, despair, lust for vengeance, sheer bloody-mindedness which were a fundamental aspect of *mentalités populaires* after Thermidor, when the people sought to impose their own standards in

---

[10] Philippe Boutry and Michel Cinquin, *Deux pèlerinages au XIXᵉ siècle. Ars et Paray-le-Monial* (Paris, 1980). The opening two chapters of this work are very sensitive and evocative, from the point of view of the clergy, of the work involved in getting men back to the church.

[11] *Histoire des catholiques*, pp. 323–5. The same section gives a very concise breakdown between male and female performance of religious duties in the nineteenth century and accentuates the emergence of the male *pratiquant saisonnier* (birth, marriage and death).

rank opposition to faceless bureaucrats and local or national politicians. This was the emotional context of the religious revival with which we are concerned. It is the story of religious survival and of how a church was reestablished from below long before the Concordat, which merely restored and placed a hierarchy on a legal footing, made peace with Rome and allowed the people to commit their spiritual well-being into professional hands. This is not to reduce the importance of the Concordat, but merely to underscore that it represented the recognition of a *fait accompli*. The people had wanted and had taken measures to secure for themselves a church of a particular kind and it would have been foolhardy for the Napoleonic state to persist in refusing to recognise that fact, particularly when the Pope was compliant. In securing this church in the aftermath of Thermidor, people and politicians joined battle and the religious issue was to prove a major defeat for the Directory.

One of the most fundamental problems for the historian is in gauging how far dechristianisation had gone by 1795, and even in defining what one understands by this term, beyond an attempt emanating from the central government to reject the paramouncy of any religious cult and to disassociate itself from institutionalised catholic worship and the dismantling of parochial worship and a professional priesthood. How does one set about estimating the preparedness of communities and individuals to renounce their religious heritage? There is no body of documentation permitting anything beyond the most impressionistic and perhaps misleading overview. Indeed, one of the liveliest controversies about the Revolution waged in recent times has been that between Michel Vovelle and Gérard Cholvy in the *Annales historiques de la Révolution française* concerning the value of records relating to the renunciation of priestly vows (*lettres de prêtrise*) and to those concerning clerical marriage.[12] Vovelle argued (and others have been prepared to follow) that the incidence of priests laying down their *lettres de prêtrise* and subsequently marrying is a proxy indicator of local attitudes *vis-à-vis* the rejection of established religion. Such a contention is based on the premise that the priest was simply a mirror-image of the community and reacted in Pavlovian fashion when pressure was placed upon him by the locals. By this means Vovelle located a dechristianised Midi-Rouge on the Mediterranean littoral and resurrected sufficient pre-revolutionary data to present such areas as ones

---

12 M. Vovelle, *Religion et Révolution. La déchristianisation en l'an II* (Paris, 1976); G. Cholvy's review is in *Annales historiques de la Révolution française*, 233 (1978), 451–64 and Vovelle's reply to Cholvy, ibid., 465–70. The same issue has a number of local studies on the district of Compiègne and on the Ouest which use Vovelle's methods, particularly the exploitation of requests for dechristianisation addressed by localities to the Convention. Cholvy's techniques which consisted of looking at *who* made requests for dechristianising measures and the past record of priests laying down their *lettres de prêtrise* drew on detailed material from the region between Pézenas and Lodève.

of latent dechristianisation merely awaiting the revolutionary impulse to become overtly dechristianised.

Gérard Cholvy, however, found such an approach unacceptable. If the priests resigning from the priesthood were oath-takers in 1791 and imposed upon parishes which were forced to lose their own non-juring priests, then they were *intrus*, outsiders, and in no way faithful witnesses of community attitudes. In any case, can one be sure that in resigning they were acting in response to local pressure, rather than to the outside pressure of the visiting *armées révolutionnaires* sent out from the big cities, which struck terror in the bosom of an already frightened priesthood? [The evidence provided by Richard Cobb's *Armées révolutionnaires* is sufficient to corroborate that such activity was precipitated from *without* the community, but that very often an internal minority pressure group could also be important in carrying the policy through.] Both the incidence of the surrender of *lettres de prêtrise* and of clerical marriage show these practices to be commonest in the provinces contiguous to Paris, the cities of the north and east and Lyon, where one could effectively demonstrate the pressure of city militants upon the rural clergy and hence the priest's response to be no genuine indicator of local attitudes.

It is impossible to refute Cholvy's critique of the evidence and other attempts to determine the frequency of patriotic names in birth registers or the abandonment of the Lenten and Advent prohibition on marriage cere-monies that these have not carried us very far towards determining the extent or degree of dechristianisation[13] or, conversely, towards knowing how tenaciously the rural parishes clung to traditional practice. Chanoine Flament identified 400 refractory priests performing services in the Orne, 300 in the Haute-Loire and 100 or more in the Sarthe throughout the Terror.[14] But such lists are compiled from very impressionistic evidence and we can confidently predict that a frequency graph of clandestine masses or a pie-chart to demon-strate how many babies had crosses slapped on their brows by midwives, whose habits died hard, will never be with us. It might be more profitable in fact to concentrate on what we can know independently of the quantitative evidence whose significance is open to challenge.

First, a regular Sunday mass, carried out in full panoply in the parish

[13] *Voies nouvelles pour l'histoire de la Révolution française*, Commission d'histoire Economique et Sociale de la Révolution française, Mémoires et Documents XXV (Paris, 1978) includes a section on religion, pp. 237–318 with articles by Le Goff and Langlois on the use of Caprara's correspondence to give an idea of the incidence and motivations of married priests, whilst the demographic section has contributions on marriages at Rouen and villages in the Vexin, Argenteuil (pp. 73–109) to show how many took place in the formerly 'closed season'.

[14] Chanoine Pierre Flament, 'Recherches sur le ministère clandestin dans le département de l'Orne sous la Révolution', *Bulletin principal de la société historique et archéologique de l'Orne* XC (1972), 45–74; E. Gonnet, *Essai sur l'histoire du diocèse du Puy en Velay (1789–1802)* (Paris, 1907), p. 209 Charles Girault, *Le clergé sarthois face au serment constitutionnel* (Laval, 1959), pp. 31–3.

church by a vested priest whose authority was freely acknowledged by both the community and the establishment, ceased in late 1793 to be a reality. During the three years which preceded this legislation communities might have been rent by loyalties to a non-juror replaced by an intruder-priest and might have rejected the intruder's parish mass in favour of one held by the non-juror at another time or in another place, or after the decrees of 1792 which made exiles of the non-jurors they may have absented themselves from the constitutional mass on offer. But, after 1793, mass availability was not to be taken for granted. There may have been the opportunity for clandestine masses but this depended upon the existence of a locale (either in a private house, a barn or by illicit securing of ingress to the parish church), of a hidden but available person to celebrate the mass, the complicity or ignorance of local authorities and the energy of the local populace in carrying out a voluntary exercise which may have put them at risk of arrest or at least to some inconvenience. *Messes clandestines* are frequently indicated to have taken place, either in communities far distant from a prying town with omnipresent officialdom or patriots in the community who might serve as informers or, in some cities, according to the impressionistic evidence of private *mémoires*, there might be the occasional gathering of a select band of faithful in a particular household in which a hidden priest or ex-monk made the sacrifice. We should note that women, most especially widows, are commonly designated as sheltering priests and providing the locale for hidden worship. None of this however detracts from the thesis of a general absence in regular public Sunday service.[15]

Similarly, one can proffer as a general rule that communities ceased to enjoy a life punctuated by the pealing of a parish bell, a bell previously used not merely to summon the faithful to mass, but to ward off hailstorms or summon the community to confront a common enemy and which, in many instances, epitomised community solidarity.[16] On Saturdays, the pealing of the bell had been a reminder of the presence of confessional services to prepare for the sabbath. The post-1793 experience was of the absence of this spiritual exercise. It is possible that here and there priests could be rooted out to hear the outpourings of a penitent soul but, equally clearly, this was not something which was readily available. The priest prepared to offer a clandestine mass did not necessarily prolong the risk-taking period by confession and absolution of the individual members of the congregation. (In time, this had an effect upon the numbers able to take communion.) Moreover, many non-

---

15 René et Suzanne Pillorget, 'Les messes clandestines en France entre 1793 et 1802', *Université d'Angers Centre de Recherches d'Histoire Religieuse et d'Histoire des Idées. Histoire de la Messe XVII–XIX siècles* (Angers, 1979), pp. 155–67, gives an excellent bibliography of local and other published work.

16 On this theme, I. Cameron, *Crime and Repression in the Auvergne and Guyenne* (Cambridge, 1981), p. 197.

jurors, forced to flee, succeeded in discrediting the constitutional clergy by insisting that they had no powers of absolution so that the absence of confessional services could be of long standing. The post-Concordat church was ubiquitously insistent upon the general loss of the confessional habit.[17]

Allied to the question of confession was that of the last rites. The lack of an available priesthood to perform this service meant a period in which communities lost the habit of recourse to a priest to perform this function. Again, even when jurors were freely available, they appear to have been rejected as unfit for this service. Again, the post-Concordat church, even in areas demonstrating a high return to conventional practice, were insistent upon their problems in re-establishing this crucial aspect of practice. Usually they allied this neglect with the absence of formal catechetical instruction during the Revolution and of regular sermons instructing the faithful of the importance of confronting one's maker with a fully shriven soul.[18]

The absence of regular informed instruction for the young also needs consideration. The 'normal' time for the instruction of children was on exit from mass, but clearly this practice no longer pertained when there was no official mass. Such instruction entailed aural inculcation by a priest using a confessional manual of the basic principles of the catholic faith and an explanation in the vernacular of the meaning of the liturgy. There was, as we shall see, little to prevent parents who could read and had the appropriate manual from taking the priest's place, but this precluded from instruction the children of the poor and illiterate. This created a generational problem. Those who arrived at the age of seven or thereabouts in 1793 might reach their teens without benefit of such professional instruction. The same generation missed out on an education which had religion as its basis. In addition, anyone conscripted for military service from 1792 spent several years in an overtly irreligious environment.[19]

[17] Jauffret (post-Concordat bishop of Metz), *Mémoires pour servir à l'histoire de la religion à la fin du XVIIIᵉ siècle* (published anon. in 1803), p. 184; Bibl. Port-Royal, Correspondance Grégoire: carton Sarthe, letter of 5 March 1796 from Prudhomme in the Sarthe, 'nous en voyons peu qui se disposent à approcher des sacrements de Pénitence et d'Eucharistie'; also B. Plongeron, *Conscience religieuse en Révolution* (Paris, 1969), p. 169. The best general overview of the situation is probably E. Sevrin, *Les missions religieuses en France sous la Restauration* (Paris, 1948).

[18] Bibl. Port-Royal, Correspondance Grégoire: carton Sarthe, letter of 13 March 1797, 'Il y sur ma paroisse trente mille âmes et il se passe des mois entiers sans qu'on porte à l'Eglise un corps mort pour que nous fassions les prières accoutumées.' On the implications of the lack of formal catechetical instruction, Sevrin, *Missions*, p. 296. It is a theme to which most of the new Beauchesne series *Histoire des diocèses* refer.

[19] This is a recurrent theme of clerical comment well into the 1820s, e.g. 'C'est un bien grand malheur que la jeunesse soit elevée sans principes religieux depuis plus de six ans dans un très grand nombre de paroisses où nous n'avons pu, jusqu'à présent, faute de prêtres disponibles, rétablir l'exercice public du culte' (Bibliothèque Municipale de Grenoble 06071, Bishop Reymond, 20 pluviôse an VII). In 1804 in this diocese 'tous les jeunes, âgés de moins de 22

One factor stands out above all others. It was fully possible to remain convinced of the rectitude of Christian doctrine throughout the Revolution; one could remain faithful, but one's religious commitment was thwarted or curtailed when it sought public expression. It had to be a largely private affair sprung from something previously inculcated or nurtured within a particular family environment. The biographies of nineteenth-century saints who were children during the Revolution, like Jean Vianney, later Curé of Ars, in the south-east, or *mémoires*, such as those of the Martin family in Franche-Comté, tell essentially of the same experience. Prayers were learnt at mother's knee; the rosary was recited within the family in the evening: when the youngest had gone to bed, the father read aloud from *L'Instruction des jeunes gens*, *Pensées sur les verités de la religion* or the *Vie des Saints* and finally before retiring a *de Profundis* was recited for deceased members of the family.[20] The Vianney family in fact sheltered a non-juror priest who prepared the future saint for his first communion. The Vianneys could usually then count on a clandestine mass though only rarely was this extended for neighbours.[21] Others had a more piecemeal experience of sporadic masses in barns or secret meeting-places but usually religion was a familial affair. In the words of the Abbé Lambert: 'Les fêtes, quand la prudence le permettait, on rassemblait les parents et les amis pour prier ensemble et faire de la religion le lien de la famille; le plus ancien, ou à son défaut celui qui lisait le mieux, récitait à haute voix les prières de la messe.'[22]

Books, literacy, a sizeable locale were all part of the experience of more affluent rural society; what about the record of more lowly folk? Again, experience varied very considerably over the question of the availability of clandestine masses. What seems, however, to have been a significant aspect of popular practice was its continued and indeed growing respect for that ancient heritage of cults and therapeutic saints which the post-Tridentine church had sought to destroy as having little to do with christianity and a great deal to do with an ingrained vestigial paganism, an amalgam of fear of the unknown and hope of the miraculous to cope with situations, sickness and misfortune, over which no individual had control. Most of these devo-

---

ans, n'avaient pas reçu une instruction religieuse normale et les autres l'avaient probablement oubliée', cited by J. Godel, *La reconstruction concordataire dans le doicèse de Grenoble apres la Révolution* (Grenoble, 1968), p. 211.

20 Boutry et Cinquin, *Deux pèlerinages*, p. 21; P. Flament, *L'Abbé Marin-Guillaume Guèrin, arrière-grand-oncle de sainte Thérèse de l'Enfant Jesus 1760–1835, Confesseur de la Foi* (Colombiers, 1973); J. M. Suchet, 'Paysans franc-comtois', *Mémoires de l'Académie de Besançon* (1887), 52–3. Sometimes nuns who had returned to their families or who existed in semi-clandestine circumstances were prepared to teach if they knew the family, e.g. Abbé Delamare, *Vie édifiante de la très honorée supérieure Marie Madeleine née Julie Postel* (Coutances, 1852), p. 10. She prepared children to receive first communion from a clandestine priest.

21 Boutry and Cinquin, *Deux pèlerinages*, pp. 21–6.

22 *Mémoires de famille de l'abbé Lambert* (Paris, 1894), p. 118.

tions were purely local, associated with a particular spring, grotto, group of rocks, trees or hillside where shrines had been established: others were associated with a picture or statuette in church or chapel representing a more generalised cult (like that of Saint Catherine): yet again, others were simply part of ordinary everyday life, like placing a cross on dough left to rise, tying *scapulaires* around the necks of children to protect them or kissing the chest of an infant in the morning as he lay in the cradle to invoke the blessing of Saint Leonidas to ward off harm for the day. Hence, throughout the dechristian-ising phase of the Terror sick cattle were marched up hills to seek the blessing of Saint Guiral and toddling children showing signs of rickets had their legs bathed in saintly waters by mothers who had no medical alternative. The popular cure for toothache continued to be myrrh if one lived near an apothecary or manual extraction by a linen thread and a prayer to Saint Apollinaire.[23] In short, it took more than a Revolution to destroy popular notions of the miraculous and this was one element which could not be grafted onto the Goddess of Reason. The latter, personified for the *fête* by a local beauty, was a direct abnegation of the miraculous and the inexplicable, and hence of no use whatsoever in the business of hope and solace. A relation-ship with this deity was like taking an ice-maiden for bedfellow. She added no warmth either to the business of living or to the process of dying. She proffered no option on crop devastation by hail; she could not be called upon when labour pains came thick and fast or when a new-born infant took a few faltering breaths and expired and the mother who had laboured in vain needed solace. Small wonder midwives continued to baptise the new born and were counted by local authorities a continuing nefarious influence, or that popular culture persisted in paying respect to its own worm-eaten pantheon of primitive sanctity.[24]

[23] Almost all these pilgrimages and devotions have a specifically local nature. The Dombes for example: 'On demande pour les chevaux l'intercession de Saint Marcel à Rancé, Saint Trivier-sur-Moignans et Saint Marcet-en-Dombes le 16 janvier, et le lendemain, c'est Saint Antoine qu'on invoque pour la conservation de la race porcine. A Mogneneins, Saint Clair guérit les maladies de la vue . . . à Jassane Saint Paul guérit le 24 janvier les convulsions et les peurs enfantines . . . On vient de très loin à Cruzilles-les-Mepillat . . . réclamer à Saint Denis le 9 octobre la prospérité de la basse cour. On porte à Notre-Dame-de-Beaumont au coeur de la Dombe d'étangs, les enfants morts-nés, qui y reviennent à la vie, le temps de recevoir le baptême.' L. Alloing, *Histoire du diocèse de Belley* (Belley, 1938), pp. 688–9. Note the onoma-topia. Saint Clair cures blindness: Saint Denis saint des nids, etc. See also *Histoire des catholiques*, p. 333.

[24] Under the ancien regime, midwives were sanctioned by the parish priest. These were not necessarily 'trained' women in any medical sense but they were women of good character, 'pious' in a religious sense. They were not necessarily devoted to the priest who appointed them and some in fact led demonstrations against non-jurors: see O. Hufton, 'Women in Revolution 1789–1796', in D. Johnson (ed.) *French Society and the Revolution* (Cambridge, 1976), p. 165 n. 51, but they were the obvious people to perform clandestine christian baptism during the absence of a formal church.

Indeed, in certain localities the range of popular devotions was extended
during the Revolution. A study of a number of parishes in the diocese of
Rennes reveals that any corpse found carrying a rosary, whether a victim of
chouannerie or a *chouan* himself was in 1793-4 popularly endowed with
sanctity and his or her grave received the floral tributes of those willing to
believe in death as an indication of martyrdom.[25]

The use of the rosary during these troubled times was most important and
offered one means whereby the simple and illiterate could try to maintain
contact with their deity without the support of a priesthood. A recitation of
the rosary was within the scope of any rural family, but it also became (it
may always have been so) a feature of *veillées*, evening get-togethers for work
in a particular house or cottage to economise on light or heat and to proffer
opportunities for social contact. In some areas, like the lace-making communities of the Pays de Velay or the stocking-knitting villages of Normandy
and the Pyrenees, the *veillées* were female in composition and the recitation
of the rosary secured a new importance when it was the only corporate
expression of adherence to the faith. The *représentants en mission*, dechristianising emissaries from the towns, *sans-culottes* or patriots in the villages, were
aware of this continuing aspect of female devotion and were often prepared
to ignore gatherings of women to chant their beads in chapels or former
religious edifices. In correspondence addressed to the *Comité de Salut public*,
they acknowledged the persistence of female religiosity in terms of derision
as an aspect of female weakness to be contrasted with male strength and
superior reasoning power. Let them have their rosaries, wrote one: 'Elles se
lasseront de cette ridicule pratique et dans peu, elles y renonceront tout à
fait.'[26] What may, of course, have softened the attitudes of bourgeois officialdom and of the most intrepid *clubistes* was the knowledge that their wives
and mothers were to be numbered amongst the bead-tellers, and we have
instances of some lively domestic clashes during the winter of 1794 in households where the male head could boast impeccable *sans-culottes* principles.
And as the bread queues grew, queues which were predominantly female in
composition, and women were confronted with the bankruptcy of provisioning policy, it suited *représentants* and local officialdom to play down the
significance of the activities of women in riot by concentrating on their
irrationality, *superstition*, *fanatisme*.[27]

25 E. Audard, *Actes des martyrs et des confesseurs de la foi pendant la Révolution* (2 vols, Tours, 1916–
    20) remains fundamental in demonstrating the growth of a saintly pantheon as a result of the
    Revolution. Delumeau (ed.), *Diocèse de Rennes* (Paris, 1979), p. 175.
26 *Actes du Comité de Salut Public* t.1, p. 353 and Pillorget, 'Les messes clandestines', p. 160.
27 Abbé P. J. B. Delon, *La Révolution en Lozère* (Mende, 1922), p. 105, gives some amusing
    instances of intra-family disputes on religious questions: e.g. the wives of patriots obliged by
    their husbands to go to a juror's mass in 1792 turned their back on the priest and the altar and
    sat on their heels. Even in Paris, at the Fête Dieu June 1793 were noted at mass 'beaucoup de
    petit peuple et *surtout les épouses des sans culottes*'. Other examples in *Histoire des catholiques*,

A general aspect of the 'privatisation' of religion was perforce its independence of the official hierarchy of the structured church (whether juror or non-juror). In large part this was the product of their physical disappearance. The non-juror clergy either left the country (estimates as to how many did so range between 40 and 50 per cent with the highest percentages on the fringes permitting escape to Jersey, Britain, Belgium, Switzerland, Germany, the Habsburg Empire or Italy);[28] suffered imprisonment or death; or they went into hiding. Many of those who chose hiding did so because they were old and frail, and after 1796 when they began to emerge from hiding, their physical condition was frequently pitiful.[29] Long-distance flight was very risky. During the early days of the war when the Prussian was making his seemingly inexorable advance and the initial wave of official persecution began, the priest in flight was associated with hostile foreign powers and many were lynched or beaten up by the rural communities who apprehended them as they attempted to pass through. This left the jurors, some of them *intrus*, not only discredited by the outgoing non-juror, but in 1793 abandoned by the state which had created them. From then on they were unpaid, either beaten into a surrender of their *lettres de prêtrise* by the *armées révolutionnaires* and perhaps also into matrimony or, if they failed to comply, imprisoned. If they chose the coward's path of resignation and marriage they became the object of derision. No spectacle occasioned greater public mirth than that of a former priest at his civil marriage ceremony.[30] As a result of the dechristianising campaign, the constitutional church suffered a credibility crisis. The religion of the people must then exist without a priesthood.

We should at this juncture stress an important distinction between the experience of most towns and that of most villages. In the village the dismantling first of the traditional catholic and then of the constitutional church and the ensuing resignation of priests, clerical marriage and the closing of the church were policies achieved under pressure from outside the community,

p. 266. Dupuy, 'Les femmes et la Contre-Révolution', pp. 67–8 again makes suggestions about sexual differences which could split families.

[28] A research project involving Timothy Tacket and Claude Langlois is aimed at clarifying and texturising what we can know of quantitative religious history during the Revolution.

[29] F. Tallett, 'Religion and Revolution. The rural clergy and parishioners of the Doubs, 1780–1797' (Unpub. Ph.D. thesis, University of Reading 1981), p. 366. Anon., *Histoire religieuse de la Touraine* (Paris, 1979), on the age structure of the clergy of the Concordat delineates the problem of the lack of ordinations during the Revolution and hence the advanced age of the available priesthood by 1801. Similarly P. Genevray, *L'Administration et la vie ecclésiastique dans le grand diocèse de Toulouse pendant les dernières années de l'Empire et sous la Restauration* (Paris, 1941), p. 35. Again the theme *le clergé veillissait* is found in all the Beauchesne diocesan histories, e.g. A. Poitrieau (ed.), *Histoire du diocèse de Clermont* (Paris, 1979), p. 221, *Histoire des catholiques*, p. 275.

[30] O. Hufton, *Bayeux in the Late Eighteenth Century* (Oxford, 1967), p. 202. Tallett, 'Religion and Revolution', p. 337 etc. J. Duval-Jouve, *Montpellier pendant la Révolution* (Montpellier, 1879), p. 298.

even if they were sometimes carried through with the connivance of a local anti-clerical minority. The inspiration and forwarding of the measures came from the towns (*promotion bourgeoise*). True, one can discern vast differences between the degree of readiness of villages to accept or adjust to change. We know that Brittany had *bleu* villages and *blanc* ones and that this distinction is in the first instance largely based on negative qualities implying an acceptance of change and in the second based on positive actions of rejection. Vovelle discerned villages prompt to respond to the dechristianising impulse in Provence, nursery of walled nuclear villages, tavern sociability and producers of the vine. Yet such discoveries do not fundamentally detract from the notion of the destruction of conventional catholic worship in the village as someone else's responsibility (*culpa tua*) which substantially reduced the degree of self-guilt the peasantry were prepared to acknowledge and increased their vindictiveness towards the patriots, bourgeois or *armées révolutionnaires* deemed responsible for the work of destruction. For the towns, the dechristianisation process was achieved from within. However much prompting came from the Paris sections or *armées révolutionnaires*, the furor of urban dechristianisation campaigns was in part self-generated. It carried with it the burden of responsibility (*culpa mea*).[31]

There is however, a further contrast to be drawn between the experience of some towns and others. In the orgiastic bursts of iconoclasm directed against particular church façades or statuary and crucifixes crowning spires, there are cities like Autun, Chartres, Rouen, Avignon and countless little towns like Mennecy and Gonesse in which women (individually if not *en masse*) are reported active. There are others in which the women absented themselves or had to be forced into action. At Arles for example the *société populaire* demanded that patriotic men bring their wives to an urban ceremony in which women and children were forced to spit on an image of Christ.[32] To impress the *représentant en mission* with their revolutionary orthodoxy the members of the *société populaire* at Le Puy ordered the burning of the black virgin, France's foremost shrine. The crowd who watched her being tossed onto the flames was entirely male, for the women feared that some terrible catastrophe would befall them and locked and bolted their doors. Priests who resigned their *lettres de prêtrise* at Bayeux, Coutances, Mende and Toulouse had to be protected by members of the *sociétés populaires* at their marriage services from physical assault by women who had been their parishioners. In the main, however, in the towns, the dechristianisation process took place without any serious effective counter-movement. Was it that townspeople in 1793–4 were afraid to register opposition? Were they convinced, unconvinced or partially convinced fellow-travellers in a movement which sought

---

31 On the town–country response to dechristianisation, Plongeron, *Conscience Religieuse*, pp. 105–6. This author is less precise on male–female responses.

32 M. Vovelle, *Les métamorphoses de la fête en Provence de 1750 à 1820* (Paris, 1976), p. 251.

so fundamentally to reverse the practice of centuries? Was political involvement and participation in civic events so engrossing that it was to some degree an effective religious substitute, as the militants of sectional and club politics urged?

These questions can only be answered in the most general way. In 1793 and into 1794 fear doubtless silenced some and even more found it possible to sacrifice commitment to an institution they saw as compromised by its association with foreign treachery. Moreover, urban women were deeply preoccupied with the implementation of the economic policy of the Terror that is, bread at a fixed price and the attendant war on hoarders and speculators. In this respect, urban working women, who much more than their men were involved in the marketplace, were Hébertistes all. The participation of women in club life was dedicated more than anything else to promoting consumer interests. As long as the maximum was in operation and the mechanism of the Terror turned against hoarders and speculators they were largely silent on religious issues. But, we note that the queues outside churches grew in proportion to the bread queues and we must assume that the queues had some common constituent at least.[33] Indeed, the recurrent use of the word *fanatisme* as a female attribute in the registers of the *sociétés populaires* and the correspondence of the *comités* in the winter of 1794 was made in two directions: first to apply to women's commitment to the principles of the maximum and insistence on retributive action against hoarders, and second to describe female commitment to vestigial catholicism. When Chaumette closed the Parisian women's club, patriots everywhere were told that the good *sans-culotte* wife stayed at home and was never a political militant, but left it to the male householder to perform his civic duty by presence at the club.[34] The *Comité de Salut public* was seeking by a sexist argument to sever some of the roots of Hébertiste and Enragé support on the issue of price fixation which had occasioned the expenditure of so much government effort and had so exacerbated relations between town and country. But they could not eliminate women from the bread queues or silence them as critics of the regime's failure to provide adequate provisioning.

When malnutrition hardened into real starvation in 1795 and the post-Thermidorean government had abandoned price controls and was associated with the hardship, women were to the fore in the riots which bore down on the Convention and tried to force a restoration of the people's price. In so doing, they were perhaps fulfilling their allotted social role as protestors for the community, but in the grisly aftermath of these risings which demonstrated

---

[33] On the twinning of mass and bread as objects of *première nécessité*, *Histoire des catholiques*, p. 266; Tallett, 'Religion and Revolution', pp. 377–9. 'Quand le bon Dieu était là, nous avions du pain', Hufton, *Bayeux*, p. 232.

[34] M. Cerati, *Le Club des citoyens républicaines révolutionnaires* (Paris, 1966), pp. 173–4; and S. H Lytle, 'The second sex (September, 1793)', *Jl. of Modern History*, XXVII (1955), 14–26.

nothing but the people's impotence we must not assume they remained passive in face of deepening distress. One protest movement had been tried and had failed. Now another replaced it. In the anarchy of the early Directorial period, when the power of pontificating authority was tempered by the weariness of local officialdom in face of the unending struggle to provision France, a female-engineered religious revival swept many of the towns. Already by the winter of 1795 much of rural France was bent on the reconstruction of a church. By the early summer in the Midi the first bloody episodes of the White Terror had occurred in the name of Christ and king. The emotions fuelling the revival varied between individuals, between social groups, between villages, between town and country. For some the anarchy of the period provided the opportunity to bring worship out into the open, fired by faith and/or the desire to re-establish community practice. For the women of the towns despair and contrition (the twinning of dearth and devotion is not after all peculiar to this period) fuelled the return to established religion. They were guilty: they must atone. Elsewhere religion proved a rallying cry, a constituent element in a movement for revenge directed against patriots in whatever guise they came: *mathevons, jacobins, bourgeois*, protestants. For an indefinable but possibly considerable proportion of the adult male populace what officials designated as an *esprit de contrariété*, a desire to find a vehicle to express dissatisfaction with the regime, may have been dominant.[35] In short, we must acknowledge that the forces contributing to reconstruction of the church were at least as varied as those contributing to its destruction.

The Thermidoreans helped the initial stages of the revival by withdrawing patronage of a state cult and pronouncing *la liberté des cultes*. How do we explain these steps which seemingly brought the threat of religious conflict into the forefront causing a great deal of government effort to attempt to control it?

The consequences of the Thermidoreans' action are obvious only to those blessed with hindsight. In part the decision to allow freedom of worship stripped of *les signes extérieurs du culte* (bells, processions, vestments, chalices etc.) and the opening of prison doors to release those who had refused to lay down their *lettres de prêtrise* was a calculated risk. In part it was a logical extension of the same policy of *laissez-faire* which abolished the maximum and opened the prison doors to a range of suspects. That is to say, the

[35] Tallett, 'Religion and Revolution', pp. 371–2 places this spirit as secondary to the genuine faith and the desire to re-establish regular worship in the Doubs but concedes its presence H. Forestier, 'Le culte laïcal', *Annales de Bourgogne*, XXIV (1952), 105–9 gives it greater prominence. In my opinion it should be regarded as a sex-specific attribute. One expression of this *esprit de contrariété* was the erection of crosses on the spot where the Tree of Liberty (levelled for the purpose) had been. The Tree represented Revolution, the cross communal hostility.

Thermidoreans' action sprang from the conviction that the repressive, interventionist policy of the Terror, directed towards the regulation of the grain trade and enforced dechristianisation, had created more problems than it had solved and that the dismantling of such a policy could only have a pacifying effect. There was certainly a risk involved but not so great as is apparent to those endowed with hindsight. True, religion was already associated with counter-revolution in the Vendée, but no one could claim it was the prime inspiration behind the movement compared, say, with conscription, and it could be argued that a policy of religious tolerance would strip the movement of any features it might have of a holy war. The reports sent by officialdom to the *Comité de Salut public* proffered the reassurance that it was women who clung most persistently to their old faith and the Thermidoreans clearly did not perceive women as a major threat. Why not let them have their god, provided, of course that they have it discreetly. At the same time, let the jews and protestants and *théophiles* have their god too. *À chacun son Dieu selon son goût.*

This kind of attitude was well rooted in the intellectual bourgeoisie, a *bourgeoisie des talents* nurtured in a tradition which believed with Voltaire that religion was an important means of social control for the masses or, like Robespierre, that the peasant had not reached the degree of intellectual maturity which enabled him to reject the idea of the supernatural. Indeed, one need only recall the reluctance of the Convention to respond to the dechristianising policy of the Paris sections, fearful that it would further alienate the peasantry from the Revolution, to realise that the Thermidoreans were merely reverting to their natural stance. They had no intention of returning to the ways of the Christian themselves, but they were intellectually committed to the notion of freedom.

Moreover, famine was raging, mortality rates soaring, especially in the towns and cities of northern France and, although it took Napoleon callously to recall the need for a belief in an after-life to console the individual dying of hunger, the Thermidoreans were not insensitive to such an approach. They certainly were not going to offer anything of material substance to improve the pauper's lot. What, however, is more surprising is that the Thermidoreans in late 1794 do not seem to have considered to *whom* the women and allied *fanatiques* would turn to administer their religion. Perhaps there is a simple explanation for this. Many non-jurors were in enemy countries and the war was now going well for France, so that their re-emergence was not perceived as an imminent threat. The constitutional clergy were, however, quite likely to re-emerge and the Abbé Grégoire was soon seeking to lend some organisation to this clergy.[36] But this was regarded by the government as a compliant clergy prepared to express allegiance to the state and the populace could take

---

[36] D. Woronoff, *La République bourgeoise de Thermidor à Brumaire 1794–1799* (Paris, 1972), pp., 143–4 gives the best short account of Grégoire's activities.

them or leave them. The state would pay no salaries, no bills. A significant burden was also placed on local authorities to see that religious sentiment was contained within proper bounds, that is, kept private. Churches were national property. Where they had not been sold to private individuals or companies and remained in the hands of the local authorities, they could only be hired out to specific individuals who were then responsible at law for their usage. If they had not been disposed of and melted down already, local authorities had control over such vessels and ornaments as the ancien regime church had possessed. They were not to let them go. They were guardians of the parish bells which were only to be used for state emergencies and certainly not to inform the parish of the hours of mass. In short, a great deal of power was placed in the hands of local authorities and in many instances the pace of the religious revival was decided by them.[37]

The attitude of local administrators varied very considerably from one canton to the next. After Thermidor, the weight of departmental and cantonal office was immense and represented an unending struggle for food supplies and taxes for or from a weary populace. Salaries were not forthcoming from a government unable to lend credence to its currency, and many local officials simply laid down office and retreated into obscurity, sometimes leaving a total vacuum of authority for several months. When someone presented himself prepared to accept an unpaid heavy job he might be a former old regime judge or official or someone whose commitment to the record of the Revolution and to the central government was far from wholehearted. At best, such people were concerned to keep local administration ticking over and adopted a quiescent attitude towards popular behaviour. Other 'royalist' officials openly colluded in actions designed to strike at former jacobins and were prepared to encourage the flouting of government legislation. In other localities jacobins and mathevons lingered on and continued to perpetuate policies and attitudes including a rigid interpretation of religious legislation. Hence, whilst Toulouse continued to pursue the burning of statues and relics, in Mende and Le Puy and other cities in Haut Languedoc, masses in vestments with the full panoply of traditional church ritual were openly taking place.

How was the process of reconstruction begun? A number of logical steps can be discerned to be taken as the obligatory prerequisite to the process of restoration. These were: the restoration of the parish church to its primitive usage; the procuring of sacred vessels and the means to summon the faithful to participation at church services; the reinstitution of Sunday (and the

---

37 Much therefore pivoted on how securely these authorities felt themselves to be as well as on their own predilictions. The Beauchesne diocesan histories in fact make one aware of considerable variations in tolerance and persecution: see also Tallett, 'Religion and Revolution', pp. 361–2. It is a theme somewhat neglected by the *Histoire des catholiques*. We are still a long way from being able to construct the geography of religious restoration.

rejection of the *décadi*) as the day of rest and the one on which an individual could hence fulfil his religious obligations and participate in a community ceremony. At some stage the decision had to be made concerning who should be asked to officiate at the parish mass, but this was seen as something secondary to the opening up of proper facilities. In short, communities had tired of *clandestinité*, of a priest whisked from hiding to perform by secret arrangement in a barn. They wanted to wallow in *les signes extérieurs du culte*,[38] with or without a priesthood.

In villages the parish church might have been used as stabling or for storing grain, but the extent of damage was usually minimal and private individuals within a parish who had these buildings on lease were unlikely to hold onto them in face of public pressure. In towns they had been used for much more diverse and damaging purposes, warehouses, quartermasters' stores, stables, fishmarkets, forges, manufactures of saltpetre, carpenters' premises or meetings of *sociétés populaires*. Many of them had been vandalised. Some required extensive repair on the eve of the Revolution and after only a short period of total neglect or non-occupancy were riddled with damp and death-watch beetle. Notwithstanding, in popular esteem, these were the proper places for public worship.

According to the letter of the law of 3 ventôse Year III/21 February 1795 which was the bedrock of the new tolerant religious legislation 'les communes ou sections de commune en nom collectif ne pourront acquérir ni louer de locale pour l'exercice des cultes'. The hiring, if the community wished to proceed by the letter of the law and not simply occupy the building in defiance of the local authorities, had to be conducted through a public auction with individuals proferring an appropriate sum. Where these auctions have been analysed, as they were in detail by the Abbé Sévestre for Normandy,[39] then women are seen to be in the forefront, a generalisation even applicable to the impious Île de France where at Gonesse *les femmes menaient l'action*. At Mende two women fought for the honour of restoring the cathedral as parish church. One, Rose Bros, offered 300 livres. Interestingly enough Rose Bros had previously been a leader of bread riots in 1789 and it is inconceivable that this 300 livres was her own money, for she was a person of very limited means. She was outbid by one Citoyenne Randon,

---

[38] This phrase as a criticism of the nature of popular religion is recurrent throughout the correspondence of the period, e.g. Panisset at Chambéry, letter cited by J. Lovie, *Les diocèses de Chambéry, Tarentaise, Maurienne* (Paris, 1979), p. 151. Cholvy writing of the south-east 'Plus que l'attachement à la personne du prêtre . . ., ce sont les rites et les croyances que défendent les populations' (*A.h.R.f.* 233 (1978), 461). Duval-Jouve, *Montpellier*, p. 327: 'On voulait donc le culte à l'extérieur, avec tout son appareil voyant et bruyant . . .' Woronoff, *La République bourgeoise*, p. 141, pithily describes this :'La clocheéta it le symbole de la reconquête; en elle s'abolissait l'Eglise du silence.'

[39] Abbé E. Sévestre, *Les problèmes religieux de la Révolution et de l'Empire en Normandie* (Paris 1924), p. 1070.

wife of an ex-district official during the Terror. It is quite clear from the actions of this second woman that she intended to make the building immediately available to the community. Was she seeking to save her husband's skin by offering the further hundred livres in expiation of his sins? Was the money out of her own funds?[40] One may never know. Were women acting on their own behalf or on behalf of the community as a whole? Were they conscious that something reported to officialdom as the work of women might secure an acceptance, a shrug of the shoulders which would perhaps not apply to the activities of men? The answer to these questions must be 'perhaps', but that we are left with a much more wholehearted female response which every interest from the Abbé Grégoire's emergent constitutional church to the national agents was prepared to accentuate. Occasionally – so occasionally that known instances perhaps do not exceed a handful per diocese – a wealthy individual stepped forward, sometimes a widow, sometimes a wealthy local *dévôt* or a crank who was prepared to find the funds for hiring. Into the last category must be placed Les Rotours (Orne), where a certain François Angot, a former *officier royal* and seigneur, provided the means to open the church and then proceeded to conduct the service

il a créé dans sa commune un culte nouveau: il fait dans la ci-devant église suivant le rite des prêtres catholiques romains, à l'exception de ce qu'il dit leur être réservé . . .

Cet office auquel assiste un si grand nombre d'habitants simples de la campagne, des deux sexes, que l'église ne peut les contenir, est qualifié *messe* dans tout le canton, et Angot dit des Rotours est si bien connu pour en être le ministre que les habitants disent qu'ils vont *à la messe de M. des Rotours*.

. . . Angot est le principal célébrant du culte que l'on exerce dans la ci-devant église des Rotours il en est donc le ministre quoi qu'il prétend qu'un père de famille marié depuis trente-deux ans et qui a le sens commun ne peut être soupçonné de vouloir se faire le ministre d'un culte . . .[41]

Other communities, because they were poor, remote or bitter did not perceive the rationale behind the demanding of money for the opening of the church and chose forcible occupation. Such was the case at Vouneuil-sur-Vienne (Vienne) where women, sticks in hand, forced the door of the church and found some vestigial relics of the presence of the *société populaire*. They tore up the Declaration of the Rights of Man, the Laws and the Constitution and smashed and burned the president's chair.[42] The news of a successful occupation in one parish could have a triggering effect and serve as inspiration to an occupation in nearby parishes. Or else, and this was the experience

---

[40] Delon, *Révolution en Lozère*, p. 51. In the riot of 1790 Rose Bros (née Castan) attacked the Chapter's grain supply (p. 740). She led the movement to hire the church, 23 ventôse an III/13 March 1795.

[41] L. Duval, 'La messe de Monsieur des Rotours', *Bulletin de la Société historique et archéologique de l'Orne*, XXVIII (1909), 156–204.

[42] M. de Roux, *Histoire religieuse de la Révolution à Poitiers et dans la Vienne* (Lyon, 1952), p. 251.

in one of the urban parishes of Bayeux, the individual who had had the church on hire since the Terror simply handed it over. The case of Madame Le Morgue whose husband, a fishmonger, had opened a fish-market in one of the churches, illustrates this point perfectly. In face of her husband's pro-testation to the municipality, she opened up the church and led a team of cleaning women to scour it out. In short, by multiple stratagems, the law of the 3 ventôse Year III made a parish church available to most people.[43] They secured a locale for their religion.

Less general was success in procuring the return of sacred vessels and the restoration of the bell which the law expressly forbade. Sometimes, the chalices and silverware had been melted down. Probably only a minority of parishes succeeded in getting the municipalities to part with the sacred vessels, unless, as at Vouneuil-sur-Vienne, the women's revolt that had opened the church reconvened to move against the municipality and succeeded in getting them handed over by a terrified official who alone could be found.[44] Without a chalice, communion could not be conducted in full panoply, but, as we shall see, this aspect of the mass was only possible where there was a fully-fledged priest to conduct it and at this stage of reconstruction such a person was not to be taken for granted. It was a similar case with the bells. Occasion-ally, as at Ribérac (Dordogne), female protest movements succeeded in getting control of this means of summoning the people to church. Pregnant and old women were lined up (having been imported from neighbouring parishes) to swell the ranks of forefront protestors, whilst the young and able-bodied of the parish brought up the rear with aprons full of stones and ashes to blind any assailants.[45] Sometimes, as in the non-nuclear villages of the Rouergue and the Auvergne, the entire community was prepared to press for the control of the bells – bells which historically were very much an aspect of community solidarity and corporate action – though they did not necessarily use them for the summons to mass. Isolated villages in the Gévaudan and the Velay were sufficiently confident that they could use them without fear of reprisals from outside officialdom.[46] Others, and there are some splendid instances to be cited from Franche-Comté, pealed the bells to symbolise local victories over officialdom after opening the church or, in 1798 when the legislation of vendémiaire inaugurated another wave of

[43] A. D. Calvados, 'Comptes décadaires', 19 thermidor an V.

[44] Roux, *Poitiers*, p. 251. See also G. Lefebvre, *Les paysans du Nord* (Laterza, 1959), p. 874.

[45] G. Bussière, *Etudes historiques sur la Révolution en Périgord* (3 vols., Bordeaux, 1897–1903), III, p. 246.

[46] *Recueil des événements qui ont lieu au Puy et aux environs depuis l'an 1775 jusqu'en 1815* (Le Puy 1931), p. 324. In the Lodévois (particularly the hilltop villages of the Causses) during May 1795 'Les cultes sont librement exercés. Le peuple est appelé aux messes et vêpres par le son de la cloche que l'on met en branle, en outre, trois fois par jour pour . . . l'angélus.' Cited by G. Cholvy, *Histoire du diocèse de Montpellier* (Paris, 1976), p. 186. Lefebvre, *Paysans du Nord* p. 874: women occupy the bell tower.

repression of non-jurors, to tell the community that attempts at priest-rescuing had been successful.[47] In spite of such instances in nuclear villages and towns the parish bell remained silent, though occasionally attempts were made to find a substitute, as when small boys were sent through the streets of Provençal and Languedocian villages – and even the city of Montpellier – with cowbells to draw attention to the holy hour.[48]

The aspect of restoration on which general cooperation was easiest to achieve and where no specific female involvement emerges was the issue of Sunday as holiday and the rejection of the *décadi*, the rationalised, laicised, ten-day week. We should at this point stress that the observance of Sunday does not necessarily bear any relationship to catholic worship. A ten-day week was far more onerous than a seven-day one and as such had never been popular. It was also compromised by association with a regime conspicuous for its intrusion into community life, its failure to provision the towns, its brutal treatment of the peasantry by the *armées révolutionnaires* and its excessive demands in terms of military personnel, food and fodder. Rejection of the *décadi* and the ostentatious leisured observance of Sunday was the pleasantest and easiest way of bucking the system and of expressing what officialdom designated as *l'esprit de contrariété*.[49] To carry that idea of protest still further by attending mass was not deemed needful by everyone. On the eve of the Concordat the mayor of Lain (near Auxerre) wrote to the prefect:

Tout le monde est catholique ici, excepté quatre ou cinq qui y vivent sans religion. Or, un bon tiers des habitants ne veulent plus observer le dimanche. On reste au cabaret; on joue aux cartes pendant les messes et vêpres; on fauche, on charroie... Nos concitoyens ont toujours tenu une conduite tout à fait opposée à tout ce que la loi prescrit. Pendant l'existence des jours de décadi tout le monde travaillait ce jour-là et célébrait religieusement le dimanche. Aujourd'hui que la décadi est supprimée, on ne veut plus reconnaître le dimanche.[50]

Time off for the working man meant drinking. The notion, throughout the period 1796–1801, of respecting Sunday whilst idling in a tavern was frequently noted. This option had not been quite as available under the ancien regime, for at least theoretically, the opening hours of the *cabaret* were

---

[47] Tallett, 'Religion and Revolution', pp. 375–6.

[48] By messidor an V however in both Lodève and Montpellier the bells were ringing. Duval-Jouve, *Montpellier*, p. 327. 'Partout il y a le son des cloches' declared the *agent national* at Pontarlier (A. D. Doubs, L 1305, 29 floréal an III, 18 May 1795).

[49] Forestier, 'Le culte laïcal', XXIV, pp. 105–9 and XXV, pp. 175–7 gives some remarkable examples of this spirit from the Auxerre: e.g., 'Ils voudraient bien que nous fissions la décade; mais pour les fair enrager, il faut toujours sonner les fêtes et dimanches et chanter en nous c.e.f. d'eux': complaint about the village of Saint-Cyr-les-Colins to the *justice de paix* of Saint-Bris nivôse an III. An inhabitant of Damblin (Doubs), when asked why he observed Sunday, said 'parce qu'il s'en fouttait de de M. Charbon' (the *agent municipal*). For this and other examples see Tallett, 'Religion and Revolution', p. 372.

[50] Cited by Forestier, 'Le culte laïcal', p. 107.

restricted on Sundays and *fêtes*. The removal of the *curé*, as a check on opening hours, the extension of sociability based on the *cabaret*, as this institution became associated with local politics and indeed in towns and *bourgs* frequently served as locale for the meetings of the *société populaire*, were factors which combined to enhance still further the notion of drink as an essential part of leisure.[51] For most of France, the tavern was a male preserve and not one available to a respectable woman. Therefore, in insisting upon the Sunday holiday, the men of the parish were still subjected to the dual pull: the choice between the 'manly' environment of the tavern and the female one of the church. One cannot be surprised that some opted for the former whilst their womenfolk went to mass.

The self-employed, a categorisation applicable to the bulk of rural society, could take the option on Sunday or the *décadi* for themselves. For apprentices and maidservants, which they chose depended upon permission from their employers. Local officials and some former jacobins clung to the *décadi* and the *fête civique*. Indeed by 1797 these groups alone (minus their wives) were the pathetic participants in processions that the populace as a whole chose to ignore. Employers in the textile cities, Rouen, Lodève, Amiens, were quick to concede Sunday to their resident female labour. Some when challenged laid the responsibility on their wives. However, the populace as a whole voted on the *décadi* with its feet.[52]

There was then the crucial question of personnel to man the restored church and here we encounter the gravest difficulties in making generalisations, because much hinged on the question of who was available as well as who was acceptable to the community; and the question of availability was linked to a range of other considerations, such as geography, individual initiative and courage and a thousand and one particular factors, like the health and stamina of the emergent priesthood. It would be very false to assume that every community could opt for either a juror or a non-juror. In the aftermath of Thermidor the Abbé Grégoire and a dozen high officials of the juror church struggled to reconstruct a working hierarchy, but the

---

[51] *Est-on plus altéré qu'autrefois?* ran a leader article in a Grenoble journal for 1810. The need of the church to extricate men from the tavern is a recurrent theme, e.g. Godel, *La reconstruction concordataire*, p. 213; see also *Histoire religieuse de la Touraine*, pp. 266–7.

[52] At Clermont-de-Lodève, known before the Revolution for impiety and irregularity of Sunday observance amongst the textile workers, 'chaque décadi, le président, les agents municipaux et moi, nous nous trouvons toujours vis à vis de nous mêmes', cited Cholvy, *Montpellier*, p. 185. God intervenes to rebuff the *décadi* at Saint Chinian where a woman paid to 'sonner le décadi' claimed 'elle avait été jetée à terre par une force invisible qui lui avait ôté la corde des mains', ibid., p. 186. At Jaulges (near Auxerre) where the *agent municipal* went to plough on Sunday 'un lièvre fabuleux s'est jeté sur lui, a épouvanté ses juments, l'a mis en fuite, l'a suivi chez-lui et ne le quitte plus' (Forestier, 'Le culte laïcal', p. 107). On Sunday as a day of rest without a devotional aspect and on the rejection of the *décadi*, Lefebvre, *Paysans du Nord*, pp. 895–7.

problems were legion. So many priests had married, resigned or fled that to know just who was available and not compromised in the eye of the public was not something to be achieved overnight. In every diocese there was at least a handful of stalwarts, deeply religious men prepared for their own kind of martyrdom, like Moulland, Curé of Saint-Martin at Bayeux, or Panisset at Chambéry, who were ready to begin the task of reconstruction and to work with the Abbé Grégoire.[53] Such men were obviously prepared to proffer themselves on their own terms to the populace, but they could only, even supposing they were acceptable, cover a small minority of parishes. Then there were the non-jurors, but the numbers and physical capacities of these in any one area varied enormously. Generally speaking, frontier regions, particularly Alsace, Franche-Comté, the Dauphiné and those regions contiguous to Switzerland soon received back a steady flow of relatively able-bodied non-jurors, though far from sufficient to man the majority of parishes.[54] Similarly, after 1796, came the return to Brittany, Normandy and Picardy some of those who had taken refuge in Britain and an antique capitular clergy emerged from obscurity.[55] Throughout the Revolution, in Brittany and the Cotentin, communities had always been willing to harbour their priests or relatives who had held priestly office elsewhere, and in the relatively permissive atmosphere of 1796 these now emerged and were warmly acclaimed by the local populace. In Pyrenean regions there was a return from Spain and in the least accessible parts of the Massif those who had practised clandestinely in hill-top villages now came into the open, but remained in the villages where they knew themselves secure and steered clear of towns. Though there was no single figure orchestrating the organisation of the non-juring church, where individual bishops in exile succeeded in organising missions or setting up effective contacts with locally established clerics who had a real appreciation of local circumstances, most could be achieved. The old arch-diocese of Lyon would appear to have been most

---

[53] Hufton, *Bayeux*, p. 264; Lovie, *Chambéry*, pp. 151–4.

[54] In some dioceses, that of the Hérault, for example, they appear to have been very thin on the ground indeed. A letter written by a non-juror, Pons-Marie Saisset, 18 June 1796, has a convincing amount of detail (cited Cholvy, *Diocèse de Montpellier*, p. 179): 'Depuis plus de deux ans, les églises sont fermées [à Montpellier] et les intrus n'exercent plus leurs fonctions. Au commencement de 1794, ils renoncèrent à leur état et cessèrent dès lors d'exercer le ministère . . . Depuis cette époque, ils ont tous disparu, il n'en reste pas un seul, de manière qu'il n'y a dans notre ville aucun vestige de schisme constitutionnel. Truchement, intrus de Saint-Pierre est allé dans son pays [le Vaucluse] où il exerce la médecine. Bellugou, intrus de Sainte-Anne, s'est retiré à Saint-Pargoire; procureur de la commune il exerce publiquement ses fonctions dans l'église où tout le monde se rend avec affluence. Barry, intrus de Saint-Denis, est au service du gouvernement et fait une fortune scandaleuse [à Paris]. Chéri, intrus de Notre Dame, est allé dans sa patrie avec une femme qu'il a épousée ici.' On Franche-Comté, Tallett, 'Religion and Revolution', pp. 384–90 and *Histoire des catholiques*, pp. 268–9. It would seem that the total potential force of jurors was no more than 15,000.

[55] Hufton, *Bayeux*, pp. 265–6.

effectively organised with mission circuits, each regularly receiving a priest.[56]

It has already been noted that exile, hiding, physical deprivation, imprisonment, the experience of being hunted, the extreme fatigue attendant on flight had all taken their toll on both sets of clergy, and it is rare to find a diocese in which allusion is *not* made to the very poor condition of those emerging from hiding, and some had to be physically forced by the local populace into the church to say mass. One at Levier (Doubs), a frontier town which had known a bitter dechristianising campaign, tried to resist and was beaten by women, sticks in hand, into the church to say mass,[57] and there are plenty of instances in the diocese of Bayeux of priests forcibly brought out of hiding against their will. In the event, given the return to persecution in 1798, the non-jurors were right to be apprehensive about the security of their position.

But whilst diffidence was the experience of those emerging from hiding, both the Abbé Grégoire and the orthodox hierarchy seeking to control events from London and Switzerland had a common characteristic: their utter conviction that the sins of the people were responsible for the rejection of the Christian church. They must atone *par le fouet et le feu*.[58] There must be no compromise with standards. The people were guilty. Each must wrestle with his or her own guilt by personal attrition.

It is easy to appreciate why the non-juring church should adopt such an uncompromising stance. Yet the jurors ceded nothing to them in this respect. In Panisset's correspondence is found the following letter written in 1796:

Les peuples ont été touchés par la persécution mais non convertis. Or, il faut les croire plus 'gâtés que bons', plus attachés à l'extérieur de la religion qu'aux sentiments

---

[56] The bishops, defined as émigrés, could not return in 1796, since under émigré legislation they would have faced arrest. They were, however, the organisers of missions: 'les réfractaires préfèrent une stratégie du mouvement: ils devinrent des "missionaires" catholiques aux interventions discrètes ou provocantes, mais toujours inattendues, avant de disparaître dans la nature. Evidemment, ils n'agissaient que dans les limites des anciens diocèses, d'ou il résultait qu'en plus de Grenoble quatre évêques s'occupaient du département de l'Isère' (B. Bligny, *Histoire du diocèse de Grenoble* (Paris, 1979), p. 180). The missions in the Lyonnais used a *chef de Histoire du diocèse de Grenoble* (Paris, 1979), p. 180). The missions in the Lyonnais used a *chef de paroisse*, a layman nominated by the leader of the mission who announced the *fête* days and on Sundays, in the absence of a priest, recited some of the liturgy of the mass. He also organised the faithful into groups in private houses to hear mass from a *prêtre à valise* 'réservant les moins prudents pour la dernière nuit' (C. Ledré, *Le culte caché sous la Révolution, Les missions de l'abbé Linsolas* (Paris, 1949), pp. 88–9). This may explain why blind masses were less common in the diocese of Lyon. Mission structure is indicated in the dioceses of Autun, Belley, and in the Vivarais, the Isère, Savoie, Jura. The bishop of Tournai sent missions into the Nord and the Pas de Calais. They also appeared in the dioceses of Le Mans and Tarbes, *Histoire des catholiques*, p. 271.

[57] A. D. Doubs L 1305, 29 floréal an III/18 May 1795.

[58] The *Annales de Religion*, the periodical founded by the little group of bishops and clerics around Grégoire resounds with this kind of vocabulary no less than the correspondence of the emergent non-jurors. On the problems of the jurors, *Histoire des catholiques*, p. 269.

intérieurs. Privés qu'ils sont de sacrements depuis trois ans, on voudrait en faire des chrétiens de la primitive Eglise. Certes quelques élus ont pu ressusciter, mais je ne crois pas que les prodiges de la conversion de Saint Paul soient devenus *vulgaires* et *quotidiens*. Ces miracles étaient du temps où on redoutait les progrès de la foi, alors que maintenant on récolte les fruits de son dépérissement.

Si bien qu'il convient d'être fort rigoureux et d'éviter tout laxisme. Rien de plus dangereux dans la direction des pénitens que cet ancien et détestable principe de condescendance, il ne faut pas *brusquer*. Il faut supporter telle chose abusive pour empêcher un plus grand mal, pour procurer plus de bien *Non, il faut brûler et couper* [my italics]. Tant pis pour les malades qui ne voudront pas supporter l'opération . . . Les peuples ne jugeront de la gravité des délits irreligieux que par la difficulté d'en être absous.[59]

Furthermore, Grégoire and his associates rejected expressly any jurors who had married or had resigned their priestly state. It was important to present a purified, uncompromised image to the people.

The jurors enjoyed two advantages. First, they were quick off the mark and second they were, in the main, acceptable to central and local authorities, prepared as well to take oaths of loyalty to the constitution. When, within days of the law of ventôse Year III Moulland went to the municipality at Bayeux and pointed out that the restoration of the church at Saint-Jean under his direction might be the best means of preserving public order, they acquiesced. The church was full to bursting and Moulland worked a nineteen-hour shift in the confessional.[60] But Moulland was merely one of ten juring priests within a thirty-mile radius of Bayeux. They were, in short, very thin on the ground. In less than three months, part of the non-juring priesthood either emerged from hiding or returned from exile. Those who had been in England had unrealistic notions about what they could hope to find in their parishes on their return, and were little prepared for the *semi-clandestinité* within which they had to operate in areas where some jacobin sentiment still lingered. What they encountered amongst a hungry, weary, disillusioned petty peasantry was a rapturous reception. For the first months they held confessions widely. Queues formed of women prepared to have their tongues scraped free of the contamination of the mass of the constitutional priest and to have babies and toddlers, many of them suffering from chronic malnutrition and vitamin-deficiency diseases, baptised.[61] If contrition was what the

---

[59] Cited by Lovie, *Chambéry*, p. 154.

[60] Hufton, *Bayeux*, p. 264.

[61] A.N. F7 7606 *Règlement provisoire donné par Monseigneur l'évêque de Bayeux aux curés, desservants, vicaires et à tous les prêtres de son diocèse 6 juin 1795* embodies careful instructions as to what should be demanded by the jurors of their flock. R. Patry, *Le régime et la liberté des cultes dans le département du Calvados pendant la première séparation 1795–1802* (Paris, 1921), p. 191 depicts these confessional queues. Also Tallett, 'Religion and Revolution', p. 382. The *conseil général* at Baume in February 1795 reported that people who had used the services of a constitutional priest for a marriage or baptism approached refractory clerics in order that the ceremony be

emergent hierarchy wanted, they certainly got it during the early months of the Directory, and they were only held back from a thorough takeover of the towns as well by the Directory's decision to wrest from them an oath of loyalty, which was a demand they could in no way respect.

There is a case for arguing that the emergent clerics somewhat over-played their hand in the demands they made of the populace and that in some cases this served as an alienating factor – though this was more visible after 1801.[62] The Abbé Grégoire's band were insistent that the people in 1796–7 were fully prepared to pay non-jurors for their services.[63] Nevertheless, there is much to suggest that after the first heady exhilaration attached to the restoration of worship something of the momentum was lost. The populace showed conspicuously little interest in the catechism, in instruction, in frequent confession, in the viaticum. A study of the Parisian parish of Saint-Sulpice shows that the full confessionals of 1796 were within twelve months replaced by a situation in which only women and the old presented themselves with any regularity. The young, particularly young men, were simply not there, and we note the emergence of what was to be the continuing problem of the nineteenth-century church; one to be aggravated by the continued secularisation of male education.[64]

The message of the emergent non-jurors was hate, hatred of jacobins, of officialdom and of the constitutional church. The last was the target of a campaign designed to discredit its powers to absolve, to celebrate mass, to baptise or marry. From mid-1797 the Abbé Grégoire's band were in difficulties wherever they came up against a non-juror. From Normandy, Franche-Comté, Poitou, the Périgord and wherever the situation has been analysed they made the same complaints. No one ever asks us for the

carried out afresh: 'Ils rebaptisent et remarient tous ceux qui se présentent à eux. Ils appellent unions illicites tous ces mariages qui ont été faits après les nouvelles lois' (A. D. Doubs L 248 ventôse an IV). Also M. Reinhard, *Le département de la Sarthe sous le régime directorial* (St Brieuc, 1935), p. 567.

[62] This was certainly the opinion of Canon Boisjugan at Bayeux who believed that many of the returning priests were under unrealistic instructions from De Cheylus in London (Hufton, *Bayeux*, p. 266). Some were prepared to obey in the short term, but once the church had been formally restored in 1801 opposition began to manifest itself. Resistance to clerical attempts to reimpose licensing hours and to secure some minimal repairs to the presbytery caused a great deal of bitterness, e.g. Genevray, *Toulouse*, p. 149. *Histoire religieuse de la Touraine*, p. 267.

[63] 'nous faisons tout gratis que les réfractaires se font payer 28 livres pour la bénédiction nuptiale autant pour le baptême et le reste à proportion. Il en est un surtout, ci-devant chanoine de la cathédrale, nommé Pouderoux, qui gagne immensément: si cela dure, me disait-on dans un an il ramassera près de 3000 livres', Gonnet, *Puy en Velay*, p. 284. Lefebvre, *Paysans du Nord*, pp. 848 and 871.

[64] S. Delacroix, *La réorganisation de l'Eglise de France après la Révolution* (Paris, 1965), vol. 1. It is to be regretted that the subsequent volumes of this thesis have not been published, since there is no better study of both the Abbé Grégoire's problems and the response of certain sectors of the population, such as selected Parisian parishes.

viaticum; we are not sought out for confession; when the people open their churches, they do not ask us to officiate. We are prepared to offer our services for nothing whilst the non-jurors demand payment. This rejection, for it was no less, the Abbé Grégoire was prepared to impute entirely to 'les femmes crapuleuses et séditieuses'.[65]

Was his imputation a fair one? In so far as the groundswell for a religious revival counted more women than men, that their attendance at mass was more to be relied upon, that they were the arbiters of who baptised their children and buried their loved ones and they were obviously more ready to accept the criticisms of the Abbé Grégoire's church by the non-jurors, it contains an acknowledgment of reality. The constitutional church was perceived as guilt-laden by its preparedness in 1791 and again under the legislation of 7 vendémiaire Year IV/29 September 1795 to make peace with the government by taking an oath of loyalty. It was a time-server making claims to popular penitence it had no right to make. If it maintained a toehold in the towns, it was because the government, in deciding to clamp down yet again on the non-juring clergy in 1798 and to initiate a second Terror in response to the White Terror, an assumption of power in the localities by royalist officials, caused a second exodus, into captivity or *clandestinité*, of the non-juring priesthood.

Yet there was an alternative to the services of a priest at all and that was the constitution of the blind mass or *messe blanche* or *messe de maître d'école*. This was a mass conducted not by a priest but by a lay figure, often a schoolmaster, who knew the form of the liturgy. These masses took place in some rural parishes, particularly in the north and east, in the diocese of Rouen – particularly the Pays de Caux, in Burgundy, the Mâconnais, Alsace and Franche-Comté.[66] In some instances the use of the *messe blanche* may have

---

[65] Ibid.; Patry, *Calvados*; Sévestre, *Les problèmes religieux* remain fundamental. Lovie, *Chambéry* p. 154; Tallett, 'Religion and Revolution', pp. 390–5 etc. Sévestre has particularly informative footnotes about women's behaviour, such as attempts by juring clergy to prevent their servants attending a non-juror's mass. He draws heavily on Bibl. Chanoine Des landes, Bayeux: Correspondence of the episcopal vicars, an V–an VII.

[66] On *messes aveugles* in Franche-Comté, Tallett, 'Diocese of Besançon', pp. 393–6. Tallett insists that they had by 1798 become the normal form of religious observance and that even with more than 400 clergy available the option most parishes chose. Pillorget, 'Les messes clandestines', pp. 163–7. Even in areas not specifically designated areas of *messes aveugles* one finds obvious analogies, e.g. Duval-Jouve, *Montpellier*, p. 282: 'A ce moment, il se passa un fait curieux et caractéristique. Des habitants de Saint Pons éprouvait . . . le besoin d'assister à des spectacles religieux et par un d'eux, le premier venu, ils se faisant chanter des messes et des vêpres. Le commissaire près la municipalité de cette commune demanda à l'administration ou départe-mentale (9 nivôse) si à cet individu, singeant ainsi les fonctions sacerdotales, il fallait faire application de la loi du 7 vendémiaire . . . Le département répondit . . . que la loi, reconnaissant la liberté de conscience et non un caractère privilégié à ceux qui veulent exercer le ministère des cultes, était applicable a tous ceux qui se présenteraient pour faire la déclaration legale. Cette réponse une fois connue, la plupart des communes voisines faisaient faire cette déclaration

reflected the unavailability of an acceptable priest or the reluctance of an emergent priest to perform anything beyond a clandestine service. Or, it may have represented a conscious option on the part of a parish as a means of obtaining a regular Sunday service which would not suddenly be terminated by the disappearance of the personnel. A third explanation is that in some instances it may have represented the extent of the community's religious aspirations.

A typical case would be that reported from Saint-Cyr-les-Colons (Yonne) on 2 nivôse Year III/22 December 1794 when a group of weavers by the names of Edme Barbette, Thomas Petit and Baptiste Bodot performed as follows:

Edme Barbette, c'est celui qui fait les fonctions de ci-devant prêtre et leur annonce toutes les fêtes qui peuvent arriver dans la semaine, comme Sainte Catherine, Saint Nicolas; mais, il le faut dire, c'est pour qu'il leur dise la messe, et ce Thomas Petit et Bodot ce sont ses chantres . . . ils font sonner les matines . . .

[A week earlier]

Pierre Dorotte, qui a sonné le second et troisième coup du rassemblement fanatique, était accompagné de Edme Barbette, qui feuilletait les livres disposés à l'office qu'ils ont chanté. Un quart d'heure après ce dernier a dit à haute voix et d'un ton ironique : 'Qu'on sonne le dernier coup.' Après cet survenu Alexis Delinotte, fils Edme, qui a sonné le dernier coup. Peu de temps après, leur prétendu office a commencé par Aspergesse me, Dominé etc., qui a été chanté par Thomas Petit, Edme Barbette a terminé . . . par Ostende nobis etc. Ensuite l'exce-messe a commencé par l'introytte chantée par Edme Delinotte, ci-devant maréchal, Jean Petit, fils Jacques etc. L'excem-esse a terminé par Pater et Filius prononcé en manière de bénédiction par Edme Barbette, qui a fait les gesticulations ordinaires de prêtre cidevant.[67]

To be noticed here beyond the assumption of the priest's role by a group of humble people is the use of noise, bells and music, the fact that this was a sung mass and reference was made to holy books which were put into use. There is no reference made here to the usurpation of clerical dress and vestments, but in other villages, like Ouanne not far away, the local schoolteacher appeared in surplice and biretta 'c'est un des chantres d'église qui pour l'absence des prêtres s'immiscent dans la célébration du culte catholique'. No attempt was made to proffer communion.[68]

Local authorities clearly did not know how to deal with this home-made priesthood. From the Ardennes in 1796 came this question to the central government: 'Ne pourrait-on pas, en les regardant comme ministres du culte, les obliger à faire la déclaration voulue par la loi et les rendre respons-ables de ce qui pourrait se commettre contre la sûreté publique dans les

par un de leurs habitants, après quoi il représentait toutes les cérémonies des dimanches et fêtes, auxquelles on assistait avec une dévote obstination. Quelque fois aussi un prêtre réfractaire sortait de sa cachette et prenait la place du déclarant . . . tel à Montpellier . . .', etc.

[67] Forestier, 'Le Culte laïcal', pp. 108–9.
[68] Both Forestier, p. 108 and Tallett, 'Religion and Revolution', pp. 388–9.

rassemblements qu'ils occasionnent?' But, the reply was explicit that under article 5 of the third section of the law of 7 vendémiaire Year IV such an oath could only be directed against recognised *ministres du culte*.[69]

The civil authorities were not alone in feeling apprehensive of these unofficial masses, though they viewed them more favourably than those of a hostile non-juror. For the constitutional priesthood they were yet another manifestation of rejection. But even the non-juror clergy were suspicious. One wrote to Monseigneur de Marbeuf:

Ces laics jaloux de présider, de charmer par leurs chants semblent oublier la nécessité du ministère. J'ai déjà trouvé quelques-uns de ces chefs d'assemblées dans les églises à qui la tête a tourné. Ils veulent réformer, faire les curés . . . Le peuple s'accoûtume à cet extérieur, à ces simulacres de culte; ils s'accoûtume à se passer de mîtres. Il s'endort, trompé par l'apparence. On n'a plus la même ardeur pour s'approcher des sacrements dans les pays où il y a de ces sortes d'assemblées.[70]

Was such fear justified? If we set aside the instances of Alsace and Franche-Comté, the areas where *messes blanches* seem to have been at their most extensive were those with the most marked tendency to slippage in the nineteenth century. The *bourgs* and rural parishes that settled for *messes blanches* were obviously content with those *signes extérieurs du culte* which both non-jurors and jurors stressed were of the least spiritual significance to the catholic faith. They carried no spirit of penitence: they were content to do without confession and absolution and even communion, but they wanted to meet regularly as a community and make their incantation in recognition of their deity. This deity had the added advantage of demanding no moral or large-scale financial sacrifice.

In much the same spirit we note the emergence of *confréries* (pious fraternities) and of parish pilgrimages to traditional shrines.[71] Both types of activity

---

[69] Forestier and Tallett, ibid. There appears, however, to have been considerable confusion about whether an oath was required or not. In Franche-Comté attempts were made to get anyone presiding at these assemblies to take an oath under the legislation of vendémiaire 1797, but this was merely an oath of hatred of royalty. Some refused on the grounds that, if anyone took an oath of any kind, *il dirait sa messe tout seul* (Tallett, 'Religion and Revolution', p. 391). We should also note that some of the *messes aveugles* had no regular leaders. See also note 66.

[70] Cited by Ledré, *Le Culte caché*, p. 229. There seems to be little doubt that this home-made priesthood was intended as a long-term alternative even to the non-jurors. 'Non contents de pervertir la jeunesse [les maîtres d'écoles] sont encore érigés en ministre du culte et président à toutes les assemblées qui continuent à se former sous prétexte de religion, et *ils remplacent ainsi les prêtres réfractaires*' (my italics) (A. D. Doubs, L 224 report of the *commissaire* 16 nivôse an VII/5 January 1798).

[71] Sometimes the *confrérie* would seem to have provided an initial basis for reorganising a parish. Hence in the region of Mont Blanc, 'La première concerne les réunions de prières tenues à l'initiative des fidèles, surtout dans les paroisses de montagne en Tarentaise et en Haute-Maurienne. Les pénitents et pénitentes y ont joué un rôle essentiel. Et ces réunions ressemblaient suffisamment à la messe avec Kyrie, Gloria, Sanctus etc. pour que les curés de retour y aient vu une concurrence' (Lovie, *Chambéry*, p. 153). Similarly, Cholvy, *Montpellier*, p. 189. Pilgrimages

appear as characteristic of those communities unable or unwilling to secure the services of a priest, and the parish pilgrimages in particular were often under the direction of the schoolmaster. The fraternities, of course, represented the male populace of the rural parishes. The spiritual content of the association was frequently small, and more than anything else the meeting was a social gathering, an expression of belonging to a community and an expression which did not contravene the letter of the law. (Notwithstanding, even the exigient Curé of Ars thought he could make a catholic out of anyone who belonged to a *confrérie*.)[72] The pilgrimages were a perfect vehicle of defiance of local authorities and one which could be emulated by the communities through which the pilgrims passed. They were not illegal so long as they did not bedeck themselves with banners, or 'process', but there was nothing to stop them chanting, nothing to stop them recounting their experiences to those they met along the way and, as they gained in confidence, little to prevent them violating the letter as well as the spirit of the law.

The refusal of communities to keep their religion quiet, the widely known activities of a priesthood which refused any compromise with the government, and the association of religion with the White Terror or with royalism lay behind the second Terror of 1798. Yet this second Terror did little to stem the resurgence of religious worship. True, a large number of non-juring clergy were driven again into hiding and many were deported or killed. But the repression varied in its intensity from area to area and where it had momentum it owed it to returned jacobins in the towns. In some instances, such as the villages of Franche-Comté or those of the Bessin, this new attempt at repression served to inject renewed vigour into a revival that was already beginning to lose its initial verve. Priest-rescuing from urban prisons and the defiant pealing of bells reminded officialdom of the limitations of their authority in the localities. Elsewhere, as in the Cotentin and Haut Languedoc, the new deportations of the non-jurors and the executions created a new set of martyrs and popular saints for incorporation in the local calendar.[73] Everywhere some form of communal religious worship could be found.

were organised in the village to traditional shrines, e.g. Saint-Maximim at Foucherons (Doubs), Tallett, 'Religion and Revolution', p. 369; to the hermitage of Saint Laurent by the women at Bessan (Hérault), Cholvy, p. 189.

[72] On the importance attached to *confréries* in the religious elevation of a parish, Boutry and Cinquin, *Deux pèlerinages*, pp. 30, 49. The *confrérie* does seem to have been crucial in winning back men to the church. 'Quand je vois un pécheur qui n'est point de confrérie je ne sais sur quoi m'appuyer pour obtenir son pardon. Mais si ce pécheur a le bonheur d'être de quelque confrérie, j'ai toujours l'espérance, malgré qu'il soit mauvais, parce que tôt ou tard les prières des autres obtiennent du Bon Dieu la grâce de son retour à Dieu' (*Sermons* (Delaroche edition of 1906) no. 15 'Sur Les Indulgences', cited by Boutry and Cinquin, p. 30).

[73] Audard, *Actes des Martyrs*, passim. M. Lagrée, 'Piété populaire et Révolution en Bretagne. L'exemple des canonisations spontanées', *Voies Nouvelles Pour l'Histoire de la Révolution Française*, pp. 265–79, is a model study in this respect. Cholvy, *Montpellier*, p. 189 has some pertinent comments on relics of 'martyrs'.

The only long-term solution was the Concordat, which represented the
triumph of the people's principles, and an immediate way of stifling religion
as a vehicle of protest. From that moment the newly established church, still
seriously undermanned, and still with many differences of opinion to sort
out between non-jurors and jurors, could assume responsibility for the care
of souls. The *esprit de contrariété* which had contributed towards the re-
establishment of catholic worship now found expression in rejecting everything from temperance movements to demands for tithes and patching up
the presbytery. Many men persisted in religious indifference: the *pratiquant
saisonnier* (he who married and died within the church and fulfilled his Easter
duties but failed to put in a weekly appearance) became an established figure
on the devotional map of France and, in areas where mass-going was the
norm, to secure anything beyond an annual confession for men defeated even
Jean Vianney. When they wrote their memoirs and in correspondence to
each other, a new theme emerged amongst the *curés concordataires*. Where had
the fervour of the old clandestine mass gone? Where was the spirit of *le culte
caché*? 'Jamais il n'y eut tant de bonnes messes que pendant la Terreur . . .
Robespierre a peuplé le Ciel, purifié, et sauvé la religion en France, et les
ignorants soutiennent et croient qu'il l'a perdue.'[74]

[74] The words are those of Chanoine Claude-Joseph Duchastanier, subsequently known as 'le Pape
de la Petite Eglise'. Cited by de Roux, *Poitiers et la Vienne*, p. 307. Compare the recollections
of Saint Marie-Madeleine Postel, 'Oh, les belles messes de minuit qu'on célébrait alors! [in
1794] on eut dit une mémoire continuelle de la crèche du Sauveur! Que notre ferveur était
grande! Comme les premiers chrétiens, nous étions constamment sous la hache du bourreau,
et comme eux nous puisions un invincible courage' (Delamare, *Vie édifiante*, p. 9).

3

Picking up the pieces: the politics and the
personnel of social welfare from the
Convention to the Consulate

COLIN JONES

If 1795 was 'the year of the loss of illusions',[1] there must be few clearer
illustrations of the principle than in the realm of social welfare. In Year II,
pious hopes had been expressed and big words uttered, as the Convention
laboured to overhaul France's poor laws, and to put in place of the motley
collection of poor relief institutions inherited from the ancien regime a
novel and comprehensive system of public assistance which, in retrospect,
represents a precocious departure in the direction of a 'welfare state'. Such
schemes, however, need time and application if they are to be successful: and
neither was forthcoming. In 1795, the high-flown welfare policies of Year II
came down to earth with a bump. Conditions in those poor relief institutions
which had survived this traumatic experience – and in practice that meant
hospitals, for virtually all the home relief agencies which had flourished prior
to 1789 (*bureaux de charité, bureaux d'aumônes, tables des pauvres, Miséricordes,*
etc.) had vanished – were appalling, and mirrored the more generalised
misery of the popular classes. Indeed, as Richard Cobb's telling study of the
social consequences of dearth in Rouen in Years III and IV reveals, many of
the worst features of popular distress – starvation, disease, demoralisation,
rocketing mortality – were to be found in all their starkness behind hospital
walls.[2]

In the eyes of many historians,[3] the aura of passivity and helplessness which

[1] Richard Cobb, 'Thermidor or the retreat from fantasy', in H. Lloyd-Jones, V. Pearl & B.
Worden (eds.), *History and Imagination. Essays in Honour of H. R. Trevor-Roper* (London, 1981),
p. 295.
[2] Cobb, 'Disette et mortalité: la crise de l'an III et de l'an IV à Rouen', in his *Terreur et subsistances*
(Paris, 1965).
[3] The best analysis of social welfare policy and its social and economic context is A. Forrest,
The French Revolution and the Poor (Oxford, 1981), which is particularly good on the period
from 1789 to about Years IV and V. Valuable too is the unpublished Ph.D. thesis, submitted
in the University of Washington, M. C. R. Gillett, 'Hospital Reform in the French Revolution',
University Microfilms, Michigan, 1980. Although most general works on the Directory contain a broad conspectus on social welfare policy and its implementation – see for example,

hovered around poor relief institutions in the face of the terrible conditions of Years III and IV casts a wider stain over the whole Thermidorean and Directorial period. Yet such a view tends to obscure another aspect of this key period in the history of French social welfare policy, namely the less eye-catching, but no less significant, work of reconstruction and rehabilitation. This was evident at the level of politics and administration, where measures were taken which would stand the test of time even into the present century. And it was present, more humbly, at local level, in the efforts of charitable administrators and their staff to place their institutions on a sound footing again following the neglect and outright hostility suffered in Year II. For all concerned, it became a question of picking up the pieces – of reconstructing certainly, but also of patching and mending – following the collapse of the 'welfare state' idealism of Year II.

I

Prior to Thermidor, the Convention had determined to revolutionise the provision of public assistance by establishing a rational, secular and nation-wide system of social welfare to replace the piecemeal and ecclesiastically dominated forms of relief which had prevailed under the ancien regime.[4] The new system was to be financed out of state taxation, distributed according to objective criteria of poverty, and was to provide appropriate forms of aid for every type of human need – sickness, old age, unemployment, unprotected childhood, motherhood, etc. – from womb to tomb. It had been the Constituent Assembly's *Comité de Mendicité* which, in a series of deeply researched and impressively argued reports in 1790 and 1791, had placed this

M. Lyons, *France under the Directory* (Cambridge, 1975), pp. 95–9 – these tend to rely heavily on much older works which have never been adequately replaced. Of these, see in particular F. Dreyfus, *L'assistance sous la Législative et la Convention (1791–1795)* (Paris, 1905); and M. Bouchet, *L'assistance publique en France pendant la Révolution* (Paris, 1908). Despite its blatant ultra-reactionary, catholic bias, L. Lallemand's *La Révolution et les pauvres* (Paris, 1898), still contains much useful material. Finally, one should note the importance of works by legal historians on this topic, though their angle of vision occasionally obscures points of interest to social historians: M. Rochaix, *Essai sur l'évolution des questions hospitalières de la fin de l'Ancien Régime à nos jours* (Dijon, 1959); and the excellent J. Imbert, *Le droit hospitalier de la Révolution et de l'Empire* (Paris, 1954).

[4] The vagaries of policy-making throughout the 1790s are best approached through the speeches, projects and legislation of the revolutionary assemblies. Particularly useful are reports of debates in the *Gazette nationale ou le Moniteur universel*, most easily consultable in the *Réimpression de l'Ancien Moniteur* (32 vols., Paris, 1863–1870), hereinafter = *Mon.*; and the collections of speeches, pamphlets and other printed materials in the relevant sections of the French revolutionary holdings of the British Library, hereinafter = B.L. There are, in addition, several handy collections of legislation relating to poor relief: notably C. Bloch, *Recueil des principaux textes législatifs et administratifs concernant l'assistance de 1789 à l'an VIII* (Paris, 1909), and A. de Watteville, *Législation charitable de 1790 à 1863* (Paris, 1863).

kind of innovation on the political agenda.[5] The reports, most of them penned by the committee's chairman, the liberal aristocrat and philanthropist the Duc de Larochefoucauld-Liancourt, had urged that the state should become more closely involved in the coordination and control of assistance so as to ensure that all citizens had equal access to relief. This recommendation was relatively novel. But the origins of the general ideas in the reports lay in the intellectual assault which had taken place during the Enlightenment on the role of charity as the mainspring of the nation's poor laws. And it was to this critique, now tinged with a modish anti-clericalism, and often as mediated by the influence of Larochefoucauld-Liancourt – though he himself was by Year II an émigré, soon to embark on an expedition to study Red Indians in Canada[6] – that the Conventionnels turned to justify and illuminate their endeavours.

Authors, from Montesquieu to Condorcet, and from Voltaire and Diderot to Cabanis and Dupont de Nemours, had viewed traditional charity as being concerned more with the spiritual welfare of the donor than the material well-being of the recipient, and as consequently encouraging sloth, improvidence and bad habits.[7] Almsgiving – now prohibited by the law 24 vendémiaire Year II[8] – and religious benefactions were thus forms of vanity and egotism rather than marks of that enlightened *bienfaisance* – altruistic, secular, grounded in a sense of social solidarity – which was now seen as the essential cornerstone of an effective and humane system of social welfare. France's two thousand hospitals – which had constituted the basis of the nation's poor laws since the so-called *grand renfermement des pauvres* in the seventeenth century – were, like charity, accused of encouraging social and economic parasitism, and as failing to respond to changing social needs. Some authors and polemicists treated the hospitals as mini-Bastilles, and their hundred thousand inmates – the aged, the infirm, the insane, the down-and-out, the abandoned and orphaned child as well as the sick – as so many political prisoners. Others pointed out that a system of state pensions orientated round the home would be far more economical than hospital care, the institutional overheads of which were likely to be high. The somewhat random geographical distribution of hospitals also militated against the provision of equal access to relief facilities.

[5] C. Bloch and A. Tuetey (eds.), *Procès-verbaux et rapports du comité de mendicité de la Constituante 1790–1791* (Paris, 1911). The best commentaries are C. Bloch, *L'assistance et l'état en France à la veille de la Révolution (1764–1790)* (Paris, 1908), p. 423; F. Dreyfus, *Un philanthrope d'autrefois: Larochefoucauld-Liancourt (1747–1827)* (Paris, 1907), p. 138; and R. Du Boff, 'Economic thought in revolutionary France, 1789–1792: the question of poverty and unemployment', *French Historical Studies* (1966). See also D. B. Weiner, 'Le droit de l'homme à la santé: une belle idée devant l'assemblée nationale constituante, 1790–1791', *Clio medica* (1970).
[6] F. Dreyfus, *Un philanthrope*, p. 200.
[7] C. Bloch, *L'assistance et l'état*, *passim*, constitutes the best guide to Enlightenment thought concerning poverty, charity and poor relief.   [8] A. de Watteville, *Législation charitable*, p. 24.

A reduction in the number and importance of hospitals was also seen as likely to improve the nation's health. Far from curing sickness, hospitals seemed to engender it.[9] This was true of the big *hôpitaux généraux*, in which the death-rate of foundlings was horrifyingly high, and in which other inmates stagnated under the care of nursing sisters who, for all their devotion, often showed a marked reluctance to implement the hygienic prescriptions of the medical profession, or to show allegiance to the Republic. It was true too of the *hôtels-dieu*, which were nominally attuned to the needs of the sick, but which often in practice seemed to be little more than 'temples de la mort'.[10] Conditions in the Paris *hôtel-dieu* were particularly appalling, one entrant in four dying there, often from diseases contracted after admission. Plans to reform this institution after its partial gutting by fire in 1772 had proved a stimulant to the burgeoning campaign against hospitals in the last decades of the ancien regime.[11] Even in 1794, nothing fundamental had been changed.

There were, it is true, a few voices raised in the last years of the ancien regime and in the early years of the Revolution in support of hospitals. Cabanis, Condorcet's brother-in-law and the future *Idéologue*, urged that a small number of institutions be used as *écoles pratiques* for clinical training. This was still, however, a minority view. Even Cabanis admitted that hospitals were essentially 'des établissements vicieux' and that, in the interests of social justice, their number should be drastically reduced and 'un nouveau système de bienfaisance générale' established.[12] Generally, moreover, hospitals were viewed as social rather than as medical institutions: the *Comité de Mendicité* had not mentioned medical education in its reports;[13] and even many medical reformers held that training in bedside medicine could be more effectively performed in private homes rather than in the noxious

9 The medical and sanitary critique of hospitals is outlined in the works cited above; see note 3. See in addition M. Foucault, *The Birth of the Clinic* (London, 1973); T. Gelfand, *Professionalizing Modern Medicine: Paris Surgeons and Medical Science and Institutions in the Eighteenth Century* (Westport, 1980); and the rather more old-fashioned works of E. H. Ackerknecht, *Medicine at the Paris Hospital, 1794–1848* (Baltimore, 1967); and G. Rosen, 'Hospitals, Medical Care and Social Policy in the French Revolution', *Bulletin of the History of Medicine* (1956).

10 P. S. Dupont de Nemours, *Idées sur les secours à donner aux pauvres malades dans une grande ville* (Paris, 1786), p. 19.

11 J. Tenon, *Mémoires sur les hôpitaux de Paris* (Paris, 1788). See too the recent studies of L. S. Greenbaum, notably 'J. S. Bailly, the Baron de Breteuil and the "four new hospitals" of Paris', *Clio medica* (1973); and '"Mesure of civilization". The hospital thought of Jacques Tenon on the eve of the French Revolution', *Bulletin of the History of Medicine* (1975). See too M. Foucault *et al.*, *Les machines à guérir (aux origines de l'hôpital moderne)* (Paris, 1979).

12 Cabanis has been the subject of an admirable recent intellectual biography: M. Staum, *Cabanis. Enlightenment and Medical Philosophy in the French Revolution* (Princeton, 1980). The citations here are from P. J. G. Cabanis, *Oeuvres philosophiques*, eds. C. Lehec and J. Cazeneuve, 2 vols. (Paris, 1956), pp. 6, 30.

13 Cf. M. C. R. Gillett, *Hospital Reform*, p. 84.

atmosphere of a hospital.[14] Furthermore, in its most radical phase the Convention had little time or sympathy for medical instruction *tout court*, performed as it always had been under the ancien regime by 'des docteurs à perruques, payés chèrement pour tenir des séances académiques'.[15] 'Nos hôpitaux,' fulminated Bo, the *rapporteur* of the Convention's *Comité des Secours publics*, 'sont une école où le médecin apprend aux dépens du malheureux à guérir le riche.'[16] Such a practice evidently struck a blow against the principle of 'justice jusqu'à l'hôpital'[17] which the radical wing of the Convention had adopted as its motto.

The case against hospitals seemed overwhelming, and the Conventionnels took a major step towards 'dehospitalising' society by erecting its system of social welfare on new foundations. Legislation on 19 March and 28 June 1793 made it clear that home relief was to be the basis of welfare policy, and this principle was to find its most celebrated expression in the system of state pensions for the rural poor – whose names were to be recorded in a *Grand Livre de Bienfaisance Nationale* – established by the law of 22 floréal Year II. The nationalisation of all hospital property by the law of 23 messidor Year II was another symptom of the government's desire to take the rhetoric of *bienfaisance* seriously. So too were the laws of ventôse, which aimed to redistribute the property of political suspects among indigent patriots.[18]

The stimulus which had brought these novel departures onto the statute-book was war. The armed struggle against ancien regime Europe transformed *bienfaisance* from a laudable virtue into an urgent political desideratum. The provision of radical social welfare policies on lines inspired by the *Comité de Mendicité* became an integral part of the programme of social radicalism introduced by the jacobins and endorsed by the Convention with the aim of securing mass support for the hard-pressed infant Republic.[19] Significantly, welfare initiatives were introduced in the assembly no longer by well-meaning nonentities from the *Comité des Secours publics*, but by the big battalions from the *Comité de Salut public*: Robespierre, Saint-Just, Barère, Collot d'Herbois ... Significantly too the projects mapped out by the *Comité de Mendicité* received an ambitious increment in the Convention's new concern for the welfare of the armies at grips with the forces of European reaction.

The walls of the Assembly now frequently resounded with enthusiastic

[14] This line of argument is developed in, for example, P. S. Dupont de Nemours, *Idées sur les secours*, p. 24. Cf. M. Foucault, *Birth of the Clinic*, p. 17.   [15] *Mon.*, XIX, p. 525.

[16] J. B. Bo, *Rapport et projet de décret sur les bases de l'organisation générale des secours publics*, B.L. FR 437, p. 8.

[17] For this phrase, *Mon.*, XVII, p. 754 (*Société des Jacobins*, 23 September 1793).

[18] Useful summary of this legislation in J. Godechot, *Les Institutions de la France sous la Révolution et l'Empire* (Paris, 1969), pp. 439–44. For the concept of 'dehospitalisation', M. Foucault, *Birth of the Clinic*, p. 43.

[19] See my article 'The welfare of the French foot-soldier', *History* (1980), p. 206.

paeans in praise of *soldats-citoyens*. 'Ce n'est point assez,' proclaimed Robespierre, 'd'épouvanter les ennemis de la patrie, il faut secourir ses défenseurs ... Toute acte de bienfaisance envers l'armée est une acte de reconnaissance nationale.'[20] The new sense of social justice in the field of military welfare was particularly clearly expressed in the law of 6 June 1793, which substantially revised the system of invalidity pensions, and accorded the rank-and-file equality of status and claims with officers.[21] The needy families of the *défenseurs de la patrie* were also the object of the government's solicitude: an earlier law of 26 November 1792 was substantially liberalised first in May 1793 and then again in pluviôse Year II. Pensions for war-widows were also pitched at a more generous level than before and, by the law of 13 prairial Year II, were made easier to obtain.[22] In addition, the Convention was always very willing to make individual grants and awards. No signal act of military patriotism was too ignoble to be passed over, and the recipients of state pensions ranged from battlefield heroes to the improbable-sounding Gottlob Titz 'femme d'un sous-officier de hussards prussiens, qui a rendu des services à l'armée du Rhin'.[23] At local level too, every devisable means was used to maintain solidarity with fellow patriots-in-arms. This often took the form of organising military hospitals for the care of sick and wounded soldiers. Although the government was simultaneously planning the run-down of France's civilian hospitals, the exigencies of the military situation caused a drastic rise in the number of military hospitals, to which the government, in the law of 3 ventôse Year II, brought some degree of uniformity and standardisation.[24]

Despite all the energy and enthusiasm expended, the political upheavals of the summer and autumn of 1794 were sufficient to lay to rest the main body of this social and military welfare legislation, conceived in the spirit of Enlightenment *bienfaisance*. With the war now going well, and with the more radical wing of the jacobins liquidated or proscribed, the urgency behind the reforms disappeared. The very idea of a 'welfare state' sketched out before 9 thermidor became a bad dream, best forgotten. Significantly, responsibility for introducing welfare legislation in the Convention passed back from the *Comité de Salut public* to the *Comité des Secours publics*, whose chairman, the

---

[20] *Mon.*, XIX, p. 54.

[21] For this aspect of military welfare policies, see I. Woloch, *The French Veteran from the Revolution to the Restoration* (Chapel Hill, 1979).

[22] For war widows, I. Woloch, 'War widows' pensions: social policy in revolutionary and Napoleonic France', *Societas* (1976).   [23] Example cited in F. Dreyfus, *L'assistance*, p. 105.

[24] *Mon.*, XIX, p. 525. For the question of medical mobilisation for the war, see D. B. Weiner 'French doctors face the war, 1792–1815' in C. K. Warner (ed.), *From the Ancien Régime to the Popular Front: Essays in the History of France in Honor of S. B. Clough* (New York, 1969); D. M Vess, *Medical Revolution in France, 1789–1796* (Gainesville, 1975;) and C. Jones, 'Welfare of the French footsoldier', p. 207. Brice and Bottet, *Le corps de santé militaire en France: son évolution, ses campagnes, 1708–1882* (Paris, 1882), p. 53 contains some still useful information.

worthy, but dull, Rouerguat physician Bo was quite unable to galvanise his fellow deputies. The laws of ventôse and a range of other welfare plans adumbrated at the height of the Terror sank without trace.[25] The law of 22 floréal found more support,[26] but it too was soon petering out. On 21 pluviôse Year III it was reported that less than a fifth of the districts of France had established their local *Livre de Bienfaisance Nationale*, and the failure of the government to despatch funds to pay the pensions soon caused the final extinction of the scheme.[27] The fate of the programme of military welfare was not much brighter: the supply of the necessary credits to keep pensions-schemes alive for *invalides*, the families of *défenseurs de la patrie* and war-widows soon began to dry up; and shortage of cash caused the state of most military hospitals to deteriorate lamentably.[28] The blueprint for a 'welfare state' was now shelved, and deputies in the Convention started gingerly to pick up the broken pieces of the ancien regime's charitable institutions, to dust them down, applying legislative elastoplast where necessary, and to set them up as the basis of the new system of poor relief.

Particularly influential in this work of legislative resuscitation and first aid were the interventions in the Convention, and then in the Council of 500, of Delecloy, the deputy for the Somme, a somewhat unbalanced character whose main prior claim to fame had been making a mess of his spell on mission in Amiens in 1793, getting drunk, consorting with a woman of dubious morals and having to be hauled back to Paris in disgrace.[29] Now Delecloy relaunched his political career in the more congenial Thermidorean

---

[25] For examples of schemes never to be followed up: *Mon.*, XIX, pp. 445–55, 611.

[26] Even Delecloy, the scourge of the *bienfaisance* of Year II, had a kind word for this scheme: Delecloy, *Rapport sur l'organisation générale des secours publics*, B.L., FR 438, p. 7 (12 vendémiaire Year IV).

[27] Saint-Martin, *Rapport et projet de décret sur un nouveau versement de fonds pour des secours extra ordinaires aux indigens de la République*, B.L., F 810, p. 5 (21 pluviôse Year III). For the rundown of the scheme in the departments, C. Jones, *Charity and 'Bienfaisance': the Treatment of the Poor in the Montpellier Region, 1740–1815* (Cambridge, 1982), p. 182; J. Dubois, *L'assistance dans le district de Bar pendant la Révolution* (Paris, 1930), p. 57; J. Adher, *Recueil de documents sur l'assistance publique dans le district de Toulouse de 1789 à 1800* (Toulouse, 1918), p. 462; C. Lefebvre, 'Pauvreté et assistance dans le district de Douai, 1788–an V', *Positions des thèses de l'Ecole des Chartes* (1955), p. 135.

[28] *Mon.*, XXIII, p. 54. For the rundown in military welfare schemes, see D. B. Weiner, 'French doctors', p. 67; I. Woloch, *The French Veteran*, p. 90; D. M. Vess, *Medical Revolution*, p. 176; C. Jones, 'Welfare of the French footsoldier', p. 208. For some local examples: F. Schierer, *L'Hôpital militaire Gaujot de Strasbourg, 1619–1939*, Strasbourg, 1955, p. 23; F. Roques, 'Les Hôpitaux militaires à Nice sous la Révolution et l'Empire', *Nice Historique* (1942), p. 6; M. Bouloiseau, 'Malades et "tire-au-flanc" à l'armée de l'Ouest, an II–an III', *Actes du congrès national des sociétés savantes* (Toulouse, 1971), p. 549; and C. Jones, *Charity and 'Bienfaisance'*, p. 220.

[29] A. Patrick, *The Men of the First Republic. Political Alignment in the National Convention, of 1792* (Baltimore, 1972), p. 21 n.

and Directorial atmosphere by becoming hatchet-man for the burgeoning lobby who wished to have done with state *bienfaisance*. In the aftermath of the *journées* of prairial, he was found intemperately attacking previous *sans-culotte* schemes for social welfare legislation.[30] But he really established his reputation in speeches from 10 thermidor Year III in which he lurched violently onto the offensive against the 'manie de nivellement, de généralisation, dans la distribution des secours' which had allegedly been displayed by 'spéculateurs arithmétiques' prior to 9 thermidor. He urged his fellow-deputies:

Il est temps de sortir de l'ornière profonde où une philanthropie exagérée nous arrête depuis l'assemblée constituante, qui très - savamment sans doute mais très - inutilement s'est occupée du pauvre. Depuis cette époque il semble que tous les spéculateurs en bienfaisance aient pris la tache de pousser sans mesure vers le trésor national toutes les classes du peuple. Qu'est-il arrivé de ce chaos d'idées? Une série effrayante de dépenses illimitées, des lois stériles et impossibles à exécuter . . .[31]

The administrative difficulties of implementing revolutionary welfare legislation to which Delecloy alluded had been only too apparent in Year II, during which speakers in the Convention were forever bemoaning bureaucratic delays which subverted the efficacy and mocked the urgency of welfare measures. Yet whereas in Year II the tendency was to ascribe these delays to a lack of republican virtue on the part of bureaucrats, by Year III the blame was being placed at the door of the legislation itself. As Saint-Martin argued on 21 pluviôse Year III, 'dans la partie réglementaire, les rouages sont beaucoup trop compliqués'.[32] Delecloy was even more down to earth: 'Quelque célérité que les bureaux mettent dans leurs expéditions, il est impossible de faire face à la fois aux demandes de 40,000 communes et de plus de 2,000 hôpitaux répandus sur la surface de la République.'[33]

In place of the ineffectual though overpowering bureaucracy which had grown up in the state's welfare services in Year II, the Delecloy lobby urged that the land expropriated from charitable institutions by the law of 23 messidor Year II be returned and that the poor laws be reconstructed around a rehabilitated network of hospitals. This change of direction did not, it is true, spring from any refound enthusiasm for hospitals. Few voices were raised to extol the intrinsic merits of hospital care, and even the *rapporteurs* of

---

30 A. Soboul, *Les Sans-culottes parisiens en l'an II. Mouvement populaire et gouvernement révolutionnaire, 2 juin 1793–9 thermidor an II* (Paris, 1958), p. 711.

31 Delecloy, *Rapport sur l'organisation générale*, p. 2.

32 *Rapport et projet de décret*, p. 4. For pungent criticism of the bureaucracy under the Terror, see the remarks of Collot d'Herbois, *Mon.*, XX, p. 630.

33 *Rapport sur la loi du 23 messidor prononcé à la tribune de la Convention nationale le 10 thermidor an troisième de la République française*, B.L., R 516, p. 3. See too his further comments in vendémiaire Year IV: *Rapport sur l'organisation générale*, p. 7.

relevant committees re-echoed the stock denigratory clichés.[34] A reversal of government policy so as to reorientate poor relief around the hospitals was, however, seen as a necessary evil: it constituted, for Delecloy, 'le système ... qui offre le moins d'inconvénients et revient le plus d'avantages ... [L']empire des circonstances est tel qu'il fait perdre de vue les idées de perfection pour ne songer qu'à ce qui est possible.'[35]

The presentation of the U-turn in policy as being a sensible step back from social and political utopianism – 'L'égalité des secours pour le pauvre dans tous les lieux', claimed Delecloy, trenchant as ever, 'est une idée aussi chimérique que l'égalité des fortunes'[36] – was particularly astute. It struck a responsive chord among deputies terrified of a repetition of the events of Year II. Equally by promoting the revival of private charity – Delecloy still talked in coded language of 'la bienfaisance individuelle'[37] – it would allow the central government to reduce its financial commitments which had been severely distended by experiments in state *bienfaisance*. The Thermidorean and Directorial regimes were both to experience chronic shortages of cash – the consequence of poor economic conditions, especially in the early years, low tax returns, inflation, monetary depreciation and the continuing strain of waging war. In these circumstances, any talk of economy was eagerly listened to by governments which, despite massive staff cuts, still found it difficult enough even to pay their own bureaucrats.[38] Both regimes also placed a premium on means of relieving distress which simultaneously doused down popular unrest. Hence, for example, their response to the appalling social conditions caused by *nonante-cinq* was to subsidise bread so as to take the edge off potential popular agitation rather than to pour money into pensions schemes or even support for hospitals. A hard-up government which would – as in 1796 – subsidise food for something like 550,000 individuals in Paris alone[39] – could afford very little else in the field of social welfare.

The remoulding of social welfare policy around the values of economy and practicality was achieved gradually between mid 1795 and the autumn of 1796. Sales of hospital property under the provisions of the law of 23

---

[34] See, for example, Paganel, *Rapport sur les prisons, maisons d'arrêt ou de police, de répression, de détention et sur les hospices de santé*, B.L., FR 437, p. 8 (vendémiaire Year IV); and Bo, speaking in the name of the *Comité des Secours publics*, Mon., XXIII, p. 236 (session 28 nivôse Year III).

[35] *Mon.*, XXVI, p. 317. Cf. J. Zangiacomi, *Rapport et projet de décret sur la proposition de rendre aux hôpitaux et autres établissements de bienfaisance les revenus des biens qu'ils possédaient avant la loi du 23 messidor an II*, B.L., R 516, p. 4 (brumaire Year IV).

[36] *Rapport sur l'organisation générale*, p. 9.

[37] Ibid., p. 3; *Rapport sur la loi du 23 messidor*, p. 5.

[38] C. H. Church, *Revolution and Red Tape: the French Ministerial Bureaucracy, 1770–1850* (Oxford, 1981), pp. 127, 230.

[39] Ibid., p. 228. The bread subsidies ceased soon afterwards; but the general situation did not much improve. For Thermidorean and Directorial attitudes towards the popular movement, and the combination of repression and charity, see R. Cobb, *The Police and the People*, passim.

messidor had continued after the fall of Robespierre.[40] But they were increasingly attacked in the Convention and local administrators, sensing which way the wind was blowing, often called a halt even before the Convention finally placed a moratorium on sales on 9 fructidor Year III.[41] By the law of 3 brumaire Year IV, the law of 23 messidor was officially abrogated: all confiscated property as yet unsold was to be returned to charitable institutions, which would also receive out of *domaines nationaux* land of equivalent value to that which had already been sold. This arrangement was confirmed by the law of 16 vendémiaire Year V which was mainly, however, concerned with hospital administration: a *commission administrative* of five local worthies elected by the municipality was established in every commune which contained a hospital.[42] The avowed aim of this 'communalisation' of hospital administration was to restore managerial stability, continuity and accountability following the chopping and changing which had gone on since 1789. The law of 7 frimaire Year V which set up similar five-man communal *bureaux de bienfaisance* endeavoured to do the same for home relief, though because of the disappearance of most ancien regime home relief bodies, most of the *bureaux* were expected to start more or less from scratch.[43] It was assumed that these *bureaux de bienfaisance* would be largely financed, as their name suggested, out of 'la bienfaisance individuelle', though hopeful noises were also made about restoring property which had belonged to their forebears under the ancien regime. Although a great many bureaux were to have no more than a fictitious existence before 1800 at least, many deputies, still subscribing to the old anti-hospital prejudices, professed great faith in these bodies.[44]

In this prevailing landscape of pragmatism and 'possibilism', there was one small oasis of attachment to the positive value of hospitals: this lay in the accredited role of hospitals as centres for clinical training. So general and comprehensive had the attack on hospitals been under the Terror that even this function, which a little earlier Cabanis among others had maintained should be widened and formalised, had been violently rejected. With the organisation of the war effort, however, hostility mellowed into a broad acceptance of the need to improve the training of the army's *officiers de santé*.[45] Even the rhetoricians on the *Comité de Salut public* came to recognise that the total abolition of hospitals – in which medical trainees could have direct and continual contact with the sick and wounded – would be dele-

[40] Cf. J. Dubois, *L'assistance*, pp. 97, 148.
[41] *Mon.*, XXVI, p. 317.
[42] A. de Watteville, *Législation charitable*, p. 41.
[43] Ibid. Cf. C. Jones, *Charity and 'Bienfaisance'*, pp. 195ff; J. Dubois, *L'assistance*, p. 43.
[44] See, for example, Delaporte, *Rapport au nom de la commission de l'organisation des secours publics*, B.L., FR 438, p. 6 (Council of 500, 13 messidor Year IV).
[45] D. B. Weiner, 'French doctors', p. 58; D. M. Vess, *Medical revolution*, p. 105; and P. Huard, *Science, médecine, pharmacie de la Révolution à l'Empire, 1789–1815* (Paris, 1974), p. 45.

terious to medical care, and thus to military effectiveness. Unable to decide whether to organise clinical training in select civilian hospitals or to attach it to the military hospitals, the *Comité* just prior to the events of 9 thermidor appointed a small committee to review the question. As a result of its recommendations, reported in the autumn of 1794, the Convention, by the law of 14 frimaire Year III, established three *Ecoles de santé* – at Paris, Strasbourg and Montpellier – a fundamental feature of whose teaching was to be 'l'observation au lit des malades', and which were to be accorded a niche for training within local hospitals.[46]

With hindsight it is clear that what started as a hesitant move of the *Comité de Salut public* to improve military medical facilities ended up as one of the foundations of medical education and research for more than a century. In the 1790s, however, the establishment and later remodelling of the *Ecoles de santé*,[47] and their orientation around hospital practice, formed only a minor part of the deliberations about the future of hospitals, which centred far more on social than on medical or educational issues: hospitals were being revamped primarily so that they could serve as the basis of the nation's poor laws. Among the deputies of the Thermidorean and Directorial assemblies who were its official progenitors, the *naissance de la clinique* was only an epiphenomenon of this more urgent process.

For all their concern with reiterating hospitals' social role, and despite the aura of sweet reasonableness and practicality in which the proponents of the new poor laws clothed themselves, there was much about the new policies that was highly questionable. The turbulence of public life in the late 1790s made the smooth reinstatement of stable hospital management difficult to achieve.[48] Similarly, in the light of the long-term attenuation of the charitable impulse over the eighteenth century, it was utterly chimerical to expect private charity to prove the hospitals' financial saviour, as Delecloy and his cronies hoped.[49] Furthermore, the practical side of organising the restitution of hospital property was to prove much more problematic than had been imagined. In many areas there were few if any *domaines nationaux* to use in compensating hospitals for property they had lost. Complaints about the non-implementation of the law were thus soon being heard – even from

---

[46] *Mon.*, XXII, 618ff. Cf. Fourcroy, *Rapport et projet de décret sur l'établissement d'une école centrale de santé à Paris*, 7 frimaire Year III; and *Rapport et projet de décret sur les écoles de santé de Paris, Montpellier et Strasbourg*, 14 frimaire Year III, both in B.L., R 405.

[47] For modifications in the law of 14 frimaire, see T. Gelfand, *Professionalising Modern Medicine*, p. 167; M. C. R. Gillett, *Hospital Reform*, p. 185; and the debates, speeches etc. in B.L. R 405 and R 601.

[48] See below, p. 78.

[49] For the decline in charity in the eighteenth century, see in particular M. Vovelle, *Piété baroque et déchristianisation en Provence au XVIIIe siècle: Les attitudes devant la mort d'après les clauses des testaments* (Paris, 1973), p. 257; C. Jones, *Charity and 'Bienfaisance'*, p. 86; C. Bloch, *L'assistance et l'état*, p. 272.

Delecloy himself – and would continue down to the early 1800s.[50] Even more serious than this, moreover, was the totally erroneous assumption which had guided the assemblies that the restoration of hospital property signified the restitution of their basic source of wealth under the ancien regime. When first launching his attack against the law of 23 messidor, for example, Delecloy had supported his arguments by citing the Paris *hôtel-dieu* which in 1795 was costing the government 60,000 livres a *décade* in upkeep but which under the ancien regime had allegedly supported itself almost entirely out of income from property.[51] This was totally erroneous: only about a third of the hospital's income – roughly the national average for all hospitals[52] – derived from this source, and this included rents of a 'feudal' nature which were not of course to be restored.[53] Very many provincial hospitals derived a much smaller proportion of their income from property: the figure was less than 5 per cent in the case of the hospitals of the department of the Hérault, less than 10 per cent for those of the Creuse and the Var.[54] This was a point which was in fact spelled out in the debates of the *Conseil des Anciens* by Durand-Maillane.[55] But he failed to sway the lower house, any more than did Lacuée who argued, basically soundly, that such property as hospitals had owned prior to 1789 had often been appallingly badly managed.[56] The deputies closed their ears too to Poulain-Grandpré, who observed that many hospitals had formerly derived a disproportionate part of their income – the *Comité de Mendicité* had suggested the figure was about a fifth – from municipal tolls of one sort or another (*octrois*) which had been abolished outright in 1790.[57]

The allegedly 'utopian' and 'illusionary' schemes of the *Comité de Mendicité* and the Convention had at least been based on an attempt at sound computation and on a close working knowledge of poor relief institutions. The smugly 'practical' and 'realistic' decisions of the Thermidorean and Directorial assemblies seem in contrast to have been made while a principle of selective deafness operated. It may be that some deputies were willing to go along with the partial and ill-informed generalisations of the Delecloy

---

50 *Mon.*, XXVIII, pp. 419, 651. Cf. Chabot, *Rapport sur un projet de loi concernant l'affectation aux besoins des hospices civils de rentes et domaines appartenant à la République*, B.L. FR 433, 1 ventôse Year IX.   51 *Rapport sur la loi du 23 messidor*, p. 3.

52 See the statistics amassed by the *Comité de Mendicité*, based on various ancien regime enquiries: C. Bloch and A. Tuetey (eds.), *Procès-verbaux et rapports*, p. 564.

53 M. Fosseyeux, *L'hôtel-dieu de Paris au XVIIe et au XVIIIe siècle* (Paris, 1912), p. 142.

54 Bloch and Tuetey (eds.), *Procès-verbaux et rapports*, pp. 564f.

55 Durand-Maillane, *Rapport sur la résolution concernant les hospices civils*, B.L., FR 432, p. 10 (Conseil des Anciens, 4 j.c. Year IV). Cf. Py, *Observations sur la suppression des hôpitaux et sur les secours à domicile* (Paris, n.d.), B.L., FR 432.

56 Lacuée, *Opinion . . . sur la résolution relative aux hospices civils*, B.L., FR 432, p. 9 (*Conseil des Anciens*, 8 vendémiaire Year V).

57 See the report of the debate in the *Gazette Nationale, ou le Moniteur Universel*, no. 22, 22 vendémiaire Year V, p. 85 (the *Réimpression de l'Ancien Moniteur* gives few details of speeches). For ancien regime figures on *octrois*, Bloch and Tuetey (eds.), *Procès-verbaux et rapports*, p. 564.

lobby because they felt that something needed to be done rapidly to avert the financial disaster in welfare policy which seemed imminent.[58] Yet if they thought that there would be a chance to modify their decision later, they were wrong. Further change was not to be forthcoming, although there was one further brief flirtation – in Year VI – with the ideas of Year II. Following the coup of fructidor Year V, the left wing in the Directory and the councils again began to preach the virtues of home relief over hospital care and, invoking many of the old jacobin arguments, including the need to guarantee equality of rights to assistance, went on to urge the reactivation of the law of 23 messidor Year II and the abolition of all hospitals in localities with less than 12,000 inhabitants.[59] The latter measure would, it was estimated, reduce the number of hospitals by 90 per cent, from about 2,000 to less than 200. It was significant, however, that the Directors did not suggest a full-scale return to the welfare schemes of Year II, and indeed they explicitly distanced themselves from any plans which endangered private charity: 'Un gouvernement qui annonceroit qu'il accordera seul des secours complets à tous les indigents, et dans tous les âges de la vie, s'imposeroit un fardeau énorme, favoriseroit l'insouciance du riche, du pauvre même, et briseroit le grand ressort de la sociabilité, la bienfaisance privée.'[60]

The councils refused to respond positively to the proposals of the Directors – a telling example of the kind of constitutional deadlock which bedevilled the Directory's hold on power – and the issue fizzled out.[61] Quite apart from having reservations about a step back towards the schemes and ideas of Year II, deputies seem to have suspected the motives of the Directors. The proposed reduction in the number of hospitals, for example, would undoubtedly – through the system of mergers envisaged – have improved the financial viability of the survivors. But surely this would have worsened the availability of assistance rather than improved it, as the Directors claimed was their intention? At the back of many deputies' minds, in addition, lurked the suspicion that the whole issue was another pretext for laying hands on hospital property so as to boost the war effort, as the Revolutionary Government had done in the law of 23 messidor. To implement the Directory's policy would be to court comparisons of an odious kind, and risk popularity which the shaky régime could ill afford to lose. As one deputy had put it:

[58] *Gazette Nationale*, 22 vendémiaire Year V, p. 85. (Contributions of Rallier and Lebrun in particular.)

[59] *Message extrait du registre des délibérations du Directoire exécutif, du 26 nivôse l'an sixième*, B.L., FR 432; and *Rapport présenté au Directoire exécutif par le Ministre de l'Intérieur* (ibid.). See too the treatment of this entire episode in M.C.R. Gillett, *Hospital Reform*, p. 162; M. Bouchet, *L'assistance publique*, p. 643; and J. Imbert, *Le droit hospitalier*, p. 123.

[60] *Message*, p. 4.

[61] Cf. Lambert, *Sur le message du Directoire exécutif relatif aux hospices civils* (no date or place of publication), B.L., R 601; and Delaporte, *Rapport au nom de la commission des hospices. Secours aux hospices civils et aux enfants de la patrie* (ibid.) (Council of 500, 24 thermidor Year VI).

'si on vendoit tous les fonds des hospices, on auroit l'air d'exproprier les pauvres'.[62]

The councils' rejection of these proposals in Year VI meant that for virtually the whole of the Thermidorean and Directorial period, social welfare was conducted within a local framework, and with little reference to a national or coordinated plan. The premise of this 'comunalisation' of poor relief – in this highly 'regionalist' era in French history[63] – was that the state neither could nor would bear responsibility for the newly reconstituted hospitals and ancillary organisations.[64] There was, inevitably, a good deal of legislation; but it was the legislation of a distant and vaguely paternalistic benefactor, not that of an organisational dynamo. Governments retained the power to intervene but chose, on the whole, not to. They respected the autonomous status which they had reconferred on poor relief institutions, and the local ambit of their activity even when, as we shall see, this necessitated turning a blind eye to the often desperate human problems which charitable administrators had to face. Administrators and their staffs had been well and truly passed the buck – as indeed Delecloy admitted. He enquired of his fellow-deputies: 'Voulez-vous donc suppléer à l'insuffisance des secours pour les hôpitaux? donnez-leur une administration paternelle; et alors reposez-vous sur elle du soin de faire fructifier les foibles ressources qui leur restent.'[65] Thus the administrators of poor relief institutions were being called on to do what the legislators had been attempting in the rarefied heights of welfare policy: namely to pick up the pieces. What were their problems and dilemmas? And how did they fare?

II

From as early as 1789, charitable institutions had been hard hit by revolutionary legislation. After all, they had occupied a small but not insignificant niche within the ancien regime nexus of privilege which the revolutionary assemblies wished to eradicate; and they depended, to a greater or lesser extent, on the managerial and ancillary services of religious personnel– nursing sisters, chaplains, curés – who were often the target of growing anticlericalism.[66] Nevertheless, there is a strong case for maintaining that these

---

[62] *Gazette Nationale*, 22 vendémiaire Year V, p. 86 (intervention of Girod de l'Ain).

[63] R. Cobb, *Police and the People*, p. 70 and passim.

[64] J. Imbert, *Droit hospitalier*, p. 103; and M. Bouchet, *L'assistance publique*, p. 99; M. Rochaix, *Essai*, p. 105.

[65] *Rapport . . . au nom de la commission de l'organisation des secours publics, . . . et au nom d'une commission spéciale*, B.L., FR 432 (Council of 500, 28 nivôse Year V).

[66] Good concise summaries of the impact of the revolution in 1789 and the early 1790s in J. Imbert, *Droit hospitalier*, p. 29; and M. Bouchet, *L'assistance publique*, p. 156. The view from the grassroots throughout the revolutionary decade is illuminated by numerous local studies, on which I have drawn heavily. I should also like to express my gratitude to the British

institutions suffered their worst damage from factors largely extrinsic to the legislative efforts of the assemblies. The effects of the depreciation of the paper currencies (*assignats*, then *mandats territoriaux*), and the inflation which this helped to fuel, were especially severe. Hospitals and other charitable institutions found it more difficult and more costly to keep adequately provisioned. It also proved, conversely, cheaper and less costly for those who owed the institutions money to discharge their obligations at a minimal rate. Tenants on hospital property, for example, who owed rents in cash rather than in kind escaped lightly by paying in *assignats* rather than in *specie*. The same was true of individuals and corporate bodies with whom the hospitals had contracted *rentes constituées*. So extreme was the monetary depreciation from Years III to V that many parties went so far as to reimburse in *assignats* not merely the interest payments but even the capital sums on which the *rentes* were fixed.[67] When one bears in mind that income from *rentes constituées* had comprised about one-third of the national hospital income prior to the Revolution,[68] it is easy to understand why many charitable administrators felt that the monetary *débâcle* had caused more permanent damage than even the law of 23 messidor. Charitable administrators were also acutely aware, moreover, of the growing demands being made on their – increasingly scanty – resources as a result of the economic situation in the 1790s. Government policy had, it is true, partly contributed to the rising demand for aid: care of foundlings was made mandatory for all hospitals, which after 1792 were also obliged to receive huge numbers of ailing soldiers. Nevertheless, the revolutionary assemblies can scarcely be blamed for economic distress caused by the emigration and the war, nor for the climatic vagaries of *nonante-cinq*. Nor – one assumes! – were they personally responsible for the tripling in the number of illegitimacies and child abandonments in the 1790s, a development which severely strained available hospital facilities.

These social and economic pressures would have crippled charitable institutions quite independently of the specifically revolutionary content of the 1790s. Monetary devaluation arising from the system of John Law – similar in many respects to the *assignat* fiasco – had caused very severe damage to hospital patrimonies in the 1720s.[69] Similarly, in the last great famine prior to 1795 – in 1709 and 1710 – charitable institutions had proved quite unable to alleviate the terrible sufferings which arose; and over the rest of the

Academy and the Nuffield Foundation for research grants which enabled me to accumulate relevant materials from national, departmental and hospital archives.

[67] C. Jones, *Charity and 'Bienfaisance'*, p. 163; M. Reinhard, *Le Département de la Sarthe sous le régime directorial* (Saint-Brieuc, 1935), p. 438; P. Clémendot, *Le Département de la Meurthe à l'époque du Directoire* (Raon-l'Etape, 1966), p. 391ff; P. Rambaud, *L'Assistance publique à Poitiers jusqu'à l'an V* (Paris, 1914), p. 585. Cf. J. Imbert, *Droit hospitaler*, p. 90.

[68] Bloch and Tuetey (eds.), *Procès-verbaux et rapports*, p. 564.

[69] C. Jones, *Charity and 'Bienfaisance'*, p. 70; O. Hufton, *The Poor of Eighteenth-Century France, 1750–1789* (Oxford, 1974), p. 153.

century, hospitals had shown themselves increasingly ill-equipped to cope with the social consequences of dearth, epidemic and structural poverty. As for charity – whose virtual absence in the late 1790s all were to deplore – this standby in time of need had shown itself to be a broken reed long before 1789.[70]

To a certain extent, then, the experience of the late 1790s was merely a repetition of a situation which had frequently occurred in French history, and the contemporary and subsequent critics who see something shockingly novel about the weak response of the Thermidorean and Directorial elite in the face of suffering commit a gross error in historical perspective.[71] The Thermidoreans and Directorials were, however, themselves guilty of a similar lack of awareness of the past when they vaunted the supposed economic independence of hospitals prior to 23 messidor. Probably the clear majority of charitable institutions had been dependent in some way on the central government under the ancien regime, and this dependence developed apace after 1789. All major institutions, for example, possessed royal letters patent, which had made them tributaries to the king for the rights and privileges there enshrined.[72] Direct state subsidies also comprised an important part of the revenue of many hospitals. The national average in the 1750s had been only about 5 per cent,[73] but this obscured marked variations round the mean, and it took no account of the drastic growth in state hand-outs from the 1760s onwards, as many hospitals found it difficult to keep abreast of social pressures, and had to be bailed out by sizeable government grants.[74] There were other types of government money available, too. Many hospitals, for example, flagrantly exploited the sums which government ministries paid for the care of sick soldiers, sailors and vagrants from *dépôts de mendicité*. After 1779, moreover, the government also began reimbursing those hospitals which admitted foundlings, and this service too might allow small profits to be made.[75]

Another, more attenuated form of financial dependence were the investments in various government bonds and annuities which charitable administrators made as a means of ensuring a steady, regular income from major legacies and windfalls. There were few institutions even of middling size

---

70 See references above, note 49. Cf. J. Imbert, *Droit hospitalier*, p. 42; and F. Dreyfus, *L'assistance*, p. 90.
71 Cf. the comments on the Directorials purported venality etc. in A. Goodwin, 'The French Executive Directory – a reevaluation', *History*, 22 (1937), 201–18.
72 C. Bloch, *L'assistance et l'état*, p. 139.
73 Bloch and Tuetey (eds.), *Procès-verbaux et rapports*, p. 508.
74 Innumerable local studies bear out the importance of the 1760s as marking the beginning of a severe financial crisis for a great many hospitals. See in particular C. Fairchilds, *Poverty and Charity in Aix-en-Provence, 1640–1789* (Baltimore, 1976), p. 131. See also O. Hufton, *The Poor of Eighteenth-Century France*, p. 152; and C. Jones, *Charity and 'Bienfaisance'*, pp. 70ff.
75 C. Bloch, *L'assistance et l'état*, p. 233.

which did not count *rentes sur l'hôtel-de-ville de Paris* – the most widespread of such annuities–among their portfolio of *rentes constituées*. After 1789, moreover, an even larger proportion of *rente* income was centred on the state, as the government assumed responsibility for servicing *rentes* which had been contracted with nationalised or dissolved bodies (provincial estates, monastic houses, guilds, etc.).[76] In addition, the revolutionary assemblies were also willing to grant provisional financial palliation to institutions which had sustained particularly heavy losses as a result of the abolition of feudalism and privilege. In this way, the picture of charitable institutions as independent became even more of a myth in the early 1790s.

The growth of financial dependence on the state did not have a ruinous effect on charitable institutions in the early 1790s. The interest on *rentes constituées* continued to be paid. Considerable government hand-outs– totalling nine million livres, according to the Ministry of the Interior[77] – were also made, and often proved of sterling worth. They were instrumental, for example, in restoring the financial health of the Grenoble hospitals, which had been in the doldrums since the 1760s.[78] Other hospitals – like those at Nemours (Seine-et-Marne) and Béziers (Hérault) used their grants to purchase new sites on the buoyant property market.[79] Still more hospitals benefited from the enforced amalgamation of small and unviable institutions: the big Parisian hospitals, for example, gained from the slimming down in the number of institutions in the capital.[80] In addition, some hospitals benefited from the state's assumption of financial responsibility for all foundlings: at Vire (Calvados), for example, the hospital received a state subsidy for this purpose for the first time in its history, and as it was able to find local wet-nurses at 2 livres less than the government allowance of 7 livres a month, it was soon making a profit of 15,000 livres a year on the service.[81]

The period of relatively easy money in the early 1790s–which helped off-set losses caused by revolutionary legislation – contrasted starkly with the late 1790s, when money was tight. Poor relief institutions were now not merely financially dependent on the state: they were dependent on governments

[76] C. Jones, *Charity and 'Bienfaisance'*, p. 164; M. Rochaix, *Essai*, p. 88.
[77] J. Imbert, *Droit hospitalier*, p. 62.
[78] A. Prudhomme, 'Introduction', *Inventaire sommaire des archives hospitalières de l'hôpital de Grenoble*, Grenoble, 1892, p. xiv. Cf. A. D. Isère, H supplément (*Hôpital de Grenoble*), B 156.
[79] A. D. Seine-et-Marne, *Archives hospitalières de Nemours* E 5; A. D. Hérault L 4625.
[80] Invaluable for public assistance in the capital until Year IV is A. Tuetey, *L'assistance publique à Paris pendant la Révolution* (4 vols., Paris, 1897). See also L. Parturier, *L'assistance à Paris sous l'ancien régime et pendant la Révolution* (Paris, 1897), p. 195. For amalgamations elsewhere in France: L. Accarias, *L'assistance publique sous la Révolution dans le département du Puy-de-Dôme* (Savenay, 1933), p. 106 (Clermont-Ferrand); J. Sahuc, 'Notes historiques sur l'hospice de Saint-Pons' in *Inventaire sommaire des archives hospitalières de Saint-Pons antérieures à 1790* (Montpellier, 1910), p. 11; C. Jones, 'Prostitution and the ruling class in eighteenth-century Montpellier', *History Workshop*, (1978), p. 22.
[81] Example cited in J. Imbert, *Droit hospitalier*, p. 59.

which, as we have seen, had neither the cash nor the political will to lend more than a token helping hand. The consequences of dependence in these changed circumstances were drastic indeed: since 23 messidor, noted the departmental administrators of the Puy-de-Dôme in Year V, with classic understatement, the hospitals 'ont été singuliérement à charge du trésor public, et n'en ont pas été pour cela plus heureux'.[82] It was a sentiment which, as we shall see, almost every charitable administrator in France could echo.

Partly, the problem was that the Thermidorean and Directorial assemblies' main concession towards establishing the independence of the hospitals – the restitution of their property – was a botched affair, which often brought as many headaches as it ended. The comments of the prefect of the Seine under the Consulate about land restored to the Parisian hospitals were not untypical. He noted: 'une dégradation considérable dans les maisons et dans les ermes, des réparations urgentes dans les meilleures, des réparations fortes dans les moins mauvaises et une reconstruction nécessaire dans un grand nombre; des pertes continuelles dans les loyers; des embarras et des lenteurs dans les recouvrements; des non-valeurs multipliées par le mauvais état des bâtiments'.[83] But at least Parisian hospitals had managed to get their land back: a great many departments found it virtually impossible to restore their hospitals' property. The land had either been sold off, or else no replacement property was available. The government showed itself unhelpfully inflexible – indeed at times deliberately obstructive – concerning conditions under which the restitution was made, and painfully slow in granting full permission.[84] It was not until the Consulate and Empire that the majority of transactions recomposing the hospitals' landed patrimony took place. Even then, the size and value of property returned did not nearly approach 1789 levels.[85] It was only from Year VIII, moreover, that the government tentatively started to give compensation for the *rentes constituées* which hospitals had had either with the government or with dissolved or nationalised bodies. Payment of these had lapsed in 1792, and the Thermidorean and Directorial assemblies proved unwilling to acknowledge their importance – or even their existence.[86]

The basis of hospital wealth in the nineteenth century was to comprise the incomes derived from land, *rentes* and from municipal tolls, or *octrois*. The

[82] A. D. Puy-de-Dôme L 2633.
[83] Cited in J. Imbert, *Droit hospitalier*, p. 208.
[84] For obstruction and even outright opposition by the government to local authorities granting hospitals land see, among numerous examples, J. Dubois, *L'assistance*, p. 107ff; and M. Reinhard, *Le Département de la Sarthe*, p. 440. Cf. A. de Watteville, *Législation charitable*, p. 105, for property restitutions achieved by ventôse Year XII: by that time, 8.4 millions livres of alienated capital had been returned, out of an estimated total of 18.1 millions.
[85] Cf. J. Imbert, *Droit hospitalier*, p. 207; M. Rochaix, *Essai*, p. 128.
[86] M. Rochaix, *Essai*, p. 88; J. Adher, *Recueil*, p. 160.

legal basis for the reconstitution of lands and *rentes* had been laid in the Thermidorean and Directorial period, though little that was concrete had been done. The picture was much the same for the *octroi*. Introduced for Paris on 27 vendémiaire Year VII and spread to other major cities between 3 brumaire Year VII and 2 vendémiaire Year VIII, it was eventually made general by the law of 5 ventôse Year VIII. There proved numerous difficulties, however, in collecting this unpopular tax: in Paris, for example, the hospitals and the home relief agencies–which here as elsewhere were allowed to share in the so-called *octroi de bienfaisance*–were chasing up the city authorities over payment in Year XII.[87]

The significance of the *octroi* for the Directorial period was, therefore, minimal, and indeed all other financial legislation introduced was nugatory in its effects. The law of 26 fructidor Year VI, for example, which granted the hospitals half the proceeds of the *personnelle, somptuaire* and *mobilière* taxes for Years V and VI seems to have been virtually ignored, the law of 6 vendémiaire Year VIII which awarded them 7.5 per cent of Year VII's direct taxes entirely so.[88] The law of 4 frimaire Year VII exempting hospitals from payment of the window tax was insignificant: hospitals proved too poor to pay it anyway.[89] The law of 8 thermidor Year V which established a municipal theatre tax (*droit sur les spectacles*, or *droits des pauvres*) from which all *bureaux de bienfaisance* and later all hospitals should benefit similarly did not amount to much: in the Sarthe, for example, there were 16 localities which contained a hospital, and 28 which contained a *bureau de bienfaisance* – but there was only one theatre, at Le Mans.[90] The *bureaux de bienfaisance*, which had less income from other sources at their disposal, suffered especially from the failure of the government to find funds with which to subsidise poor relief institutions. A large number of departments had few if any home relief agencies outside the departmental *chef-lieu*, and although efforts were made from Years VIII and IX to breathe life into these new creations, significant improvements did not come until after Years XI and XII.[91]

[87] M. C. R. Gillett, *Hospital Reform*, p. 194. The text of the law of 5 ventôse Year VIII may be found in A. de Watteville, *Législation charitable*, p. 67. For the importance of the *octroi de bienfaisance* in restoring the fortunes of charitable institutions in the early years of the nineteenth century, J. Dubois, *L'Assistance*, p. 116 (Bar-le-Duc); A. Giost, 'Histoire de l'hôpital général de Limoges', manuscript in 8 vols., 1883–7, located in A. D. Haute-Vienne (for Limoges); L. Boniface, 'Les établissements de bienfaisance sous le régime français de 1800 à 1814', *Nice Historique* (1942) (for Nice); and J. Imbert, 'La centralisation administrative des hôpitaux et de la bienfaisance dans les communes du département de la Dyle', *Tijdschrift voor Rechtgeschiednis*, 1951. Cf. too the general comments of J. Imbert, *Droit hospitalier*, 203; and M. Rochaix, *Essai*, p. 131.

[88] A. de Watteville, *Législation charitable*, pp. 48, 67. Cf. Levallois, *Motion d'ordre sur les hospices*, B.L. FR 433 (13 prairial Year VII).   [89] A. de Watteville, *Législation charitable*, p. 62.

[90] Ibid., pp. 45f; M. Reinhard, *Le Département de la Sarthe*, p. 441.

[91] C. Jones, *Charity and 'Bienfaisance'*, pp. 217 and 229; J. Dubois, *L'assistance*, pp. 98, 122; L. Lallemand, *La Révolution et les pauvres*, p. 225.

The financial plight of poor relief institutions would have been greatly attenuated had governments been willing and able to pay the bills which they ran up with individual hospitals. Hospital treatment for soldiers and sailors, and the upkeep of foundlings and orphans under hospital tutelage, were in theory the state's financial concern. But that was theory. In practice, nothing seems to have been paid for foundlings in the whole of Years III and IV, and the situation regarding soldiers and sailors does not appear to have been much better. Even though there was a slight improvement in the supply of funds in Year V, this did not last long, and the situation in Year VIII was especially bad.[92] The big *hôpital général* at Limoges was by then a year outstanding in receipt of funds for either soldiers or foundlings, and the administrators claimed that they were unable to keep alive any child who passed through their hands.[93] The hospitals of the department of the Dyle, and the institution at La Fère (Aisne) were by then still awaiting payments going back to Year III, and this was doubtless not untypical.[94] Indeed, the hospital at Bar-le-Duc was still waiting patiently in Year X.[95] So long had many institutions hung on, so substantial were the sums involved, that the eventual honouring of these bills under the Consulate was of considerable importance in restabilising hospital finances.

The bureaucratic jungle which had sprung up around communication between the provinces and the capital made the plight of poor relief institutions all the more poignant. The wish to be assured that the nation's good faith was not being duped had led governments from early on in the 1790s to insist on a high level of supporting evidence behind every claim for assistance which charitable administrators made. Ironically, however, by asking for every i to be dotted, every t to be crossed, every claim for compensation accompanied by abundant certification, every communication countersigned by local authorities, the Ministry of the Interior lost itself in its own red tape.[96] Even though their number was far higher than under the ancien regime, the Ministry's clerks found it impossible to cope with the mountains of bureaucratic bumf which poured in from the departments. Hospital administrators consequently found it almost impossible to get a straight answer from Paris. The administrators of the Limoges hospitals, for

[92] L. Lallemand, *La Révolution et les pauvres*, passim, and A. Forrest, *The French Revolution and the Poor*, passim, both contain a great deal of material relating to miserable conditions in Years III and IV. For Year VIII, cf. J. Dubois, *L'assistance*, p. 102; C. Jones, *Charity and 'Bienfaisance'*, pp. 216ff; A. D. Haute-Vienne H Supplément, *Hôpitaux de Limoges* E 125; A.N. F 748.

[93] E. Vincent, 'La grande détresse de l'hôpital de Limoges à l'époque révolutionnaire', *Bulletin de la Société d'archéologie de Limoges*, 1954, p. 466.

[94] J. Imbert, 'La centralisation administrative', p. 87; A. Forrest, *The French Revolution and the Poor*, p. 132.

[95] J. Dubois, *L'assistance*, p. 114.

[96] Problems caused by bureaucratic niceties go back at least to 1791. Cf. J. Imbert, *Droit hospitalier*, p. 58.

example, having despatched copies of the same request and accompanying documentation on three separate occasions, only to receive a note from a clerk that no communication had been received, concluded that the government was acting in a deliberate and machiavellian manner to reduce its financial outgoings.[97] It would, however, be more plausible to assume bureaucratic incompetence than malice. Moreover, the fault was not always with the clerk: the scribbled and poorly laid-out scraps of paper purporting to be regular accounts which they received from semi-illiterate hospital administrators bore witness to that.[98] But, whichever way the blame is apportioned, the new bureaucratic formality of the 1790s further aggravated an already desperate situation for a great many poor relief institutions.

The bureaucratic medium through which negotiation was conducted gave substantial opportunities for skilful fraud. The treasurer of the hospital of Saint Pons (Hérault), for example, was accused of grossly exaggerating the number of inmates in his hospital so as to attract greater government aid.[99] At one stage in the 1790s, the administrators of the *hôpital général* at Limoges were claiming they had lost 61,000 livres as a result of revolutionary legislation: in fact this sum had been lost in the John Law farrago in the 1720s![100] Later in the decade, they were claiming they had been despoiled of over 100,000 of their pre-revolutionary income of 120,000 livres: yet in fact this sum represented state subsidies for foundlings which the hospital was still in theory receiving.[101] In these circumstances, it was understandable that the bureaucrats should be ultra-cautious, especially as they had the politicians breathing down their necks: 'Que de surprises ont été faites à la religion du Gouvernement?', asked Delecloy. 'Combien d'états mensongers ont été fournis?'[102]

Given this suspicion which requests for aid provoked in Paris, any prudent hospital administrator found it expedient to ensure that his petitions tugged on the heart-strings. That such men occasionally let their pens run away with them is not to deny the appalling conditions under which most hospitals laboured in the late 1790s: only to serve as reminder that a situation of extreme economic dependence inevitably produces a rhetoric of pity and sycophancy. Such gilding the lily was not new: hospital administrators had always been 'quémandeurs obstinés'[103] on the frequent occasions on which

---

[97] E. Vincent, 'La grande détresse', p. 456. Cf. J. Dubois, *L'assistance*, p. 102; and C. Jones, *Charity and 'Bienfaisance'*, p. 186.

[98] The numerous petitions and accounts sent into the Ministry of the Interior and classified in the series F 15 of the *Archives Nationales* contain numerous examples of this.

[99] A.N. F¹⁵ 748.

[100] A. D. Haute-Vienne H Supplément, *Hôpitaux de Limoges* E 2.

[101] Ibid., E 130. For a similar case involving the Montpellier hospitals, cf. A. D. Hérault, *Archives de l'hôpital général de Montpellier. I. Antérieures à 1790 E 31*, and *II. Postérieures à 1790 E 56*.

[102] Delecloy, *Réflexions... sur l'organisation de l'administration des hospices civils*, B.L. FR 432 (16 fructidor Year IV).   [103] C. Bloch, *L'assistance et l'état*, p. 300.

they proffered the begging-bowl. Yet the sense of helplessness and passivity which their petitions for aid exude obscure the patient and humdrum work they were simultaneously engaged in, to try to make ends meet.

The sense of adjustment to expediency which emerges in the fraudulent petitions to the government came out in the other activities of charitable administrators. No strategem or fund-raising device was turned down, if it helped keep hospitals open and in service. Many *hôpitaux-généraux* – as at Poitiers, Montpellier and Bar-le-Duc[104] – set their inmates to work for outside textiles manufacturers. Other hospitals saw care of soldiers as a means of attracting additional revenue: the administrators of the Poitiers *hôtel-dieu* even turned their civilian inmates onto the street in August 1796 to make way for an influx of soldiers[105] (though the wonted tardiness of the government in paying its bills soon revealed the hollowness of this strategem). Local authorities were badgered into allowing hospitals many of their ancient rights and privileges. The old monopoly of coffins which the hospitals of Lamballe, Dinan and Guingamp (Côtes-du-Nord) had enjoyed was re-established. So too was the right of the hospitals of Saint-Brieuc, Condéac, Lannion and Tréguier to hold the franchise for street clearance.[106] Proceeds from fines levied in the courts were soon being directed into the coffers of local poor relief institutions. And the ancient practice of hospital children and inmates being hired out to follow funeral processions was also allowed very generally throughout France. Although in theory manual almsgiving was still against the law of the land, the public authorities were inveigled into turning a blind eye to the charitable collections which many hospitals now resumed: the first full-scale municipal *quête* since 1792 was organised in Montpellier in brumaire Year V, and other localities in the department, as indeed in France generally, soon followed suit.[107] These expressions of 'la bienfaisance individuelle' hardly constituted that torrent of giving which Delecloy and his cronies had dreamt of: but in the circumstances, every little helped.

Probably even more widespread than these fund-raising activities were attempts to save money by reducing commitments. The most effective way of doing this was to cut down the level of inmates. Every hospital found itself turning away individuals who in happier times it would have admitted.[108] A closer eye was kept to ensure that the able-bodied were excluded, and that the children of indigent parents did not find their way among the foundlings. Outsiders to the community also tended to find it more difficult

---

[104] P. Rambaud, *L'assistance publique*, p. 568; A. D. Hérault, *Archives de l'hôpital général de Montpellier. II. Postérieuers à 1790* E 1; and J. Dubois, *L'assistance*, p. 104.
[105] P. Rambaud, *L'assistance publique*, p. 173. Cf. for the hospital at Lodève (Hérault), A.N. F15 284.   [106] J. Imbert, *Droit hospitalier*, p. 215.
[107] A. D. Hérault, *Archives de l'hôtel-dieu de Montpellier. I. Antérieures à 1790* E 31, E 32. Cf. J. Imbert, *Droit hospitalier*, p. 138.
[108] The points made about hospital conditions are all so amply borne out in the series F 15 of the *Archives Nationales* that exact detailing becomes otiose.

to secure admission.[109] By the late 1790s, hospitals in the department of the Meurthe contained one-fifth fewer inmates than under the ancien regime.[110] Reductions elsewhere in France may well have been even more sizeable. A number of hospitals – it may have been over a third[111] – closed down permanently, many others shut their doors temporarily. The administrators of the tiny *hospice* at Castanet (Tarn-et-Garonne), for example, reported in Year VII that 'notre hospice n'a pas des dettes, n'ayant pas osé les contracter, crainte de ne pouvoir les acquitter, ce qui a privé l'hospice du pouvoir de secourir l'humanité souffrante'.[112] Even quite substantial institutions followed a similar tack: they reduced levels of inmates to next to nothing, and compensated by giving more home relief. A large number of *soi-disant* hospitals in the Lodévois, the local sub-prefect reported in Year VIII, were 'plutôt des établissements de bienfaisance pour secours à domicile'.[113] Other hospitals adopted the money-saving device of the administrators of the hospital at Condé-sur-Noireau (Calvados), who discharged all inmates save three homeless *vieillards* and two foundlings, who were all sent out daily to beg their bread, returning to the hospital at night to sleep.[114]

In these hard times, possession of property, which had managed to survive expropriation as feudal in 1789 or nationalisation under the law of 23 messidor, was a particularly useful financial prop. Land was the best possible hedge against insolvency and dependence. The administrators of the hospital at Embrun (Hautes-Alpes) had, for example, purchased some *biens nationaux* in the years of easy money in the early 1790s, and although some were lost in Year II, the remainder allowed the institution to sail through the late 1790s relatively unbothered.[115] Much the same was true at Nuits-Saint-Georges

---

109 For hospitals in the district of Bar, J. Dubois, *L'assistance*, p. 105; in the Maine-et-Loire, J. Imbert, *Droit hospitalier*, pp. 84, 169; in the Sarthe, M. Reinhard, *Le Département de la Sarthe*, p. 439; in the Dyle, J. Imbert, 'La centralisation administrative', p. 92; in the Hérault, C. Jones, *Charity and 'Bienfaisance'*, p. 189; and in the Hôtel des Invalides, I. Woloch, *The French Veteran*, p. 169.

110 P. Clémendot, *Le Département de la Meurthe*, p. 347.

111 C. Jones, *Charity and 'Bienfaisance'*, p. 255 for calculations concerning the department of the Hérault. For national figures, contrast the 2,188 institutions cited by the *Comité de Mendicité* in 1790 (Bloch and Tuetey [eds.], *Procès-verbaux et rapports*, p. 567) with the 1,270 institutions in existence in the middle of the nineteenth century: A. de Watteville, *Statistique des établissements de bienfaisance. Rapport à M. le Ministre de l'Intérieur sur l'administration des hôpitaux et des hospices* (Paris, 1851), p. 5.

112 J. Adher, *Recueil de documents*, p. 558 n. For the similar case of the hospital at Magnac-Laval (Haute-Vienne), A. Leroux, 'Notice historique sur l'hôpital de Magnac-Laval en Basse Marche (1610–1793)', *Bulletin de la Société archéologique et historique du Limousin* (1880), pp. 195ff.

113 A. D. Hérault 131 M 1. Cf. J. Dubois, *L'assistance*, p. 92; C. Jones, *Charity and 'Bienfaisance'*, p. 189; and A. D. Lozère H 1083 (Hospital at Mende).

114 R. Cobb, *Reactions to the French Revolution* (Oxford, 1972), p. 281. Cf. L. Lallemand, *La Révolution et les pauvres*, p. 200 (cases recorded at Angers, Marvéjols, Brives, Quimper . . .). See also, for Pézenas, A. D. Hérault 1 X 64.

115 *Archives départementales des Hautes-Alpes* 1 X 190, 1 X 191.

(Côte-d'Or), whose hospital derived more than two-thirds of its income from vineyards which were looked after, it was said, 'comme l'est le ménage d'un père de famille sage et économe'.[116] The hospital's administrators in the late 1790s offset hardship by raising rents, collecting in kind rather than in cash and developing a sophisticated system of barter against its excellent burgundy–thus ingeniously exploiting the discriminating palate of the Thermidoreans and Directorials![117] Other hospital administrators also used their imaginations in utilising what property remained them to palliate their distress. There was much cultivation of hospital gardens and allotments, for example, both to provide substance for barter and to improve inmates' diets. The inmates of the Poitiers *hôpital général* even started breeding rabbits and poultry with similar ends in view. Any spare capacity – chapels, unused rooms, untended gardens – might also be leased out.[118] Other administrators, more crudely, went in for something like asset-stripping: the hospital at Marvejols (Lozère) sold off all its furniture, that at Bar-le-Duc the contents of its stables, that at Montpellier its empty wine-barrels, that at Mons the silver from its chapel . . .[119]

Hospital administrations also mitigated their predicament by resorting to massive borrowing and by endlessly deferring settlements. Loans and contracts were agreed on the understanding that payment would occur when promised government aid finally arrived. Given the customary delays the latter involved, this entailed brazenly abusing the good faith of hospital creditors, suppliers and servants. Hospital wet-nurses, for example, had to wait months, even years for payment.[120] Servants had to habituate themselves to going without wages, too–though it was often found that, such were levels of poverty in the outside world, there was no shortage of individuals willing to serve gratis, as long as they were given free bed and board. Doctors and surgeons too had to abandon any pretence of being properly remunerated for their services.[121] Hospital bakers, butchers and other suppliers ran up huge bills which imperilled their businesses–indeed one merchant in Bordeaux was driven to suicide by his account with the local hospital.[122] Credit could always wait; but, as the administrators of the hospital at

---

[116] R. Laurent, 'La situation financière et économique de l'hôpital de Nuits-Saint-Georges, ans III–IV', *Annales historiques de la Révolution française* (1952).

[117] For similar cases at Saint-Etienne and at Malzieu, see A. Forrest, *The French Revolution and the Poor*, p. 43; and A. D. Lozère H 453.

[118] A. Rambaud, *L'assistance*, p. 566; A. Prudhomme, 'Introduction', p. xviii; A. D. Hérault, *Archives de l'hôpital général de Montpellier. II. Postérieures à 1790* E 56, E 68.

[119] J. Imbert, *Droit hospitalier*, p. 84; J. Dubois, *L'assistance*, p. 104; *Archives de l'hôpital général de Montpellier (II)* E 33; L. Lallemand, *La Révolution et les pauvres*, p. 373.

[120] See, for example, A. D. Lozère H 1083 (hospital at Mende) – one case which could be multiplied a hundredfold.

[121] E. Vincent, 'La grande détresse', p. 245; L. Lallemand, *La Révolution et les pauvres*, p. 116ff; A. D. Hérault L 2891 (hospital of Saint-Pons).   [122] M. C. R. Gillett, *Hospital Reform*, p. 176.

Morlaix remarked, 'la faim ne s'ajourne pas'[123] – and consequently administrators too found themselves digging deep into their own pockets to help ease their institutions through the darkest days. The administrators of the hospital at Tulle lent 150,000 livres, the treasurer of the big *hôtel-dieu* at Montpellier half a million livres – and borrowing on this scale was probably far from rare.[124] In human terms, it was difficult for many administrators merely to shrug their shoulders at the sight of such distress: 'nous n'avons pas des âmes de bronze', commented the administrative board of the hospital at Brive.[125]

The predicament of the administrators was all the more galling in that, for most of the 1790s, it was clear that they were fighting a losing battle. They could do little without cash, and forced government economy and financial stringency denied them this. Inevitably, then, the quality of care plummeted.[126] Maintenance of buildings was usually the first to go – with a consequent increase in leaking roofs, holed windows and damp walls. Stocks of linen were then run down – with the result that most of the hospital population in the late 1790s were shoeless and in rags, and the hordes of abandoned children had scarcely a nappy between them. Food deteriorated: meat and wine rations fell away to next to nothing; experiments were made with bread substitutes (rice, potatoes, etc.); and the size of the daily ration was cut back. At La Salpêtrière in Paris, it was said that inmates could choose between not consuming rations and dying of hunger on one hand, and eating them and risking death by choking on the other.[127] The fear expressed here – lest 'l'azille réservé à l'humanité devienne son tombeau'[128] – held true for a good many institutions. The nauseous stench of hospital rooms and the growing familiarity of rats and vermin attested a sharp drop in hygiene as environmental conditions worsened. Epidemics too became more general, and the fear which occasionally surfaced that hospitals had been invaded by the plague[129] revealed how panic-stricken the popular imagination had become at the misery to be found behind hospital walls.

It was understandable, given such conditions, that many individual administrators should feel overcome by the enormity of the task confronting

---

123 Cited in F. Dreyfus, *L'assistance*, p. 92.
124 C. Jones, *Charity and 'Bienfaisance'*, p. 188.
125 Cited in F. Dreyfus, *L'assistance*, p. 92. Cf. L. Lallemand, *La Révolution et les pauvres*, p. 279; M. Reinhard, *Le Département de la Sarthe*, p. 441.
126 L. Lallemand, *La Révolution et les pauvres* contains large numbers of horror stories about conditions in the hospitals, and also a large number of *pièces justificatives* drawn from the series F15 of the *Archives Nationales*, which form a sampler of reports and petitions requesting government aid.   127 A.N. F15 1863.   128 Ibid.
129 M. C. R. Giliett, *Hospital Reform*, p. 1978 (Paris *hôtel-dieu*, 1793); C. Caizergues and S. Rogéry, *Rapport fait à l'Ecole de médecine le 23 ventôse an VIII sur la nature, la marche et le traitement de la fièvre observée dans les hôpitaux de cette commune pendant les six premiers mois de l'an VIII*, Montpellier, an VIII, p. 6 (Montpellier *hôtel-dieu*, Year VIII).

them. As continued sniping in the Directorial assemblies suggested, the law of 16 vendémiaire Year V did not always bring that stability and continuity in hospital administration which had been its intention. Indeed, in some places, frequent resignations left many institutions bereft of sound management, and thus worsened conditions.[130] In many small localities, it proved difficult to find enough individuals disinterested – and even literate! – enough to serve on the *commissions administratives des hospices civils*, as indeed on the *bureaux de bienfaisance*.[131] Elsewhere, an unwillingness to allow common management for all hospitals within a single commune caused initial teething troubles.[132] The political dangers of hospital administration persisted too, especially in Paris, where accusations were soon flying around that the administrators – who were roundly reproached for 'leur table splendide, leurs voitures élégantes, tout ce luxe qu'étalent à nos yeux ces hommes fiers' – were encouraging royalism in the hospitals and making their fortunes out of the poor.[133] Some 35 individuals passed through the five places on the Parisian hospital board in the late 1790s, and the joke began to be told that the administrators lasted a shorter time in the hospitals than the patients.[134]

Nevertheless, despite these problems, the law of 16 vendémiaire was slowly but surely restabilising hospital administration. Although there is a case for arguing that – as was certainly true of the *bureaux de bienfaisance* – the major work of consolidation was achieved after Year VIII, by which time the government started working through prefects and sub-prefects to regularise and encourage, but also to control, the communal aspect of poor relief administration, the foundations of better management were laid in the late 1790s.[135] The example of Paris notwithstanding, turn-over of personnel was less high, and there was a clear improvement in administrative standards, with individual administrators showing a greater sense of commitment in what were depressing and demoralising circumstances. If the 'bienfaisance individuelle' of which Delecloy had made so much had had little financial pay-off, at least it manifested itself positively in altruistic service which came, moreover, from all points of the political and religious spectrum. At Bar-le-Duc, the appointment of the ancien regime *receveur* of the hospital brought immediate stability to the institution's affairs: he served down to 1807, by

130 A good example of the turbulence of hospital administration is provided by Paris. L. Parturier, *L'assistance à Paris*, passim; F. Dreyfus, *L'Assistance*, p. 106; A.N. F15 1863. Resignation and replacements of hospital administrators abound in the dossiers of series F15.
131 J. Imbert, *Droit hospitalier*, pp. 115, 303; J. Imbert, 'La centralisation administrative', p. 303; A. D. Hérault L 2899 and 2 X 39.
132 J. Imbert, *Droit hospitalier*, p. 111; L. Lallemand, *La Révolution et les pauvres*, p. 103; A. D. Hérault, *Hôpital général (II)* E 23 and *Archives de l'hôtel-dieu de Montpellier. II. Archives postérieures à 1790* E 13, E 17.
133 Important dossier on the affair in A.N. F15 1863.
134 The joke is recorded in L. Parturier, *L'assistance à Paris*, p. 23.
135 J. Imbert, *Droit hospitalier*, pp. 113, 153; C. Jones, *Charity and 'Bienfaisance'*, p. 217.

which time recovery was total.[136] In Montpellier, Etienne Barthélemy and in Paris Benjamin Delessert initiated terms of service on the hospital commissions which were to last uninterrupted down to 1833 and 1846 respectively.[137] The unglamorous slog, the humdrum perseverance which such men manifested in the late 1790s were crucial to the limited but practical gains of the period, and indeed to the very survival of many institutions through appalling conditions: they belie the appearance of passivity and helplessness which exude from the – consciously heart-tugging – petitions to the central government and they contradict the conventional nostrum that the social elites of the Thermidorean and Directorial periods were uniformly hard-hearted and insouciant in the face of distress.

III

Even more altruistic than charitable administrators in the services which they rendered the beleagured hospitals were the nursing sisters attached to many institutions: for all had to undergo a change in lifestyle, and most a measure of humiliation and persecution as a result of the Revolution.[138] Although most communities of nursing sisters had enjoyed a good reputation at the beginning of the Revolution, the drift of events had gradually turned against them. Despite the opposition of most communities to the Civil Constitution of the Clergy, only relatively few – as at Le Mans and Vire[139] – were driven out for refusing to acknowledge the constitutional clergy. Most local administrators seem to have shrunk from dismissing their nurses on the grounds that it would prove difficult to find adequate replacements, and this view was shared by many national politicians. Thus even the law of 18 August 1792 which formally abolished all nursing and teaching communities charged individual sisters to remain at their posts, on pain of losing their

---

[136] J. Dubois, *L'assistance*, p. 94.

[137] C. Jones, *Charity and 'Bienfaisance'*, p. 195; J. Imbert, *Droit hospitalier*, p. 154. Cf. E. Vincent, 'La grande détresse', p. 462.

[138] No convincing treatment of the history of nursing sisters during the revolutionary decade exists. We get glimpses of them in local hospital archives, in the series F15 and F19 of the *Archives Nationales* and in local studies on hospitals and religion. There is some material to be gleaned too from the hagiographical works of historians of the different nursing communities. For the largest community of nursing sisters, the Filles de la Charité see, for example, P. Coste, *Les Filles de la Charité. L'Institut de 1617 à 1800* (Paris, 1933); L. Misermont, *Les Filles de la Charité d'Arras (1794)* (Cambrai, 1901); P. Coste, *Une victime de la Révolution. Soeur Marguerite Rutan, Fille de la Charité* (Paris & Lille, 1908); and the *Livre d'or des Filles de la Charité, ou simple aperçu des plus belles notices des soeurs* (2 vols., Paris, 1938–48). Interesting information is also available on all communities in C. Molette, *Guide des sources de l'histoire des congrégation féminines françaises de vie active* (Paris, 1974). An excellent insight into the general dilemmas and problems of the nursing sisters is given in the study of the Paris Augustine community: D. B. Weiner, 'The French Revolution, Napoleon and the nursing profession', *Bulletin of the History of Medicine* (1972).

[139] J. Imbert, *Droit hospitalier*, p. 39. Cf. L. Lallemand, *La Révolution et les pauvres*, p. 133.

pensions.[140] The increasing polarisation of attitudes over religion, however, left the nurses increasingly dangerously exposed. In Mézières they were accused of comprising a 'milice ultramontaine'.[141] Recriminations in the Jacobin Club in September 1793 against the best-known and most widely spread of all such communities, the *Filles de la Charité*, eventually led to the Convention passing a law on 15 vendémiaire Year II which stated that all *hospitalières* who refused to take the oath of liberty and equality were to be dismissed and replaced by 'des citoyennes connues pour leur attachement à la Révolution'. This law, reiterated on 9 nivôse Year II, the oath on which it insisted, together with the growing anti-clericalism apparent in public life led to the stepping up of the tempo of dismissals and expulsions.[142]

The implementation of legislation against nursing sisters tended to depend very much on local issues: the perceived local importance of the religious question, for example, the nature of the involvement of the sisters in un-revolutionary activities (support of non-jurors, etc.), the prior popularity of the sisters and so on. Though sisters rarely seem to have attracted outright enemies, personal antipathies might also come into play: the expulsion of the *Filles de la Charité* from the *hôtel-dieu* at Bayeux, for example, well suited the purposes of local physician and official Le Tual, who in the last years of the ancien regime had fought tooth and nail with the sisters over responsibility for the hospital's medical services.[143] Local jacobins and sectional personnel with axes to grind could also have significant influence. They were notably critical in Paris, for example, of the activities of the *Filles de la Charité*: the latter were accused of turning the Invalides into a 'foyer d'aristocratie' and at the Enfants-Trouvés of having 'insinué dans l'esprit des enfants les principes les plus dangereux, jusqu'à leur persuader que s'ils communiaient de la main d'un prêtre assermenté, ils recevraient le diable au lieu de Dieu'.[144] Local militants were largely responsible for the coerced dissolution of the *maison-mère* of the community in 1792.[145] Where local militancy did not suffice, moreover, the arrival of a radical *représentant en mission* could do the trick. Joseph Le Bon, for example, threw local sisters into gaol on his arrival in Boulogne, and was instrumental in the arrest and execution of four sisters from Arras; Laplanche vigorously purged the Loiret and the Cher of hospital sisters; and Barras and Fréron congratulated themselves on rooting out a 'nest of nuns' from the hospital at Embrun.[146]

---

[140] Cf. A. Aulard, *La Révolution française et les congrégations* (Paris, 1903), p. 226.

[141] A.N. AD XVII 43.

[142] J. Imbert, *Droit hospitalier*, p. 90; L. Lallemand, *La Révolution et les pauvres*, p. 133.

[143] O. Hufton, *Bayeux in the Late Eighteenth Century: a Social Study* (Oxford, 1970), p. 245.

[144] I. Woloch, *The French Veteran*, p. 139; F. Dreyfus, *L'assistance*, p. 115.

[145] A.N. S 6157 and L 1054.

[146] L. Misermont, *Les Filles de la Charité d'Arras*; L. Lallemand, *La Révolution et les pauvres*, p. 127; D. M. Vess, *Medical Revolution*, p. 97.

The impact of revolutionary legislation and of this semi-official 'dechristianising' persecution was, however, not nearly as ruinous and widespread as is sometimes claimed. Local interest cut both ways: local officials in Montpellier, for example, mindful of the sterling services which the *Filles de la Charité* had performed in the city, administered the oath in a very anodyne form, merely asking the sisters to 'promettre à Dieu à continuer à servir les pauvres comme par le passé'. Similarly at Bar-le-Duc, local officials unhesitatingly awarded local nursing sisters their *certificats de civisme* 'à raison de ce qu'elles soulagent l'humanité'.[147] Nationally, too, there was no great hecatomb, no massive round-up. In only 3 of the 426 localities served by the *Filles de la Charité*, for example, did the sisters actually go to the scaffold; they were severely mistreated in about half a dozen other localities; they were imprisoned in another twenty places, and expelled from about the same number.[148] The experience of other nursing communities was not dissimilar.[149] Furthermore, it was not long before those sisters who had been expelled were being recalled. In Le Havre, the sisters had only been dismissed for a couple of months before changed political circumstances led to their being invited back. The year 1795 saw such recalls coming thicker and faster: Morlaix (ventôse Year III), Béziers (messidor Year III), Romorantin (nivôse Year IV), Le Puy, Libourne, Loudun . . .[150] By Year VI, even the Minister of the Interior was encouraging their return, and was turning a blind eye to the reconstitution of the national network of the *Filles de la Charité*.[151] The recrudescence of dechristianising activity in poor relief institutions following the coup of Fructidor caused barely a hiccup in the slow process of normalisation.[152] Eventually in nivôse Year IX, the Minister of the Interior Chaptal officially recognised the existence of the *Filles de la Charité*'s central organisation, allowed them to recruit new members, and even made them a state grant of aid to assist their recovery. With the Concordat soon bringing an end to the bulk of politico-religious dissension, the floodgates were opened, and recognition of other nursing and teaching communities soon followed.[153]

---

[147] *Documents historiques sur l'oeuvre de la Miséricorde de la ville de Montpellier* (Montpellier, 1840), p. 16; J. Dubois, *L'assistance*, p. 84. Cf. J. Boussoulade, *Moniales et hospitalières dans la tourmente révolutionnaire: les communautés de religieuses de l'ancien diocèse de Paris de 1789 à 1801* (Paris, 1962), p. 107.

[148] *Livre d'or*, vol. I, p. 319.

[149] C. Molette, *Guide*, p. 64; A. Le Moign Klipffel, *Les Filles de la Sagesse* (Paris, 1947), p. 118.

[150] L. Lallemand, *La Révolution et les pauvres*, pp. 138, 147; J. Imbert, *Droit hospitalier*, p. 144; A. D. Finistère, *Archives hospitalières de Morlaix* 47 H 28; A. D. Hérault, *Archives hospitalières de Béziers* II E 14.

[151] A. D. Seine-et-Marne, *Archives hospitalières de Nemours* F5 Cf. J. Imbert, *Droit hospitalier*, p. 144.

[152] I. Woloch, *The French Veteran*, p. 135; A. D. Hérault, *Archives hospitalières de Montpellier* (*Hôtel-dieu*). *II. Postérieures à 1790* E 1.

[153] J. A. Chaptal, *Mes souvenirs sur Napoléon*, Paris, 1893, p. 71f; C. Molette, *Guide*, p. 65f; D. B. Weiner, 'The French Revolution', pp. 291ff.

By the end of the Consulate, the communities were even beginning to take on new branches for the first time for a decade and a half.[154]

The communities of nursing sisters did see a marked shrinkage in the size of their operations – the Filles de la Charité, for example, were only serving in some 250 institutions in 1804, as against the 426 institutions they had staffed in 1790[155] but factors extrinsic to the purely political persecution of the radical phase of the Revolution played the most important part in this. The prohibition of vows, the closure of the maison-mère and consequent organisational disarray caused a sharp fall in recruitment to the Filles de la Charité, and the experience of other communities was probably the same.[156] Religious divisions following the Concordat also seem to have lost the communities some of their more recalcitrant sisters.[157] Even more important in the disappearance of the nursing sisters from many localities was the fact that many of the institutions which they had served either disappeared in the revolutionary maelstrom, or else could no longer afford to pay for the sisters' upkeep. Many small branches of the Filles de la Charité under the ancien regime had effectively been discharging by proxy seigneurs' duties towards their peasants: the raison d'être behind such establishments disappeared with the abolition of feudalism.[158] The income of a great many of the institutions in rural localities which the sisters served was, moreover, so exiguous, that even with the slightest mismanagement or ill-luck it dwindled away to nothing. Nursing sisters were consequently less likely than before to be met with in rural localities: their geographical diffusion was temporarily 'urbanised' as a result of the upheavals of the 1790s.[159]

In one way or another, the networks of institutions to which nursing sisters were attached were thrown into disorder by the events of the 1790s. Not only that: these years traumatised the individual members of the communities. Nursing sisters had always viewed the service of the poor as a

---

154 For the restoration of the nursing communities, see the important dossiers in A.N. F[15] 2562 and F [19] 6244. Cf. Précis historique de la Congrégation de Saint-Charles de Nancy (Nancy, 1845).

155 C. Molette, Guide, p. 65. Cf. the census of nursing communities in 1808 (A.N. F[15] 6244), which cited 274 outposts of the Filles de la Charité.

156 D. B. Weiner, 'The French Revolution', p. 283; C. Jones, Charity and 'Bienfaisance', p. 199; A. D. Seine-et-Marne, Archives hospitalières de Provins K 4. Cf. P. Adam, Histoire des hospices et hôpitaux de Sélestat (Sélestat, 1960), p. 200.

157 Information on religious defections in A.N. F[15] 2560, 2561.

158 The establishment of nursing sisters in seigneuries was something of a 'pieuse vogue' in the late seventeenth and eighteenth centuries: 'Appendice', N. Gobillon, La vie de la vénérable Louise de Marillac, veuve de M. Le Gras (revised edition, Paris, 1862 – originally 1769 – p. 351). The archives of the Filles de la Charité which were confiscated in the 1790s contain numerous contracts relating to establishments of this sort. A.N., S 6160 to 6180.

159 See in particular the dossier concerning the hospital at Pons (Charente-Inférieure), A.N. F[15] 2560. Comments on the change in the geographical diffusion of the Filles de la Charité are based on a provisional comparison between localities served under the ancien regime, according to A.N. S 6160 to 6180 and the census of establishmnents in the late 1830s in A.N. F[19] 6244.

religious state; and it was this that they were called upon to renounce. They gave up their ecclesiastical dress – even their *noms de religion* at the Limoges *hôpital général* – and were obliged to don the revolutionary cockade.[160] The traditionally religious character of the hospital environment was deliberately overturned. Hospital chapels were closed down, religious, royal and 'feudal' emblems destroyed. Busts of revolutionary martyrs appeared. The spire of the ancient hospital chapel at Beaune was provocatively decked with a *bonnet rouge*.[161] Trees of liberty sprouted abundantly in hospital premises – though the administrators of the *hôtel-dieu* at Nemours prudently drew the line at planting one in the middle of the main ward; and their counterparts in Montpellier evidently found it difficult to restrain inmates from urinating against the newly planted trees in the hospital courtyard![162] The Constitution and the Rights of Man now replaced hymns and catechisms, and *enfants trouvés* – or *enfants de la patrie*, as they were now called, the bearers of revolutionary rather than christian names[163] – were paraded out to temples of reason rather than on religious processions. Even the nomenclature of hospital life changed: '*hôpital*' and '*hôtel-dieu*' were replaced by the more neutral '*hospice*'; saints' names disappeared from the titles of hospitals and individual rooms – the latter often being renamed after revolutionary virtues or martyrs.[164] The *modus vivendi* which most hospital sisters had worked out with lay administrators under the ancien regime was now viewed with the deepest suspicion: sisters were suspects, and local officials had to keep them on a tight rein. The keys of the hospitals – formerly in the hands of the local superior – were now consigned to the safe keeping of administrators or communal officials, who locked sisters and inmates in at night and opened up in the morning. Sisters could be forgiven for regarding themselves as prisoners.

These trials and tribulations appear to have, if anything, only strengthened the resolve of the nursing sisters to remain faithful to the customary precepts of their vocation. Even though by law they were not permitted until after the turn of the century to don their religious uniforms,[165] the conditions of

---

[160] A. Aulard, *La Révolution française et les congrégations*, p. 41; *Livre d'or*, vol. I, p. 106; A. Giost, 'Histoire de l'hôpital général de Limoges'.

[161] J. Imbert, *Droit hospitalier*, p. 99. For dechristianising activities within the hospitals see in particular ibid. p. 100; C. Jones, *Charity and 'Bienfaisance'*, p. 196; and I. Woloch, *The French Veteran*, p. 134.

[162] A.D. Seine-et-Marne, *Archives hospitalières de Nemours* E 5; A.D. Hérault, *Archives hospitalières de Montpellier* (*Hôtel-dieu*), *II, Postérieures à 1790* E 1.

[163] A. Soboul, *Les Sans-culottes parisiens*, p. 675; E. Vincent, 'La grande détresse', p. 458; R. Cobb, 'Thermidor', p. 279; M. Lyons, *Revolution in Toulouse: an Essay on Provincial Terrorism* (Berne, 1978), p. 160.

[164] I. Woloch, *The French Veteran*, p. 135; M. C. R. Gillett, *Hospital Reform*, p. 124; L. Lallemand, *La Révolution et les pauvres*, p. 143; C. Jones, *Charity and 'Bienfaisance'*, p. 197.

[165] P. Coste, *Les Filles de la Charité*, p. 136; J. Imbert, *Droit hospitalier*, p. 195; *Archives hospitalières de Dijon* F7 18.

service which they were able to extract from administrators in the late 1790s and early 1800s showed only too clearly that their value was highly prized.[166] The salary levels of the *Filles de la Charité* prior to the Revolution had not exceeded 120 livres per annum, and had often been around 60 or 80 livres: now, they were able to insist on a figure of 200 livres. In some cases, additional benefits were extracted: the Soeurs de Saint Thomas de Villeneuve who returned to the Rennes *hôpital général*, for example, were granted extra food privileges, including wine and cider.[167] The hospital keys were now returned to the local superiors – a powerful and satisfying symbol of the refound authority of the sisters.[168] The hiring and firing of ancillary personnel was entrusted to them. The communities would be allowed to live their collective religious life without hindrance – the way thus being cleared for the hospitals to become – as they did, down to the Concordat at least – storm centres of popular catholicism and royalism. Charges were soon being made of the sisters neglecting the welfare of inmates with pronounced revolutionary views, and bullying them into changing their opinions: the Lieutenant Jacques Baumès admitted to the lunatic asylum at Charenton in Year VIII 'se disant poursuivi et tourmenté par quatre filles hospitalières qui font grand tapage à ses oreilles surtout la nuit', was, it would appear, only an extreme victim of the sisters' over-enthusiastic proselytising.[169]

The nursing sisters saw in their recall or reinstatement the vindication of their traditional view of the hospital as a material and spiritual refuge for the poor and needy.[170] The idea of hospitals serving as laboratories for republican morality seemed defunct. In addition, many sisters seem to have been equally critical of the clinical concept of the hospital being generated by the medical profession. There had been numerous disputes in the last decades of the ancien regime between doctors and nursing sisters over their respective roles and responsibilities within the hospitals, and these now reasserted themselves. The greater prestige which the medical professions had acquired as a result of their involvement in the war effort made it, in theory, more difficult for the sisters to oppose doctors having a greater sway in the internal running of institutions. From about this time, moreover, the Ministry of the Interior

---

166 Numerous contracts of service from the early nineteenth century in the series F 15 of the *Archives Nationales*: see in particular F¹⁵ 192, 193, 2560, 2561.

167 R. Capsie, 'L'hôpital général de Rennes sous la Révolution et l'Empire', unpublished thesis, *Ecole nationale de santé publique* (Rennes, 1968/9), p. 15.

168 See, for example, the contracts with the hospitals of Thiers in Year X (A.N. F¹⁵ 192), of Cambrai (approximately the same period) (ibid.) and of Moulins in Year X (F¹⁵ 1540). This clause does not seem to have appeared in contracts under the ancien regime.

169 A.N. AJ² 99. Cf, L. Accarias, *L'assistance publique*, p. 107; and C. Jones, *Charity and 'Bienfaisance'*, p. 202.

170 D. B. Weiner, 'The French Revolution', p. 275; C. Jones, *Charity and 'Bienfaisance'*, p. 202; L. S. Greenbaum, 'Nurses and doctors in conflict. Piety and medicine in the Paris hôtel-dieu on the eve of the Revolution', *Clio medica* (1979), passim.

began to ensure that the major hospitals were properly equipped with full medical facilities for training purposes.[171] The effective 'rechristianisation' of hospitals at the hands of the sisters in the later 1790s, however, meant that the battle for medical control of the hospitals was far from over. Indeed, the anti-clinical disposition of the nursing sisters seems to have been instrumental in blocking the full implementation of the law of 14 frimaire Year III relating to the provisions of clinical facilities in the hospitals of Paris, Montpellier and Strasbourg. Although the Parisian *cliniques* were soon well established, that at Montpellier had to labour under considerable disadvantages well into the nineteenth century; and that at Strasbourg was not put on a proper footing until Year VIII.[172] The sisters' influence thus worked to minimise the medical role of the hospitals, at the expense of the institutions' social and religious functions.[173]

Yet if the 'rechristianisation' of hospitals – and indeed of other poor relief institutions – following the dechristianising activities of the revolutionary decade often frustrated the reforming intentions of the medical profession, it also signified, at a more mundane level, the reimposition of sound managerial technique and the return of competent levels of care for inmates, which had been sadly lacking while their influence had been eclipsed. The undignified rush by hospital administrators to secure the services of sisters from the main nursing communities in the late 1790s and the early 1800s[174] showed how closely administrators associated the care proffered by the sisters with the more general task of restabilising hospital administration and finance. Sisters were willing to work around the clock, to skimp on wages when need be, to persevere in often repulsive tasks and to exhibit an honesty and integrity which had been sadly lacking in their replacements in the 1790s. The experiment of staffing the hospitals with *citoyennes patriotes* had proved a barely qualified disaster. When in 1791 there had originally been talk of replacing the Augustine sisters who ran the Paris *hôtel-dieu* with 'mercenaires', the superior of the Parisian community had argued that only religious vocation made nursing life at all bearable: 'il faut avoir fait la sacrifice de sa vie pour

---

171 J. Imbert, *Droit hospitalier*, p. 166.

172 For Strasbourg, E. Wickersheimer, 'L'hôpital de Strasbourg au XVIIIᵉ siècle', *Archives internationales d'histoire des sciences* (1963), p. 274; for Montpellier, C. Jones, *Charity and 'Bienfaisance'*, pp. 204ff.

173 For other regional examples of continuing opposition between nurses and medical staff in the early nineteenth century see, for example, A.D. Hérault, 1 X 1; *Archives hospitalières de Dijon* E 1 52; and A.D. Ille-et-Vilaine, *Archives hospitalières de Vitré (Hôpital général)* 1 J 2. Cf. the general comment of M. Candille, 'Les soins en France au XIXᵉ siècle', *Bulletin de la Société française d'histoire des hôpitaux* (1973), p. 56.

174 There are numerous examples of often unavailing efforts by hospital administrators to acquire the services of nursing communities in the late 1790s and early 1800s in the A.N. F¹⁵, F¹⁹ and in local archives. For a single example: A.N. F¹⁵ 3963; request of the administrators at Le Vigan (Gard) for *Filles de la Charité*, Pluviôse Year XIII.

prendre un si triste et si laborieux état, et en avoir fait la consécration la plus réfléchie pour y persevérer'.[175] Events seemed to prove her right. At Dijon, it was recorded that the sisters' replacements 'se faisaient passer pour patriotes et volaient le linge et toutes sortes de hardes'; at Angers, their counterparts were guilty of 'rapine et détournement des denrées'; at Montpellier, they never won the confidence of inmates, who tricked and teased them into demoralisation.[176] It had proved immensely difficult to find women of the necessary dedication and integrity to brook the trials and tribulations of hospital life. Though some administrators were to support the *mercenaires* – the old sisters were nothing but 'bougresses et salopes' according to the local authorities at Vilaine, 'misérables et nuisibles au service' according to the administrators at the Tournai hospital[177] – in general, the return of the sisters was popular both with the administrators with whom they were to work to reorganise the institutions, and with the poor themselves who would be the recipients of their care. The steady hand of the nursing sisters was as important as the selflessness and devotion of charitable administrators in ensuring survival of poor relief institutions and in building the foundations of their modest prosperity in the nineteenth century.

IV

The final decades of the ancien regime and the early years of the Revolution had seen the development of a passionate and eloquent critique of all aspects of the organisation of social welfare in France, and in particular the central role of the country's two thousand hospitals as the basis of poor relief. By the time of the Consulate, in contrast, this critique had virtually sunk without trace, and there was a general acceptance that existing forms of relief, though not perfect, were quite adequate to the tasks confronting them. Welfare reform was no longer conceived of as totally recasting the nation's poor laws, but as a matter of piecemeal tinkering and marginal adjustments. The number of hospitals had been slimmed down somewhat – from two thousand to about thirteen hundred[178] – but their central position in the state's welfare system was not contested. The missionary zeal of welfare reformers which had climaxed in the pre-Thermidorean Convention had been canalised in the late 1790s into the sententious meanderings of neo-jacobinism and the hollow

---

[175] A.N. AD XVII 43.

[176] A.D. Côte d'Or, 1 F 271; M. Bouloiseau, 'Les "tire-au-flanc"', p. 548; C. Jones, *Charity and 'Bienfaisance'*, p. 198. Similar tales of woe recorded in O. Hufton, *Bayeux*, p. 245; L. Lallemand, *La Révolution et les pauvres*, p. 138; A.D. Isère, *Archives hospitalières de Saint-Marcellin* K 1; and J. Gardère, *Inventaire sommaire des archives hospitalières. Hospices de Condom* (Auch, 1883).

[177] L. Lallemand, *La Révolution et les pauvres*, p. 149; J. Imbert, *Droit hospitalier*, p. 290. Cf. ibid., p. 194.

[178] See above, note 111.

pseudo-philosophical posturing of theophilanthrophy.[179] Once these petered out, the whole movement which had championed the values of Enlightenment *bienfaisance* lost any intellectual heirs–down to the 1830s and 1840s at least, when a new wave of polemic against the premises of the nation's poor laws emerged.[180] Significantly, however, these latter-day critics who mouthed the old arguments – against the over-reliance on private charity, against over-numerous hospitals, for home relief, for greater equality in the right to assistance – did so under the impression that what they were saying was novel: to that extent had the intellectual moorings with the *bienfaisance* of the Enlightenment and the early years of the Revolution been snapped.

Changes in the social and economic context of welfare policy – evidently too general and too numerous to be investigated in the present essay – played a part in this remarkable transformation of attitudes between the Convention and the Consulate. Many men who, under ancien regime conditions, would have joined the serried ranks of the 'sturdy beggars' who so frightened both government and its critics were now, for example, to be found striding purposefully across Europe clad in military uniform; and whereas the *Comité de Mendicité* in 1790 had diagnosed France's social ills as deriving from a shortage of employment, by the early 1800s farmers and manufacturers were complaining bitterly of the high wages and labour shortages caused by the displacement of so much able-bodied manpower to the front.[181] In ways such as this, the shape, the perceived intensity of the problem of poverty seemed less threatening, less urgent than before–and this obviously contributed to the decline in the concern with questions of social welfare.

Besides these general contextual points, however, there were a number of aspects of the experience of poor relief organisations and welfare policy over the course of the late 1790s which contributed to the decline of interest in remoulding welfare provision, and to the revaluation of hospital care. The association of science with poor relief, for example, which had its origins in the last decades of the ancien regime, was now warmly welcomed back by the 'République des professeurs'.[182] The clinical training which took place

---

[179] See sporadic but revealing references to 'bienfaisance' in both I. Woloch, *Jacobin Legacy: the Democratic Movement under the Directory* (Princeton, 1970), and in A. Mathiez, *La Théophilanthropie et le culte décadaire 1796–1801* (Paris, 1904).

[180] For the critique of provision of assistance, see the early pages of H. Hatzfeld, *Du paupérisme à la sécurité sociale, 1850–1940* (Paris, 1971), and the final sections of F. Dreyfus, *Un philanthrope*. Cf. M. Rochaix, *Essai*, p. 150.

[181] R. Cobb, *The Police and the People*, passim, for changing perceptions of the threat constituted by the popular movement. For labour-shortages, cf. D. Woronoff, *Les Thermidoriens et le Directoire* (Paris, 1972), p. 122; J. Godechot, *La vie quotidienne en France sous le Directoire* (Paris, 1977), pp. 38, 62.

[182] For the association of science and poor relief institutions under the ancien regime, C. C. Gillispie, *Science and Polity in France at the end of the Old Régime* (Princeton, 1980), esp. p. 244. The phrase 'la République des professeurs' comes from F. Furet and D. Richet, *La Révolution française* (Paris, 1973), p. 466.

under the eye of the Faculté de Médecine in Paris hospitals – if not yet at
Strasbourg or Montpellier – was the most brilliant example of how hospitals
could serve both scientific and philanthropic ends, but there were others.[183]
The newly established *Maison Nationale de l'Aliénation mentale* offered means
of studying and researching insanity, the *Sourds-muets*, deaf mutes.[184] Even
administrative reorganisation could serve scientific purposes: the *Apothicairerie
générale*, for example, established in Paris in Year III to supply drugs for all
Parisian hospitals, was acknowledged as providing 'un vaste moyen d'étude
et d'instruction'.[185] Welfare policy was sufficiently flexible, furthermore, to
accommodate fresh scientific endeavours in the guise of private philanthropy:
the *Société philanthropique* – which had been abolished under the Convention – was reorganised and was soon promoting schemes as diverse as
Rumford soups, smallpox vaccination and dispensaries; and the *Société
de Charité Maternelle* was also re-established in its ancien regime form in
the same period, and assisted poor mothers at the same time that it encouraged research into better childbirth conditions.[186]

These reforms and developments – many of them located in the capital –
helped to defuse much of the criticism which welfare reformers and medical
men had levelled against the system of poor relief. The same was true of
hospital reform in the capital. Much ancien regime hostility towards hospitals
had focused on the state of Parisian hospitals, and in particular the *hôtel-dieu*.
The simplification and rationalisation of Paris hospital administration over
the 1790s – in spite of the occasional managerial scandal – thus took some of
the wind out of the critics' sails.[187] Many of the smaller and more un-
economical institutions disappeared. A degree of institutional specialisation
was introduced: hospitals for children's diseases and for venereal disease
appeared, for example; special provision for women in childbirth was
established; at Charenton, treatment for the insane was provided; and so on.
The bigger hospitals improved too. The more repulsively repressive aspects
of Bicêtre and La Salpêtrière were attenuated. Single beds had finally been

---

183 M. Foucault, *Birth of the Clinic*, p. 74; T. Gelfand, *Professionalising Modern Medicine*, p. 173;
E. H. Ackerknecht, *Medicine*, p. 33.

184 For Charenton, see A.N. AJ² 87; M. Foucault, *Folie et déraison. Histoire de la folie à l'âge
classique* (Paris, 1961), final chapters; J. Imbert, *Droit hospitalier*, p. 119; D. B. Weiner, 'Les
handicapés et la Révolution française', *Clio medica* (1977).

185 Clavereau in Year X, cited in M. Bouvet, *La pharmacie hospitalière à Paris de 1789 à 1815*
(Paris, 1943), p. 10.

186 O. Festy, 'La société philanthropique de Paris, 1800–1847', *Revue d'histoire moderne et con-
temporaine* (1911); R. G. Dunbar, 'The introduction of the practice of vaccination into
Napoleonic France', *Bulletin of the History of Medicine* (1941); F. Redlich, 'Science and charity:
Count Rumford and his followers', *International Review of Social History* (1971); G. Vauthier,
'La société de charité maternelle sous l'Empire', *Revue des études napoléoniennes* (1917).

187 E. H. Ackerknecht, *Medicine*, p. 16; Duchanoy, *Précis de l'état actuel des hôpitaux et hospices de
Paris comparé à ce qu'ils étaient avant la Révolution* (Paris, 1808).

introduced in the *hôtel-dieu*, and this helped produce an impressive fall in the death-rate, from between 20 and 25 per cent to about 13 per cent under the Consulate and Empire.[188] Things in the hospital were far from perfect: and it is notable that when the city authorities had to erect ramshackle overspill infirmaries in the city abattoirs in 1814 and 1815, the death-rate within them was only a fraction of the *hôtel-dieu*'s![189] Nevertheless, the state of the hospital was no longer the invitation to shock and disgust which it had been prior to 1789.

These points about poor relief institutions in general, and hospitals in particular, doubtless had their importance in dissipating the potentially damaging hostility of the medical intelligentsia. But hospitals were still, nonetheless, viewed essentially as social rather than as scientific institutions, and the decline in criticism of them rested more on their social functions than on their medical potential.[190] An enthusiast for hospitals was still, in the 1800s, something of a rare bird. But there were few close to the mechanisms of policy-making who did not feel that, given the flirtation with state *bienfaisance* in the 1790s, organising the poor laws around these flawed institutions was a necessary evil. The cost of the pension schemes sketched out in Year II had been too high; the bureaucratic remodelling of the poor laws had been over-ambitious; the numbers of the needy seemed too great; and – given the social radicalism and the state terror which had accompanied the schemes – the political alternative to the tried old system seemed too awful to contemplate. Furthermore, the adaptability which surviving poor relief institutions had exhibited in the appalling conditions of the Thermidorean and Directorial periods – resulting in particular from the steadfast response of charitable administrators and nursing sisters – highlighted the resilience and the flexibility of the old system. Relations between poor relief institutions and the state were, moreover, very different from what they had been under the ancien regime. The institutions had been forced out from behind the protective skirts of the church, and were now more directly exposed to the manipulation of the central government than ever before.[191] The Consulate and the Empire were to witness the pouring forth of a plethora of state

[188] A. Husson, *Etude sur les hôpitaux, considérés sous le rapport de leur construction, de la distribution de leurs bâtiments, de l'ameublement, de l'hygiène et du service des salles de malades* (Paris, 1862), p. 249; *Tableaux à joindre au rapport sur les hospices civils de Paris* (Paris, Year XI).

[189] A. Husson, *Etude sur les hôpitaux*, p. 37.

[190] I differ on this point from M. C. R. Gillett (*Hospital Reform*, see esp. p. 196), who sees the Revolution defining the future of France's hospitals primarily in medical educational terms. My view is also rather distinct from C. C. Fairchilds (*Poverty and Charity*, esp. chapter 7 'From charité to bienfaisance', p. 147) who sees the trajectory of the 1790s as leading towards 'a national system of bienfaisance' (p. 160), and thus seriously underestimates the force of the U-turn back towards ancien regime charitable practices from Year III onwards.

[191] A. Cherubini, *Dottrine e metodi assistenziali dal 1789 al 1848. Italia, Francia, Inghilterra* (Milan, 1958), p. 118.

regulations – whose volume and abundance contrasted strikingly with the same regimes' niggardly attitude to dispensing hard cash – which, through the effective agency of the prefectoral system, brought all manner of hospital business (borrowing, accounts, buildings, staff–patient ratios, medical personnel, etc.) under the direct and watchful guidance of the clerks of the Ministry of the Interior.[192] The network of hospitals and poor relief institutions was thus a far more malleable instrument in the hands of government.

The careers of two men who in the early years of the Revolution had been among the most eloquent promoters of the ideas of *bienfaisance* offer a telling commentary on the changed social and intellectual atmosphere of the early nineteenth century. Larochefoucauld-Liancourt, the egregious chairman of the *Comité de Mendicité*, had returned from exile after the 18 brumaire to be appointed to the *Conseil général des hospices* which ran the Paris hospitals.[193] He had studiously placed his 'welfare state' idealism behind him now, and down to his death in 1827 he threw his abundant energies into a variety of forms of 'improvement': vaccination, friendly societies, technical education, prison reform, dispensaries, soup kitchens and much else besides. The career of Cabanis, ardent proponent early in the 1790s of the creation of 'un nouveau système de bienfaisance générale', and a key figure in the rationalisation of assistance in Paris over the decade, described a similar trajectory, from advocacy of total overhaul of welfare arrangements to an acceptance of piecemeal social engineering and private charitable initiatives.[194] A professor in Paris' new medical faculty, a member of the councils and a luminary in the *Idéologue* movement, Cabanis by the 1800s was commenting on society in quite a different way from formerly. His erstwhile passion for social justice had drained away under the influence of the events of Year II, and he now saw remedies to the problem of poverty in terms of generalising public education, making minor institutional and administrative amelioration and preventing public disorder. The scales of philanthropic idealism had fallen from his eyes, and he perceived social reality in sharpened, economistic focus: philanthropy had its virtues, but not the least of them was making the world safe for entrepreneurs.

In social welfare, much had been learnt over the revolutionary decade. And it is remarkable that, although politicians, charitable administrators and their staffs had, in their different ways, engaged in little that was more ambitious than the work of salvage and retrieval, their pragmatically arrived-at solutions would have a long and honoured history. Numerous measures – the laws of 16 vendémiaire and 7 frimaire Year V, the *octroi de bienfaisance* and so on – were to prove cardinal features of public assistance even into the present

---

[192] C. Jones, *Charity and 'Bienfaisance'*, for a fuller discussion of this point, p. 218. Cf. J. Imbert, *Droit hospitalier*, p. 165.

[193] F. Dreyfus, *Un philanthrope*, p. 248.   [194] See above, note 12.

century.[195] Though largely intent, as I have suggested, on 'picking up the pieces', they did their work so effectively that short-term, stopgap measures to get over the specific problems of the Thermidorean and Directorial periods proved far more influential, in the nineteenth century, than the more progressive programmes mapped out earlier in the 1790s, which for many subsequent decades were either frowned upon or forgotten. A return to the themes and policies adumbrated under the Terror had eventually to come in French history of course; but it took place far more gradually than the rapidity of conception and execution with which the Conventionnels had acted, and with which the Thermidoreans and Directorials had performed their U-turn. It was not to be until well into the Third Republic that the principles of social security came to be inscribed on to the statute-book.[196] The men and women involved in 'picking up the pieces' of the state's welfare system in the Thermidorean and Directorial period would doubtless have derived a certain smug satisfaction that the nineteenth century preferred to march in step with them, and not with their more radical and more prophetic predecessors of Year II.

[195] J. Imbert, *Les hôpitaux en France*, 2nd edn (Paris, 1966), p. 41; M. Rochaix, *Essai*, p. 144.
[196] J. Imbert, 'L'assistance et les oeuvres', *Encyclopédie de la Pléiade: la France et les français* (Paris, 1972), p. 416.

4

❖◇❖

Conscription and crime in rural France during the Directory and Consulate

ALAN FORREST

During the period of the Directory and the Consulate the Revolutionary Wars gradually lost their former libertarian glamour and turned into a seemingly endless campaign of attrition, accompanied by increasingly bureaucratic demands for additional manpower. The Loi Jourdan of Year VI abolished the revolutionary *levées* and replaced them with annual conscriptions, whereby men in their early twenties were placed in the military *classes* out of which the battalions would be drawn.[1] And though hundreds of thousands of young men dutifully accepted the inevitability of their lot, there were many others, who themselves would number hundreds of thousands by the end of the Napoleonic campaigns, who resisted, either hiding in the surrounding hills, remaining unperturbed on their farms or deserting from their regiment before their service had even begun. Richard Cobb is right to see in these men a major element in the breakdown of law and order which so blighted this period in the French provinces.[2] At a time when policing techniques were still in their infancy and the goodwill of the local community was essential if any respect for the law were to be maintained, the fact of resistance had implications far beyond the military context. Of course the success of the call to arms varied considerably from region to region, and indeed from village to village. Allegations of unfairness or of nepotism, of social differentiation whereby those with money or with family influence could avoid the rigours of services on the frontiers, of fraud in the organisation of the *tirage* on the village green, all could result in an ominous silence when the names of the communal battalion were read out to the villagers.[3]

---

[1] For the implications of the Loi Jourdan see any of several recent doctoral and *maîtrise* dissertations on local case-studies; a good example is J.-A. Castel, 'L'application de la Loi Jourdan dans l'Hérault: Les levées directoriales de l'an VII', thèse de maîtrise (Montpellier, 1970).

[2] There are several references to desertion and its concomitant problems in *Les armées révolutionnaires*, but see especially *The Police and the People*, pp. 93–104.

[3] Instances of alleged injustice resulting in popular anger can be found in many departments

But in general it is possible to distinguish between those areas where a certain military tradition was already engrained in the population and where soldiering was regarded as a natural part of the process of growing up – areas like the rolling plains of the Île-de-France or the frontier departments of the east – and those regions, equally numerous, where almost any price was seen as preferable to that of the *corvée* in blood demanded by the state. Departments like the Cantal and the Lozère in the southern Massif Central, or like the Ariège and the upland parts of the Haute-Garonne in the Pyrenees, regarded military service as something quite foreign to their experience, as a sinister and deadly interference by Paris in the assured tenor of the agricultural or pastoral year. To many Frenchmen the call to arms in defence of the nation-state was a totally meaningless notion which lacked any emotive appeal. In such circumstances an act of defiance, whether to the *levées* of 1793 or to the annual conscriptions after Year VII, represented a collective choice by entire communities, which would connive openly at the flouting of the law and offer every assistance to men on the run from the authorities. In this way the individual crime of desertion or *insoumission* would often become generalised into collective criminal activity by the recruit's family, neighbours and friends, by mayors and village officials, by fellow-villagers seduced or terrorised into compliance. In consequence the recruitment laws could have the most drastic effect on village politics and village attitudes and plunge whole communities across that uncertain dividing-line between obedience and lawlessness.[4]

Whether this plunge was lightly taken depended very much on local circumstances. The stationing of a military garrison in a nearby town, for instance, could do much to concentrate the minds of the local population on their patriotic duty, a circumstance which may go far to explain the relative submissiveness of the area around Versailles, always a powerful military centre where there were constant reminders of the army's presence and authority.[5] Or again, areas regularly exposed to the passage of troops, accustomed to periodic billeting and requisition, might take the fact of service very much for granted. Such seems to have been the case along the valley of the Rhône, constantly criss-crossed in this period with battalions marching to and from active service with the *armée des Alpes*.[6] But it was local topography that was the principal determinant, encouraging or discouraging disobedience in proportion to the opportunities it furnished for

(see, for instance, A. D. Cantal L 253; A. D. Drôme L 369; or A. D. Seine-et-Oise 16 L 36); in the Haute-Garonne this led to the organisation of a riot against the gendarmerie (A.N. F⁹ 306).

[4] A.N. AF^IV 1043, analysis by Minister of Police of the effects of conscription on village society.
[5] Versailles was also a town with a long military tradition; in Year VIII it was reported that conscripts here demanded to be attached to particular regiments (A.N. F⁹ 250).
[6] A.N. F⁷ 3592, report of prefect of Drôme on the contrasting responses to conscription in his department an XIII.

escape and concealment. Mountains, dispersed habitation, lonely upland pasture, rocks and caves, treacherous marshlands familiar only to the local population, smugglers' hill tracks that were part of village *connaissance*, these were the very stuff of escape or evasion. *Commissaires* and prefects, reduced to near-despair by the demands of Paris and by the inadequacy of their policing resources, placed the blame for poor conscription records on all kinds of local circumstance, but again and again they turned to geography as the main impediment to their endeavours. Only the detail varied: in the Puy-de-Dôme the gendarmes were thwarted by the mountains, in the Gironde by the coastal marshes and the close secrecy of the fishing communities they contained, in the Nord by the marshy terrain and mine workings, in the Mayenne by the natural protection offered by the *bocage*. In the Île-de-France there was easy access to the anonymity of Paris, in the Cantal the dispersed settlement and the absence of large towns: each prefect seemed to have particular problems emanating from the peculiar geography of his own patch.[7] Some administrators were even more unfortunate. In Cantal the well-established habit of seasonal migration to the Mediterranean littoral and especially to Spain provided the ideal cover for a young farmworker seeking to escape the draft.[8] And in frontier departments, especially those on the unpoliceable Spanish frontier, the opportunity to slip across some mountain pass under cover of darkness was always present – shepherds with their flocks, smugglers with their mule trains, local villagers who were permanently unsure of the exact whereabouts of the frontier, all were sources of the kind of help the young soldier required if he were to make his escape.[9] Regardless of questions of commitment, whether political or religious, there were so many areas of France where effective policing during the Directory and Consulate was sheer self-delusion, and where local people remained ignorant both of the state of the law and of the duties of citizenship so beloved of Parisian orators.

That is not to say that all young men on the run were equally liable to be welcomed with open arms by a village community. There were, after all, dangers for local people implicit in aiding deserters and refractories, and for much of the period the attentions given to a particular community by the local gendarmerie could depend substantially on their recruitment record. Few villagers relished the prospect of the arrival of a company of gendarmes, far less the later involvement of the *colonnes mobiles*, quite simply because so

7 Reports on the topographical problems of these departments are mostly classed in series F9 of the *Archives Nationales* (for instance, F9 310, 312, 217, and 250); for the Gironde, see F7 8440 and A.D. Gironde 2 R 284.

8 Cantonal reports on the effects of migration are especially detailed and indicative of the authorities' helplessness in the face of migration (A.D. Cantal L 250, 263, 265, 266, 271, and 277); a more general analysis is contained in A.N., F9 165.

9 See, for instance, reports on the emigration from the Basses-Pyrénées in A.N. F1cIII Basses-Pyrénées 7.

many of their other activities might be exposed to the judicial authorities.
There can have been few rural communities where smuggling and poaching,
petty theft and breaches of the forest laws were not taken largely for granted,
even regarded by the majority of the inhabitants as necessary expedients to
avoid cold and starvation. It was in the interests of no one that these irregularities should come to light, and the local *notables* were therefore generally
concerned to maintain a respectable record on recruitment that would keep
the enquiring instincts of the authorities at bay. Again, there were few communities which were not accustomed in the eighteenth century to travelling
vagabonds and beggars, who had come with the passage of the century to be
regarded more and more as parasites to be hustled on as quickly as possible
to the next town or parish. Deserters from a regiment in Italy or from a ship
anchored in Toulon or Dunkirk would have to travel many weary, hungry
miles to regain their native village, miles of deprivation and near-starvation
which made them indistinguishable in the eyes of many of their hosts from
the hated *vagabonds* who bullied and terrorised them.[10] Nor were deserters
immune from the same temptations as wandering beggars – the temptation
to band together for company and impact, the temptation to rob and
threaten in order to extort food or shelter, the temptation to turn themselves
into thieving gangs indistinguishable from the various brigand bands which
so terrorised France after Year III.[11] In this respect the most crucial distinction
is perhaps that between the deserter and the *insoumis*, the refractory conscript
who had never joined his regiment but who continued to live in his village,
disappearing into the woods and fields whenever the gendarmes hove into
view, yet for most of the time an active member of local society. Unlike the
deserter, who besides being unfamiliar presented something of a threat to the
village even by his presence on its soil, the refractory was one of their own
sons, playing his part in the village economy, dancing at the *bal champêtre* and
drinking in their local *auberge*. Whereas attitudes to passing deserters might
vary violently, the local conscript draft-dodging on his father's smallholding
would generally be assured of a warm and protective reception from the
villagers.

Both the *insoumis* and the deserter could be relied upon to add to the
village's crime statistics, but they were wont to do so in rather different
ways. In the eyes of the village the offences of refractories were far easier to
comprehend and to assimilate. Since they were not generally desperate and

---

[10] The distances travelled by deserters could be enormous, from one end of France to the other.
On 13 messidor XII, for instance, Gabriel Marquion, who had deserted at Arras (Pas-de-Calais),
was arrested at Courthézon (Vaucluse). Details in A.N. F9 317.

[11] The sheer misery of life on the run is manifest, especially on cold winter nights in the mountains. It could lead to death from exhaustion and malnutrition (A.N. F7 8429); in the Nord a
refractory was found dead from simple exposure in an isolated wood (A.D. Nord 1 R 230).
But it could also lead to violence, as in the Var, where it was reported that conscripts were
forced by hunger to 'mettre à contribution les voyageurs' (A.N. F9 317.)

hungry, ill-clad and far from home, the *insoumis* had no reason to rob or defraud the villagers or pillage their property; they were, after all, living at home for the greater part of the year, working the fields or practising their trade and in receipt of some form of wage, however meagre. They were, of course, young and male, usually – because of the terms of the conscription laws – unmarried and without family responsibilities; in short the very groups in local society which could be expected to commit the lion's share of petty crime. It is therefore no surprise to find that such men figure prominently among those arrested for drunken behaviour, for taproom brawls and disturbances at fairs and markets. But these were misdemeanours which village society was well accustomed to assimilate, offences which could easily be attributed to the pressures of growing up. Similarly, conscripts might become involved in the ordinary crime of the community – most notably poaching and *délits forestiers*, probably the most commonplace of offences in the eighteenth-century countryside. But again this caused neither anger nor great inconvenience: as *conscrits réfractaires* they were doing neither more nor less than they might have been expected to do had there been no question of military service. Such crimes were committed jointly by conscripts and civilians: in one instance, in the Ariège, a father and his two sons, both refractories, were arrested for breaches both of the forest laws and of the conscription laws, and it emerged that their father hid them in a hut occupied by a village blacksmith close to the Spanish frontier, where 'ces jeunes gens venaient parfois couper du bois sur les montagnes, le père le vendait ensuite, soit à Seix, soit ailleurs'.[12] There was nothing unusual about the crime, and the fact that they spent much of their lives in hiding merely gave them the time and opportunity to forage illegally for wood. Nor did the participation of conscripts in smuggling cause any animosity amongst local people. For involvement in a smuggling ring would seem to have incurred little obloquy in the community, even when the operation involved passing goods to a country at war with the French Republic. In brumaire Year III, for instance, the Haute-Garonne reported that villagers from the frontier commune of Aspet, near Saint-Gaudens, were passing mules across the mountains into Spain under cover of darkness; but despite the protests of the authorities, the village was quite unmoved.[13] Indeed, in those cases where customs men tried to make arrests, it was not uncommon for the local population to riot in defence of the smugglers, as happened in the villages of Suc and Lavalanet in the Ariège in 1810.[14] In such areas whole villages were directly implicated in contraband, with local *notables* occupying prominent positions in the rings.[15]

---

[12] A.N. F7 8514, accusation against Pierre Amilhat and his sons, 29 January 1808.
[13] A.N. F1cIII Haute-Garonne 8, report from the District of Mont-Unité, brumaire III.
[14] A.N. F7 8516, report of prefect of Ariège on 'deux rébellions pour fait de contrebande' in Suc and Lavelanet, 8 October 1810.
[15] A.N. F7 8516, police report on a band of smugglers at Sorgeat (Ariège), 4 July 1810.

Smugglers were treated with a certain respect, admired for their boldness and bravado and protected from the prying inquisitions of officialdom. When conscripts merged into such enterprises they had little to fear from local opinion, since they claimed their full share in the risks and glory. In some cases conscripts even formed themselves into bands of smugglers and, like one band near Maubeuge, could organise themselves with paramilitary efficiency. Commenting on this band, the *juge de paix* makes it clear in Year VI that their activities were public knowledge in the villages they frequented:

Je passais dernierèment dans une auberge à portée de Mons. J'y vis plusieurs hommes robustes, armés de gros bâtons de chêne à bourlette, chapeau rabattu, manteau bleu, tous en pantalons et en bottes, ayant chacun leur monture à l'écurie. Je fus fort étonné d'un tel rassemblement, et je vous avoue qu'il m'a d'abord donné quelqu'inquiétude; mais aussitôt j'ai entendu l'ordre du départ, qui fut exécuté comme et avec la même promptitude que les soldats les mieux disciplinés.[16]

Such refractories had little cause to shun public exposure, since they were as well integrated into their local community as the most law-abiding of its citizens .

Of course the strains of spending days and even weeks in hiding could tell on refractories, and there are incidents of theft and violence that must have put at jeopardy their relatively calm relations with the rest of the commune. But there is little evidence that they were liable to be denounced or handed over to the authorities as a result of crimes against local people. Where *insoumis* were denounced, indeed – and there are numerous cases where jealousies and petty hatreds led to surreptitious visits to the *mairie* or the local gendarmerie – criminal activity was not even mentioned. By far the most common denunciations came from the parents of young men forced to serve in place of refractories, where these same refractories were openly enjoying the luxury of work on their holdings or drinks in the village inn. In ventôse IV, for instance, a young man from Balatre in the Somme was reported to the authorities for draft-dodging; while others served in their regiments he had been offered the protection of the municipal officials in Roye, 'au grand mécontentement des parents de cette commune dont les enfants sont aux frontières'.[17] Elsewhere jealousy could acquire a more unctuous flavour. At Hesdin in the Pas-de-Calais, again in Year VII, a recruit wise enough to get married just before the date laid down in the conscription law took it upon himself to denounce those of his contemporaries who had no such alibi. With all the feverish enthusiasm of a police spy he offered corroborative detail of their wilful behaviour: 'il assure que c'est dans les cabarets, les jours de dimanche, que les réquisitionnaires et les conscrits se rassemblent et forment

[16] A.N. BB[18] 584, Minister of Interior to Minister of Justice on the organisation of *contrebandiers* in the area around Maubeuge (Nord), 8 ventôse VI.
[17] A.N. F[9] 316, denunciation of Charlemagne Pican *fils*, 27 ventôse IV.

leurs complots'.[18] In similar vein, those overstaying their *congés* when they
ought to have been back in their battalions,[19] or those reformed for reasons
of health or deformity which their fellows knew to be false, were liable to
be reported to officialdom: typical of many victims of rural malice was
Antoine Lambaut from a commune near Lesparre in the Gironde, who had
been seen at the annual carnival in the town dancing with his friends with
rare spice and vigour, in spite of the debilitating leg injury which had
supposedly prevented his military service.[20] Jealousy and a sense of searing
injustice usually lay at the root of these and many similar denunciations; it
is no accident that many of them were written by the young men of the
village who were already incorporated and who resented the freedom enjoyed by their more devious friends. Occasionally, inter-communal rivalries
stimulated a flood of denunciations, towns jostling in a rather undignified
way to present the efforts of the other in a dismal light: Saint-Flour's
attempts to ingratiate themselves with the revolutionary authorities by
pointing to the shortcomings of their rivals in Aurillac can only be inter-
preted in this way.[21] But in none of these cases is criminality cited as a reason
for police action: refractories offended against the spirit of *égalité*, they
antagonised others by their insolent presence in their homes and communes,
but they did not cause further offence by flagrant criminal activity.

The attitude of the local population towards deserters, usually men from
other areas who could not rely on local patronage and protection, was more
circumspect, largely because it was widely believed, and with some justice,
that their presence in a commune automatically invited trouble. The government itself was in no doubt that crime was increasing dramatically in those
areas of France where deserters were prone to hide while on the run: a report
in 1813, surveying the whole period, concluded that acts of violence had
become particularly frequent and that the huge increase in the numbers of
men involved – in 1810 they totalled over 160,000 according to official
figures – constituted the primary cause.[22] The range of crimes listed is very
wide, the vast majority of them thefts and pilfering necessary if the deserters
were to keep themselves alive. In the Nord, thefts of food were predictably
numerous, 'le tout pout parvenir à se dérober aux poursuites qu'on faisait
après eux'.[23] Sometimes the fugitives would become rather more ambitious,

---

18 A.N. F9 312, report from Hesdin (Pas-de-Calais), 14 frimaire VII.
19 A.D. Vosges L 533, letter from 'plusieurs volontaires de la commune de Saule (Vosges),
   8 pluviôse VI.
20 A.D. Gironde 2 R 287, denunciation of Antoine Lambaut by conscripts from Lesparre, 15
   April 1814.
21 A.D. Cantal L 255, letter from *vice-procureur-syndic* of Saint-Flour to commune of Aurillac,
   16 August 1793.
22 A.N. AFIV 1147, report of *police générale*, 11 May 1813.
23 A.N. BB18 587, letter from *directeur du jury* of the *arrondissement* of Dunkerque, 13 frimaire
   VIII.

like those in the commune of Arsac who burgled homes, waylaid one of the richest farmers in the district and drove away two flocks of sheep in one brief orgy of criminal activity.[24] Areas harbouring deserters were also prone to poaching and woodland offences, again the kinds of petty criminality that could not be avoided if the deserters were to survive during their weeks and often months on the run.[25] In a few cases, the patience demanded by their hazardous life-style finally broke, and deserters would steal horses from local stables, either to sell them at a fair to obtain money for food or, more rarely, to make a brisk dash for home and a nostalgically recalled liberty and creature-comfort.[26] Local farmers were the most frequent victims of these thefts, though in certain areas of the Nord deserters would seem to have shown a predilection for the easy pickings they found in the *coffres* of isolated parish churches, generally left unlocked and unguarded even after nightfall.[27] Few of these crimes involved injury or great sums of money; but their frequency did much to tarnish the image of deserters in villages which had previously offered them a degree of protection.

Given the straitened circumstances of many young deserters, it is hardly surprising that theft should constitute such a high proportion of their criminal activity. Fear of detection if they ventured openly into towns and villages by day made crime even more necessary if they were to avoid starvation; and the fact that they were often hundreds of miles from their homes, frequently unable to communicate clearly and directly with the local population, both increased their sense of insecurity and reduced any feelings they may have retained of social responsibility. The incidence of thefts among reported crimes was in any case rising during the revolutionary and Napoleonic years, a fact commented upon by several *commissaires* and prefects and ascribed largely to the increased numbers of men wandering from place to place, deserters, *insoumis*, soldiers with *congés*, new recruits passing from one *ville d'étape* to another on their way to their regiments. Away from the calming influence of the village community, the opportunities were legion and the level of social control diminished. Crime statistics for the period reflect this concern. Of 312 reported crimes in the Department of the Gironde for 1805, for instance, the majority were crimes against property, although a measure of violence may have been involved. The official statistics[28] reveal the balance of crime in the department:

---

[24] A.N. F⁷ 8555, letter from mayor of Arsac to prefect of the Gironde, 9 August 1809.
[25] A.N. F⁷ 8445, report from Fours (Gironde), 22 January 1806.
[26] A.D. Nord 1 R 213, report from Valenciennes (Nord), 1 April 1811.
[27] A.N. BB¹⁸ 591, letter from prefect of the Nord, 30 frimaire XIII.
[28] A.N. BB¹⁸ 361, breakdown of the crimes committed in the Gironde during 1805 and 1806, dated 3 February 1807.

Assassinats	19
Meurtres	5
Incendies	12
Empoisonnements	1
Infanticides	3
Viols	7
Vols avec effraction	67
Faux	14
Banqueroutes frauduleuses	9
Rébellion à la gendarmerie	8
Fausse monnaye	1
Vols simples, filouteries et escroqueries	120
Recels de conscrits	27
Outrages envers la magistrature	20
Jeux prohibés	0
Total crimes	313

These figures find their echo in reports from all over France; the only element that may have been less important in other areas was that of frauds and commercial deceits, crimes that were particularly common in trading communities like Bordeaux. They are supported by the national statistics collected by the Napoleonic Ministry of the Interior, which again show a disturbing level of theft and burglary in all regions of the country.[29]

If thefts were the most numerous of the offences committed by soldiers on the run, they were far from being the most notorious or the most resented. For in rural areas in particular, where isolation made the inhabitants more vulnerable and more fearful, deserters came to enjoy a somewhat lurid reputation for violence and banditry in an age when *brigandage* inspired fear in many peasant families. Rumour was rife, and acts of terrorisation by deserters in neighbouring towns and villages were soon the subject of feverish and exaggerated gossip. *Vols simples* could possibly be forgiven by families whose own sons had to face the terrible lottery of the *tirage*; but other forms of crime, whether committed out of desperation or greed, were less easy to tolerate. Village girls were exposed to yet another possible source of assault and rape, and parents were rightly apprehensive. When the daughter of an innkeeper, Cathérine Claudel from the commune of Ainvelle in the Vosges, was found raped and murdered in a wood in 1810, opinion was quite naturally outraged. She had been savagely attacked with blows to her stomach before being strangled with 'une ficelle' with such violence, indeed, that the gendarmes were at first inclined to believe that more than one man

---

[29] A.N. AF^{IV} 1042, *Tableau des crimes qui ont donné lieu à des poursuites devant les cours de justice en l'année 1810* (Ministry of Justice).

was responsible. They revised their opinion only after the arrest six weeks later of a deserter from La Folie in the Haute-Loire, 'refusé dans les auberges et arrêté sur la route par des charretiers à cause de son travestissement en fille ... Les habits qui formaient son déguisement ont été reconnus être ceux de laditte Claudel.'[30] Of course, soldiers did not have to have deserted to commit rape, and popular distrust extended to garrisons and passing regiments as well. In the same department, for instance, and in the same year, a 12-year-old girl from Nomexy in the *arrondissement* of Epinal was the victim of rape by the fencing-master from the local regiment.[31] Such cases left a lingering bitterness in local communities which could threaten the security of all deserters, for smouldering anger could be difficult to extinguish and the desire for vengeance could take indirect forms. In Year IX, at Saint-Quintin in the Ariège, the mayor had given protection and work to a conscript of the previous year, Pierre Besmas, who had, after his condemnation, seduced and raped a local girl and had then persuaded the mayor to marry them. The dossier was closed, but the bitterness of the girl's mother was quite unquenchable, with the result that in 1809 she denounced the mayor and two village craftsmen for protecting another refractory in a similar manner. The peaceful existence of this soldier, who had been living quietly on the mayor's farms for nearly four years before his offence was brought to the attention of the authorities, was put at risk through no action or careless slip on his own part, but through the undying hatred of an embittered widow determined to avenge her daughter's suffering.[32]

The presence in a commune of men on the run, in urgent need of food and money and under very severe psychological strain – particularly once the forces of repression were more effectively turned against them after the introduction of the Loi Jourdan in Year VI – was always liable to lead to violent assaults and killings. It should cause little surprise, therefore, to discover that when murders were committed in small towns and villages, or when bodies were found in ditches by lonely roadsides, the gendarmerie were wont to see deserters from local regiments as prime suspects. So did local opinion, which was liable to panic in a manner reminiscent of the *Grande Peur* of 1789. When an obscure individual was murdered on a lonely road near the departmental boundary between the Cantal and the Puy-de-Dôme in Year XI, *le bruit public* was quite adamant that deserters were responsible and such exaggerated rumours were circulating that 'on ne voyageait plus dans cette contrée qu'en caravane'. The sub-prefect at Murat was sufficiently alarmed that he ordered an immediate search of the woods, mountains and *burons* – the huts occupied by shepherds on the higher slopes – in order to

---

[30] A.N. F7 8628, report of *inspection générale de la gendarmerie* on a rape at Ainvelle (Vosges), 2 June 1810.

[31] A.N. F7 8628, report of 5 May 1810.

[32] A.N. BB18 8, dossier on a case of *recel* at Saint-Quintin (Ariège), 15 September 1809.

assuage local fears, but with no success.[33] In that case it was the sheer random-
ness of the killing which most alarmed the local population, the fact that
almost any traveller seemed to be placed at risk. Elsewhere particularly
vicious attacks were reported which could only exacerbate ill-feeling towards
deserters. At Galgon, near Libourne, an old lady living alone was bludgeoned
to death by her *domestique*, a deserter from a neighbouring village: the motive
was presumably gain and there was evidence of premeditation, but it was the
excessive violence of the attack which horrified opinion. 'On lui avait
fracassé le crâne à coups de massue, et sa poitrine était frappée de plusieurs
coups de couteau.'[34] Even more callous was the brutal killing of two women
and a baby in an isolated farmhouse at Sainte-Croix, near Die in the Drôme,
in Year XI. The killers were both deserters, *cultivateurs* from Die, who had
called at the farm claiming that they were looking for two *remplaçants* to
whom they had paid sizeable sums the previous Sunday. This was, however,
no more than a cunning pretext to gain admission to the house. On asking
whether there were no young men around, they were told that the women
were alone, the husband and uncle being away at the fair in Saillans and the
brother-in-law out in the woods collecting a load of firewood. They then
attacked the occupants, leaving them all for dead, and set fire to the house to
destroy any evidence of their crime. The story sent a *frisson* of horror through
the locality, and large crowds turned out to witness the execution of the two
murderers on the main square of Valence.[35] Deserters already condemned in
their absence faced severe military penalties if they were recaptured, and some
of them responded as men with nothing to lose, killing and robbing with
carefree abandon. But few can have been as indiscriminate as Pierre-François
Fautrel, who had deserted from several different regiments in and around
Lille, and who on the eve of his execution for murder confessed to a whole
series of killings over the previous few years. A Norwegian soldier, an Italian
whom he had met on the road, the mayor of a Belgian town through which
he passed and a woman in whose company he had staged one of his escapes,
all figured on his list of victims, usually for purposes of theft. Even more
horrifying, if Fautrel is to be believed, was his admission that for two of the
crimes other men, themselves soldiers or deserters, had been convicted and
shot.[36]

Many of the killings ascribed to deserters were not of local people, however, but of other travellers and frequently of other soldiers. Conscripts
leaving home to make the often long and hazardous journey to join their
regiments could be counted upon to have a certain amount of money on
their person, generally in the form of the *prime* they had received from the

---

[33] A.N. BB[18] 216, report from *sous-préfet* of Murat, 8 prairial XI.
[34] A.N. BB[18] 31, report of the trial of André Boussaye, 3 May 1808.
[35] A.N. BB[18] 280, report of the trial of the two murderers at Valence, 21 vendémiaire XI.
[36] A.N. BB[18] 594, report of the confession of Pierre-François Fautrel, 14 April 1806.

recruiting-officer, supplemented by gifts from parents and relatives. They therefore made obvious targets for theft, especially by those who knew the timetable and the habits of new recruits, and the discovery of their bodies on public highways caused considerable anger among government officials.[37] Young conscripts could be terribly naive and trusting, lured into a false sense of security by their uniform and by the comradeship of the journey. At Asnières-sur-Oise (Seine-et-Oise) in 1806, the body of a conscript was found, hurriedly concealed, in a communal wood; on investigation it was revealed that he had been persuaded by another conscript to take a short-cut away from the main road shortly before his disappearance, that the two men had been discussing money in a bar before the murder and that the victim had revealed to his companion that his father had given him several gold coins before he set out on his long tramp from Mende to join his battalion at Boulogne. His fate was sadly predictable.[38] The full extent of that predictability is underlined by another such murder, at Autreville in the Vosges, where passers-by found a conscript dying in a derelict *baraque* by the roadside. Again, he had been robbed of all his cash by his two companions, to whom he had vouchsafed the information that he had received three hundred francs to help him on his long journey to the front. Almost clinically they had steered him towards the shed and 'à une portée d'un coup de fusil et à coups de sabres le laissèrent pour mort, le déshabillèrent et répandirent ses habits pour ôter la trace qu'il fut un militaire'.[39] In this case, the gendarmes seem to have known exactly what procedure to adopt, searching the local bars, dilapidated and disreputable inns known to shelter criminals, where they quickly arrested one of the murderers. Again, it became clear that this was a killing among soldiers, since all three had come from hospital in Nancy and were on their way to rejoin their unit. It was the second killing of its type on the same lonely stretch of road within six months; on the previous occasion a *militaire réformé* had attacked another young recruit in almost identical circumstances.

While individual crimes of violence caused alarm and anger, it was collective acts of terrorisation which could turn whole communities against deserters and which occasionally led to active cooperation with the authorities. In the years of general lawlessness that followed the removal of revolutionary government such crimes became almost commonplace. Alarmist reports flooded into Paris from all over France in Year III and Year IV, talking in agitated terms about the activities of organised bands of deserters turning to looting and highway robbery. Near Bourganeuf in the Creuse bands of between fifteen and twenty able-bodied conscripts, 'des plus beaux hommes', were sighted roaming the countryside, begging for food at remote farms

---

37 A.N. F7 8627, report from prefect of the Vosges, 5 January 1808.
38 A.N. BB18 839, BB18 75, reports on the trial for the murder of David Pouge.
39 A.N. BB18 915, report on the murder at Autreville (Vosges), 30 December 1807.

with abundant use of threats and menaces.[40] They would hide in the woods during the day and emerge only at night, protected by the knowledge that the whole community lived in fear of their ravages. Often, indeed, they would lurk near departmental boundaries, ready to cross into a neighbouring department should police activity become unpleasantly threatening.[41] Most of these *bandes* were receiving a degree of protection, or at least of mute tolerance, from the local community; and the fact that they became so organised and established made them very difficult to hunt down. They were, indeed, often indistinguishable from the ordinary civilian bands of *brigands* and *chauffeurs* who caused so much havoc and disruption in the French provinces during the Thermidorean and Directorial years, and in several notable instances they merged with civilians in such awesome groupings as the *Bande de Salembrier* which ravaged the Nord, the Pas-de-Calais and wide tracts of the *départements réunis* in Year IV and Year V, using the frontier as a welcome means of escape when they felt themselves threatened.[42] Salembrier's enterprise was on a considerable scale, with around sixty brigands, men and women, at his beck and call. But he was not unique in making use of deserters, whose life-style of forced clandestinity made them particularly suited to the requirements of brigandage. In the Drôme in 1809 the authorities were convinced that the problem of lawlessness would be solved if desertion were effectively stamped out, and the dossiers of captured brigands would seem to bear out their judgement. They talked openly about their military service:

répond qu'il a servi pendant six ans dans la 100ᵉ demi-brigade; il s'est retiré avec son congé;

répond qu'il n'a servi que quatre mois il y a sept ou huit mois, dans un bataillon auxiliaire qui fut ensuite licencié;

répond qu'il a servi neuf mois dans le 11ᵉ Bataillon de la Drôme, qu'il vint à son pays en convalescence, et qu'il s'est marié depuis.[43]

In the Mayenne, the prefect reported that deserters were being openly recruited into bands of *chauffeurs* by local brigands who threatened to harm them or reveal their whereabouts if they refused to turn to crime.[44] So tight was the link between brigands and deserters, indeed, that in the countryside around Nyons, in the Drôme, thieves and highway robbers sought anonymity by passing themselves off as deserters: the *sous-préfet* observed in frimaire

---

[40] A.G. Vincennes B¹³ 36, letter from Simon to the District of Bourganeuf, 27 messidor III.

[41] A.N. AF^III 148^B, Minister of War to the Directory on brigand activities in the eighth *Division Militaire*, 23 brumaire VI.

[42] A.N. BB¹⁸ 582, dossier on the *Bande de Salembrier*, Bruges, 18 pluviôse V.

[43] A.N. F⁷ 8428, dossier on several brigands arrested in the Drôme, interrogations dating from Year IX.

[44] A.N. F⁹ 310, report from prefect of the Mayenne, 15 May 1809.

X that by means of this disguise 'les brigands ont trouvé un abri dans les montagnes de cet arrondissement, sans faire naître la méfiance ou le soupçon'.[45]

Brigandage is a somewhat indiscriminate term used by the authorities to cover a confused multiplicity of crimes. In the revolutionary period especially, the word has a clear political connotation, and some at least of the activity of the *brigands* would appear to have had precise and political targets. Where mail coaches and *voitures publiques* were held up and robbed, as happened with increasing frequency in the months following Thermidor, distinctions were often drawn between private property and that of the state, and it was the moneys of the Republic that were stolen.[46] Other favoured targets included arms dumps and granaries belonging to the Republic, crimes which again could be shown to have possible political connotations. Deserters in the Aisne ravaged grain stocks, particularly in the area around Chauny: they inspired fear among local farmers, giving themselves chilling *noms de guerre* drawn from the annals of war and banditry (Dumouriez, Cartouche, Lafayette, Mandrin . . .) and warning local peasants that they would not require any hired labour for the harvest, since they would find their crops harvested for them.[47] In the Drôme, arms would appear to have been the principal goal, especially those hidden in isolated farmsteads, but some bands at least were rather particular about their ownership. At Taulignan, bands of deserters, led by a convicted counter-revolutionary, terrorised those citizens of known republican loyalties, extorting from them both their papers and their firearms: in this way at least sixty *patriotes* were disarmed in the course of Year V.[48] Among the most likely victims were those members of the local community who had bought *biens nationaux* during the Revolution, whether out of jacobin commitment or with an eye for profit. At Ayrens, near Laroquebrou in the Cantal, several attacks, always at night and involving both refractories and deserters, seemed to have a decidedly religious context, with the result that the authorities suspected priests of stirring up discontent. In one such incident, a 'troupe' of *brigands* 'ont arraché la clôture d'un jardin dépendant d'une chapelle acquise de la Nation par le citoyen Lavergne, absent pour raison de son commerce, que les brigands ont menacé de faire brûler la femme Lavergne dans ladite chapelle, lieu de sa résidence, si elle

---

[45] A.N. F⁷ 8428, report from the *sous-préfet* of Nyons (Drôme), 3 pluviôse X.
[46] See, for instance, cases of brigandage in the Gironde in Year IV and Year V brought before the *tribunal criminel* in Bordeaux (Arch. Mun. Bordeaux, D112, D174, D176). The evidence of these and other cases suggests, to the author at least, that much allegedly political brigandage was criminal first, and only secondarily political. In this I concur with the conclusions drawn about banditry in the Department of the Drôme by Richard Maltby in his unpublished thesis, 'Crime and the local community in France: the Department of the Drôme, 1770–1820', Oxford University D.Phil. 1981.
[47] A.G. Vincennes, B¹³ 35, minute of the Department of the Aisne, 21 prairial III.
[48] A.N. F¹ᵇ II Drôme 15, letter from *commissaire du Directoire Exécutif* in Valence, 8 pluviôse V.

continuait de l'habiter et n'en abandonnait la propriété . . .'[49] Since royalists
were known to be active in the department, it is not surprising that the
authorities concluded that this crime smacked of counter-revolution, of
royalism and *fanatisme*.

If brigandage had overtones of counter-revolution in many regions of
France – the Massif Central, Languedoc and the various cities previously
party to the federalist revolt are all held to be highly suspect – it became
heavily implicated with *chouannerie* in Brittany and the departments of the
west. Here brigands and *chouans* blended easily in the same bands, which
often united under *chouan* leaders, men with military experience who could
bring effective discipline and leadership to otherwise disparate robbers.[50]
These qualities were shown in their operations, often conducted with a
military precision rare in other areas of the country. Deserters who attacked
farms at night in the region around Locminé were well armed with sticks and
guns, and four members of the band wore military uniform. They appeared,
villagers reported, to obey orders from one of their number whom they
addressed as captain; and they claimed, with supreme irony, to be gendarmes
empowered to search the premises to make 'une perquisition de déserteurs'.[51]
By Year III the government was probably justified, in departments like the
Finistère and the Morbihan, in its assumption that deserters were liable to be
chouans, recruited into *chouan* bands as soon as they returned to their homes.[52]
Conscripts could, after all, escape from the army by the simple device of
crossing into *chouan*-held territory;[53] and such was the rate of desertion in
these areas that there was a serious fear that when the old *chefs de chouans*
returned to their villages, they would be able to raise a powerful force of
republican deserters.[54] In peasant areas there were always sizeable stockpiles
of weapons which could be turned against the Republic, and the prefect of
the Morbihan was already warning Paris in Year IV that the countryside was
really in a state of permanent militarisation.[55] The danger was very real.
Centres of recruitment for the *chouan* armies had been established throughout
the west, like the one at Hennebont in the Morbihan.[56] Mayors in rural
communes were terrorised by *chouan* units into hiding weapons and ammuni-

[49] A.N. F1b II Cantal 7, suspension of the *agent national* of Ayrens (Cantal), 11 germinal VII.
[50] A.N. AFIII 150A, report from Rieux (Morbihan), 1 frimaire VII.
[51] A.N. F7 8386, report on *chouan* activities in the *arrondissement* of Napoléonville (Morbihan),
4 October 1813.
[52] A.D. Morbihan L 593, interrogations of deserters, Years III and IV.
[53] A.N. AFIII 146, report from Minister of Interior to the Directory, 2 pluviôse IV.
[54] A.N. FIc III Morbihan 6, letter from department of the Morbihan to Minister of Police,
11 nivôse V.
[55] A.N. FIc III Morbihan 6, letter from *commissaire du Directoire Exécutif* in Vannes to Minister of
Interior, 13 vendémiaire IV.
[56] A.N. FIc III Morbihan 6, letter from *commissaire du Directoire Exécutif* to Minister of Interior,
30 frimaire V.

tion for future use.[57] And the tactics of terrorisation which they had long used to good effect in rural hamlets were coming to be effective in the towns and cities.[58] Public officials were always vulnerable to threats and blackmail, and a number of mayors in the Breton departments had been forced to flee to the towns, abandoning their office and often their wives and families to avoid *chouan* reprisals.[59] As for conscripts, those serving the Republic risked the vengeance of their *chouan* neighbours, whereas those staying at home could always be ordered or bullied into joining the rebels. Whole villages were forced to hand over their young men to the *chouans*: reports came in daily to Vannes of the mass exodus of the young from their communes, often in response to a peremptory order, backed with threats: 'Dans le canton du Faouët les jeunes gens ont reçu de la part des chefs des rebelles l'ordre formel de se tenir prêts à marcher sous peu de jours.'[60] Despite occasional glimmers of hope – a few conscripts expressing the intention to join the rebels were handed over to the gendarmes by republican villagers – the overall picture was a gloomy one. By Year VIII, the rebels were recruiting more or less at will in the departments of the west, their forces swelling daily through the incorporation of the previous year's conscripts, and Dubois-Crancé could think of no adequate remedy other than the suggestion of his *commissaire* in the Sarthe that stability in the west demanded the forcible removal of all young men of military age from communes known to favour royalism and counter-revolution.[61]

Even where royalism was not an overt issue, public officials were prone to be assaulted and terrorised by deserters and *insoumis* embittered by their lot and filled with implacable hatred for those whom they held to be responsible. Village mayors, compelled by law to organise the *tirage* and supervise recruitment, were especially vulnerable to reprisals from the young men of their communes, and reports from all over France emphasise the extent of that vulnerability. Since rural mayors and their *adjoints* were often themselves peasants or more substantial farmers, crops and animals were frequent targets of night attacks, attacks reserved for those whose enthusiasm for the *levée* and vigour in chasing up offenders were deemed to be excessive. Being country boys themselves, the deserters would know only too well how to wreak the maximum damage. At Poujols in the Hérault, for instance, the vineyards of the *agent municipal* were seriously damaged in a surreptitious night raid: all the buds were chopped off his vines over an area of three *ares*,

[57] A.N. F^{1b} II Morbihan 8 and 10, dismissals of Mayors of Gestel (18 messidor IX) and Augan (5 brumaire X).

[58] A.G. Vincennes X^w 70, extract from the municipal records of Ploërmel (Morbihan), 5 floréal V.

[59] A.N. F^{1c} III Morbihan 6, letter from *commissaire du Directoire Exécutif* to Minister of Interior, 14 frimaire VIII.

[60] A.N. F^{1c} III Morbihan 6, letter from *commissaire du Directoire Exécutif* to Minister of Interior, 30 vendémiaire VIII.

[61] A.N. AF^{III} 151^A, report of Minister of War to the Directory, 16 brumaire VIII.

and young plants in another part of the estate were systematically uprooted.[62] The rich vines of the Gironde would appear to have been particularly at risk, and mayors throughout the Bordelais were made to pay dearly for their zeal. After one particularly severe attack at Mouliets in 1811, the *procureur-général* in Bordeaux explained to the Minister that the department had been subjected to such outrages for years and that the devastation was done 'par des individus qu'on croit être des conscrits réfractaires ou insoumis. Il paraît que ceux-ci ont voulu se venger du maire qui a donné des renseignements à la colonne mobile sur le lieu de leur retraite.'[63] Elsewhere deserters caught committing offences against the forest laws would turn on the *gardes-champêtres*, and *juges de paix* rash enough to try to bring charges against them would themselves be subjected to attack: in one such incident, at Landrecies in the Nord, a horse belonging to the justice of the peace was killed by deserters as it was grazing in a field, a symbolically powerful reminder to a rural community that could never quite make the necessary distinction between law enforcement and personal interest that it was deserter bands which effectively held sway across large tracts of peasant France.[64] In the Nord, indeed, terrorisation of this sort was especially widespread, since deserters simply adapted for their own use the terror tactics already used by local bandits, the device of the *sommation minatoire*. The *sommeurs* would leave a chilling note with their chosen victim, generally a farmer in the heart of rural Picardy, instructing him to place a designated sum of money at a selected spot, 'sous différentes menaces et particulièrement sous celle d'incendie'; those refusing to answer this summons would find their barns, outhouses and hayricks destroyed in an unexplained blaze. The crime was almost unknown outside the north, where governments had been grappling with it throughout the eighteenth century. In 1722 the Parlement of Douai had attempted to force farmers to declare any *billets* they received from *sommeurs*; in 1763 it had been noted that the crime was reaching epidemic proportions, in spite of the most draconian punishments (*sommation* was regularly punished by breaking on the wheel); and in 1812, such was the increase in the offence, mostly by deserter bands, that a *Cour Spéciale Extraordinaire* was established in Douai with exceptional powers.[65] For throughout the period of the Directory and the Consulate, fire-raising was being used by deserters as a weapon against over-zealous mayors, justices of the peace and even gendarmes sent out to hunt them down.[66]

[62] A.N. F⁹ 307, report from Poujols (Hérault), 4 prairial VII.

[63] A.N. BB¹⁸ 363, report from the *procureur-général* in Bordeaux to Minister of Justice, 11 July 1811.

[64] A.N. BB¹⁸ 580, report from *commissaire du Directoire Exécutif* in Avesnes (Nord), 16 messidor IV.

[65] A.N. BB¹⁸ 598, report from the *procureur* in Douai (Nord), 28 April 1812.

[66] A.N. BB¹⁸ 53, letter from Minister of Interior to Minister of Justice, 9 January 1806; A.N. BB¹⁸ 591, case reported from Haverskerque (Nord), 1 thermidor XII.

Under the Empire the death penalty was again being imposed on convicted *sommeurs*.[67]

It would be quite unrealistic to deny that such acts of terror and collective banditry seriously undermined the government's recruitment efforts in the countryside. Mayors were frequently dissuaded from carrying out their duties too punctiliously, as persistent complaints from *commissaires* and *sous-préfets* bear eloquent witness. In the Ariège, attention is drawn to their lack of cooperation with the authorities; in the Cantal, to their unhelpful attitude and 'esprit municipal'; in the Dordogne, to their sheer apathy.[68] Almost everywhere there was a marked lack of enthusiasm, and often the more prosperous local farmers were resolutely refusing to assume an increasingly dangerous burden. From Maubeuge it was reported in Year VII that *gens aisés* had no longer any interest in public office and that 'il en résulte que la plupart des agents de la commune ne sont que des journaliers qui ont besoin de tout leur temps pour se procurer la subsistance'.[69] The gendarmerie, too, had every reason to be discouraged, since patrols which did succeed in capturing deserters and *insoumis* were regularly ambushed by other deserters on their way down from the hills and forced to free their captives. Refusal to do so often led to serious injury and even to lynching by angry crowds of friends and relatives; the pattern is strikingly similar all over France, and the regard in which the gendarmes were held in the rural community suffered accordingly. Examples are legion. In the Deux-Sèvres, two gendarmes were killed when a band of deserters discharged forty or fifty shots at them in the course of freeing two of their comrades.[70] In the Pas-de-Calais, deserters again freed one of their number from the hands of the gendarmerie in an attack which reportedly enjoyed widespread local support; the attack took place on a path near the commune of Blessy, hidden from the village by high hedgerows, where fifteen or twenty men appeared 'armés de fusils, fourches, et autres instruments aratoires'.[71] Even when such attacks were effectively repelled, the atmosphere was almost always laden with local resentment of the role which the police were compelled to play. Parents and relatives of the prisoners were frequently prominent in the crowds that blocked their path, and whole villages would turn out to prevent the arrest of one of their own. Typical was an incident on the road between Tulle and Aurillac, when two gendarmes and their captures were ambushed by thirty local cowherds and carters angered by the arrests, the *bouviers* 'armés de longues piques en fer qui

---

[67] A.N. BB[18] 598, conviction of two *sommeurs* in Douai, 4 June 1812.

[68] For instance, A.N. F[9] 156, F[9] 176, F[7] 3589, reports on the *esprit* of local mayors over conscription.

[69] A.D. Nord L 2635, letter from *commissaire du Directoire Exécutif* in Maubeuge to his counterpart with the department of the Nord in Douai, 25 fructidor VII.

[70] A.N. AF[IV] 1156, report of attack on the gendarmerie at Clazay (Deux-Sèvres), 3 February 1806.

[71] A.N. F[9] 312, report of *police générale* on armed attack at Blessy (Pas-de-Calais), 27 messidor

leur servaient à conduire des boeufs'.[72] For the gendarmerie the arrest and
escort of conscripts was not only a dangerous and unpopular assignment; it
was an activity which lost them much of the local goodwill on which even
the most basic policing was dependent.

This in turn threw open the countryside to terrorisation by the deserters
themselves. Some of the incidents seem random and indiscriminate, with the
result that few isolated farmsteads could be regarded as safe from attack.
When three deserters forced an entry into a farm at Sulniac in the Morbihan,
their technique was that classic formula of the *chauffeur*: they threw themselves on the farmer, tied his hands behind his back, and threatened him with
a shotgun, and when he said that he did not have money hidden on the
premises they 'ont dans le moment arraché de la paille de son lit, ayant
allumé le feu lui ont mis les pieds dedans pour lui faire dire où était son
argent'.[73] The sheer violence of many of these attacks helped spread panic in
the community. The gratuitous destruction is well illustrated by a break-in
near Remiremont (Vosges) in Year V, the work of around fifteen men who
smashed down the door and then:

y ont brisé toute la vaisselle de terre et de faïence, les verres et les bouteilles; y ont fait
cuire un fromage, avec trois douzaines d'oeufs qu'ils ont pris, avec deux à trois livres
de boeure (*sic*) frais et recuit, s'en sont regalé, en se rendant maîtres de la maison;
ensuite ont fracassé toutes les vitres.

They also stole all the money in the house and broke up any other cheeses
they could find; but what is really striking is that the incident took place at
five o'clock in the afternoon and that no one sought to intervene. In this part
of the Vosges such attacks were commonplace, and the whole community
had been hushed into silence by the fear which united them all.[74] Burglary,
destruction, fire-raising: the same picture of threats and violence is recorded
throughout the country, almost always leading to a conspiracy of silence
among local people. The *juge de paix* at Cadillac in the Gironde expressed
very pithily the fears of his fellow-citizens when he outlined the general
trends of violent crime in the area:

Des jeunes gens échappés au service et que l'on n'occupe pas pour ne pas contrevenir
aux lois s'introduisent dans les maisons écartées le jour et la nuit, brisent portes et
fenêtres, pratiquent des ouvertures et enlèvent tout ce qui peut se déplacer, entr'autres
la volaille et les troupeaux ... La crainte d'en courir le ressentiment des malfaiteurs
comprime ceux qui pourraient en déposer judiciairement et enhardit les coupables.[75]

---

[72] A.N. F⁷ 8531, report on attack on the gendarmerie between Tulle and Aurillac, 30 December
1808.

[73] A.N. BB¹⁸ 553, report by *juge de paix* at Elven (Morbihan) on an act of *chauffage* at Sulniac,
4 germinal IX.

[74] A.N. BB¹⁸ 913, report of Grosjean *aîné* from Remiremont (Vosges), 25 frimaire V.

[75] A.N. BB¹⁸ 355, report from *juge de paix* of Cadillac (Gironde), 6 floréal VIII.

In such circumstances, fear was an integral part of everyday life, and it was even being doubted whether the arrest of individual deserters could have any effect on the morale of the countryside.[76]

Of course the main purpose of all the criminal activity of both deserters and refractories was to remain at large and to avoid the threat of military service: other aims were no more than ancillary: of providing the food and money necessary for existence, of helping their friends escape the attentions of the recruiting officer or of profiting from their unwanted freedom to rob and pillage where opportunity beckoned. Hence it is only logical that some of the most spectacular crimes were those perpetrated in order to destroy the evidence on which recruitment was based, the dossiers of the *état civil* which designated the dates of birth and marriage and which, after the introduction of conscription in Year VI, were the principal documents used to condemn 20-year-olds to army life. Criminal damage to these documents was not uncommon, with mayors and their staff often deeply implicated; more news-worthy were acts of arson by the conscripts themselves aimed at destroying the hated evidence of their obligations. At Murat in the Cantal, for instance, only the alertness of a 12-year-old boy, playing near the stables of the *sous-préfecture* when he stumbled across a lighted wick near piles of straw and fodder, averted a serious disaster: the sub-prefect was in no doubt that the conscription records were the target of the incendiaries and strongly suspected that the men of that year's requisition were to blame.[77] In one department, the Ariège, a whole series of fires was reported which effectively rendered conscription quite impossible to carry through. In Year VII, conscripts were believed to be responsible for a fire which swept through the *maison commune* in Saint-Girons, always the most refractory of towns in the area, destroying not only the *état civil* for the entire district but also the local prison, thus making it impossible for the gendarmerie to take any effective measures against such deserters as they surprised in the surrounding hills.[78] The destruction of the records was enthusiastically welcomed by the lads of the local villages, especially after another fire in Year XII, which not only burned the duplicate records held in the prefecture in Foix, but destroyed the entire building in an uncontrollable sheet of flame. All the administrative records were destroyed in the blaze, which had been started by setting light to a pile of firewood directly below the library. Witnesses reported smelling traces of sulphur in the debris, and the delighted reactions of local people left the authorities in little doubt that the fire was an act of deliberate *malveillance*: one witness recorded that:

[76] A.N. BB[18] 15, report on an *attroupement* in Saint-Urcize (Cantal), 8 nivôse XII.

[77] A.N. F[7] 8418, report from *sous-préfet* of Murat (Cantal), 15 brumaire XIII.

[78] A.D. Ariège 5 L, canton de Saint-Girons, *cahiers de correspondance*, reports on the effects of the fire of 5/6 nivôse VII.

au moment où les flammes se manifestèrent, il entendit plusieurs personnes parler, sur la place publique, et dire *voilà le joly feu*. Un autre avoir aussy entendu dire, *Ça va et ça ira*. Un troisième avoir ouy dire à un individu inconnu, rencontré sur le chemin de Foix à Pamiers le matin de l'incendie, que la Préfecture de Foix avait été incendiée et que malheureusement on n'avait pu y brûler les oizeaux.[79]

The consequences, especially in the rural villages of the district of Saint-Girons, were extremely grave, since the only records still extant were those held by individual mayors, often kept in chaotic disorder and constantly open to fraud and forgery. For all practical purposes the government was no longer able after Year XII to maintain even a pretence of orderly recruitment in the villages towards the Spanish border.[80] The burning of the prefecture turned the *mairies* of the Ariège into preserves of deceit, forgery, oversight and destruction.

In other words, the deserters and *insoumis* were by their actions and by their very presence in rural communes involving third parties in their crimes and unleashing a whole gamut of secondary criminality. Parents, friends, mayors and public officials, farmers offering casual employment, villagers taking pity on young men on the run, all were committing crimes and all were running increasing risks as the level of policing was systematically increased in the course of the period. They were accomplices, often willing accomplices to what the government saw as a serious crime undermining the effectiveness of the war effort, but what was often dismissed by local people as nothing more than common hospitality or the natural protective instinct of parents and relatives. The government was increasingly outraged that local people showed such limited sympathy for the law of the land and such overt fellow-feeling for deserters. It feared, and with some justice, that law and order was being chipped away by the obvious alienation suffered by the gendarmerie as a result of their drives against conscripts. And its attempts to cow local opinion by collective fines or even by laying siege to recalcitrant communities – this measure was especially common where mobs of villagers had attacked and injured gendarmes[81] – were met with sullen hatred and a general refusal to cooperate. Deserters and refractories were seen as a major threat to public order, since they not only increased the crime rate by their own actions but also turned thousands of law-abiding citizens into accomplices and criminals.

The most widespread and spontaneous of all these crimes was that of sheltering deserters from the gendarmerie or the *colonnes mobiles*, an offence

---

[79] A.N. BB[18] 139, letter from the Grand Juge to the *commissaire* in the department of the Ariège, 6 brumaire XII.

[80] A.N. F[7] 8405, letter from prefect of the Ariège on the consequences of the fire at the prefecture in Year XII, 29 frimaire XIV.

[81] For instance, in Year IV Pontivy in the Morbihan was placed under siege; it is one of many cases where this punishment was used to counter collective violence (A.N. F[1b] II Morbihan 15).

which was frequently condemned by the government and which continued to be punished even in periods of amnesty for the deserters themselves.[82] To constitute a criminal offence, harbouring had to be entered into 'sciemment', which did, of course, provide numerous loopholes and give juries multiple grounds for acquittal. When the gendarmes made a dawn raid on a farm near Charmes in the Vosges where two *réquisitionnaires* were believed to be hiding, they overheard the farmer shouting a warning and saw the two young men running off naked from a barn: yet the court refused to believe that the conscripts were employed on the farm or that the farmer knew of their presence. He was therefore acquitted.[83] All kinds of personal and sentimental ties could lead people to harbour deserters, and public sympathy was aroused. Mothers were charged with sheltering their own sons; wives were occasionally taken to court for protecting their husbands; and there are instances where widows harbouring deserters were known to be living with them in the full sexual sense of the term.[84] Village attitudes and loyalties were far too deeply engrained for the government to expect to root out the problem. It did attempt to deprive deserters of any opportunity for employment by punishing most severely those found giving them casual or temporary work while they were on the run. But this again was a vast enterprise, and the fact that young, able-bodied men desperate for money provided a valuable source of cheap labour in a country denuded of its best workers by the demands of conscription ensured that most communities again closed rank behind the offenders. For village society needed the labour of deserters and *insoumis* in key sectors and at key moments of the year – as casual labour in agriculture and in vineyards, but also in local industries, especially those located away from main centres where a degree of concealment was guaranteed. Thus we find deserters employed as *cardeurs de laine* in the villages of the Gironde, as stonemasons in the woods of the Yonne, as woodworkers and labourers on the timber trains from the Nièvre to Paris;[85] they were equally welcome in the forges of the Ariège and the Vosges, the coalmines of the Nord and the quarries of the Seine-et-Oise.[86] Nor was the answer to be found in swingeing penalties or exemplary convictions, since in the words of the *commissaire du Directoire* in Epinal in Year V, 'les loix pénales trop rudes sont toujours éludées' and juries would simply refuse to convict, as they were already refusing to convict those harbouring émigrés and refractory priests,

[82] A.N. BB[18] 31, letter of complaint about the law of 13 prairial XII, dated ventôse XIII.

[83] A.N. BB[18] 914, case of Talotte, heard at the *tribunal criminel* at Mirecourt (Vosges); letter from *commissaire du Directoire Exécutif* to Minister of Justice, 14 brumaire VII.

[84] Examples can be found, for instance, in BB[18] 53 and 54, F[7] 8539, for the departments of the Nord and the Drôme.

[85] These examples are drawn from A.D. Gironde 11 L 67, A.N. F[9] 319 (Yonne), and A.N. F[9] 225 (Nièvre).

[86] These examples are drawn from A.G. Vincennes X[w] 7 (Ariège), A.D. Vosges L 533, A.D. Nord L 2635, and A.N. F[7] 3611 (Seine-et-Oise).

for whom the death penalty had been instituted.[87] Sheltering conscripts might constitute a breach of the law, but it never came to be seen as a *criminal* activity in the eyes of the community.

A more positive act of collusion was the connivance which often accompanied the frauds and deceits employed by conscripts to avoid service. For though many of these frauds were purely individual acts by the young men themselves, everyone in the village knew what had happened and the vast majority silently approved. Self-mutilation is a case in point. Since the conscription law insisted that those liable to serve should be able-bodied, and since it was common knowledge among village boys that none could be considered for the army who lacked either the trigger finger of his right hand or the front teeth required for reloading a musket, one possible if very painful road to salvation was clear to all, and from all over France came reports of drastic acts of homespun surgery by conscripts desperate for a *réforme* and abundantly anaesthetised at the local *auberge*. A report by the Minister of War in Year VII lamented the alarming increase in such incidents, regretting that 'des pusillanimes incapables de vouloir contribuer au succès de nos armées ont néanmoins le lâche courage de s'abattre un pouce ou un doigt de la main droite pour se soustraire au service militaire'.[88] In one village in the Gers, indeed, four conscripts had all perfected the technique and ritualistically chopped off their index fingers to defy the recruiting officer.[89] There are even cases where brothers made pacts to inflict agreed injuries on one another as they approached the age of conscription.[90] In such circumstances, *enquêtes* would frequently be arranged to try to establish the circumstances of the injury and to allocate responsibility for it, but the stubbornness and recalcitrance of fellow-villagers made this task well-nigh impossible. When Baptiste Sauzeil cut off his index finger in 1807 he was working alone in the communal wood at Vicdessos (Ariège) and claimed that because of rheumatic pains he was obliged to saw left-handed: it was an unlikely story which raised the suspicions of the authorities, but various villagers agreed rather uninformatively that he had indeed been observed cutting with the saw in his left hand.[91] Similarly, local society connived at a rich variety of implausible marriages during this period between conscripts and village women three and even four times their age. Some small communes were recording 'une foule de mariages' in the weeks after the promulgation of the conscription law, and the scale of abuse was worrying the military authorities.[92]

[87] A.N. BB¹⁸ 913, letter from *commissaire du Directoire Exécutif* with department of the Vosges to Minister of Justice, 13 nivôse V.

[88] A.N. AF^III 149, report from Minister of War to the Directory, 5 brumaire VII.

[89] A.N. AF^III 158, letter from commune of Simorre (Gers) to Minister of War, 20 frimaire VII.

[90] A.D. Gironde 2 R 287, case of Jacques Biralleau from Saint-Antoine (canton de Saint-André-de-Cubzac).

[91] A.D. Ariège 2 R 94, report from commune of Vicdessos, 10 October 1807.

[92] A.N. F⁹ 286, report from department of Basses-Pyrénées, 8 pluviôse VIII.

Women of seventy and even eighty were offering their services as brides to lads threatened by the requisition, an abuse which neither the Consulate nor the Empire managed to erase. In the Drôme, in the last years of the Empire, the prefect was still complaining about the widespread nature of these 'mariages disproportionnés', which were given the blessing of entire village communities. One conscript had married a woman of seventy-five to escape service, while two others, from Erôme and Larnage, had married widows from their own communes aged seventy-seven and eighty-two respectively.[93] The prefect of the Calvados, commenting on the same abuse, noted that the conscripts involved were usually young men of considerable means, whereas the women frequently used marriage as an escape from the poorhouse.[94] What is clear in all these cases, however, is the open connivance of local people: the only opposition came from other conscripts, who saw their own chances of escape cruelly diminished.

That connivance and evident sympathy could easily be turned into perjury and false testimony. Doctors and medical orderlies were notoriously easy to convince or to bribe into complaisance, and minor ailments would frequently serve as the basis for a *réforme*. In some areas a third or even a half of those presenting themselves for medical examination were being exempted, much to the annoyance of the military. And the situation was only exacerbated in those cases where evidence of infirmity could not be provided on the spot, for instance for epileptics, where the 'evidence' consisted of sworn statements from ten of the young man's fellow-villagers.[95] Under the Empire the demands became more exigent, and mayors were asked to provide testimony that they personally knew that a conscript was deaf or that another had been seen having an epileptic fit.[96] The whole area of medical *réformes* was fraught with suspicion and assumptions of fraud. Individual hospitals were well known in their localities as places where medical certificates could be easily obtained – in the Somme, for example, the *hôpital militaire* at Amiens was much favoured by men seeking an exemption.[97] And individual *médecins* and *chirurgiens* obtained a certain local notoriety through the ease with which medical evidence would be issued. In the Gironde, indeed, the prefect was moved to intervene to avoid fraudulent exemptions being recommended by the doctors employed by the *conseil de révision* itself: from 1806, the name of the *chirurgien* called by the council was announced only fifteen minutes before the hearing, and the doctors on duty were changed daily, since 'celui de la

---

93 A.D. Drôme 1 R 6, letter from the prefect of the Drôme to *sous-préfet* at Valence, 5 May 1813.

94 A.N. F7 3583, letter from the prefect of the Calvados to Minister of Police Générale, 6 January 1813.

95 A.N. F9 286, letter from the *commissaire du Directoire Exécutif* at Chinon to Minister of Interior, 12 nivôse IV.

96 A.N. F9 189, report from the prefect of the Gironde, 8 June 1807.

97 A.N. F9 316 report from the *commissaire du Directoire Exécutif* in the Somme, 21 floréal VII.

veille est immédiatement accablé de visites et de lettres'.[98] Certain doctors were themselves worried by the incidence of fraud and deception. The ruses resorted to by conscripts were highly ingenious: one lad from Luzarches in the Seine-et-Oise convinced the recruitment authorities that he was deaf and dumb;[99] in the Creuse, in Year IV, there were complaints that conscripts were swallowing concoctions which affected their pulse;[100] while the 'maladies simulées' of conscripts in the Seine-Inférieure over the period of the war were graphically described by the prefect in Rouen in 1812. They:

s'étaient fait arracher toutes les dents pour ne point servir, d'autres étaient parvenus à les carier presque toutes en employant des acides ou en mâchant de l'encens, quelques-uns s'étaient fait des plaies aux bras ou aux jambes par l'application de vésicatoires, et pour rendre ces plaies pour ainsi dire incurables, ils les ont pansées avec de l'eau impregnée d'arsenic. Beaucoup se sont fait donner des hernies soufflées, quelques-uns appliquèrent sur les parties de la génération des caustiques tellement violents que les médecins doutent qu'ils puissent échapper à la mort.[101]

Of course these ruses did not all deceive the authorities, nor did all the men operated on in these ways live to tell the tale: but permanent disability and even death were risks which conscripts and their medical accomplices were willing to take in their bid to escape from military service.

In other types of fraud it was mayors and public officials who were most likely to be involved, especially in those rural communes where they came under considerable pressure from local opinion. It was mayors, after all, to whom the conduct of the conscription procedures was entrusted, and it was on them that local influences and inducements bore most heavily. By the time of the Directory and Consulate, some of the early problems of organising the *levées* had been finally ironed out and the most flagrant abuses removed. The blatant unfairness of the method of selection *par scrutin*, for instance, whereby the local citizenry turned out in force to vote other people's children into the army, had been recognised and the method abandoned. Nor were there in Year VII the widespread complaints which had accompanied the early *levées*, to the effect that mayors were omitting to include their own children or those of their more influential friends in the ballot-box. No longer were the *bouviers* of outlying hamlets, barely known by the rest of the village and therefore more immediately dispensable, so certain of being included in the battalions, as had been the case in certain parts of the Cantal in 1793.[102] At least the annual conscriptions that were introduced by the Loi Jordan from Year VII could be seen to be fair in principle and difficult to manipulate in

---

[98] A.N. F⁹ 189, letter from prefect of the Gironde to *Conseiller d'Etat*, 31 August 1806.

[99] A.N. BB¹⁸ 75, report from Luzarches (Seine-et-Oise), 20 July 1807.

[100] A.N. F⁹ 315, letter to Minister of Interior from two deputies from the Creuse, 18 nivôse IV.

[101] A.N. F⁹ 247, letter from prefect of the Seine-Inférieure to Minister of War, 11 November 1812.

[102] A.D. Cantal L 248, report of the *scrutin* in the canton of Laroquebrou, 13 March 1793.

practice. But all this meant was that public officials were induced to resort to more devious means of diverting the interest of the recruiting-officer from the rich or the favoured. The *état civil* remained the key to a young man's liberty, and forgeries of widely disparate kinds were perpetrated to allow conscripts to claim a *réforme* or exemption. The dates of births and of marriages were deliberately falsified; the papers of younger brothers were accepted to enable exemptions to be given on the grounds of height; dead relatives and neighbours were exhumed from their administrative graves to help provide *réformes* for the living.[103] There were communes where by some freak of nature only girls were being born so that, twenty years hence, no one from the village would find himself faced with military service; there was often little sense of guilt at this fraud, since in very catholic villages it was difficult to persuade parents of the necessity or morality of civil registration.[104] On all sides the registers of the *état civil* were being adulterated, torn, erased or in some cases burnt altogether: one mayor in the Ariège calmly set fire to the civil records of his village for the previous fifty years.[105] In some communes traditions of fraud and bribery were established which no amount of policing and vigilance could break. Often, indeed, the gendarmes were frustrated by the refusal of anyone in the village to testify against the forgers.[106] In consequence, there was a real danger of local government breaking down completely in certain rural parts of the country, notably along the Spanish frontier, where the respect for law and order, never very deeply engrained, was further jeopardised by the state's military demands. The scale of the problem in the badlands around Saint-Girons is well illustrated by the crime statistics passed to the Minister of the Interior during the Empire, and by the fact that the staff of the sub-prefecture themselves were implicated. In all, the reports lists fifty-one communes where crimes of *faux*, *recel* and *escroquerie* had been committed; and sixteen communes where armed attacks had been mounted on the gendarmerie.[107]

These cases almost invariably involved bribery of some kind – of mayors, or *adjoints*, *secrétaires*, or *agents municipaux*, of gendarmes, even of *fonctionnaires* on the payroll of the army itself, employees of the prefecture or sub-prefecture, members of the jury or of the *conseil de révision*.[108] The price of an oversight or of a deliberate forgery might vary from place to place and in accordance with local sympathies: in one instance a mayor was found to have forged papers not for a monetary reward but out of simple friendship,

---

[103] A.N. F⁹ 286, cases of *fraudes* declared to the Minister of War.

[104] A.N. F⁷ 3581, report from prefect of the Puy-de-Dôme, dated March 1807.

[105] A.N. F¹ᵇ II Ariège 13, case of the former *maire* and *adjoint* of Larbont, who had burned the communal *état civil* from 1751 to 1790, reported 9 May 1808.

[106] A.N. BB¹⁸ 20, case of forgery at Coulombier-le-Vieux (Drôme), 1 brumaire XII.

[107] A.N. F⁷ 8514, 8515, 8516, enumeration of cases brought against *maires* and municipal officials in the Ariège.

[108] A.N. F⁹ 286, contains case-studies of the various kinds of frauds employed.

stimulated by a few bottles of wine.[109] This was, however, a rare exception, and sizeable sums of money regularly changed hands. For the demand for exemptions and false papers was so persistent that crime-rings soon formed to take advantage of the desperation of those conscripted and of the gullibility of their families. It was a terrain tailor-made for tricksters and racketeers, and many of the frauds were being committed at the expense of the conscripts rather than to bring them succour. In the Nord, gang members scoured the countryside looking for young men of the age and build to provide *remplacements*, and an almost professional trade in *remplaçants* was rapidly organised.[110] In Aurillac, swindlers were touting for business among the country lads who had just arrived to present themselves for their medical;[111] in Bordeaux, they were waiting like vultures on the quayside for young recruits to disembark.[112] In many cases the replacements they offered failed to meet the army's specifications, or simply slipped off with the money, leaving the conscript to serve in person. Bars were a favoured haunt of the *escroc*, and innkeepers were frequent accomplices: they would note the arrival of new customers, naive and uncertain as they made their way to the barracks for the first time, and they would make their premises available to the gangs, usually sharing in the profits of the trade as recompense. It was an unscrupulous form of fraud, one which grew more widespread and more profitable as the repeated conscriptions of the Empire successively drained the countryside of labour and forced up the real value of a *congé* or a replacement. Money might be handed over for a magic intervention to prevent a son or husband from drawing a low number in the *tirage*: sorcery and black magic were still a potent force in the lives of simple peasant families, and conscription offered an excellent opportunity to exploit their simplicity.[113] As the prefect of the Gironde recognised in 1810, when faced with tales of ghosts in the commune of Saint-Laurent-en-Médoc, 'les contes populaires trouvent encore quelques accès dans l'esprit faible des habitants des campagnes', and this made the task of the *fraudeur* so much easier.[114] The case of three *sorciers* operating from Year XIII in the rural Gironde illustrates the full gullibility of rural opinion; they played mercilessly on local superstition and turned it to their profit. Two of them were former priests, itself an undoubted advantage when they claimed magical powers of healing, since the faithful needed no further conviction: the remoter parts of the department, noted the prefect, were full of such men, 'médecins empiriques', known for their

---

[109] A.N. F¹ᵇ II Cantal 8, case of Brioude, *maire* of Deux-Verges (Cantal), Year XII.
[110] A.N. F⁷ 3605, interrogation of Georges Allin at Lille, 8 June 1807.
[111] A.N. BB¹⁸ 15, letter from the *substitut du procureur* in Aurillac to the *procureur* in Riom, 14 June 1811.
[112] A.D. Gironde 2 R 285, report of the *procureur* in Bordeaux, 5 December 1808.
[113] A.N. BB¹⁸ 75, case of Nicolas Lecomte, *charpentier* at Asnières-sur-Oise, 5 April 1809.
[114] A.N. F¹ᶜ III Gironde 5, report of the prefect of the Gironde for the fourth *trimestre* of 1810.

powers to cure sterility between man and wife, or revered because they cured 'hommes et bêtes avec des prières et des signes de croix'. Palais, the principal accused in this case, was arrested for offering to provide conscripts with the false symptoms of a disease and later cure it; his reputation in the countryside, however, was much more deeply based, since he was known as a *devin* with magical powers: 'Pour se mettre en réputation, il fit enlever sa femme par le diable. Elle criait de toute sa force que le diable l'enlevait: tout le quartier accourut.'[115] Village culture and popular superstition were powerful accomplices for *fraudeurs* preying on the fears and anxieties of mothers who would clutch at any straw to prevent their sons from leaving for the army.

And here, perhaps, we come up against the nub of the problem facing recruiting officers in large areas of rural France during the Directory and Consulate: that the government never succeeded, either by publicity or by policing, in persuading many communities that military service was a direct corollary of citizenship. Village custom and popular superstition, sometimes directed by outside forces like religion and counter-revolutionary movements, remained stronger formative influences than the law and the state police. The religious element present in the response of many villagers serves only to emphasise the cruelty of their dilemma. In the Finistère, for instance, conscripts went timorously to the *tirage* clutching talismans and sacred medallions to fend off a low number; throughout that highly superstitious department they and their families went on repeated pilgrimages to *calvaires* and the shrines of their Breton saints, to Rumengol, to Le Folgoët, to Sainte-Anne-la-Palu;[116] and in 1813 the prefect was moved to remark that:

La manière dont la plupart des bons habitans des campagnes du Finistère quittent leurs enfants appelés à la défense de la patrie est touchante et digne de remarque. Ils vont les conduire jusqu'à une certaine distance, là ils les embrassent en leur disant un éternel adieu, puis, après les avoir quittés, ils retournent chez eux en récitant des prières, quelques-uns le De Profundis...[117]

In such circumstances, even although the *insoumis* might be a destabilising element in the commune, even though deserters passing through on their way home might be cursed for their nuisance value or slightingly dismissed as little better than *vagabonds*, it is not difficult to see why most villagers came to their aid and why denunciations to the gendarmerie were rare. The crimes they committed on the run were similarly tolerated by villagers who could only too easily envisage themselves or their own children reduced to the same plight. And the crimes which they committed in helping or sheltering conscripts only fortified the wall of silence towards the outside world and

---

[115] A.N. F7 8442, dossier on *escroquerie* in the rural Gironde, an XIII – 1808.
[116] L. Ogès, 'La conscription et l'esprit public dans le Finistère sous le Consulat et l'Empire', *Mémoires de la Société d'histoire et d'archéologie de Bretagne* (1962), p. 106.
[117] J. Waquet, 'La société civile devant l'insoumission et la désertion à l'époque de la conscription militaire', *Bibliothèque de l'Ecole des Chartes*, 126 (1968), 191.

ensured that no one cooperated with the gendarmes. *Insoumis*, in particular, being village boys who understood not only the terrain but the collective mentality of the village community, were tolerated and defended against outsiders.[118] Often their crimes were totally compatible with the balance of criminal behaviour in the commune itself; and thanks to the increased level of repression during this period, the entire commune was directly or indirectly involved. The presence in the commune of deserters or *insoumis* was a shared secret that helped cement the close-knit village community against the authorities; the crimes were an inevitable, perhaps a necessary, concomitant.

[118] On the closed nature of community and village society in the southern Massif Central, for instance, see Peter Jones, 'Parish, seigneurie and community of inhabitants in southern central France during the eighteenth and nineteenth centuries', *Past and Present*, 91 (1981).

5

Common rights and agrarian individualism
in the southern Massif Central 1750–1880

PETER JONES

Ever since Marc Bloch's seminal article[1] on the growth of agrarian individualism, the struggle against common rights has been associated with the second half of the eighteenth century. The bureaucrats of the late ancien regime launched the debate, the Revolution resolved it by consecrating the principle of private property. Subsequent regimes had merely to complete the mopping-up operation. That such a linear perspective should have survived for so long despite the nuanced judgements of historians like Henri Sée[2] and Georges Lefebvre[3] and, indeed, Bloch,[4] owes much to the pervasive quality of the revolutionary myth. Few would dispute the claim of the French Revolution to mark the beginning of a new political era, but its impact in the field of economic policy and development calls for careful assessment. As evidence accumulates which casts doubt upon the Revolution as the point of convergence of maturing economic, social and political processes, the old assumptions have been undermined. The champions of 1789 continue to assert its specificity, but with faltering conviction. Arguments are adjusted to acknowledge recent research, but even where this points strongly in other directions the categories of debate and the conclusions remain unchanged. By destroying seigneurial privilege and collective rights the Revolution accelerated the dissolution of the rural community, asserts Albert Soboul.[5]

[1] M. Bloch, 'La lutte pour l'individualisme agraire dans la France du XVIIIᵉ siècle: l'oeuvre des pouvoirs d'ancien régime', *Annales d'histoire économique et sociale*, 2 (1930), pp. 329–81 (reprinted in M. Bloch, *Mélanges historiques* (2 vols., SEVPEN, 1963), vol. 2, pp. 593–637).

[2] H. Sée, *La vie économique de la France sous la monarchie censitaire, 1815–1848* (Paris, 1927), chap. one; ibid., 'La vaine pâture sous la Monarchie de Juillet d'après l'enquête de 1836–1838', *Revue d'histoire moderne* (1926), pp. 198–213.

[3] G. Lefebvre, 'La Révolution française et les paysans', *Annales historiques de la Révolution française* (1933), pp. 97–128.

[4] M. Bloch, *Les caractères originaux de l'histoire rurale française* (2 vols., Paris, 1952, 1956), vol. I, pp. 239–51.

[5] A. Soboul, 'Problèmes de la communauté rurale en France (XVIIIᵉ–XIXᵉ siècles)' in *Ethnologie*

He concedes that the process was slower in the regions of 'petite culture' and accepts that revolutionary legislation was not always implemented; nevertheless he rejects the idea of a 'compromise' proposed by Lefebvre[6] and prefers to use the term 'paradox' instead.[7] According to Lefebvre, the anticapitalist instincts of the small peasantry prevented bourgeois revolutionaries imbued with the principles of economic liberalism from fully executing their historically appointed task. Soboul shifts the emphasis: cautious revolutionaries failed to remove the obstacles lying in the path of a potentially kulak peasantry. If once these interpretations were sustained by our very ignorance of post-revolutionary rural history, neither is adequate today. They narrow the variety of experience in the countryside to an unacceptable degree.

In the past decade the orthodox view has come under attack from several angles. The notion of an agricultural revolution and a parallel growth of agrarian individualism has been reassessed and, on the whole, relegated to the second half of the nineteenth century.[8] At the same time the Revolution has been placed beneath the microscope and its legacy in the agricultural domain revealed as tentative and unambitious. The fragmentation of the rural community to which Soboul and others allude doubtless owed something to the policies of successive revolutionary legislatures but owed more, perhaps, to secular demographic and economic pressures which were already evident before 1789 and which would continue to shape the destinies of the countryside throughout the nineteenth century. The so-called 'pays de petite culture' pose a further problem. The orthodox opinion treats them as a minor and backward appendage to a burgeoning market-oriented agricultural economy, and yet the most recent research suggests that these regions formed the backbone of the French economy until the 1850s, if not later.[9] If we allow, too, that the impact of the Revolution on traditional agrarian structures was by no means as doctrinaire as is often supposed, it seems reasonable to query some of the premises on which so much writing on French rural history has hitherto rested.

Schematisation sacrifices a certain, if baffling, diversity in favour of a comprehensible, but illusory, uniformity. The study of peasant civilisations or

et histoire: forces productives et problèmes de transition, hommage à Charles Parain (Paris, 1975), p. 369; P. Léon et al., *Histoire économique et sociale de la France* (Paris, 1976), vol. III (1), pp. 61, 117.

[6] Lefebvre, *La Révolution française*, p. 127; Lefebvre, *Les paysans du Nord pendant la Révolution française* (Bari, 1959), p. 912.

[7] Soboul, 'Problèmes de la communauté rurale . . .', p. 387. Also Soboul, 'Georges Lefebvre (1874–1959): pour le centième anniversaire de sa naissance', *Annales historiques de la Révolution française* (1975), pp. 188–92.

[8] M. Morineau, *Les faux-semblants d'un démarrage économique: agriculture et démographie en France au XVIIIᵉ siècle (Cahier des Annales 30, Paris, 1971); T. Kemp, Economic Forces in French History* (London, 1971); R. Price, *The Economic Modernisation of France* (London, 1975); H. Clout, *Agriculture on the Eve of the Railway Age* (London, 1980).

[9] Clout, *Agriculture on the Eve*, pp. 223–5.

cultures within a national context poses this problem in its most acute form and it is all but insurmountable. As one modern analyst has remarked,[10] the complexity and variety of French agrarian conditions is such that almost any generalisation is deficient as soon as it is formulated. Rural history is perforce local history and must first be studied as such. The physiocratic edicts of the 1760s and 1770s on the subject of the commons and fallow grazing (*vaine pâture*) constituted an impressive and doctrinaire body of law, which in certain respects went beyond anything the Revolution was to introduce, but were they enforced? It seems doubtful and consequently Bloch's thesis must be regarded as highly speculative. A healthy scepticism is an indispensable aid to research in French local history: legal forms and physical realities imperfectly coincided. The ancient distinction between written or Roman law and Customary law which survived until the Revolution is a case in point. Juridically speaking, *vaine pâture* and its corollary, free grazing between communities (*droit de parcours*), was unknown in those parts of southern France subject to Roman law. The proprietor enjoyed full and sole access to his land, whether arable, meadow or wooded, at every season of the year. Thus the sub-delegate of the *élection* of Aurillac in the Haute-Auvergne – an area bisected by the frontier between Customary and written law[11] – could maintain, in 1768, that the *droit de parcours* did not exist in his district.[12] Strictly speaking he was right, but collective agricultural practices were enforced in this region and throughout parts of Guyenne[13] and Languedoc,[14] nonetheless. Jurisprudence yielded to usage and usage to social and ecological environment. Where customary institutions seemed most suited to the prevailing conditions, they were transplanted by private treaty between interested parties. These *servitudes* developed as a body of prescriptive rights coexisting alongside, but at variance with, codified law. In this as in other matters French rural history is full of traps for the unwary,[15] and it is essential to resist the temptation of neat categorisation.

These cautionary remarks might equally be directed towards the legislation of the Revolution and succeeding regimes. Unlike the edicts of the ancien

---

[10] G. Wright, *Rural Revolution in France: the Peasantry in the Twentieth Century* (Stanford, 1964), p. v.

[11] J. Yver, *Egalité entre héritiers et exclusion des enfants dotés, essai de géographie coutumière* (Paris, 1966).

[12] C. Trapenard, *Le pâturage communal en Haute-Auvergne (XVIIᵉ–XVIIIᵉ siècles)* (Paris, 1904), p. 115.

[13] H. Sée, 'Une enquête sur la vaine pâture et le droit de parcours à la fin du règne de Louis XV', *Revue du dix-huitième siècle* (1913), 270.

[14] E. Appolis, 'La question de la vaine pâture en Languedoc au XVIIIᵉ siècle', *Annales historiques de la Révolution française* (1938), 97–132.

[15] Even Lefebvre assumed that landowners possessed 'absolute right' under Roman Law: G. Lefebvre, 'The place of the Revolution in the agrarian history of France', in R. Forster and O. Ranum (eds.), *Rural Society in France: Selections from the Annales, Economies, Sociétés, Civilisations* (Baltimore, 1977), p. 36.

regime, the new *décrets* and *lois* applied unreservedly to the entire national territory, but their uniformity was more apparent than real. With the notable exception of the forest codes,[16] this was nearly all enabling legislation. Communities – or rather their institutional descendants, the municipalities – were empowered to alter or curtail collective practices, but were not required to do so. As a result, statute law was refracted through a prism of local agrarian structures which no historical model has yet been able to comprehend. If we could share Soboul's[17] confident belief that the nineteenth-century peasantry was polarising into owners of capital and owners of labour, it might be possible to attribute to specific social groups stereotyped responses on questions such as enclosures, the division of commonland or the abolition of *vaine pâture*. But Soboul's model is a simplification of the processes of post-revolutionary change in the countryside. In those areas of France in which the proprietorial segment of the peasantry increased as the century progressed, it makes no sense at all. Alignments and confrontations on the issue of collective agricultural practices in such regions were by no means clear-cut. Often poor plot-holders (*colons*) fought tooth and nail to prevent big landowners from clearing and enclosing the commons for arable cultivation, but over time and space the roles might easily be reversed. Large stock-owners in regions lacking meadows or fodder crops (*prairies artificielles*) were doughty advocates of traditional grazing rights on common, fallow or stubble. No typology could do justice to this diversity. The perpetuation or demise of collective rights over common and private property depended upon a host of factors which together made up the balance of the local economy. Prominent among these factors were the conditions of access to common pasture and the common flock; the extent and quality of common-land available; the existence of enclosed meadows and the precise terms of any proposed revision or abolition of common rights.

Fifty years have passed since Bloch drew attention to the paucity of secondary works on nineteenth-century agrarian history. Although synoptic studies have since been published under a variety of titles,[18] there are still considerable gaps in our knowledge. We theorise about the decline of the commons, but are unsure as to how, when and where this came about. We lack a comparative study of customs governing access to commonland, as an ethnologist[19] pointed out over a decade ago. A comprehensive account of the peasantry during the French Revolution has only recently been published[20]

---

[16] See below pp. 29–31.

[17] P. Léon *et al.*, *Histoire économique et sociale*, vol. 3 (I), p. 117.

[18] F. Braudel and E. Labrousse (eds.), *Hsitoire économique et sociale de la France* (4 vols., Paris, 1970–80); G. Duby and A. Wallon (eds.), *Histoire de la France rurale* (4 vols., Paris, 1975–6); J.-P. Houssel (ed.), *Histoire des paysans français du XVIIIᵉ siècle à nos jours* (Roanne, 1976).

[19] C. Parain, 'Contribution à une problématique de la communauté villageoise dans le domaine européen', *L'Ethnographie*, 64 (1970), 54.

[20] A. Ado, *Le mouvement paysan pendant la Révolution française* (Moscow, 1971) – in Russian: for

and the obscurity surrounding the long-term effects of the agrarian legislation of revolutionary and post-revolutionary assemblies is nearly total. As more research is undertaken and interest in peasant history increases these lacunae will doubtless be filled, and it is with this aim in mind that we propose to explore the impact of agrarian individualism on a rural civilisation which retained many archaic characteristics.

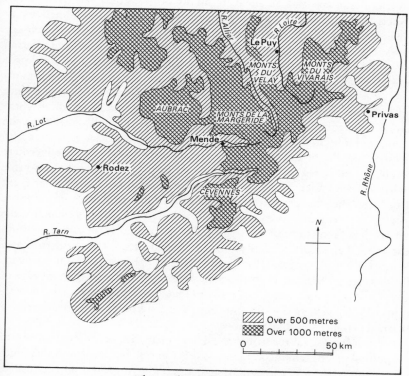

The southern Massif Central

The southern and south-eastern flanks of the Massif Central (see map) harboured a peasant society of unusual richness and vitality in the nineteenth century. Insulated from outside pressures by a curtain of mountains and the calcerous ramparts of the *causses* (arid plateaux), it formed a classic 'pays de petite culture'. Agriculture was totally geared to the satisfaction of the carbohydrate needs of an expanding population. An ingenious 'economy of makeshifts' resting on polyculture, increasing resort to cereal substitutes, such

a French *résumé*, see A. Soboul, 'Sur le mouvement paysan dans la Révolution française', *Annales historiques de la Révolution française* (1973), pp. 85–101.

as the sweet chestnut and potato, and the voluntary expatriation of superfluous mouths by means of rural migration during the dead season generally achieved this objective in normal years. Such was the difficulty of communications that the provisioning of this hinterland in times of dearth was scarcely feasible before the final decades of the century. Consequently market networks remained localised and specialisation embryonic as even those communities most ill-suited by nature for arable cultivation devoted their best energies to ensuring an adequate supply of foodstuffs.

Subsistence agriculture in the southern Massif Central exhibited many archaic features which to impatient eighteenth- and nineteenth-century observers were signs of incorrigible backwardness. A simple biennial rotation of rye and fallow was the norm, except in a few lowland hollows and on a handful of large estates where the planting of fodder crops had been pioneered. On the highest slopes even biennial rotation proved too demanding and an irregular slash-and-burn agriculture (*écobuage*) was practised which involved the rotation of fields cut out of the heath at will rather than the rotation of crops. In the absence of new crops, artificial fertilizers and adequate supplies of animal manure, the fallow period survived longer here than in any other region of France. Only a tiny proportion of the cultivable land stock was under the plough in any one year. In the future department of the Ardèche, this proportion has been calculated to have been no more than 15 per cent on the eve of the Revolution.[21] While, nationally, the surfaces left fallow declined significantly in the course of the nineteenth century, and especially after 1850, in the departments of the southern Massif Central (Aveyron, Lozère, Haute-Loire, Ardèche) progress was much slower. The 1882 agricultural survey[22] revealed the existence of a recalcitrant core of heavy fallowing embracing the most mountainous portions of the departments of the Aveyron, Lozère and Cantal. In the Lozère over 30 per cent of the arable land regularly lay fallow.

Backwardness is a recurring theme in many monographic studies of agricultural practices in the southern Massif Central, but this is a facile judgement. It is reasonable to argue that heavy fallowing, like polyculture in general, was an intelligent and even sophisticated response to difficult ecological conditions. Agronomists were doubtless correct in condemning the peasant habit of extending the area of land under the plough without heed to the supply of manure in the belief that greater productivity would result.[23] But in the same breath the advocates of enlightened farming recommended the division of commonland, enclosure of meadows, restriction of

[21] A. Molinier, 'En Vivarais au XVIIIᵉ siècle: une croissance démographique sans révolution agricole', *Annales du Midi*, 92 (1980), 308.

[22] P. Léon et al., *Histoire économique et sociale*, vol. 3 (2), p. 672.

[23] For example, A. Rodat, *Le cultivateur aveyronnais: leçons élémentaires d'agriculture pratique et vues sur la science de l'exploitation rurale* (Rodez, 1839), p. 229.

free grazing and the introduction of fodder crops. This was contradictory: cereal cultivation on poor soils at altitudes of up to 1,300 metres was only viable when integrated with a pastoral economy, and fodder crops were not easily added to a rotation in which the staple cereal – rye – required ten or eleven months in the soil before it reached maturity.[24] The fact remains that, for all its 'backwardness', traditional polyculture demonstrated a remarkable capacity to adapt. Between 1750 and 1880, the southern Massif Central experienced a rapid, and in some localities headlong, increase in population. While some of the growth merely took up the slack in the rural economy left over from earlier demographic crises, the expansion continued and pushed the existing agrarian system to its limits. In the high Cévennes those limits were soon reached, and from the 1860s the population began to leave in droves for the plain, but elsewhere the pressure was accommodated with only minimal alterations to the traditional structure.

In the wooded gullies of the Ségala (Aveyron) and on the highland plateau of the Velay (Haute-Loire), the potato was adopted on a large scale,[25] but otherwise the additional mouths were fed by clearing more land, intensive exploitation of the commons and an adjustment in the balance between cereal and chestnut cultivation. The sweet chestnut was a traditional alimentary resource in times of demographic growth and was aptly dubbed the 'arbre à pain'.[26] Although chestnuts had a lower calorific value than rye grain, the trees produced heavy and, on the whole, regular yields once they had reached maturity. They could also be planted in thin, acidic soils and on steep hillsides which generally defied tillage. The century after 1750 was the heyday of the chestnut in the southern Massif Central. Vast groves were established to meet the shortfall in bread grains. In the Lower Ardèche, where population growth was precocious, it has been calculated that the production of chestnuts nearly doubled between 1731 and 1811.[27]

Demographic pressure within a closed economy did more to focus attention upon the commons and collective practices than any number of legislative pronouncements. In the southern Massif Central common and heathland was extensive, though not as extensive as in the mountain departments of the Vosges, the Jura, the Alps and the Pyrenees.[28] But whereas the commons, like the fallow, were progressively slimmed in the course of the nineteenth

---

[24] A. Fel, *Les hautes terres du Massif Central: tradition paysanne et économie agricole* (Paris, 1962), pp. 16, 65–6.

[25] Clout, *Agriculture on the Eve*, pp. 90–3 and figure.

[26] Ibid., pp. 136, 144–6; J.-R. Pitte, 'Les origines et l'évolution de la chataigneraie vivaroise à travers un document cadastrale du XVIIIᵉ siècle', *Bulletin de la section de géographie*, 82 (1975–7), 165–78.

[27] Molinier, 'En Vivarais', p. 312.

[28] J. de Crisenoy, *Statisque des biens communaux et des sections de communes* (extrait de la Revue Générale d'Administration) (Paris, 1887), pp. 22–3, table; R. Graffin, *Les biens communaux en France: étude historique et critique* (Paris, 1899).

century in many 'pays de petite culture',[29] along the southern flanks of the Massif Central they largely survived the attacks made upon them. French agricultural statistics permit a rough ordering of magnitudes and it is estimated that roughly 15 per cent of the land surface of the department of the Lozère was held under communal tenure in 1863. By 1914 this figure had scarcely declined and may actually have risen as the beginnings of rural depopulation transformed more land into *de facto* common pasture.[30] This situation contrasts strikingly with the agrarian evolution experienced by the department of the Creuse. In 1863 the Creuse had even more commonland than the Lozère, but by the end of the century much of it had been enclosed.[31]

Communal tenure was, in any case, something of a misnomer in the Massif Central, since ownership of pasture and woodland designated as 'common' was vested not in the commune, but in its constituent elements, the villages and hamlets. These outlying settlements were defined as 'sections' in administrative terminology. In essence this was merely a recognition of the dispersed habitat which had evolved in southern central France. In the great majority of departments the commune was superimposed upon a well-nucleated habitat and hence was both proprietor and custodian of the community's assets. Such was the case, for instance, in the Alpine and Pyrenean departments. In the Hautes-Pyrénées[32] where common pasture and woodland covered 43 per cent of the land surface in 1863, these holdings were almost entirely owned and managed by the communes. Of 453 communes possessing commons, only 20 had sections with assets of their own. By contrast, in the Haute-Loire[33] 256 communes out of 260 had dependent sections and the commons were overwhelmingly the property of these villages and hamlets. Just 461 hectares or 1.3 per cent of the departmental stock of commonland was at the disposal of the communes.

Inequalities and chronic enmities were the natural by-product of such a regime. The distribution of pasture and woodland was haphazardly related to population patterns and access was determined either by residence or 'immemorial right' customs. Gross disparities both between and within communes existed. Some communes were sub-divided into a dozen or more sections each having its own commonland; in others only a handful of sections had significant holdings of common property, which they jealously guarded against villages less well endowed. The commune of Saint-Privat-

[29] For example, in the Gironde, Landes, Creuse and the Breton departments: J. Tessier, *La valeur sociale des biens communaux en France* (Paris, 1906), pp. 149, 153, 156, 273.

[30] Crisenoy, *Statisque*, p. 23, table; P. Roqueplo, *La dépopulation dans les arrondissements de Mende et de Marvejols (Lozère)* (Rodez, 1914), p. 147.

[31] Crisenoy, *Statisque*, p. 22, table; Tessier, *La valeur sociale*, p. 273. But note, too, the comments of A. Corbin, *Archaisme et modernité en Limousin au XIXᵉ siècle, 1845–1880* (2 vols., Paris, 1975), vol. I, pp. 287–96 and notes.

[32] Crisenoy, *Statistique*, p. 23, table.

[33] Ibid.; C. Best, *Dissertation sur les biens communaux de la Haute-Loire* (Le Puy, 1860).

d'Allier (Haute-Loire) is a case in point: it comprised twenty-six sections possessing commons whose area ranged from a little over 20 hectares to 88 square metres.[34]

As the countryside recovered from the debilitating crisis decades of the late seventeenth and early eighteenth centuries, the pressure to clear the wastes and even a portion of the commons (*défrichement*) became irresistible. While the threat to the integrity of the commons during the late ancien regime stemmed mainly from seigneurial *triages*, bourgeois encroachments (*grignotage*) and physiocratic legislation, the challenge under the Empire, Restoration and July Monarchy took the form of creeping *défrichement* by plot-farmers desperately seeking the means of subsistence. The decline of sharecropping (*métayage*) and rural handicrafts encouraged this trend towards micro-property. Large landowners deplored the tilling of verges, drove roads, sheep-runs and rocky slopes and accused the *colons*[35] of a variety of sins ranging from spoiling the market for day labour to destroying the soil structure by spade cultivation, but to little effect. On the stony and arid, but otherwise fertile, *causses* tillage became a veritable mania. At La Cavalerie[36] on the Causse du Larzac obsessive clearing of waste and common – encouraged in part by the *arrêté* of 1767 which exempted reclaimed land from the tithe and royal impositions – threatened to dislocate the local economy completely. Rich flock-owners unctuously preached respect for ancient custom and defended grazing rights on common, fallow and stubble; peasant cultivators ignored the prescriptions concerning tillage and hacked fields out of the pasture more or less at will. Meanwhile, the Commander of the Order of Malta which had originally ceded one of the commons, subject to certain conditions, actively encouraged the clearers in the knowledge that their industry would swell seigneurial revenues. Indeed, the Commander, Mirabeau,[37] went further and in 1779 divided up this common on a basis which foreshadowed the egalitarian legislation of the Revolution.

Often the big proprietors found themselves the victims of their own example, although they rarely viewed their plight as objectively. In the *causse* around Sévérac (Aveyron) wealthy landowners had repeatedly encroached upon the commons and had never been held to account. The

---

[34] J.-B. Meyronneinc, 'Des communautés villageoises aux sections de communes: l'exemple de quelques communes du Devès et de Margeride', Université de Clermont-Ferrand, Institut de géographie, Mémoire de maîtrise, 1975, pp. 22–3 and table.

[35] For example, Cabrières *fils*, 'Sur l'état de la domesticité en France et particulièrement dans le département de l'Aveyron', *Annales de l'agriculture française*, 32 (1807), 5–82.

[36] H. Guilhamon (ed.), *Journal des voyages en Haute-Guienne de J. F. Henry de Richeprey* (2 vols., Rodez, 1952, 1967), vol. I, pp. 120–7; vol. 2, pp. 461–3 and note. Also P. M. Jones, '*La République au Village* in the southern Massif Central, 1789–1799', *The Historical Journal*, XXIII (1980), 796.

[37] Jean-Antoine de Riqueti de Mirabeau, younger brother of the Marquis de Mirabeau and uncle of the revolutionary.

labourers and plot-holders of the *bourg* responded in 1793 by invoking their right to a statutory division and one of the commons was marked out for parcelling into 630 roughly equal plots.[38] The fate of this democratic initiative is unclear, but it probably came to grief in the political reaction following Thermidor.[39] At any event, popular pressure was renewed in the aftermath of the commotions of 1830. When a petition to the prefect demanding the punishment of the usurpers elicited no response, the commons were engulfed in a frenzy of unlicensed clearing. The municipal council requested immediate police action, but the higher authorities were embarrassed and unsure how to respond. As the *colons* were not slow to point out, the councillors were themselves the most notorious usurpers. 'Comment donc poursuivre les uns tandis qu'on laisserait les autres jouir en paix du fruit de leurs usurpations?'[40] noted the sub-prefect of Millau in a letter to his superior.

Bureaucrats and embattled councils packed with village bigwigs were apt to blame the 'mania' for *défrichement* on the laws of the Revolution just as, later in the century, they would blame the division of inheritances on the same source. In 1820 the prefect of the Lozère characterised the uncontrolled clearing of land as: 'une épidémie née des principes révolutionnaires qu'il sera très difficile de déraciner au moyen des voies ordinaires'.[41] In fact the problem of *défrichement* long ante-dated the Revolution in many districts of the southern Massif Central, and merely coincided with it in others. In the highest mountain communes, on the other hand, it only became a serious issue under the July Monarchy. Although egalitarianism and individualism were to make some inroads in the latter half of the nineteenth century, land clearance was a symptom of a quite separate development. Nearly all the evidence confirms that it was a sign of rapid population growth and, in some districts, of relative overpopulation.

In any case the pronouncements of the Revolution on the subject of common rights were far from monolithic and unremittingly radical. The apotheosis of private property in constitutional instruments was not translated into practice. Instead of disavowing the cautious tone of government policies in the late 1780s, the first revolutionary assemblies continued this pragmatic approach. The seigneurial right to alienate a portion of the commons (*droit de triage*) was swiftly revoked as a relic of the 'feudal complex', but *vaine pâture* and the *droit de parcours* were effectively retained. The Rural Code of 1791 merely removed the legal basis for these practices.

---

[38] A. D. Aveyron, 2E 275 24, Sévérac, partage des biens communaux des Fonds et dépendances, 22 Sept. 1793.

[39] See below p. 131.

[40] A.D. Aveyron, 48 J 35, Famille Rouvelet: correspondance, 14 July 1834.

[41] A.N. F II[le] Lozère 1, prefect of Lozère to Directeur général de l'administration communale et départementale, Mende, 17 Nov. 1820.

Indeed, although a procedure for contracting-in was progressively substituted for the facility to contract-out, *vaine pâture* was never abolished in the nineteenth century.

Conventional opinion had long preached the merits of converting commonland into private property by division and enclosure, but here, too, the revolutionaries were concerned to weigh the consequences of their actions. A decree passed on 14 August 1792 authorised the division of land held in common, but offered no guidance as to how this was to be accomplished. In effect, therefore, the measure did little more than reiterate the conditions that obtained in many provinces at the end of the ancien regime. The following year some of the ambiguities of this proposal were resolved by the law which is often regarded as the corner-stone of the agrarian legislation of the Revolution. The decree of 10 June 1793 seems, in fact, to have been a political gesture made at the height of a *sans-culotte* offensive in Paris. It empowered a municipality to convene a general assembly of all inhabitants in order to debate the division of non-wooded commonland into equal plots, 'par tête d'habitant domicilié',[42] regardless of age or sex. If a third or more of those attending opined in favour of division, it became compulsory. Former seigneurs who had previously invoked their 'right' of *triage* were excluded from the proceedings and a separate measure[43] stipulated that sectional commonland might only be divided among the inhabitants of the village or section to which it belonged. On 15 January 1794, a further decree extended the egalitarian principle of 'par tête d'habitant' to wood-cutting rights (*affouages*) in communal forests.

Although this legislation remained on the statute book until 20 thermidor X/8 August 1802, it was a product of the exceptional atmosphere of the Terror. Thermidor opened the door to a moderate reaction which, in the agrarian sphere, was manifested in a marked hostility towards equal *partage* and a doctrinaire attempt to withdraw meadows from the ambit of *vaine pâture*. Little commonland was divided up after 1794 and ways were found to forestall those divisions which had not already been implemented, or which had given rise to disputes. Finally, two laws passed on 21 prairial IV/9 June 1796 and 2 prairial V/21 May 1797 suspended indefinitely the alienation of the commons which the decree of 1793 had made possible. On 25 thermidor III/12 August 1795, meanwhile, the Thermidorean Convention took steps to enable proprietors to restrict access to the second growth of hay (*regain*) in their meadows. As for common woodland, systematic management had virtually ceased at the outbreak of the Revolution, but on 9 brumaire XIII/31 October 1804, even the principle of the 1794 reform was abandoned and *affouage* rights were graded according to ancient custom once more. The Imperial regime took steps to guarantee the commons against revolutionary encroachments and yet, paradoxically, was responsible for

[42] Section II, article one. [43] Law of 13 June 1793.

potentially the most damaging assault upon their integrity of all. Driven to
extremes by the financial strain of the Russian campaign, Napoleon initiated
the sale of commons put out to lease and the investment of the proceeds in a
sinking-fund which he could then raid.[44] The scheme caused deep resentment
in the countryside but, in the Lozère at least, few communes were actually
parted from their property.[45]

The impact of the decree of 10 June 1793 has been much discussed,[46] but
until a broad-based study of the agrarian history of the revolutionary and
Napoleonic epoch has been undertaken no firm conclusion can be reached.
In the southern Massif Central only a small number of villages sought to
implement the law. This was less an indication of general satisfaction concerning the way in which the commons were managed, than an acknowledgement of the pivotal position they occupied in the rural economy of the
region. In addition, it was possibly a sign that in the highland communes
where the most extensive pastures were located, population pressure had yet
to register significantly.[47] But there were marked local variations determined
by social as well as ecological factors. In the districts of the Puy-de-Dôme
bordering the fertile Limagne plain there was little resistance to division,
apparently,[48] while in the Ardèche[49] only five communes appear to have
acted upon the decree of 10 June 1793.

An analysis of the deliberations of communes and sections which did
proceed to divide up their commons brings to light a number of recurring
themes. *Partage* was often invoked where encroachment by local bigwigs had
got out of hand and caused ill-feeling, and it was invoked where an outlying
– but populous – village was too far away to send its stock to join the common herd and therefore was unable to benefit from common grazing. There
were other reasons, too, such as promiscuous grazing of sheep, cattle and pigs
which had so damaged the pasture that there was little choice but to plough
it up for arable use. The considerations which weighed against division have
largely to be inferred. Although the late eighteenth- and early nineteenth-
century plot-farmer persuaded cereal crops to grow in even the most hostile

44 On the abuses to which the law of 20 March 1813 was subject, see Tessier, *La valeur*, p. 41;
    Duby and Wallon (eds.), *Histoire de la France rurale*, vol. 3, pp. 127–30.
45 A.N. F³ II Lozère 1, prefect of Lozère to Directeur général de la comptabilité des communes
    et des hospices, Mende, 7 June 1813.
46 Tessier, *La valeur sociale*, pp. 139, 244–5; G. Bourgin, 'Les communaux et la Révolution
    française', *Nouvelle revue historique du droit français et étranger* (1908), 690–751; Soboul, 'Prob-
    lèmes de la communauté rurale', pp. 206–7; A. Ado, 'Le bilan agraire de la Révolution
    française', *Cahiers d'histoire de l'institut Maurice Thorez*, vol. 37 (1978), p. 46.
47 See R.-J. Bernard, 'Démographie et comportements démographiques en Haute-Lozère,
    XVIIᵉ–XVIIIᵉ–XIXᵉ siècles', *Revue du Gévaudan*, NS, 21 (1975), 99–100.
48 M. Laurent, 'Le partage des communaux à Ennezat à l'époque révolutionnaire', *Revue
    d'Auvergne*, 92 (1978), 171.
49 P. Bozon, *La vie rurale en vivarais: étude géographique* (Valence, 1963), p. 152.

of environments, the bulk of commonland in the southern Massif Central was fit only for pasture. This was a fact of nature which might exceptionally be questioned, but which always reasserted itself in the end.[50] Accordingly, communities were generally agreed on the mode of exploitation to which their commons were most suited. They bickered endlessly about conditions of access to the common herd or flock, but decisions affecting the balance between arable and pasture were rarely a matter for genuine choice. Cereal production on thin soils required large quantities of manure; manure pre-supposed animals and – in the absence of fodder crops and stall-feeding – animals presupposed pasture. Even where commons were divided, whether in 1793 or in the late nineteenth century with the trend towards temporary parcellisation[51] (*allotissement*), this cycle was rarely subverted. Few com-munities countenanced division unless they already possessed an adequate stock of pasture, or unless the interlocking components of subsistence agriculture had already begun to break down. The logic of the agro-pastoral economy was irrefutable and it demanded the retention of the commons.

While economic imperatives were clearly paramount some allowance should be made for social and political pressures, too. Village *notables* played an undoubted, if generally imponderable, role in the debate over the com-mons. At Chaudesaigues (Cantal) the proprietorial bourgeoisie welcomed the law of 10 June 1793 until it discovered the principle upon which the division was to be based: 'le mode décrété est désastreux et impraticable, les domes-tiques acquièrent une propriété dans une commune où ils n'ont aucune habitation au détriment des propriétaires qui les salarient'.[52] This was prob-ably a common reaction; certainly landowners in this region were quick to condemn the egalitarian legislation as soon as it became safe to do so after Thermidor. What was beyond immediate redress at the parliamentary level could, in any case, be sabotaged at the local level by procrastination and law suits in most instances. Many projected divisions were abandoned as a result of this kind of pressure. A few proved more tenacious and survived for a time the attacks of the rural bourgeoisie and the Thermidorean administra-tion. Their slow demise illustrates well the ambivalence of the Directory and the Consulate towards the agrarian heritage of the Revolution.

The three largest villages of the commune of Estables[53] (Lozère) voted to split up their commons in or around messidor II/June–July 1794. In the

---

[50] The experience of land clearance for arable cultivation in the Lozère in the late nineteenth century demonstrated that, 'à 1400 mètres d'altitude les résultats sont nuls et donnent lieu aux plaintes des paysans. A partir de 1,250 mètres l'expérience prouve qu'ils n'occasionnent que des déceptions; le sol reste en friche, la culture étant impossible': Tessier, *La valeur sociale*, p. 280.

[51] See below pp. 144–5.

[52] A. Rigaudière, E. Zylberman and R. Mantel, *Etudes d'histoire économique rurale au XVIIIᵉ siècle* (Paris, 1965), p. 52.

[53] A.N. F³ II Lozère 4, dossier for Estables.

ensuing ballots the plots appear to have been distributed 'par tête', except at La Bastide where the villagers ignored the terms of the law of 10 June 1793 and proceeded on a household basis. Little is known of the *prise de conscience* which precipitated this unusual step. Estables was situated in cattle and sheep country: almost all of its commonland lay at altitudes in excess of 1,200 metres and was quite unsuited to prolonged arable cultivation. Nor was the commune especially populous, unlike Le Malzieu[54] to the north, where in July 1793 a significant minority of *bourg* artisans and labourers had opined in favour of division. Some indication of what may have happened is contained in a hostile *mémoire* published by local proprietors in the course of the Year V (1796–1797). They alleged that, 'ces partages ont été le fruit des manoeuvres clandestines pratiqués par trois ou quatre individus seulement et notamment par Velay et Chassary experts, ce dernier secrétaire de la commune qui dans le temps où tout paroissoit permis aux intriguants, surpris quelques signatures'.[55] Evidence, perhaps, of a coterie of village jacobins led by two individuals who had everything to gain from a demarcation of the commons.

Be that as it may, the conflict over types of communal exploitation (*jouissance*) at Estables became something of a trial of strength under the Directory, pitting proprietor against small peasant and the Ministry of the Interior against the recalcitrant authorities of the department. On the first *jour complémentaire* of Year IV/17 September 1796, the malevolently royalist *administration centrale* of the Lozère passed a measure unilaterally revoking the *partages* carried out in accordance with the legislation of the Terror. The plot-holders were dispossessed and triumphant flock-owners drove their beasts onto the arable. In the subsequent polemical exchanges the issues at stake became much clearer. The 'gros tenanciers' argued that, since the commons were originally a seigneurial concession in return for a *censive* assessed on landholding they had, in effect, purchased a right of privileged access to the commons which the egalitarian principle of the law of 10 June 1793 had flouted. They also pointed out all manner of irregularities in the execution of the decree. The 'petits tenanciers' retorted that the landowners had agreed to abide by the decision to divide and enclose at the time; that since 1789 the tax burden on the commons had been levied uniformly upon all beneficiaries whether rich or poor, and that the proprietors were employing underhand means to secure their economic position as monopoly suppliers of grain to the local population. Velay, one of the architects of the *partage*, complained that these village bigwigs had replaced the seigneurs to all intents and purposes: 'le gros tenancier accoutumé à nous vendre les

54 C. Riffaterre, 'Les revendications économiques et sociales des assemblées primaires de juillet 1793', *Bulletin trimestriel, Commission de recherche et de publication des documents relatifs à la vie économique de la Révolution* (1906), pp. 332, 362.

55 A.N. F³ Lozère 4, *mémoire que les gros tenanciers du lieu d'Estables fournissent à l'appui de l'arrêté de l'administration centrale du Département de la Lozère en datte du 1ᵉʳ complémentaire de l'an 4ᵐᵉ.*

denrées bien cher sont intéressés [*sic*] à ce que l'abondance ne vienne jamais d'un très grand nombre de défrichements'.[56]

The *administration centrale* of the department, meanwhile, was taken to task by the Ministry for straying beyond its authority and issuing an *arrêté* which formally contradicted the law of 21 prairial IV. Far from retreating, however, the department compounded its non-compliance as the tide of reaction flowed ever more fiercely throughout the Year V. How consistently the administration prosecuted this policy during the years that followed is unclear, but the wrangle seems to have continued into the Consulate. From a letter of the Minister of the Interior addressed to Jerphanion, the first prefect of the Lozère, it would appear that the prefecture had confirmed (or reinstated) the *administration centrale*'s retrospective prohibition of *partages*. The 'petits tenanciers' persisted in their efforts to obtain redress, but the ultimate fate of their enterprise is not recorded. It may be guessed at, however. In the commune of Fournels[57] on the north-western frontier of the department, an egalitarian division had also been overturned in the Year V and the commons reverted to pasture. Ironically, the law of 9 ventôse XII/29 February 1804, which marked a final attempt to stabilise the contentious legacy of the Revolution in this field, inspired the dispossessed with fresh hope. At the instigation of poor plot-holders the sub-prefect of Marvejols conducted an enquiry and concluded that the original division had been legal after all. The prefecture enshrined this decision in an *arrêté* which threatened to rekindle old animosities in the commune and in several other localities. However, the case was evoked before the *Conseil d'Etat* which ruled, on 12 July 1806, that the revolutionary *partage* of the commons of Fournels was invalid.

Even if the attempts to convert the pastures of Estables and Fournels into private property had been allowed to proceed, it is doubtful whether the experiment would have survived for long. Division was a desperate remedy espoused by poor peasants who could find no other way of gaining sufficient access to the commons. Quite apart from the rational objections to land clearance at high altitude, there existed an engrained prejudice against short-sighted solutions of the kind proposed. In some villages at least, there was a sense in which the commons defined the community. They were a patrimony for the use of each succeeding generation which it would be immoral to alienate. Unusually, this conviction was put into words by the municipal councillors of Chanaleilles (Haute-Loire) when, in 1868, several inhabitants of the village of Le Villeret d'Apchier requested a division of the common-land:

l'on peut se demander ici où en seraient plusieurs familles actuelles si les anciennes ne consultant que leur seul intérêt avaient largement profité des lois qui à une certaine époque avaient autorisé le partage ou la vente des communaux qui nourissent tant de

---

[56] Ibid., Velay to Minister of the Interior, Mende, 27 flor. year V.
[57] Ibid., dossier for Fournels.

bêtes bovines et ovines et d'où l'on retire par des défriches, céréales et pommes de terre . . .[58]

Indeed, when *partage* had been mooted in the commune on 20 prairial II/8 June 1794,[59] only one inhabitant voted in favour.

Legislative innovations on the subject of enclosures provoked a more energetic reaction. Along the southern and south-eastern escarpments of the Massif Central, the right of *vaine pâture*, or *compascuité* as it was sometimes called, was stubbornly defended by the peasantry. The Parlement of Toulouse had attempted to restrict and even abolish it several times in the eighteenth century, but on each occasion the mountain dioceses successfully invoked 'immemorial rights'.[60] Even the freedom to enclose and thereby withdraw meadows, vines and chestnut orchards from common pasturing was by no means generally established. Moves to hinder the passage of the common flock brought swift retaliation and such was the interlocking complexity of grazing customs that communities and parishes could not easily step out of line. In 1785, efforts to reduce the *droit de parcours* on the Causse de Gramat[61] produced a minor rebellion. Landowners clearly expected the Revolution to bring relief from onerous *servitudes* which in bad years might deprive them of the entire yield of their grass land. In a petition to the National Assembly, the Comte de Rochefort[62] argued that it was unfair that tenants should be entitled to redeem their seigneurial obligations whilst landowners were unable to escape from common rights. Such pleas went unanswered until 1795 when the problem of the meadows was tackled once more. It was one thing to legislate that the proprietor was the sole owner of his hay crop and quite another to enforce it, however. The measure was fiercely resisted and nowhere more so than in the Monts du Velay. At Allègre[63] (Haute-Loire) enclosures were demolished and the *regains* consumed by the common herd on three occasions – in 1796, 1801 and 1802. The municipality called for troops and the *juge de paix*, who happened to be one of the largest proprietors, handed out fines, but to little avail. Similar incidents were reported from the commune of Cayres[64] (Haute-Loire) and from near Pradelles[65] (Haute-Loire).

[58] Meyronneinc, 'Des communautés villageoises', p. 45.

[59] Ibid.

[60] Bloch, 'La lutte pour l'individualisme agraire . . .', pp. 609–11; Appolis, 'La question de la vaine pâture en Languedoc . . .', pp. 110–21; G. Frêche, *Toulouse et la région Midi-Pyrénées au siècle des lumières vers 1670–1789* (Mayenne, 1974), pp. 276–8.

[61] Guilhamon (ed.), *Journal des voyages*, vol. 2, p. 100 and note 40.

[62] P. Sagnac and P. Caron, *Les Comités des droits féodaux et de législation et l'abolition du régime seigneurial (1789–1793)* (Paris, 1907), p. 169, *doléances du Comte de Rochefort, commandant des Cévennes*, Marvejols, 29 March 1790.

[63] M. Saby, *Allègre et sa région au fil des siècles* (Le Puy, 1976), pp. 167, 274–7.

[64] R. Chamonard, 'Les structures agraires du Velay occidental', *Cahiers de la Haute-Loire* (1967), p. 173.

[65] A.D. Haute-Loire 154 0 III Petition of Jean Guilhon, *propriétaire foncier* to prefect of Haute-Loire, Pradelles, August 1808.

If, by and large, the rural community vindicated its claim upon the meadows, landlord hegemony over the commons survived until late in the century. When, in 1874, the prefect of the Haute-Loire revoked a resolution of the municipality of Bains which graded access to the commons against tax contribution, it marked the waning of an era. 'Je ne puis approuver la disposition délibérée par votre conseil', he observed, 'qui porte que le nombre de bêtes que chaque propriétaire sera autorisée à faire paître dans les communaux sera proportionnel à l'impôt. Cette disposition est illégale, les communaux appartiennent indistinctement à tous les habitants, les pauvres y ont autant droit que les riches'.[66] The poor had always shared an ancient conviction that it was sufficient to be a member of the community in order to profit from the commons, but this was only superficially the case. Considerable disparities existed between and within communities. Access and the question of membership (*ayant-droit*) were matters settled by convention and hence susceptible to abuse.

The custom of the Auvergne was formal on the subject. One could put out to graze on the commons the beasts '. . . que l'on a hiverné et nourri des foins et pailles provenant des héritages qu'on l'on tient'.[67] This condition, known as the rule of *foins et pailles*, applied generally throughout the southern Massif Central. Technically it excluded from the commons the stock of any peasant who was not a proprietor, or at least a householder, with more than a plot of land. In practice the rule was bent slightly and landed proprietors allowed the poor to add a small number of animals to the common herd. The management of the commons acquired, thus, an eminently censitary character. Access was geared to taxation or landholding, which amounted to the same thing. Briefly, during the Revolution, these restrictive practices were relaxed and in pastures earmarked for division they succumbed altogether. But the 'tête d'habitant' principle was not without ambiguity as the strictures of the bourgeoisie of Chaudesaigues[68] made plain, and the resultant confusion gave strength to those who opposed any alteration in the existing agrarian regime. As the egalitarian impulse was neutralised, the censitary custom which enabled large landowners to treat the commons as an extension of their own property revived. At Laguiole[69] (Aveyron), an assembly of inhabitants had voted overwhelmingly for the division of a large area of commonland in August 1793. The municipality, which was dominated by large proprietors engaged in a lucrative fat-stock and sheep-rearing trade, blocked the decision. By 1810 the *status quo ante* was fully restored and the municipality promulgated a new *compoix cabaliste* for sheep grazing on the commons. Access to

---

[66] Meyronneinc, 'Des communautés villageoises', p. 37.
[67] Parain, 'Contribution à une problématique', p. 53.
[68] See above, p. 133.
[69] *L'Aubrac: étude ethnologique, linguistique, agronomique et économique d'un établissement humain* (4 vols., 1970–3), vol. 2, pp. 78, 91.

the common flock was geared to the tax roll. Proprietors were licensed to pasture between 20 and 250 animals, whilst non-proprietors – mere inhabitants – were limited to 6.

From the point of view of the poor peasant, the struggle for agrarian individualism seemed to have been lost by the end of the Empire. The division of commonland in order to facilitate private cultivation had not been ardently desired in the southern Massif Central. But where such a desire had been formulated, it had often been thwarted. More widespread had been the ambition to revise the conditions of admission to the common flock but, on this front, too, there had been little apparent change. In fact, if not in name, the custom of *foins et pailles* continued to apply for much of the nineteenth century. No government, indeed, would return to the strictly egalitarian agrarian legislation of the Montagnard Convention. Future measures would seek to conciliate the rights of the family or household groups and not those of individuals. The law of 18 July 1837, which first introduced the principle of leasehold sub-division of commonland, conferred the status of *ayant-droit* on resident family heads (*chefs de famille*) rather than proprietors. But if the exclusive rights of the proprietor were thereby challenged, those of the individual were by no means vindicated. In 1896, the *conseil municipal* of Pelouse[70] (Lozère) refused to lease a communal allotment to Charles Antoine because the petitioner lived with his father and did not, therefore, constitute an independent household.

The most bitter disputes over grazing rights occurred in the communes situated along the Margeride spine where the cultivation of cereals at exceptionally high altitudes coexisted with extensive sheep pastures. Commonland accounted for up to a third of the territory of parishes such as Arzenc-de-Randon, Saint-Jean-la-Fouillouse, Chaudeyrac and Luc in the north-eastern Lozère and up to two-thirds of the adjacent parishes of the Ardèche (Cellier-du-Luc, Saint-Etienne-de-Lugdarès and Le Plagnal). These mountain communities were rarely capable of overwintering sufficient stock to exploit fully their herbage and during the summer months they took in transhumant flocks driven up from the Languedoc plain. In the 1880s, when transhumance was beyond its peak, the Lozère provided pasture for between 250,000 and 300,000 lowland sheep annually, to which should be added an indigenous flock of similar proportions.[71] The seasonal invasion of sheep brought with it the indispensable adjunct to arable cultivation: dung. As far as the peasants were concerned this was the principal object of the exercise, although the lowland shepherds generally paid a money rent for the use of the pastures as well. The collection and distribution of the manure was achieved by means

---

[70] A.D. Lozère 2 o 1104, Administration et comptabilité communales: Pelouse.

[71] Fel, *Les Hautes Terres du Massif Central*..., p. 271; P. Léon et al., *Histoire économique et sociale*, vol. 3 (2), p. 700. In 1846, according to the minutes of the *conseil général* of the Lozère, approximately 800,000 transhumant sheep and 200,000 cattle pastured in the department.

of an elaborate system of night folding of the animals (*nuits de fumature*) on the property of each *ayant droit*. The common flock was deployed in the same way. The rota for folding became the object of considerable in-fighting.

In the seventeenth and eighteenth centuries the mountain communities fought long and costly court cases with their seigneurs over the apportionment of the *nuits de fumature*. Led by a rural bourgeoisie of well-to-do proprietors and village notaries and lawyers, they generally carried the day, but only to fall into the clutches of these self-appointed guardians. By the mid-nineteenth century the issue had become more complex, as anarchic clearings threatened to spoil the sheep-runs. The wealthy landowners, who had appropriated the lion's share of the *nuits de fumature* during earlier anti-seigneurial struggles, justified their retention by invoking the rule of *foins et pailles*, whilst the growing numbers of plot-holders practised a miserable, manureless and shifting agriculture on the edge of the common. In the commune of Chaudeyrac the mayor, Vital Augustin Dubois, waged a relentless campaign against local land-clearers and the information he gathered on their activities and grievances serves to underline the close relationship between demographic growth, arable cultivation and the *nuits de fumature*.

In the village of Le Cheylard-L'Evêque[72] (commune of Chaudeyrac), significant population increase did not begin to register until the Empire – a characteristic shared by a number of communities in the north-eastern Lozère.[73] On the eve of the Revolution, the village comprised about sixty families, but by 1831 this figure had risen to seventy-eight. A small portion of the commonland had always been cultivated by the poor, and at first the growth was accommodated without any recorded signs of stress. Around 1827, however, large-scale land clearing commenced which, by 1831, had reduced the area under pasture by half. Seriously alarmed, the half-dozen principal proprietors petitioned the prefect for redress. Led by Dubois, they complained that the precious *nuits de fumature* were being jeopardised. Originally, the commons, together with private property subject to *vaine pâture*, had been capable of nourishing a Languedoc flock of 1,300 beasts in addition to the village flock of about 400. Since the clearing, this capacity had been reduced by about a third. The *colons* protested their need for plough land upon which to grow cereals, potatoes and root vegetables, but their pleas were brushed aside by the prefect, who called in surveyors to draw up a fresh rota for *nuits de fumature* based upon the common pasture remaining and the territory contributed by each proprietor to *vaine pâture*. This detailed list of landholdings makes plain the balance of power in the community: forty-three households owned under an *arpent* (3,419 square metres) of land each and of these twenty-seven owned 3 perches (103 square metres) or less, that

[72] For this paragraph, see A.D. L. 2 0 484; 2 0 510.
[73] Bernard, 'Démographie et comportements démographiques', pp. 99–100.

is to say just a house and garden. The mayor, Dubois, was by far the largest landowner. His property was three times as extensive as that of his nearest rival and eight times that of the third largest proprietor. The proposed allocation of *nuits de fumature* naturally took account of this state of affairs. Those who contributed no land for grazing could not expect to reap any benefits therefrom. As the major proprietor and flock-owner, Dubois took twenty-eight *nuits* from the village flock, his nearest rival eight and fifteen other landowners smaller fractions. The manure of the Languedoc flock was divided in approximate fashion with Dubois receiving twenty-one *nuits*. In each case, the remaining sixty-three families (81 per cent of the community) were entirely excluded. In conditions such as these, it is hardly surprising that *défrichement* continued to be a problem in the sections of Chaudeyrac throughout the 1830s and 1840s; the poor had very little to lose.[74]

The struggle between flock-owners and plot-holders at Le Cheylard-L'Evêque was complicated by a dispute over common rights in the neighbouring forest of Mercoire.[75] For centuries, the eleven adjacent communities had shared privileged access to the forest in order to pasture stock and cut forage and wood. Shortly before the Revolution a large portion of the forest had passed into private hands as a result of sales by the Polignac family, and in 1794 the remaining portion followed suit when the estates of the Abbey of Mercoire were auctioned as *biens nationaux*. The local inhabitants exploited the change of ownership and the confusion of the revolutionary epoch to extend their customary rights and, for a brief period, they virtually occupied the forest. By the end of the Empire, however, the implications of unrestricted access were becoming apparent to all. The communities drew up fresh *affouage* regulations, based on landholding and tax contribution naturally, and settled down to enjoy a period of more prudent management. The new owners felt neither bound nor inclined to admit the 'immemorial rights' of a peasant society which acknowledged only customary law, however. They refused to recognise the *affouages* and established guards to bar access to their woodland. With the discreet support of resident flock-owners, they even encouraged the felling of trees in the belief that the 'forest' was more valuable as private pasture which could be leased to the Languedoc flocks than as a source of commercial timber. Throughout the Restoration, there were clashes between the *ayant droit* communities and the forest guards. Each autumn as the season for wood-cutting approached, tension rose as apprehensive peasants were arrested whilst trying to collect their winter firewood.

74 For similar disputes over the allocation of *nuits de fumature*, see A.D. Lozère 2 0 484, Villeneuve de Mercoire (commune of Chaudeyrac); A.D. Lozère 2 0 1292, Le Charzel (commune of Saint Alban); A.D. Lozère 2 0 438, Daufage (commune of Chasseradès); A.D. Haute-Loire 234 9 III, Rognac (commune of Saugues) and Rouliac.

75 P.-M. Weyd, *Les forêts de la Lozère* (Paris, 1911), pp. 139–45; A.N. BB16 423, prefect of Lozère to Minister of Justice, Mende, 25 July 1819; F7 4065 *Rapports de gendarmerie, Lozère*, November 1829, August 1830, September 1831.

In November 1829, the gendarmerie reported widespread rebellion in the communes bordering the forest of Mercoire.

The conflict over the exploitation of forest and woodland brought the competing interests of private landlord and rural community into especially sharp focus. The struggles surrounding the forest of Mercoire were reproduced in many parts of the southern Massif Central. Indeed, they were endemic to every region of southern France[76] in which the traditional rural economy still held sway and would not be swiftly resolved. As a rule proprietors were concerned to consolidate rather than delete their holdings of timber – the case of the Margeride with its intensive arable cultivation, poor quality woodland and accessibility to transhumant flocks is unusual. Everywhere the consequences were similar, however; a round of assaults and unending litigation as communities sought to vindicate in the courts a much older concept of property.

The most acrimonious, violent and prolonged disputes were fought over forests which had become public property during the Revolution. Although the state was slower than private proprietors in applying a policy of conservation, it proved much the more formidable and resourceful adversary. With the promulgation of the Forest Code in 1827 and its vigorous enforcement in this region from the 1840s, the degrees of anarchy which had prevailed in state forests since the Revolution were rapidly curbed. The change of regime came as a considerable psychological shock in a number of districts. In joyfully invading the woods as the old forest administration (*Maîtrise des Eaux et Forêts*) crumbled after 1789, many communities mistook physical possession for legal title. Some even destroyed the charters detailing their *affouage* rights on the anti-feudal pyres of 1793 and 1794. This had happened in the Aubrac,[77] where the state had withheld from auction the wooded assets of the Domerie d'Aubrac. As the original donors, the monks had never disputed the *affouage* rights of the eight contiguous communities situated at the junction of the borders of the Aveyron, the Cantal and the Lozère, but the state forest bureaucracy was not so minded. Two of the *ayant droit* communities in the Lozère were involved in litigation for forty years before their wood-cutting rights were recognised in 1842.

The residue of problems stemming from the revolutionary epoch had scarcely been resolved before the state added afforestation to its policy of stabilisation and amelioration of existing woodlands. In this area, the

---

[76] Forest disturbances in the Pyrenees have received much attention, see notably, L. Clarenc, 'Le code de 1827 et les troubles forestiers dans les Pyrénées centrales au milieu du XIXe siècle', *Annales du Midi*, vol. 77 (1965), pp. 293–317; J. M. Merriman, 'The Demoiselles of the Ariège, 1829–1831', in J. M. Merriman (ed.), *1830 in France* (New York, 1975), pp. 87–118. For conflicts over forest management in Provence, see M. Agulhon, *La République au village* (Paris, 1972), pp. 49–92.

[77] Weyd, *Les forêts de la Lozère*, p. 146; *L'Aubrac: étude ethnologique*, vol. 2, pp. 99–100; A.D. Lozère 2 0 876, Administration et comptabilité communales: Malbouzon, contentieux.

governments of the nineteenth century exhibited a dynamism and determination to intervene which contrasts strikingly with their cautious attitude on the subject of common rights. The first afforestation schemes (*reboisement*) were stimulated by the Forest Code and applied to rocky outcrops and wasteland. They were justified on ecological grounds as a means of arresting soil erosion and guarding against landslips and flash-flooding. In 1830, the first of 13,765 hectares of pines were planted along the slopes of Mount Aigoual in the Cévennes and in 1850 a similar operation began on the Montagne du Goulet at the southern extremity of the Margeride chain.[78] Such enterprises aroused little opposition because they did not conflict with traditional agricultural practices, but the same could not be said of subsequent schemes. In 1860, the Imperial government promulgated the first in a series of measures[79] to promote afforestation, partly as a long-term commercial exercise and partly, it would seem, as an indirect assault upon commonland which conventional wisdom insisted was under-exploited. Subject to certain conditions, uncultivated private and common land was made liable to compulsory afforestation and the agents of the forest administration were instructed to carry out a survey and assessment of the territory of every commune.[80]

In the southern Massif Central the bulk of uncultivated land was not waste, but unenclosed pasture closely geared to cereal production, and the communes reacted with dismay, prevarication and concealment. Dismay turned to anger as forestry workers arrived to fence off pastures and plant seeds or seedlings in the turf. As a coordinated scheme to plant both the Haute-Loire and Ardèche flanks of Mont Mézenc gathered momentum, the impoverished villages situated on its slopes watched their highland pastures grow slimmer. The inhabitants of the hamlet of Les Pradoux[81] (Ardèche) warned the prefect that they would have to sell their stock which would leave them destitute, but his attention was focused on the long-term benefits and he refused to intervene. The afforestation of the Mézenc seems to have passed off without serious violence and in 1879 an English traveller[82] reported trekking through a forest of infant pine trees. Further south, however, there were bloody confrontations. At Loubaresse[83] (Ardèche) in the Tanargue, extensive highland pastures provided the wherewithal to nourish 1,700 transhumant sheep

---

[78] Fel, *Les hautes terres du Massif Central* . . ., p. 258; Duby and Wallon (eds.), *Histoire de la France rurale*, vol. 3, p. 198.

[79] Laws of 28 July 1860; 8 June 1864 and 4 April 1882.

[80] A.N. F¹⁰ 2315 Agriculture: mise en valeur des communaux, enquête de 1860, dossiers for the Aveyron and the Ardèche.

[81] A.D. Ardèche O series (unclassified) no. 109 Borée, petition of inhabitants of Les Pradoux (commune of Borée), 22 May 1864; *réclamation* of inhabitants of Tempeyrac (commune of La Rochette), 1862; *délibération* of municipal council of Borée, 7 May 1865.

[82] E. Barker, *Through Auvergne on Foot* (London, 1884), p. 116.

[83] A. Gleyze, 'La rébellion de 1877 à Loubaresse', *Revue du Vivarais*, vol. 61 (1957), pp. 106–13, 128–34.

and a village flock of 500. The forest administration proposed to annex approximately half of this territory and restrict the number of sheep grazing on the other half. When labourers arrived under armed escort in June 1877 to begin the planting, frantic villagers tried to disrupt the proceedings. The gendarmes shot one protester dead and several others received bayonet wounds. State-sponsored afforestation and supervision of existing woodland were widely regarded as an intolerable intrusion into the life of the rural community. Few government policies provoked as much anger and frustration in the course of the nineteenth century. When resistance and even rebellion proved fruitless, the peasantry demonstrated the depth of its disillusionment by systematically pillaging forests that were about to be subjected to the straitjacket control of the Forest Code. One night in 1903, the inhabitants of the village of Combret[84] (commune of Venteuges, Haute-Loire) hacked down 2,855 trees and bushes in a wood which had been earmarked for scientific management by forestry officials.

The restive spirit of agrarian individualism which Bloch detected in the 1760s and 1770s and which Soboul and others have associated with the egalitarian impulses of the Revolution did not have a significant impact upon the southern Massif Central until the second half of the nineteenth century. Although there were signs of a political awakening in the countryside by the end of the century, the process owed more to the profile of population growth during previous decades (see figure). The attack on the integrity of the commons and common rights was launched by poor plot-holders and squatters whose numbers had swollen dramatically since the Revolution. In effect, the roles of upholder and opponent of collective exploitation of commonland were becoming more fluid. At the end of the ancien regime, large proprietors had often championed division – secure in the knowledge that by *grignotage*, seigneurial and censitary privilege they would always receive the lion's share. The poor, for their part, generally favoured the retention of traditional forms of exploitation, despite the iniquitous rule of *foins et pailles*. Arable land was not at a premium, except in the valleys, and population congestion was not yet acute. By the 1870s, the balance of interests seeking advantage from the commons had shifted and attitudes began to change accordingly. As demographic pressure caused the rural economy to bulge at the seams and many traditional handicrafts contracted, competition for land – any land – on which to grow crops became intense. In place of *défrichement* which had caused such dissension in the 1830s and 1840s, the poor demanded the selective partition of commonland into individual, or rather family, plots. Confronted by a challenge to their social and economic pre-eminence in the community, the landlords fought a bitter rearguard action against *allotissement*. They claimed that plot cultivation wore

---

[84] Meyronneinc, 'Des communautés villageoises', p. 45.

out the soil and that the high administrative costs involved would nullify any short-term gains. More specifically, since they were often stock-owners and raisers with a commercial interest in the Languedoc flocks, as well as cultivators, they argued that even a modest partition would disrupt the sheep-runs and reduce the *nuits de fumature*.

The leasing of commonland *en bloc* as an alternative to collective exploitation had been encouraged during the Empire and the Restoration, but it

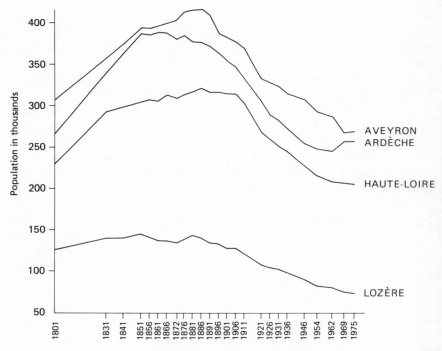

Population change in the southern Massif Central, 1801–1975

failed to evoke much enthusiasm in the southern Massif Central. In 1837,[85] a more flexible measure permitting the sub-division of commonland into small leasehold plots was passed. The plots or allotments were to be of equal value and allocated by ballot to every resident household for a maximum term of eighteen years. It was around this law, bolstered by subsequent legislation, that the struggle for agrarian individualism in the southern Massif Central crystallised.

In the Lozère, its impact is discernible from the 1870s. Petitions addressed

[85] See above, p. 138.

to the prefect by poor cultivators betrayed a growing impatience with the collective mode of exploitation of commonland. Even where the rule of *foins et pailles* had been successfully challenged, the rich continued to be the principal beneficiaries of common pasture by virtue of the quantity of stock they owned or leased. A state of affairs which had once appeared pre-ordained, now seemed intolerable. The battle over methods of exploitation was fought out in the municipal council for, although the commons were generally the property of the sections, their management fell within the competence of the commune.[86] Municipal jurisdiction in this sphere was enhanced further by legislation which vested the power to hire the common shepherd in the mayor.[87] Despite the latitude of the law, *allotissement* was usually the fruit of a long war of attrition by the poor. Deference, tradition and, until 1884, an imperfectly democratic system of local government, were obstacles not easily overcome. In 1868, pressure for a measure of *allotissement* in the section of Le Villeret (commune of Chanaleilles) was resisted by the municipality with the observations:

considérant que lorsque ces pâtures auront été morcelées en 40 ou 50 fractions, chaque famille verra bientôt, à son détriment quelle différence il y a entre ces vastes pâtures où tant d'animaux peuvent paître sans être exposés à passer sur les pâtures d'autrui, et ces petites fractions d'où à chaque moment ils pourront s'écarter sur les voisines . . .

and,

. . . considérant qu'il y a aussi fausseté ou grande exagération à dire que les riches profitent seuls des communaux . . .[88]

The villages of the southern Margeride and Mont Lozère provided summer pasture for transhumant flocks and the large proprietors were determined to resist any change that might curtail their stock-raising capacity. At Les Fagoux[89] (commune of Luc, Lozère), several inhabitants petitioned for an *allotissement* in 1876, but the municipal council ignored all pleas and leased the commons as it had in the past. The law proved a weak restraint when vital economic interests were at stake. At Chasseradès[90] (Lozère), the five principal landowners simply ignored the institutions of local government and unilaterally leased the commons to a Languedoc shepherd. The mayor and forty other households of the village learned of the arrangement only on the arrival of the flock in the spring. The five proprietors shared out the *nuits de fumature*. What became of the monetary element of the lease is not recorded, but it is far from certain that it benefited the whole community. In the

---

[86] Law of 18 July 1837, article 17.   [87] Law of 5 April 1884.

[88] Meyronneinc, 'Des communautés villageoises', p. 72.

[89] A.D. Lozère 2 0 864, Administration et comptabilité communales: Luc, petition of inhabitants of the section of Esfagoux (Les Fagoux) to prefect of Lozère, Les Fagoux, 17 Aug. 1876.

[90] A.D. Lozère 2 0 438, Administration et comptabilité communales: Chasseradès, mayor of Chasseradès to prefect of Lozère, Chasseradès, 29 June 1899; petition of inhabitants of Chasseradès to prefect of Lozère, Chasseradès, 25 June 1899.

Lozère, landowners generally contrived to impose a censitary distribution of the cash proceeds of leasing as well. When, in 1904, the inhabitants of the village of Chareylasse (commune of Altier) on Mont Lozère divided up the 608 francs 74 centimes paid as rent for their pastures, they did so disproportionately according to time-honoured custom. The prefect agreed to endorse the *procès-verbal*, but 'à titre exceptionnel'.[91]

Where the pressure for an egalitarian mode of exploitation of the commons proved irresistible, the local *notables* were forced to give way, but they did so slowly and tactically in the knowledge that municipal decisions could often be revoked at a later date. In 1870, the poor of the village of Laveis (commune of Venteuges) complained that, '. . . sur 17 maisons, 5 seulement profitent des communes parce qu'ils ont beaucoup de bêtes à envoyer au pacage, les autres sont pauvres et que même les riches, dont certains sont membres du Conseil municipal, chassent des pacages les bêtes des malheureux suppliants'.[92] Six years later, the municipality agreed to an *allotissement* in this section, but on condition that it should only run for six years. This stratagem seems to have been fairly frequently employed in the communes of the Margeride. In 1865, the municipality of La Villedieu[93] (Lozère) consented to an eight-year experimental *allotissement*. In the event many such experiments were renewed on expiration for a full eighteen-year term and again thereafter, but the arguments advanced by the defenders of traditional collective exploitation were not always coloured by self-interest. Sometimes the slopes cleared proved too high, too steep or too water-logged for arable cultivation;[94] often poor households were unable to meet their portion of the costs of the operation. Forced to lease his plot the moment he received it, the *colon* remained landless to all intents and purposes.[95] In the final analysis the pangs of land hunger were eased not by *allotissement*, but by the voluntary expatriation of tens of thousands of surplus mouths in the final decades of the nineteenth century.

Whatever their origins, the struggles over common rights had acquired a political dimension by the 1870s and 1880s. In a region in which the great landed proprietors were either Legitimists or Bonapartists, it was inevitable that the agitation for agrarian individualism should borrow some of the rhetoric, if not the substance, of republicanism. Political upheaval radicalised secular conflicts, endowed them with ideological reference points and thereby gave them a new lease of life. During the Revolution, and at intervals throughout the nineteenth century, the politics of opinion and slogan spilled

[91] A.D. Lozère 2 0 114, Administration et comptabilité communales: Altier, approbation of prefect of Lozère, Mende, 22 Nov. 1905. See, also, L. Aucoc, *Des sections de commune et des biens communaux qui leur appartiennent* (Paris, 1864), pp. 558–62.

[92] Meyronneinc, 'Des communautes villageoises', p. 72.

[93] Ibid., p. 73.   [94] See above note 50.

[95] A.D. Lozère 2 0 1104, Administration et comptabilité communales: Pelouse, extract of *délibération* of municipal council of Pelouse, 21 Oct. 1894.

into the countryside to produce a pale imitation of party alignments at the centre. But the ideological affiliations which disputes over the commons and common rights thus acquired were highly circumstantial and owed more to an identification made by anxious administrators than by the protagonists themselves. In the southern Massif Central, at least, there is scant evidence for a revolutionary umbilical linking the *partageurs* of 1793 with the *allotisseurs* of the 1870s and 1880s. When the upheaval of 1830 brought to a head disputes about the management of the commons in *bourgs* like Sévérac[96] or Campagnac[97] (Aveyron), it was the local sub-prefect who invoked the ideological precedents, not the *défricheurs*. 'L'esprit de trouble,' he enquired rhetorically, 'se réveille-t-il en France, et nos contrées doivent-elles subir son influence funeste de même que Lyon, St Etienne, Marseille, Paris?'[98]

With nuances, this pattern prevailed throughout the century. In the mountainous hinterland of southern France, commonland and collective agricultural practices were crucial to the functioning of the rural economy. They tended to focus village tensions and that tension was endemic. In moments of political crisis and expediency, local *notables* and officials projected their own intellectual stereotypes onto these conflicts. In the aftermath of the *coup d'état* of December 1851, the mayor of Le Recoux (Lozère) complained about the activities of a rabble-rouser named Pourquié who had encouraged the poor to demand the partition of the commons. Once the population had lived in harmony, he insisted, but, 'aujourd'hui il n'est plus ainsi; le parti qu'on nomme les rouges s'accroît d'un jour à l'autre . . .'[99]. The refrain is taken up again during the traumatic crisis of 1871. In the wake of the Paris Commune, the municipal council of Paulhac in the Haute-Loire resolved to liberalise the *foins et pailles* rule which had hitherto restricted access to the commune's rather exiguous pastures. Although the censitary principle governing the composition of the common flock (two sheep per hectare of private property) was not entirely repudiated, the right of poor households to put six sheep and one cow with calf on the common was vindicated. The riposte of the landlords was swift and uncompromising. A petition to the sub-prefect offered their interpretation of what had happened: 'ce conseil composé presque entièrement de gens imbus des tristes doctrines du club de Brioude [a centre of democratic propaganda] dont ils ont été les zélés auditeurs et qui n'a dû sa très faible majorité dans les dernières élections qu'en faisant des promesses mensongères telles que partage des communaux

[96] See above pp. 129–30.

[97] A.D. Aveyron 48 J 33 Famille Rouvelet: correspondance, mayor of Campagnac to sub-prefect of Millau, Campagnac, 15 Apr. 1835.

[98] A.D. Aveyron 48 J 35, Famille Rouvelet: correspondance, sub-prefect of Millau to prefect of Aveyron, Millau, 1 March 1834.

[99] A.D. Lozère IVM⁴ 10–12, Elections législatives, 1849–1852, mayor of Le Recoux to sub-prefect of Florac, Le Recoux, 27 Sept. 1852.

... profite aujourd'hui ...'[100] In a letter to the prefect, the mayor rejected this gratuitous politicisation of the issues: 'on veut abuser de votre bonne foie [*sic*] en nous fessant passer pour des communants [communards]'.[101]

The pseudo-politicisation of communal tensions was most pronounced in the Lozère during the early years of the Third Republic. The growing imbalance of subsistence agriculture and commercial stock-raising has already been noted, but in the 1880s the department became the theatre for an exceptionally bitter conflict between church and state as well. The struggle contaminated municipal government and added a further dimension to every local issue. In 1892, a routine squabble over the arrangements for leasing pastures belonging to the village of Mirandol (commune of Chasseradès) to the Languedoc shepherds became the pretext for a general call-to-arms in the commune. The municipality stood accused of having under-rented the herbage of its dependent section and the prefect was urged to use his power to revoke the lease. The aggrieved inhabitants presented their case in terms calculated to evoke the sympathy of the administration. In a letter to an unnamed official in the prefecture, one local landowner painted a dire picture of ideological confrontation: 'Je prends la respectueuse liberté de vous prier de vouloir bien, dans l'intérêt du parti républicain de la C[ommu]ne de Chasseradès, *faire vos possibles* pour que la police de la ferme des des terrains communaux de *Mirandol* ne soit pas approuvée par Monsieur le Préfet. Parmi tant de tripotages à l'actif de ce conseil il seroit à désirer qu'il en échoue un [*des derniers* !]'.[102]

The administration was by no means the dupe of such clever pleading or the alarmist reports of minor functionaries. Amid the rival accusations of disloyalty, the authorities believed what it suited them to believe. In the embattled atmosphere of the Lozère in the late nineteenth century, it was not implausible to view the behaviour of the municipality of Chasseradès as a clerico-legitimist conspiracy against the republicans of Mirandol. On the other hand, when the sub-prefect of Florac passed on to the prefect the complaints of the mayor of Le Recoux in 1852 he omitted the political dimension altogether.[103] Sometimes the administration was itself instrumental in harnessing the question of common rights to the broader issues of party strategy. This was particularly the case during the Second Empire when the prefectoral corps acted as an electoral organisation quite openly. In the commune of La Cresse[104] (Aveyron) where a number of the inhabitants were calling for an

---

[100] A.D. Haute-Loire 147 0 III, Paulhac: biens communaux, 1845–1951, 'inhabitants and electors' of Paulhac to sub-prefect of Brioude, Paulhac, 2 July 1871.

[101] Ibid., Mayor of Paulhac to prefect of Haute-Loire, Paulhac, 15 July 1871.

[102] A.D. Lozère 2 0 438, Administration et comptabilité communales: Chasseradès, Rabanit to *chef de division* (prefecture of the Lozère), Belvezet, 12 March 1892.

[103] See above p. 147 and note 99.

[104] A.D. Aveyron 5 M 10 Elections législatives, correspondance, 1863: *mémoire* on commune of La Cresse.

allotissement of the pastures, the agents of the official candidate promised his best offices and a contribution towards the costs involved should he be returned in the legislative elections of 1863.

It is difficult to discern a coherent and sustained assault upon the commons and common rights in the southern Massif Central and a corresponding growth of agrarian individualism. Nevertheless, a few instances in which division was both prompted and accompanied by an authentic *prise de conscience* have been documented. The precocious example of La Cavalerie[105] has already been mentioned and is discussed elsewhere;[106] more remarkable, perhaps, were the villages squatting on the edge of the rich pastures of the Aubrac plateau. For reasons which are obscure, but which may owe something to demographic trends, the communities on the Aveyron side of the plateau were slower to challenge the traditional methods of exploiting the commons than were their counterparts in the Lozère and the Cantal.[107] In the Aveyron, on the other hand, the revolt against landlord domination seems to have left a deeper imprint upon the psyche of the small peasantry. The revolution in modes of *jouissance* began in the 1900s. At Les Enfruts,[108] the highest and most northerly village of the commune of Saint Chély-d'Aubrac, *allotissement* was conceded in 1905 and each household received a 4-hectare plot; at Born,[109] a section of the commune of Prades-d'Aubrac, the reform was pushed through in the same year. The evidence is most plentiful on the subject of the village of Born and it is clear that in this community the attack on ancient practice was the product of a sudden political awakening instilled from outside. During a by-election campaign in 1904, a plot-holder pinned to the door of his cottage the *profession de foi* of the local 'red' (Republican) candidate. Several months later the same individual went to see the deputy whilst he was passing through Saint-Geniez and the partition of the commons was set in motion as a result of that encounter.

Communal tenure and *vaine pâture* were twin pillars of an agrarian system which retained its vitality throughout the nineteenth century. When subsistence agriculture reached its limits, it was demographic and settlement patterns that faltered and not the mode of production. *Allotissement* represented a compromise between individualism and collectivism, between a rural bourgeoisie of proprietors and flock owners and a rural proletariat of plot-farmers. Yet much commonland continued to be exploited jointly as heath and rough grazing. Indeed, arable cultivation of the commons was

---

[105] See above p. 129.

[106] Jones, '*La République au Village* in the Southern Massif Central', p. 796.

[107] *L'Aubrac: étude ethnologique*, vol. 2, pp. 102–3 and A.D. Cantal o 241, La Trinitat; o 216, Saint Urcize.

[108] C. Royer, 'Les buronniers de l'Aubrac' (Université de Paris, Institut d'ethnologie, Thèse de doctorat de troisième cycle, 2 vols., 1966), vol. I, p. 199.

[109] *L'Aubrac: étude ethnologique*, vol. 3, pp. 117–18; and Royer, 'Les buronniers de l'Aubrac', vol. I, pp. 173–6.

viable only if an adequate area of pasture remained. In the western Massif
Central specialised animal husbandry developed and *vaine pâture* declined
steadily. It had virtually died out in the Cantal by the end of the century. In
the damper and more accessible declivities of the Atlantic watershed, forage
was abundant and the logic of subsistence agriculture less pressing. On the
high plateaux of the south and south-east, however, the agro-pastoral
economy evolved in response to its own rhythms, largely unaffected by the
revolution in communications and the pressures of the national market.
Forage and manure remained scarce resources and demanded thrifty management. *Vaine pâture* was the mechanism that achieved this objective.

Proprietors of well-rounded estates naturally sought permission to enclose
and to withdraw their stock from the common herd, but the community
discouraged such initiatives. Legislation provided small consolation and
proved a perpetual disappointment to the landed bourgeoisie. Apart from the
Thermidorean Committee of Public Safety, no government was prepared to
launch a full-scale offensive against common rights during the period in
question. The laws of 9 July 1889 and 22 June 1890 did not formally abolish
vaine pâture,[110] they merely shifted the emphasis. Communes wishing to
retain free grazing were now required to 'contract-in' by means of a petition
addressed to the prefect. In some highland villages *vaine pâture* was abandoned. When the large stock-owners of Chasseradès[111] insisted on withdrawing their cattle and sheep from the common herd, the municipality
resolved to discontinue the custom in 1892. In most of the villages of Mont
Lozère, the Montagne du Goulet and the Margeride it survived into the
middle of the twentieth century, however. At Combret the common herd
was disbanded in 1933, only to be reconstituted briefly between 1938 and
1940. At La Villedieu it dwindled to extinction in the 1950s, whereas it
survived until 1962 in the communes of Chanaleilles and Estables.[112] As for
the department of the Ardèche, a number of villages in the Tanargue and the
Monts du Vivarais invoked the right to practise *vaine pâture* until 1936 at
least.[113]

In the absence of quantifiable data, it is difficult to chart the evolution of
the commons and collective agricultural practices in the southern Massif
Central in anything more than a bold outline. We have precise and reasonably reliable statistics on the legal status and physical extent of the commons
as between departments, but that is all. The impact of enclosures, scale of
afforestation and *allotissement*, and ramifications of *vaine pâture* remain largely

[110] The *droit de parcours* was abolished, however.
[111] A.D. Lozère 2 0 438, Administration et comptabilité communales: Chasseradès, *délibération* of
municipal council of Chasseradès, 11 Sept. 1892.
[112] Fel, *Les Hautes Terres du Massif Central*', p. 40; Meyronneinc, 'Des communautés villageoises',
p. 68.
[113] H. Aldebert, *Usages locaux: recueil et commentaire: département de l'Ardèche, arrondissement de
Largentière* (Largentière, 1936), p. 106.

imponderable. If not quite infinite, the variations over time and space are such as to require interpretation within a broad chronological span if they are to make sense. Clearly the rural community of the southern Massif Central – in its agricultural dimension – did not disintegrate as swiftly and as inexorably as some historians have supposed. Arguably it did not disintegrate at all, but merely evolved within the constraints of an archaic subsistence economy. By 1900, concessions had been made to individualism, but they were not concessions which jeopardised the edifice. Rather they resembled the adjustments that any society based on subsistence agriculture might make to its structures in a period of demographic pressure. It follows from this that the contagion of individualism which undoubtedly infected the southern Massif Central during the latter part of the nineteenth century carried with it few of the overtones of emancipation and self-awareness associated with the assault on the commons and common rights elsewhere in France. Despite exceptions, the drive for *allotissement* and the decline of *vaine pâture* (such as it was) were not the concomitants of revolutionary liberty.[114] In this region, the growth of agrarian individualism was episodic and cyclical, rather than linear. The year 1789, the abolition of feudalism and the legislation of the Convention were epiphenomena, for the rhythms of evolution were biological and not political.

[114] Soboul, 'Problèmes de la communauté rurale', p. 386.

6

◇–◇

Themes in southern violence after 9 thermidor

COLIN LUCAS

Violence, intimidation, and murder quickly established themselves as an integral part of the revolutionary process in the south-east of France. However, from the Year III the violence attained a wholly new dimension in its intensity, its pervasiveness and its persistence. In the spring and summer of the Year III, jacobins in a broad area of the Midi fell victim to a massive wave of assassination and violence within the more general anti-jacobin revulsion of the Thermidorean Reaction that did not attain this level of murderousness elsewhere in France. In subsequent years, the level of this violence fluctuated. In the Year IV, it became more sporadic as a jacobin-minded Directory sought to instal jacobins in positions of local authority and gave them some fairly ineffectual support. Coinciding with the resurgence of ultra-conservatism and crypto-royalism around the elections of the Year V, the violence was renewed in what was sometimes called locally 'the second reaction'. Strong government after 18 fructidor damped it down again in the Year VI. It resurfaced more sporadically from the later Year VI into the Consulate, exploding again in the White Terror of 1815. Although the pattern becomes less compelling after 18 fructidor, there was an essential continuity in this violence until then at least. It was one long bloody struggle between opposing groups of jacobins and counter-jacobins. In towns and villages, and even in a city like Marseille, essentially the same individuals were involved from one year to another. Very few new names appear in the documents; by and large, those missing are the victims of the previous round. Moreover, although the jacobins did indulge in some violence in the Years IV and VI, the main initiators and protagonists were the counter-jacobins.

In two striking passages, Richard Cobb has established with characteristic verve the grim catalogue of this phenomenon and has anatomised some of its

The research for this essay was completed with the help of a grant from the Leverhulme Foundation.

rhythms and its classic features.[1] These pages remain the most perceptive general observation available to historians. In some respects, however, his picture is contradictory. Thus, for example, he writes first that counter-jacobinism 'was neither blind, nor anarchical, nor spontaneous'; yet, later he argues that it was anarchical and highly personalised, the work of amateur enthusiasts.[2] Of course, in one sense, Cobb is right even in his contradiction. The counter-Terror was a highly contradictory phenomenon, both anarchical and organised, both deliberate and accidental, both structured and random. Above all, southern violence in these years was a compound of separate though overlapping and intertwining strands. It is important to try to distinguish its component elements in order better to reach an eventual understanding of the decay of the Revolution in the Midi during the late 1790s.

One should not confuse three rather different types of violent disorder in the south-east. The first is the peasant disturbances and the brigandage of the mountains, especially in the Haute-Loire, the interior of the Ardèche and the Lozère. The second is the counter-revolutionary conspiracies in both high-land and lowland which maintained small bands of insurgents and from time to time gathered large bodies of men for attacks upon republican strongholds. The third is the communal violence surrounding the passage from the Terror to the Directory which gave the Thermidorean Reaction its bloody connota-tion and which was perpetuated in continuing confrontations under the Directory. This last type of violence was characteristic above all of the Rhône Valley and the southern plain.[3] Its northern end was marked by the city of Lyon and the lowlands in the Loire; it penetrated the foothills on either side of the Rhône – for example, roughly as far as Largentière (Ardèche) in the west and Crest (Drôme) in the east; at the southern end, it included the southern Var as far as Grasse whilst it petered out in the Hérault along a frontier that still needs definition.

Of course, these three types shared common features beyond the recourse to murderous violence, beyond the coincidence in time and beyond the rejection of the Republic and its institutions. For all, the revolutionary struggle provided a language for other conflicts of a social, communal or personal nature. All had some association with the refractory church, for the religious issue was but one dialect of the language of conflict and protest

---

[1] R. Cobb, *The Police and the People* (Oxford, 1970), pp. 131–50 and *Reactions to the French Revolution* (Oxford, 1972), pp. 19–62.

[2] *Police and People*, p. 140; *Reactions*, p. 22.

[3] It is possible that the Ain should be included on the strength of the attack on the prisoners being transferred from Bourg-en-Bresse in the Year III. Although this event is very similar to southern incidents, the region seems too remote from the heartland of communal violence and it does not appear to display to any significant degree the other patterns of violence discussed here. Similar considerations apply even more strongly to the prison massacre and convoy attack in prair. III at Lons-le-Saulnier.

offered by the Revolution. Each was the most recent episode in a continuum of violence and conflict that stretched back into the early years of the Revolution and beyond. In all three, *insoumis* and deserters provided a large element of the manpower of violence. Furthermore, there are clear connections between the types. Although our knowledge of counter-revolutionary conspiracy in the south-east is imperfect, the most prominent insurgents were at least loosely bound into conspiracies that related them to each other and to militant émigrés.[4] The English agent Wickham certainly thought that he was pouring money into wide-ranging conspiracies; the Baron de Saint-Christol had been in and out of France as often as he had been in and out of the French nation's jails; the Marquis de Bésignan's plots took him from the Rhône Valley to the hill villages of the Monts du Forez. Inasmuch as local gentry were involved in the communal violence of the Year III and beyond (and the degree to which this was the case is difficult to determine), they were presumably liable to be in some sort of diffuse contact with circles in which counter-revolutionary plots flourished. On the other hand, it is clear that the groups of armed young men organised by men like Saint-Christol and Lestang in the Rhône Valley were both locally recruited and participated in communal violence in a limited range of small towns and villages around their centre.[5] Indeed, particularly well-connected local reactionary groups could occasionally get quite formidable counter-revolutionary help in their communal struggles. For example, Dominique Allier came down from the mountains of his pre-Terror exploits to lead a murder gang at Bagnols (Gard) in the Year III.[6]

Nonetheless, the fact that royalist insurgents like Allier or Saint-Christol operated counter-jacobin gangs in the Year III does not mean that all or even a majority of counter-jacobin groups were part of a broad counter-revolutionary conspiracy, however loosely linked. The fact that such insurgents organised their men into a formal structure, to which the title of *Compagnie de Jésus* or *Compagnie du Soleil* was frequently attached, does not mean that all those anti-jacobin groups that took some organised form were necessarily part of a grand design under some superior command structure. The title of *Compagnie de Jésus* was one used above all by jacobins about their persecutors.

[4] G. Lewis, *The Second Vendée* (Oxford, 1978). Other material in J. Barruol, *La Contre-révolution en Provence et dans le Comtat* (Cavaillon, 1928) and E. Daudet, *Histoire des conspirations royalistes du Midi* (Paris, 1881).

[5] R. Maltby, 'Crime and the local community in France: the Department of the Drôme, 1770–1820' (Unpublished D.Phil. thesis, University of Oxford, 1979), pp. 308–15. More details on recruitment and activity in A.D. Drôme L 1854, 1856 and 1892. Saint-Paul-Trois-Châteaux offers a clear case of noble involvement with the organising hands of de Castellane, de Lestang and Genton de Barsac. Yet, even here, the action is not clearly related to any general royalist concept: much of Lestang's time seems to have been taken up in getting Genton's confiscated land back from its purchasers by intimidation (A.D. Drôme L 1854, enquiry of 28 frim. VI).

[6] Lewis, *Second Vendée*, p. 94.

They used it indiscriminately. Indeed, the jacobins were the first to argue that they were the victims of a general royalist conspiracy linked to émigré centres abroad and aimed at undermining the Republic by the physical elimination of its most zealous defenders. It was a notion that came naturally to the jacobin concept of 'l'ennemi en dedans et l'ennemi au dehors'. This assumption underlay the great majority of the enquiries and comments by jacobin officials when they were back in office in the Years IV and VI.[7] Since these documents constitute in fact the great bulk of the information about the events, the historian often has great difficulty in not accepting the assumptions of the documents along with their information.

The confusion into which the historian of the south-east is liable to fall in this subject does not derive only from the shared features and connections between these three types. It is also due to the fact that the coherence of counter-revolutionary militancy and also the clarity of communal violence both declined during the Directory. The republican offensive against counter-revolutionary insurgency was in fact quite successful, particularly after 18 fructidor Year V/4 September 1797. Already, the seizure of Bésignan's papers in early Year IV had destroyed what appears as a major insurrectionary conspiracy radiating out from Lyon.[8] Lestang was arrested in ventôse Year IV and his group disintegrated.[9] Saint-Christol's insurrection at the end of the Year V was a miserable failure. Lamothe-Picquet was captured in floréal Year V and died in mysterious circumstances at Le Puy. Dominique Allier and Surville, forced back into the high country, were captured on the frontier of the Loire and the Haute-Loire in the late Year VI and executed.[10] It was very much the débris of royalist bands that confronted the military repression of the Consulate. As for communal violence, on the other hand, it is clear that even during the 'second reaction' of the Year V the precision of retribution and revenge was becoming blurred. The structure of violence that this essay will seek to demonstrate was decreasingly visible as the Directorial years went by. The choice of victims became more indiscriminate; the features of pillage and restitution of goods turned increasingly into uncomplicated acts of theft and rapine. In sum, during the Directory, although jacobins remained obvious targets of violence, one can see a progressive conflation of originally different types of violence into a single, diffuse

---

[7] E.g. the j.p. of Orgon in the Year VI concluded that the Year III murders had been part of a great plot 'secondant par l'assassinat des plus chauds défenseurs de la liberté le projet liberticide des conspirateurs ligués avec les princes étrangers pour renverser la République et poignarder le gouvernement' (A.N. BB[18] 186, enquiry of 1 ther. VI). The standard jacobin interpretation of the Year III is presented by L. M. S. Fréron, *Mémoire historique sur la réaction royale et sur les massacres du Midi* (Paris, an IV).

[8] A.N. AF[III] 332 d. 1411.

[9] Fréron, *Mémoire historique*, p. 45 and A.D. Vaucluse 1 L 224 d. Bollène. However, Fréron's claim that he was executed seems optimistic, since he was tried *contumax* (A.D. Drôme L 1981).

[10] E. Daudet, *La Conspiration de Pichegru* (Paris, 1901), pp. 294–316.

criminal violence of small *bandes*, which were the residue of communal struggles and broken royalist organisations.[11]

The pattern of this development is rendered more confused by the fact that not all groups lost coherence or drifted to more ordinary criminal violence at the same time. Of course, the ordinary criminal element had always been there. A number of obvious common-law crooks are to be found among the rank and file of reactionary militants.[12] Moreover, the opportunities of the Year III were far too good for the traditional criminal *bande* not to seek to profit under spurious invocations of anti-jacobinism. The frightful murder of Polier in his country house near Avignon in pluviôse Year III was a classic case. He was in fact murdered by the long-established Liotard gang and the motive was robbery, for Polier was the agent for a consortium of Swiss (including Laharpe) purchasing national lands. Yet, he wàs done to death to cries of 'nous cherchons ici un Robespierre' and the identity of the victim as a purchaser of national lands lent some superficial credence to the notion of a counter-jacobin act.[13] Nonetheless, in the Year III, such common-law criminality was not in the least typical of either communal or counter-revolutionary violence and it is a great mistake to generalise from a few instances. Later in the Directory, however, many of the younger men who had indulged in counter-jacobinism were to carry over their anti-republican language and predilections into common-law criminality.[14]

It was a natural development. Many of these young men were footloose and armed. For most, settling down was difficult even if they were so inclined. However indulgent the judiciary may have been, and in most departments here it was remarkably so, they were nonetheless marked men in their localities with a record of violence which was public knowledge. As we shall see, there was a great localism in the pattern of communal violence, while even those involved in counter-revolutionary 'armies' do not seem to have operated far from home. Historians have insisted on how trapped many jacobins were in their localities by jobs and commitments. Many reactionaries were equally trapped though, in the case of younger men, more by instinct and horizon. Deserters in particular had often been brought home by *le mal du pays* as much as anything. Instinctively, they would tend to stay within

---

[11] Cf. A.N. BB[18] 186, j.p. of Orgon to Min. Just., 9 vend. VII, 'L'impunité et la protection que trouvent les assassins royaux dans cet arrondissement de ce département les enhardit d'une telle manière que les voyageurs ne peuvent plus aller. S'ils sont escortés par la force armée, on les fusille dans leurs voitures; et s'ils ne le sont point, on les dépouille de tout.'

[12] E.g. A.N. BB[18] 177, report to the Consuls, n.d., on Jean Girard, a professional thief, 'depuis 24 ans, il ne cesse d'aller de la prison aux galères et des galères à la prison'. Cf. Cobb, *Reactions*, p. 25.

[13] Musée Calvet 2530 p. 13.

[14] A clear description of a regional example of this process in Maltby, 'Crime and community', pp. 299–335. See also the account of the disintegration of St-Christol's army in A.D. Vaucluse 1 L 226 d. Orange, Mun. admin. of Orange to central admin., 25 vend. VI.

reach of home and to operate within the reassurance of familiar terrain. Much of the confusion of the later Directorial scene in the south-east derived from the fact that banditry had become a means of earning a living without straying too far from one's locality. It was rendered more necessary by the economic distress of these years, which brought out into ambushes and rural break-ins the day labourers and the unemployed alongside the deserters, the former dispersing into the anonymity of hamlets or of the alleyways of *bourgs* while the latter disappeared back into the *garrigue* or the wooded hills.[15] Those who cried 'Vive le Roi' when pillaging a stage-coach in the Year VII or the Year VIII should not fool us into thinking that they were necessarily royalist militants even if they had once been so. Those who shot at *commissaires du Directoire* in those same years were not necessarily accomplishing gestures of the same significance as those that they had undertaken in communal violence in the Year III or the Year V.

It seems, then, that these three species of violent anti-republicanism should remain distinct, despite their flowering in the same soil of south-eastern anarchy. Each had really a quite separate identity drawn from a distinct prehistory.[16] As far as the mountains are concerned, one can certainly observe in some areas the kind of factionalism consequent upon the rivalries of a local bourgeoisie that is discernible in the communal violence of the lowlands.[17] Yet, other factors gave a distinctive quality to this violence. The mountain disturbances were partly the perennial brigandage of the secret places long given over to deserters and bands of *rouleurs*; the violence was the habitual recourse of this hill population which defied the declining rates of physical violence recorded elsewhere; the hatreds were those of religiously fervent, poor, xenophobic peasants in isolated, dispersed villages against small-town profiteers, lawyers and protestants. As for counter-revolutionary conspiracy, it had been endemic since the very beginning of the Revolution and its dominant personalities were much the same after the Terror as before. Its roots lay among those deprived of office and privilege early in the revolutionary struggles in a region which, in the lowlands at least, was liberally endowed with both office and privilege. Finally, the communal violence of the lowlands after 9 thermidor was very much internal to the community in which it took place and had its roots both in the direct experience of the Terror and in a pre-history of personal, municipal and inter-communal struggles that

---

[15] Coulet, a poor *tafetassier* at Avignon, recorded in his diary for the Year IV: 'Coment voullez-vous que le peauvres monde vive, tout les jours on entant dirre on a vollez a tel androit . . . il faut que les peauvres monde sest fasse volleur par force, car il peuvent plus thenir' (quoted by H. Chobaut, 'Le Journal historique de la révolution d'Avignon de Joseph Coulet', *Ann. d'Avignon et du Comtat Venaissin*, 1931, p. 94).

[16] A general background is provided by C. Lucas, 'The Problem of the Midi in the French Revolution', *Trans. Royal Hist. Soc.*, 5th ser., 28 (1978), 1–25.

[17] P. M. Jones, '*La République au village* in the southern Massif-Central, 1789–1799', *Historical Journal*, 23 (1980), 793–812.

characterised this area in the earlier revolutionary years and before. The purpose of this essay is to explore further this third type of violence, not by a complete analysis of the problem but by drawing attention to some aspects which seem hitherto ignored. It is concerned principally with the phenomenon in villages and smaller towns, but where the patterns seem equally visible in large towns and cities reference will be made to them also.

It is easy to become obsessed by the most spectacular and ghastly aspects of this violence. It is easy, therefore, to believe that murder and massacre were its essential features. In fact, these were only two manifestations of a more complex structure of violence whose significance is only apparent when viewed as a whole. There were at least six broad types of incident. The most spectacular was the prison massacre, which took place only in the Year III. The worst, but by no means the only examples, were at Marseille in which over a hundred people were put to death, at Lyon which accounted for another hundred and at Tarascon (Bouches-du-Rhône) where forty-seven died in two separate massacres. Much more frequent and persistent, however, were the other types of murder. On the one hand, there was the assassination of political prisoners during their transfer from one place to another. They were killed either by their escort or by another group with or without the complicity of the escort. This was the fate, for example, of the prisoners from the Vaucluse massacred on the bridge at Pont-Saint-Esprit (Gard) in prairial Year III. On the other hand, the commonest killing was the simple murder of a victim either seized on the street or dragged out of his house. All these murders, however, took place within the context of four other types of incident – insults, beatings, the pillage of possessions and arrests. These were by far the most usual manifestations of the violence. For instance, at Graveson (Bouches-du-Rhône), only four people were killed but fifty-two were put in prison.[18] Much of the confusion of the picture derives from the fact that the same perpetrator and the same victim were often involved in several incidents: thus, frequently, someone who was murdered had already been beaten up and possibly arrested before. The bread and butter of militant counter-jacobins, known to their victims and to us as 'égorgeurs' or 'sabreurs', was not in fact throat-slitting and slashing so much as beating up, insulting, harassing, humiliating and wrecking the households of the men and women who were their enemies. By far the commonest feature was not strictly violent: it was verbal violence in the form of insult. The next commonest feature was simply physical assault not accompanied by wounding or arrest.

[18] A.N. BB[18] 183, Tableaux des assassinats: Graveson. These annotated tables of victims in the Bouches-du-Rhône provide the most coherent single source for counter-jacobin violence in its various forms. Drawn up by commune in pluv. VI, the tables are unfortunately incomplete (Marseille is missing for example) and of uneven value.

The most immediately striking feature of this violence of the Thermidorean months and beyond is the very local context within which so much of it took place. It was predominantly a local phenomenon perpetrated by locals on other locals. At Salon (Bouches-du-Rhône), to cite but this example, the jacobins were quite clear that the murders had been done 'par les soi-disant honnêtes gens de cette commune'.[19] This could be true even of those most unlocal of events, the prison massacre. The fort at Tarascon served as a collecting-point for prisoners from the whole of the western Bouches-du-Rhône. The first massacre on 6 prairial Year III/25 May 1795 caused the death of twenty-four people, all Tarasconnais. The second massacre, in the night of 2–3 messidor Year III/20–1 June 1795, claimed twenty-three lives, all of people from outside Tarascon. Indeed, after the first massacre one Tarasconnais was heard to remark that 'eux avaient fait périr ceux de leur pays et que c'était aux autres à en faire de même'.[20] Other evidence shows that men from the surrounding area marched into Tarascon and did indeed dispatch their jacobins, though certainly with the complicity of the men of Tarascon guarding the fort. Indeed, during this second massacre, some killers seized one man, but 'l'ayant examiné, ils dirent: "c'est un étranger, cela ne nous regarde pas" et on le laissa'.[21] It seems moreover that this localism was felt by participants to be a necessary element. Thus, when Boniface Fréguier of Puyloubier (Bouches-du-Rhône) was murdered in the Year V by a counter-jacobin group, one man going to view the body in the fields met three young men from the village of Pourrières who made haste to tell him that 'ce n'était pas eux qui avaient assassiné ledit Fréguier mais bien les jeunes gens de Puyloubier'.[22] In this case, it was in part obviously necessary to prevent the incident from becoming a further subject of inter-communal hatreds, but it was also necessary to establish thereby its specific relationship to a local context in Puyloubier.

It is clear from the evidence at later judicial enquiries, cautious discreet

[19] A.N. BB[18] 176, Mun. admin. Salon to centr. admin., 17 germ. IV.

[20] A.D. Bouches-du-Rhône L 3051. This same feature was perhaps present, though less completely, in the Aix prison massacre of 22 flor. III. The contemporary *procès-verbal* suggests that people came (from Marseille?) to attack 'les prévenus de Marseille'. On the other hand, Aixois were clearly involved. Thirteen of the dead were from Marseille and ten from Aix (together with an administrator of the depart. who would have been well known at Aix). Only a small minority of five were from elsewhere (Manosque, Saint-Chamas, Salon and Saint-Maximin). During the incident, a couple of men from other towns were brought from the prison to the municipality which was asked to investigate them, revealing once again an unwillingness to attack men whose conduct was not properly known (Fréron, *Mémoire historique*, pp. 165–72 and A.D. Var 2 L 982, trial of Royère, Year V).

[21] A.N. BB[18] 177, director of jury of Tarascon, 8 mess. VI. Similar phrase as far north as Bourg-en-Bresse where, during the attack on prisoners leaving the jail, one killer was restrained by another on the grounds that 'il ne fallait point frapper sur celui-là, qu'il n'était point d'ici, qu'il ne le connaissait pas' (A.D. Haute-Loire L 10, evidence of J. C. Perdrix).

[22] A.D. Var 2 L 983, evidence of Jouvencel.

evidence though it mostly is, that witnesses and victims usually knew who the killers and thugs were, just as the latter usually knew who their victims were. One would, of course, expect this not to be the case in cities. Evidence for Marseille is thin, but even here a man can give the name and occupation of at least the most prominent of those who invaded his house or beat him up.[23] Populous, artisanal Saint-Etienne (Loire) was a much smaller city than Marseille, the third largest in France, but even here its 14,000 inhabitants might have been thought to confer a certain anonymity. Nonetheless, a gunsmith watching a murder was addressed by name by a thug who, as clerk to a silk merchant, came from quite a different milieu – 'Morin, recule-toi', he cried.[24] In smaller towns, such as Tarascon or Saint-Paul-Trois-Châteaux (Drôme) or Montbrison (Loire), the trait is even more marked. When the killers visited the house of Curtil at Montbrison, his son tried to protect a relative helping out during his father's absence by saying that the man sharing his bed was not his father. 'Nous connaissons bien Curtil' came the disdainful reply.[25] At Saint-Paul-Trois-Châteaux, the *veuve* Tourangeau (Payan's housekeeper) was heard to cry 'Marron, ne me tuez pas' as Jacques Marron cut her down.[26] At Tarascon, Claude Roman spent the night of the first massacre locked in his cell but could identify fourteen killers by their voices.[27] As for the villages, such intimacy was by and large the rule. To cite but one example, a man hiding out in the mountain above Orgon (Bouches-du-Rhône) was pursued by another man 'que je reconnus à sa voix et que je vis ensuite'.[28]

Of course, not all the incidents obeyed this rule. It is clear, for example, that the anti-jacobin forces hastily raised at Aix and Marseille in floréal Year III against insurrectionary Toulon committed a number of aggressions along their line of march.[29] Similarly, it is certain that a number of men from Lyon and Paris turned up at incidents in Marseille and Aix and that Marseillais travelled up the Rhône.[30] Some of the killers in the Forez had previously been active in Lyon.[31] Counter-revolutionary groups contained men who travelled

---

[23] E.g. A.N. BB[18] 178, 'mémoire pour le citoyen Galibert', 3 fruct. V; BB[18] 179, enquiry of 15 mess. IV; A.D. Bouches-du-Rhône L 3048, proceedings of Year IV. Note also the case of Mouren of Marseille who had just been arrested and, leaving his house under escort, 'un nomme Latrève, demeurant même rue que lui, lui a plongé son sabre dans le corps' (Fréron, *Mémoire historique*, p. 89).

[24] A.N. BB[18] 690, evidence of Morin.

[25] Ibid., evidence of femme Curtil.

[26] A.D. Drôme L 1856.

[27] A.D. Bouches-du-Rhône L 3051, evidence of Roman; similar sort of evidence by Bonnet.

[28] A.N. BB[18] 186, enquiry by j.p. of Orgon, therm. VI.

[29] E.g. A.N. BB[18] 186, enquiry at Le Beausset, 22 prair. VI.

[30] E.g. A.N. BB[18] 179, interrogation of Mirvault, mess. IV; A.D. Bouches-du-Rhône L 3048, enquiry of Year VI, evidence of Cayol Richaud.

[31] A.N. AF[III] 298 (1181), denunciations to Reverchon.

around the Midi.[32] The situation was further complicated in the Year III by the habit that reactionary authorities had of sending National Guards of the most dubious nature to keep order in various places, such as the departmental force established in the Vaucluse in prairial Year III or the group that Lestang was able to lead from Saint-Paul-Trois-Châteaux to Montélimar (Drôme).[33] On closer inspection, however, the number of incidents devoid of local context seems fewer than one might believe. In the first place, even though strangers were present in a large centre like Marseille or Lyon, it still seems that the majority of militant counter-jacobins were local men. Certainly, those later charged with such murders at Lyon and Marseille were in very great majority from those cities.[34] Indeed, the Forezien killers at Lyon were recorded above all as attacking fellow Foreziens visiting the city.[35] Even clearly counter-revolutionary leaders often worked in their local context, at least in the Year III: Bagnols was Dominique Allier's home town and Lestang had been a prominent figure at Saint-Paul-Trois-Châteaux early in the Revolution.[36] In the second place, armed groups travelled from some villages and small towns in order to capture victims who had fled. The men killed at Morières (Vaucluse) in the Year III were in fact from the Bouches-du-Rhône and were killed by their compatriots come to get them; similarly, men from Aubagne (Bouches-du-Rhône) seized Jullien and his two sons at Brignolles (Var) and shot them on the way back.[37]

A hidden form of localism was also present in some of the murders of prisoners under escort. For example, the convoy from Orange, which was to suffer so badly on the bridge at Pont-Saint-Esprit in prairial Year III, had already been attacked at Mondragon (Vaucluse) on the road. But, only men from Mondragon died.[38] Indeed, the closer that one looks at murders or assaults by people from out of town, the more likely one is to find a direct connection between persecutor and victim, even if this was not necessarily a connection of locality. Thus, for example, Grange was assaulted in his house at Avignon in messidor Year III by Allègre of Apt (Vaucluse) and a man from Orange. Allègre had in fact been born at Avignon, the man from Orange was the fiancée of his sister and Grange was assaulted because he intervened

[32] E.g. A.D. Ardèche Fonds Mazon, t. 19, p. 221; A.D. Vaucluse 7 L 84, denunciation by Croisi, 11 brum. IV.

[33] P. Vaillandet, 'Le procès des juges de la Commission révolutionnaire d'Orange', *Ann. hist. Rév. fran.*, 6 (1929), 137–63; A.D. Drôme L 1981, enquiry of niv. IV on Lestang at Montélimar.

[34] A.D. Haute-Loire L 31, jury d'accusation of Yssingeaux, Year VI; A.N. BB[18] 174, petition to 500, 3 pluv. VI.

[35] A.D. Rhône 31 L 166, 8 and 18 vent. III.

[36] A.D. Drôme L 200.

[37] Musée Calvet 2530 p. 73, *Tissot, administrateur du Département, et Blaze, administrateur du District, à la Convention nationale* (14 them. III), p. 26; A.N. BB[18] 177, indictment, 17 niv. VIII; see also A. Mun. Avignon 3 D 7, 20 germ. III, for men from Bagnols come seeking a man, and A. Mun. Montélimar, *registre de police*, 17 flor. III, for Mornas sending to collect an arrested jacobin.

[38] A.D. Vaucluse 1 L 225 d. Mondragon.

when Allègre tried to arrest Grange's wife who had given evidence against Allègre's father at the Commission d'Orange, which had sent him to the guillotine.[39] Similarly, the apparently inexplicable murder of Jay in the village of Magnieu-Haute-Rive (Loire) by a few men from Montbrison in fact occurred because Jay had belonged to the Year II municipality, which had sent fatal evidence against a man whose cousin came to Magnieu that day, together with the cousin's brother-in-law and the latter's bosom friend.[40] It was widely claimed in the Year III and later that murders and assaults were the work of strangers. Once again, one should not be misled about this. Complicity, fear, tacit rules about giving evidence to justice and a general village dislike of the outside combined to render it a convenient fiction. At Clansayes (Drôme), a jacobin enquiry in floréal Year IV into two murders met with the blanket assertion that no one recognised the killers. The relatives of the dead did not even testify. It was only in another judicial enquiry in ventôse Year VI, originally concerned with another killing in a neighbouring village, that it began to come out that, although strangers had been present, the principal authors were known local men.[41]

Localism was not however so precise that it must be confined to the interior of one locality. Villages in the lowlands and foothills were not isolated communities; their inhabitants were recognisable individuals within a neighbourhood which grew wider the greater their substance. At the same time, towns and markets had villages in their skirts, rendering some faces recognisable in both localities. This was true even of the city of Marseille: the *canton du centre* listed an area within a circle bounded by Cassis, Aubagne and Gardanne as being habitually supplied from Marseille.[42] This situation meant that cities were not particularly safe for jacobins from nearby. It also meant, in reverse, that for example the inhabitants of the village of Malemort (Vaucluse) were perfectly able to identify two jacobins from Carpentras and Pernes.[43] Similarly, a group of men from Solliès (Var) met Lazare Bernard of Hyères in the countryside in prairial Year III and seized him saying 'ce n'est pas toi que nous cherchons, ce sont les patriotes de Solliès, mais c'est égal, il faut que tu périsses comme les autres'.[44]

Such a definition of localism that allows people to remain in a local context outside their immediate locality inevitably encounters the vexed and obscure question of inter-communal relations. Historians have always emphasised the rivalries between communities. These were certainly real and often bloody. Indeed, inter-communal violence is a theme in southern revolutionary

39 A.D. Vaucluse 7 L 84.
40 On this rather tortuous business, see C. Lucas, 'Violence thermidorienne et société tradition-
   nelle: l'exemple du Forez', *Cahiers d'histoire* 24 n° 4 (1979), 35.
41 A.D. Drôme L 1869 d. Pelisse.   42 A. Mun. Marseille 1 D 19, 5 fruct. VI.
43 A.D. Var 2 L 981.   44 A.D. Var 2 L 798.

violence before as after the Terror and it frequently expressed itself in the polarised language of the Revolution. However, there were also alliances between communities, presumably based upon a common dislike of some third party, whether for intimate reasons, such as grazing rights or past insults, or else for some regional disequilibrium, such as the alliances surrounding the rivalry between Carpentras and Avignon. The young men of a village did not stone or fight the young men of every other village within reach. What happened to the young men of Aubignan (Vaucluse) in thermidor Year V is instructive. They had been invited by 'la jeunesse' of Vacqueyras to dine with them and, stepping out defenceless in their best clothes and rolled-up sleeves, they were set upon by the youth of Beaumes.[45] These were villages of the bitter lands of the Comtat civil war, riven by struggles at least since then.[46] It is clear enough that at least some groups in different villages or small towns were ready to cooperate with each other. Thus, to take another example from the Comtat, fifty men from Sainte-Cécile (Vaucluse), Tulette (Drôme) and Visan (Vaucluse) went in prairial Year III to Vinsobres (Drôme) to look for people from their own communes.[47] However, the men of these three villages retained their own identity and would only concern themselves with their own compatriots. It seems that in the Thermidorean and early Directorial period the role of reactionaries not members of the community in which they found themselves was governed by a number of tacit conventions. It was only later, and as another manifestation of the decay of communal violence, that groups of reactionaries began to behave themselves indiscriminately wherever they happened to be.[48] Earlier, one could lend support and encouragement to local men; one could participate in many of the rituals associated with these acts and which we will examine below. However, it seems that by and large one did not take a direct part in thuggery unless one had a personal connection with the victim. This would be to violate the unwritten rules of Thermidorean violence.[49] Thus, the most important feature of Lazare Bernard's encounter with the men of Solliès was perhaps not that they knew who and what he was, but that he was in fact not harmed at all despite their ferocious promise. Indeed, groups of counter-jacobins who did try to operate in places where they had no consorts were liable to encounter the blank wall of communal solidarity. Three men came up from Saint-Paul-Trois-Châteaux to the next-door village of Saint-Restitut in floréal Year IV looking for jacobins. Saint-Restitut does not appear to have been a particularly patriot village. Yet, no one would tell them

[45] A.D. Vaucluse 1 L 224 d. Aubignan, agent mun. of Aubignan to centr. admin., 15 therm. V.

[46] For some background, see in particular A.D. Drôme L 197, troubles at Vacqueyras, 1793.

[47] A.D. Drôme L 112, proc. general synd. to proc. synd. district of Nyon, 17 prair. III.

[48] E.g. A.N. BB[18] 183, Tableaux des assassinats, Senas.

[49] A clear example of this pattern is provided by the *tapages* at Montélimar in late therm. III (A. Mun. Montélimar, *registre des delib.*, 26 therm. III, complaints, and 3 vend. IV, copy of letter from patriots to Boisset).

where the men lived. The *agent municipal* was quite firm about it: 'je ne peux concéder à votre demande, ma conscience me répugne, je ne peux consentir à faire faire du mal à ces personnes qui sont nos frères'.[50] It must have been a rule that counter-jacobins understood, for no reprisals were taken for this resistance.

Communal violence seems naturally to imply crowd violence. In particular, stories abound of hapless petty jacobin tyrants brought back to succumb to a screaming crowd in the Year III. It is certainly true that crowd violence did form part of counter-jacobinism up to the end of the Year V. Juge of Valréas (Vaucluse) and Philippon of Saint-Galmier (Loire) were examples of men falling to large and incensed crowds on their return to their small towns.[51] In fact, however, both of these cases took place in the Year IV when they were returning as *commissaires du Directoire*. It was perhaps the fact that they were powerful rather than that they were defenceless that moved the crowd to action. At Valréas, the crowd fought Juge's military escort of 170 men for six hours. In larger towns, riots linked to political struggles were in practice primarily associated with jacobin enterprises – for example, the riot of 5 vendémiaire Year III/26 September 1794 at Marseille and the Toulon insurrection of late floréal Year II/mid-May 1795 or else the food riots of 4–6 nivôse Year IV/24–6 December 1795 at Arles and 19–20 pluviôse Year IV/8–9 February 1796 at Montpellier, from both of which jacobin groups sought to profit.[52] Indeed, if one defines a crowd action as one involving a large body of people without any clear structure, then it is in fact relatively difficult to find upsurges of this nature assaulting jacobins in the Year III. Perhaps the clearest example is the death of Nappier, *huissier* of the Commission d'Orange, at Avignon in messidor Year III. Unlike the judges, he was sentenced only to prison and *exposition au poteau*, but was torn from the pillory and done to death by the crowd. Once again, however, he brought it on himself in a certain sense, because he was attacked only after he had insulted the crowd jeering at him.[53]

---

[50] A.D. Drôme L 1892, enquiry of 29 flor. IV.

[51] A.N. F¹ᵇ II Loire 17 d. Saint-Galmier, inhabitants of Saint-Galmier to General Montchoisi, n.d.; A.N. BB¹⁸ 888a, *Adresse individuelle des administrateurs municipaux et habitants de . . . Valréas au . . . Directoire executif* (Year IV) and Grivet to Min. Just., 15 germ. IV. At Valréas, the crowd dispersed the moment that the murder was accomplished.

[52] G. Martinet, 'Les débuts de la réaction thermidorienne à Marseille', *Actes du 90ᵉᵐᵉ Congrès national des Sociétés savantes. Nice 1965* (Paris, 1966), 149–66. On Arles, A.N. F⁷ 7090. On Montpellier, A.N. F⁷ 7102. It seems that the very complex events at Avignon in pluv. V also fall into this category: see A.N. F⁷ 7233; there was also a jacobin riot in this city on 5 prair. III (Ch. Soullier, *Histoire de la Révolution d'Avignon et du Comté-Venaissin* (2 vols., Paris, 1844), vol. 2, pp. 276–7).

[53] Soullier, *Révolution d'Avignon*, vol. 2, pp. 284ff. Of course, there were cases of armed attack by crowds of villagers organised against reputed republican centres – for example, the attack against Avignon in vend. IV. However, these belong much more to the intersection of counter-revolutionary agitation and traditional hostility to urban centres. Patriots were clear enough

It is easy here to be misled once more by the documents. Local authorities could hide their complicity or justify their incompetence by alleging great crowd movements. For discreet or terrified witnesses it was a convenient variant on the theme of strangers. Thus, all the Year III reports established by the administrations about the prison attacks at Tarascon made them the work of large unrestrainable crowds.[54] It is quite clear that this was simply untrue. Similarly, the municipality of Mondragon stated in prairial Year III that the convoy going to Pont-Saint-Esprit had passed with prisoners from the village 'sur lesquels s'étaient jetés une immense quantité de femmes, d'enfants, de vieillards'.[55] Yet, one prisoner from the convoy later stated that, passing Mondragon, 'il apperçut dix hommes armés qui bordaient la haye sur le grand chemin et qui voyant arriver les détenus fondirent sur eux en choisissant leurs victimes'.[56] Nonetheless, it is certain that large crowds were present at many of the most characteristic incidents of harrassment and murder. However, one should not confuse the presence of large numbers of people with crowd action. Closer inspection frequently reveals a different pattern. Take, for example, the murder of Lascalet Pascal, done to death in prairial Year III on the highroad from Uzès to Nîmes whither he was being escorted. The gendarmerie (for the most part a relatively neutral witness in the Year III) reported that a crowd of men and women had appeared and that several individuals with drawn swords had stepped out of the crowd to kill him.[57] At Saint-Etienne, a substantial crowd was present at the street murder of Robert, but a witness later mentioned incidentally that a number of men had in fact kept the crowd back whilst the murder was accomplished.[58] Jean Mamille of the village of Orgon was precise in his description when he later reported that 'il a été frappé par les assassins royaux qui l'ont saisi à la gorge et ont failli l'étrangler en présence de près de cent personnes'.[59]

It is possible to argue, therefore, that the role of the crowd was primarily that of a spectator or a witness. Certainly, the noise and the shouted threats that almost ritually surrounded murders or harassment were bound to attract spectators, even if it was only the woman who, 'la curiosité l'ayant

---

about that – 'aux armes patriotes, les villages sont ici' was the cry at Orange in germ. V (A.D. Vaucluse 7 L 85).

[54] A.B. BB[18] 8 176 and 177.   [55] A.D. Vaucluse 1 L 225 d. Mondragon.

[56] A.N. BB[18] 317, evidence of François Onde.   [57] A.N. BB[18] 317, report of 28 prair. III.

[58] J. B. Galley, *Saint-Etienne et son district pendant la Révolution* (3 vols., 1903–7), vol. 3, p. 169. An exactly similar instance at Aubagne (A.D. Bouches-du-Rhône L 3049, evidence of Pignol on murder of Domergue). At Aix, clearly large crowds milled around the opened prison in the massacre of flor. III, but the actual action appears to belong to a group of somewhere between 30 and 60 men (Fréron, *Mémoire historique*, pp. 165–72, *procès-verbal* of the Mun., 23 flor. III: compare with the claim (same date) by the criminal trib. that it was the work of 'une multitude immense, furieuse et armée', printed p. 174).

[59] A.N. BB[18] 183, Tableaux des assassinats, Orgon.

portée à savoir ce qui se passait à la rue . . . se mit doucement à la fenêtre' or
the timid observation of the man who followed an event 'de loin en loin' as
it moved down the street to its fatal conclusion.[60] A killing was in a certain
sense a public spectacle which one turned out to see – at Aix, one man said
to another 'qu'il était temps de venir voir lou pendouleau (la pendaison)'.[61]
Large crowds turned out to see the prisoners arriving at Pont-Saint-Esprit
and watched the killing on the bridge. The escort must have waited for this
audience just as much as for the dramatic neatness of heaving the bodies over
the bridge, since they themselves had not touched the prisoners all the way
from Orange until then.[62] The thugs did indeed frequently go out of their
way to seek publicity. They deliberately sought the public gaze. Even in
night-time killing, victims were frequently dragged out into the street.
Counter-jacobin incidents were not silent, but deliberately noisy. The thugs
wrapped up their behaviour in a public display on streets and squares at all
hours that went far beyond loud-mouthed loutishness. The population was
being solicited to spectate. Such behaviour suggests that counter-jacobins saw
spectators as an important element in their action and that the crowd, even
if it did not participate directly, had the function of witness. Where the
crowd did intervene more directly in murders, it seems (in the most clearly
documented cases at least) to have obeyed a tacit rule to intervene only when
the main work had been done. Thus, jacobin evidence about the death of
Fréguier *pere* and *fils* on the road to Aix makes it clear that the crowd set
about mutilating the bodies after the deaths.[63]

It was, therefore, predominantly groups of people who killed or assaulted,
not crowds. Moreover, it was groups rather than individuals. The lone
encounter between a jacobin and his persecutor was a rarity. When it did
occur, it was likely to result merely in a lot of threats. The numbers involved
in incidents varied from place to place. Thirty-six men took part in the prison
massacre at Saint-Etienne.[64] In smaller towns, such as Aubagne or Montbrison or even Aix, the *égorgeur* group seems to have been about thirty
strong, although in the day-to-day routine of violence the actual number of
them involved in any one incident might be between four and eight.[65] In

---

[60] E.g. A.N. F[7] 7090 d. 40, evidence of Thérèse Allée. A typical statement by witnesses at later
enquiries would be that 'le déclarant s'avance par un motif de pure curiosité' (A.D. Var 2 L 982,
affair Royère, evidence Marriot). This does not seem to be a case of proclaiming one's innocence,
though it might establish impartiality. In practice, it would be easier to claim to have seen
nothing specific which is what many other witnesses do.

[61] A.D. Bouches-du-Rhône L 3043.

[62] A.N. BB[18] 317, complaint of Etienne Besson, 22 therm. III.

[63] A.N. BB[18] 175, denunciation by Decomis, flor. IV. See similar pattern in the murder of
Vincent at Marseille (BB[18] 179, enquiry of j.p., 15 mess. IV, evidence of Mallet).

[64] A.N. BB[18] 125, evidence of Escomel.

[65] Aix: composite evidence from A.D. Var 2 L 982, A.N. BB[18] 175; Aubagne: BB[18] 176, 'Etat
des assassins de ce canton d'Aubagne'; Montbrison: Lucas, 'Violence thermidorienne'.

villages, the *égorgeur* group would be half a dozen or possibly ten.[66] It seems probable moreover that a distinction should be made in many places between a small hard core of men prepared to kill, whom one would properly term 'égorgeurs', and a larger group of counter-jacobin activists around them who participated in all the other forms of counter-jacobinism and were often in attendance at murders.

Leaving aside speculations about predisposition of character or of particular trades, one must emphasise that the hard core in particular (though not only them) mostly had strong personal motives for militancy. The dominant figures at least were men who had suffered personally during the Terror. They had either been in prison or had fled during the Terror. More than that, many had lost relatives to the guillotine and had lost possessions to the nation through seizure and forced sale. One militant reactionary in the Loire had lost twenty-five relatives on the scaffold.[67] Most had had the ordinary course of their lives and business badly disrupted, their income jeopardised through absence or inattention and sometimes their possessions dilapidated. They may have had their names circulated as wanted men or put on official lists of émigrés which meant automatic proscription. Indeed, a significant proportion of those later listed by jacobins either as their persecutors or as associated with them were émigrés who had returned after the Terror. Twenty-seven of the sixty-four people against whom arrest warrants were issued over the Tarascon troubles were on the *Liste générale des émigrés*.[68] However, although it is evident that, among the returning émigrés, there were men of the ancien regime elite with substantial counter-revolutionary commitment and connections, this was not the overwhelming characteristic of returned émigrés.[69] One must be careful to remember that the pervasive character of the Terror in this most active of all the areas of federalism had meant that large numbers of people from different social levels had been classed as émigrés. Many had not even gone abroad, but had disappeared into the hills or the *armée d'Italie*. There is no obvious social connotation to the term. Certainly, such people were likely to be royalists, just as were deserters. However, it is possible to suggest that for many counter-jacobins royalism

---

[66] E.g. BB¹⁸ 183, Tableaux des assassinats, Noves; BB¹⁸ 317, enquiry of j.p. of Pont-Saint-Esprit, 29 vend. IV, evidence of Onde.

[67] A.N. F⁷ 5203 d. Lesgallery, petition of niv. VIII.

[68] A.N. BB¹⁸ 177, *mandats d'amener*, 9 germ. VII. The presence of émigrés in most militant groups particularly in the deep south is attested by many documents, of which one example is the analysis of Aubagne in A.D. Bouches-du-Rhône L 3049, enquiry of prair. VI, evidence of Pignol.

[69] Note the letter from Mun. admin. of Le Beausset to Fréron, 1 niv. IV: 'Dans le courant de la troisième année, la loi a rappelé tous les cultivateurs; ils sont tous rentrés sous ce nom; mais il y a beaucoup de bourgeois, de notaires, de négociants et autres' (Fréron, *Mémoire historique*, p. 239). Note how careful Freron was to specify 'des émigrés de 91 et 92' when making his accusations about the massacres (p. 30)

was essentially only a name for their hostility to the republican regime which had been espoused by their local enemies. Although they wore white cockades, shouted *vive le roi* and sang royalist songs, that was all part of the uniform of counter-jacobinism and of the culture of reaction, an antithesis rather than a programme. Obviously, they were more or less available to counter-revolutionary conspirators in a general sort of way and the more sophisticated of them had some kind of view of what a restored king might do for them, if only in a general sense of a return to 'le bon temps'.[70] But it was this negative, emblematic quality of counter-jacobin royalism in the villages and the small towns that made counter-revolutionary conspiracy ultimately so sterile in the Midi.

Thus, personal revenge for personal suffering exacted upon known individuals within a community context was a classic characteristic of counter-jacobin violence throughout the Years III, IV and V. 'Je viens de venger la mort de mon père' was the commonest of all counter-jacobin phrases after a murder, much more so than 'Vive le Roi'.[71] This far, at least, the Thermidorean administrators were not misrepresenting matters when they invariably presented the murderous violence as the result of personal revenge born of an impatience with delays in government action against jacobins. This direct relationship between persecutor and victim is also visible in assaults. 'Rends-moi la cuvette que tu m'as prise,' cried one counter-jacobin as he beat the man who had been the *garde-séquestre* at his family house in the Year II.[72] We have seen how this kind of relationship tended to lie behind attacks by men from out of town. Indeed, this personal quality in the violence was clearly felt to be necessary. Witnesses noted that when one member of a detachment marching against Toulon in the Year III maltreated a man at Tourves (Var), 'ses complices frémissaient de le voir si acharné contre ce citoyen qu'il ne connaissait pas'.[73] His violence was beyond what counter-jacobins themselves deemed correct. In this land of vendetta, the personal relationship legitimised certain acts but, by the same token, it prohibited others. It was not merely sophistry (although it was certainly that) which prompted the *agent national* of Laudun (Gard) to disclaim all responsibility of his compatriots in murders at Pont-Saint-Esprit by saying that 'on comprendra que nous ne pouvions pas être ennemis des gens que nous ne con-

---

[70] E.g. A.N. BB[18] 175, accusation against Roman, vent. III: 'est-ce qu'on n'était pas bienheureux alors? est-ce qu'on n'était pas bien payé en travaillant? les choses n'étaient point aussi chères et l'on ne manquait de rien; on était libre alors; on allait à la chasse quand on voulait'.

[71] Note that at Tarascon, the only one who seems to have made a point of crying 'Vive le Roi' was the only identifiable noble involved (A.N. BB[18] 183, Tableaux des assassinats, Graveson).

[72] A.N. BB[18] 690, evidence of Aubert; cf. A.D. Bouches-du-Rhône L 3051, evidence of Veuve Liotard: 'ton mari m'a pris 35 francs et s'il ne me les rend pas, je lui donnerai une bonne bastonnade'.

[73] A.N. BB[18] 186, Mun. admin. of Tourves to Mun. admin. of Aix, 19 prair. VI.

naissions pas'.[74] He was invoking those common rules of southern behaviour which are emerging in this analysis of the pattern of violence.

Socially, counter-jacobin activists were drawn from a diverse milieu. Clearly, the dominant figures were often well-to-do in the local context, belonging to landed, professional and occasionally noble families or else from local better-off merchant families. However, one should not be drawn into stating that these elements typified the group. When the authorities later attempted to prosecute the *égorgeurs*, they issued warrants against men drawn from a social spectrum that included day labourers and notaries, landowners and artisans.[75] Certainly, prosecution often aimed to implicate local personalities seen as promoters of counter-terrorism, but who were not necessarily personally involved in assaults. This widens the social group and above all the age group identified as *égorgeurs*; but this does not alter the picture of social diversity that emerges from the identifications based on evidence in later judicial enquiries. In many villages and small towns, counter-jacobins seem drawn from much the same social area as jacobins whose social recruitment was also diverse. Although it is clear that at least in some parts of this region the struggle between jacobins and reactionaries brought into play a struggle between poorer and richer ends of the community, the cohesiveness of the general counter-jacobin group did not derive from a social cohesiveness in a class sense. It was rooted in other sources of group identity. These related in part to the common personal experience of these men; but they are to be found above all in the nature of the local community.

The dominant characteristic of counter-jacobin activists, with a few exceptions, was their youth.[76] Many of these young men were deserters or refractory conscripts. Indeed, it is by no means the least irony in a period rich in ironies that the other characteristic of these young men should have been that they so often organised themselves militarily. In the early summer of the Year III, they either took over or substituted themselves in very many places for the National Guard.[77] They were indeed encouraged to do this by the higher administrations and even some *représentants en mission* in the fear

---

[74] A.N. BB[18] 317, letter to *accusateur pub.* of Nîmes, 30 niv. IV.

[75] A careful analysis of the composition of these groups has yet to be undertaken. To my knowledge, the only case-study so far is that contained in my article, 'Violence thermidorienne'. For the Bouches-du-Rhône, the enquiries and correspondence contained in A.N. BB[18] 175, 176, 177 provides the basis for this paragraph. Evidence is more fragmentary for other departments in the BB[18] series and must be supplemented from tribunal papers in departmental archives. The footnotes in Cobb, *Police and People*, also make accessible some evidence.

[76] The most significant exception is Tarascon.

[77] E.g. A.N. BB[18] 174, *Précis des cruautés arrivées à Beaucaire*; BB[18] 175, patriotes of Port Chamas to Min. Just. (Year IV) and Paillet, j.p. of Aix, to Min. Just., 28 flor. IV; BB[18] 176, report by commander of Arles, 5 niv. IV, and *Précis des cruautés exercées à Barbentane*; A.D. Drôme L 200, order of the Depart., 26 therm. III; A.D. Loire L 126 fols 274 and 297.

generated by the Toulon insurrection.[78] They formed elite companies, called *hussards* or *grenadiers* or *chasseurs* according to the place. These were the companies that were called *Compagnies de Jésus*.[79] Many of the incidents in which counter-jacobins were involved found them dressed in elite company uniforms (possibly no more than a distinctive tassel with a white cockade) and many of their operations had a military style – they guarded the prisons where they massacred, they escorted prisoners whom they killed on the road, they surrounded and searched areas of town, they claimed orders to arrest, they patrolled the streets and beat up jacobins whom they encountered. Indeed, elite companies were so prevalent in the south-east that *représentants en mission* later in the Year III and then Fréron, as government *commissaire* in early Year IV, issued blanket orders for their abolition.[80]

This double characteristic – youthful and military – was so evident that neutral witnesses who did not wish to use partisan terms such as 'égorgeurs' or 'royalistes' referred to them in many places as 'les hussards' or 'les chasseurs' or 'les grenadiers' or else, and much more frequently, as 'la jeunesse' or 'les jeunes gens'.[81] In other words, they were frequently identified as a youth group. They themselves, indeed, identified themselves as a group – their peculiar hairstyles, their white cockades, their songs, their slogans, all these were symbols of their collective identity. The paramilitary organisations also reflected a search for a collective identity. They deliberately wore uniforms which defined them in the eye of those who watched them. Witnesses knew full well that this was not the real Guard but a disguise, for their later testimony carefully specified 'des individus habillés en gardes nationaux', 'habillés en hussard'.[82] This military character was in fact a typical manifestation of the traditional youth group. Maurice Agulhon has shown how youth groups became incorporated into the traditional civic military institutions of southern France before the Revolution (such as the *bravade*, a sort of gun-firing parade on important local occasions).[83] In this sense, therefore, the counter-jacobin youth was accomplishing a traditional gesture by taking over the Guard. The link was explicit in the more formal acts of the counter-jacobin youth in the Year III. They escorted local reac-

---

[78] E.g. Fréron, *Mémoire historique*, p. 253; Musée Calvet 2530 p. 8. It was not merely Toulon which worried Thermidorean administrations; jacobin resistance and threats were recorded in several centres, especially Avignon and Orange.

[79] E.g. A.D. Bouches-du-Rhône L 3049, interrogation of Monnier, 'cette Compagnie de Jésus et du Soleil était nommée la compagnie des chasseurs et des grenadiers'.

[80] E.g. A.D. Vaucluse 1 L 137, *arrêté* of Boursault, 19 therm. III; A.N. BB[18] 186, *arrêté* of Depart. of Bouches-du-Rhône on Fréron's order, 25 brum. IV.

[81] E.g. A.D. Bouches-du-Rhône L 3049, enquiry of prair. VI, passim; A.N. BB[18] 690, enquiry of Year VI, passim; A.N. F[7] 7090, *commissaire du Direct.* of Gard depart. to Min. Int., 10 niv. IV.

[82] A.N. BB[18] 182, enquiry of brum. VI into Graveson, evidence of Barthelemy; BB[18] 690, evidence of femmes Phalipon, Farjon and Seigneur.

[83] M. Agulhon, *Pénitents et Francs-Maçons de l'ancienne Provence* (Paris, 1968), pp. 43–62.

tionary officials, they drilled on the square, they searched areas of town under the eye of local officials, they burned the Liberty Tree in front of the administrators.[84] All this had strong links with the municipalised and militarised rituals of ancient regime southern public life.

However, these echoes of traditional youth groups did not constitute the substance of *égorgeur* action, neither did the simple act of wearing a uniform suffice to make one an *égorgeur*. The quality of being a deserter, the title of victim, the condition of being an ex-émigré, all predisposed the local core of militants to admit a man to their ranks; indeed, these were the attributes that allowed the inclusion into the group of a few men outside the traditional contexts of town quarter or parish.[85] However, as with all youth groups, there existed here rites of initiation, of which murder itself constituted the *chef d'oeuvre en maîtrise*. All had to excel in threats, almost in a competition of outrageous exaggeration in tavern and street. But it was not enough to claim verbally one's right of entry to the group. Sometimes the jacobins themselves distinguished between an 'égorgeur' and a 'persécuteur des patriotes qui a mis en oeuvre tous les moyens pour les mettre sous les poignards'.[86] It was not enough to set someone up for the knife; one had to plunge it in oneself. This was the act of initiation. We see it clearly in the abortive murder of Perraud at Montbrison. Two groups met in the street over the unhappy Perraud, one composed of novices like Achard and the other of old hands like Lesgallery. When Achard's pistol failed to go off, Lesgallery cried 'retirez-vous – vous n'êtes que des enfants' and himself buried an axe in Perraud's chest.[87] Thus, this rite of initiation possessed strong overtones of a virility test. Equally, murder was the necessary gesture that tied the individual to the group and compromised each in the same fraternal complicity of blood shed. One of the *veuve* Tourangeau's killers cried 'nous sommes ici huit, il faut que chacun de nous la frappe et celui qui ne la frappera pas il faut le frapper lui-même'.[88] Indeed, it was the accomplishment of this initiation that probably identified the hard core of young killers inside the wider group of youth who surrounded them and formed the counter-jacobin companies devoted to the performance of general brutality.

If counter-jacobin activity often seems very much an outgrowth of traditional youth activities, it sometimes becomes difficult to establish a frontier between action significant in the structure of the Reaction and action

---

[84] E.g. A.N. BB¹⁸ 175, patriots of Port-Chamas to Min. Just. (Year IV); BB¹⁸ 183, Tableaux des assassinats, Noves and Cassis; BB¹⁸ 690, enquiry of Year VI, passim.

[85] See, for example, how Faure-Pibrac was able to get himself accepted by the reactionary *jeunesse* of Montélimar after making a reputation for himself at Crest (A.D. Drôme L 1689 and L 1829.

[86] A.N. AFᴵᴵᴵ 298 (1181), information sent to Reverchon, Year IV.

[87] A.N. BB¹⁸ 690, evidence of Perraud (who survived). A very similar incident at Clansayes (A.D. Drôme L 1869 d. Pelisse).

[88] A.D. Drôme L 1856, evidence of Veuve Berenger.

more properly construed as youth leisure adorned with some contemporary idiom. At Arles, a pitched battle raged between two sets of youth at a wedding dance in frimaire Year VI.[89] One side cried that 'nous ne voulons plus de muscadins' and the other that 'il emmerdait la nation'. It was a typical venue for a typical fight between two *jeunesses* who would have used other terms eight years before. Yet, one side were sailors, and sailors provided the jacobin base at Arles, where there had been endless confrontations of this nature between patriots and reactionaries. This incident illustrates the intertwining of local political expression and popular sociability. On the other hand, one should not see counter-jacobin youth as a mere replica of traditional youth groups of pre-revolutionary society. For one thing, there was frequently a minority of married men and older men mixed up in counterjacobin actions. One or two would not necessarily be incompatible with a youth group especially in its militarised form: an older man as commander of a Thermidorean 'National Guard' could have had a function derived from the traditional 'capitaine du guet'. Others were doubtless brought into action by a need for revenge so urgent that it could not be delegated to the *jeunesse*, as it might have been in an earlier time, while the legitimacy of vendetta allowed their inclusion into groups whose young men would probably have excluded them before. Nonetheless, there may be an additional explanation. Youth groups inhabited a kind of twilight zone of tacit tolerance by their community. From time to time, one can see the counter-jacobin youth benefiting from this attitude: one *cafetier* at Aix prevented his clients from intervening in an incident by saying 'que c'étaient des jeunes gens, qu'il n'était pas nécessaire de descendre, qu'il fallait les laisser battre'.[90] However, it is clear that older men could intervene in the affairs of youth if need be, although it required some judgement, and that by so doing they made the business much more serious. A conversation at Montélimar as an incident built up at the end of the Year III is explicit in this sense. One man said that 'pour cette fois les hommes s'en mêleraient. Ce à quoi le déclarant répondit que puisque les hommes voulaient s'en mêler, lui ne s'en mêlerait pas, parce que les affaires de jeunesse ne devaient pas se traiter sérieusement.' A third man remarked that they should 'aller ... donner mainforte à ces jeunes gens s'ils n'étaient pas assez forts'.[91]

However, the identification of a strong element of the traditional youth group in counter-jacobin action is important because whoever speaks of youth group in traditional society is also speaking of forms of social regulation. From the vantage point of the tacit tolerance of their often ritualised excess, youth groups traditionally expressed reproach and exacted sanctions

[89] A.N. BB[18] 181, report of 6 frim. VI. Cf. a similar incident at Cavaillon in Year V (A.D. Vaucluse 1 L 220 d. Cavaillon).

[90] A.N. BB[18] 175, indictment of Roman and Péchot, 24 vent. III.

[91] A.D. Drôme L 1829, affair Faure-Pibrac, evidence of Blanchot *fils*.

for behaviour outside the unwritten norms of conduct in this southern society, as well as protecting the interests of their own age group. We are therefore immediately brought to the question of whether this counter-jacobin youth was accomplishing traditional tasks of regulation in the local community.[92] In some measure, the very fact that this youth took over the National Guard is itself revealing. It could be said to be not a fortuitous act. It was a sort of *jeu à double entente*. Those who watched this guard knew that it was an unauthentic guard. But its uniform, its title, its hierarchy of ranks, its relations with municipal officials conferred on it a semblance of reality. Indeed, it is rare to see anyone questioning its right to arrest and search. Whilst not being National Guards, they were in a certain sense national guards all the same. By definition, the National Guard's function was to maintain good order in the community. Thus, by acquiring this institution and its appearance, the youth was in a sense attributing this role to itself. By no means all youth action in the Year III took place in the context of a 'National Guard', but the widespread use of this form is significant of the relationship which these young men at least attempted to have with the community.

If one looks at the action of the youth, one can see with ease many actions characteristic of traditional attitudes and modes of collective regulation within the community. Murder poses some particular problems which will be examined later in this essay. However, as was stressed earlier, murder constituted only a part, though the most spectacular, of the whole action of these people. A great deal of the daily business of counter-jacobins repro-duced traditional acts. The *farandole* was danced before and after incidents, both as a means of raising the temperature and of celebrating as well as a means of bringing in a crowd round the event.[93] The staple diet of songs and shouted insults in front of the door of an unpopular local figure, together with the throwing of stones, deliberately noisy and insulting behaviour in the street, constituted a *tapage*. In the ancien regime, *tapage* was consistently used as a form of public reprobation and its use here was no different. The inten-tion of this action was to humiliate. Public humiliation associated with an act of punishment or public expiation lay at the heart of all the work of the militant reactionaries. Frequently, the action was relatively anodyne. For example, it could take the form of a kind of inverted reiteration of the reproved act – hence, in the Year III one sees members of the jacobin club obliged to uproot the Liberty Tree under the hoots and catcalls of the youth and the women in an obvious parody of the ceremonial planting under the

---

[92] On youth groups, see Agulhon, *Pénitents et Francs-Maçons*, pp. 43–64; Y. Castan, *Honnêteté et relations sociales en Languedoc, 1715–1780* (Paris, 1974), pp. 31, 420–6; N. Castan, *Les Criminels du Languedoc* (Toulouse, 1980), pp. 104–5, 126, 139, 202–7.

[93] E.g. A.N. BB¹⁸ 177, annotated copy of report of Mun. of Tarascon, 6 prair. III; A.D. Vaucluse 1 L 225 d. Mondragon, report of j.p. of Mornas, 9 therm. V.

applause of the club.[94] Humiliation and punishment could frequently be much more explicit and painful. People were often forced to beg for pardon on their knees, once again sometimes being taken to the Liberty Tree or to the locale of the former club.[95] Even more frequent were beatings. However, in all these cases, the scenario was the same. It always took place outside, in the street – it was indeed essential that punishment and humiliation should be seen by all, not perhaps quite so much as a deterrent to the individual as to endow the punishment with a collective communal significance. We have seen how the counter-jacobins went out of their way to obtain an audience: here is one of the principal functions of the crowd. For all these victims, the punishment was direct and brutal, but short. For others, however, it was more elaborate. The *tapage* became a *charivari*. Essentially this consisted in parading a victim through the locality before locking him or her up in the local jailhouse. The *charivari* was frequently copied directly from those of the ancien regime. Perhaps the victim's hair was burned or cut off or else the victim was placed on an ass and dragged round the locality.[96] In all cases, the *charivari* was designed to show the victim to the population and to expose him or her to mockery. Often he or she was taken to special places – in front of a church, in front of a particular cafe, on a square – at each of which there was a pause during which the population came out to jeer.[97] For some, the humiliation was made even worse by being loaded with chains like a common criminal and by being deliberately put in cells with common criminals.[98] In this masculine southern society, there were some humiliations that were deeply galling: one jacobin told his guards that 'je crains que les femmes ne me viennent insulter'.[99] Mockery was indeed one of the prime functions of women in this structure.[100]

---

94 E.g. A.N. BB[18] 690, evidence of Billard. At Sainte-Cécile, one man was told 'vous étiez trop content quand on la plantait, chacun à son tour' (A.D. Vaucluse 7 L 85, enquiry of germ. IV, evidence of Maurie).

95 Ibid., evidence of Granier and Maurie.

96 E.g. A.N. BB[18] 186, enquiry at Le Beausset, prair. VI; BB[18] 888a, *Jean-Baptiste Mauric . . . au Directoire executif* (n.d.); A.D. Drôme L 1892, attack on Jalade of Saint-Restitut.

97 E.g. A.N. BB[18] 174, enquiry by j.p. of 5e *arrond.* of Marseille, evidence of femme Coqueluche; BB[18] 183, Tableaux des assassinats, Graveson; BB[18] 690, evidence of femme Forest.

98 E.g. A.N. BB[18] 183, Tableaux des assassinats, Saint-Chamas: Laveirerie 'toujours lié, garrotté comme un grand criminel'.

99 A.D. Drôme L 1892, enquiry into murder of Coulon.

100 There are a very few cases of women seizing, roughing up and jailing other women (e.g. A.D. Bouches-du-Rhône L 3051, evidence of femme Michel and Veuve Monnier on Tarascon). Women do not seem to kill, except perhaps as a crowd. Cobb is too hasty in attributing this to them (*Police and People*, p. 146). Women certainly urge men on, providing encouragement, applause and the kind of general information that a crowd of partisan supporters would offer in the heat of action. They attack dead bodies (and most of Cobb's examples refer to this). On the other hand, women have a substantial role as restrainers and intermediaries, as their sex allows them to be.

The Liberty Tree was everywhere a favoured spot to which to take people for beating or even for murder.[101] This symbolised that the act was retribution for behaviour in the Revolution of which the Tree was itself the symbol. For, in the eyes of the counter-jacobins, these acts were acts of punishment.[102] Obviously, there were accidental events. The *égorgeurs* were after all violent, impatient, angry men. Yet, counter-jacobin actions were not characteristically random but deliberately aimed at chosen victims. It is very clear in all accounts of the prison massacres that the victims were carefully selected and had often been sorted into separate cells beforehand.[103] In the second massacre at Tarascon, some of the prisoners from villages which had sent killers were not touched. When the convoy of prisoners on its way to Pont-Saint-Esprit was attacked at Mondragon, not only did the witness observe that the ten assassins chose their victims but we also know that they did not touch two of the five men from Mondragon in the convoy.[104] Indeed, throughout the south-east, only a minority of the people who had played roles in the Terror were sought out. Thus, at Saint-Etienne, the local *bien pensants* held a meeting in the Year III to discuss the political morality of local jacobins. About half of those discussed were exonerated and half incriminated. Yet, each group contained men who had served in the terrorist administration, revolutionary committee and local *armée révolutionnaire*.[105] To the eye of even the well-informed local historian they do not appear very different from one another. At the same time, the severity of counter-jacobin action contained a crudely gradated but clear structure of punishment – derision and insults were less severe than beating which was less severe than arrest, etc. Thus thirty-two people were arrested at Eyragues (Bouches-du-Rhône): fourteen were kept for short periods in the local lock-up; seven were sent down to the prison at Saint-Rémy, which was one step up in humiliation and danger to life; eleven were sent to Tarascon which constituted the nastiest and most dangerous imprisonment; but only two of these actually perished in the prison massacres there.[106]

It follows, therefore, that the counter-jacobins did not reprove the Terror as such. One could well have been a member of even one of the Terror's repressive and coercive institutions, provided that one had respected tacit but imperious rules of conduct. It is possible to argue that these rules were largely

[101] E.g. A.N. BB¹⁸ 183, Tableaux des assassinats, Maussanne and Aix.
[102] Note that the statement by the men trying to seize cannon at the town hall of Aix in flor. III that they wanted it for 'la punition des malfaiteurs' (A.N. BB¹⁸ 176, *procès-verbal* 22 flor. III).
[103] E.g. Marseille: A.D. Bouches-du-Rhône L 3048, proceedings of Year VI; Tarascon: A.D. Bouches-du-Rhône L 3051, enquiry of Year VII; Saint-Etienne: A.N. BB¹⁸ 125, evidence of Escomel, and BB¹⁸ 8 690, 'tableau indicatif des noms des citoyens égorgés'.
[104] A.D. Vaucluse 1 L 225 d. Mondragon; Musée Calvet 2574 p. 109, list of prisoners.
[105] A. Mun. Saint-Etienne 1 D 10 (5) fols 81–2.
[106] A.N. BB¹⁸ 183, Tableaux des assassinats, Eyragues.

those of traditional society which Yves Castan has explored.[107] The first sin
of the reproved jacobin was to have failed to display what Castan calls
honnêteté, not because he sympathised in general with the Terror but because
he behaved in some specific way. The local community was always ready to
accept and to tolerate personal and group rivalries, provided that they did
not endanger communal equilibrium. To achieve this, each person had to
respect in his personal behaviour those limits which allowed others to know
not perhaps so much what to expect from him, as what not to expect. One
should never be wholly intractable, one should be conciliatory in so far as
that did not impugn one's personal honour. One had to be able to accommodate the roles played by others so that they might accommodate those
played by oneself. Now, these were precisely the qualities of which protagonists of the Terror had often been devoid. They had often been intractable
and unpredictable. One could perhaps have tolerated the arrest, even the
execution of some personalities provided that trial and execution had happened on some distant stage such as Paris. That was not the case in the south-
east which saw massive arrests and lengthy imprisonments either in the
locality or nearby, files of prisoners in chains on the roads, lightning trials
and multiple executions. All this jarred the habits of ancien regime justice
which permitted all sorts of transactions and ambiguities in the legal proceedings of one man or group against another, a justice which admitted that
men might have recourse to it as a manoeuvre and never in fact wish it to
pronounce. Counter-jacobins could argue that their opponents had broken
the tacitly accepted equilibrium. They had introduced an external power into
the community. They had appeared to do this in order to become abnormally
powerful within the community, without respecting the roles played by
others. They had not simply defeated their rivals, but they had attempted to
forbid them from playing any kind of role at all even at the cost of physically
eliminating them.[108] Thus, when local officials tried to justify the murder of
Juge at Valréas, they recounted the invasion by National Guards from
neighbouring centres and said: 'ce n'est pas d'eux dont nous avons à nous
plaindre, mais de ceux qui les ont trompés, qui les ont fait tomber dans un
piège dont les suites ont été si funestes aux habitants de Valréas'.[109]

[107] Y. Castan, *Honnêteté et relations sociales* upon which the next two paragraphs are based. A
rather more elaborate exploration of this idea with reference to a single example is found in
Lucas 'Violence themidorienne'. Cf. T. Le Goff and D. Sutherland, 'The Revolution and the
rural community in eighteenth-century Brittany', *Past and Present*, 62 (1974), 96–119.

[108] Cf. Musée Calvet 230 p. 1, *Adresse de la Municipalité de Visan au public impartial* (n.d.). Estève
'se comportait en vrai despote et . . . il était dangereux de ne pas céder à sa volonté, attendu les
liaisons qu'il avait au-dehors avec des gens puissants'. He is said to have kissed the girls, bought
cheaply at sales of émigré effects as *commissaire* of the Dist., to have kept 'aristocrates' away
from the sales, to have exchanged his poor land for good land and to have demanded money
which he claimed owing to him by threatening to use his power on the rev. committee.

[109] A.N. BB[17] 888a, *Adresse individuelle*. An equally clear statement in BB[18] 176, inhabitants of
Auriol to Corps Législatif, 26 vent. IV.

Counter-jacobins could say that their opponents had innovated brutally. Traditionally, the community feared innovation. An innovator had to justify this departure from the accepted rules of behaviour by using arguments sufficiently credible in the local context to gain general acceptance. Doubtless, this was what the jacobins were trying to do with their appeals to the notions of *patrie*, defence of the Revolution, and counter-revolutionary plots. Indeed, it may be that this quest for collective approbation was one important function of the jacobin clubs in the south-east. However, the jacobin argument inevitably encountered reticence in many quarters. It belonged to a train of thought and assumption that was not traditionally that of the community. It did not reside upon the commonly accepted morality and it was not appropriate in important respects to the needs of continuing daily life within the community. The jacobins called upon criteria and considerations that were external to the community in order to justify political repression and they constructed a system of public order based upon almost abstract concepts, which were foreign to the tangible and traditional customs. Arresting, imprisoning, sequestrating and selling the possessions of someone whom one had known all one's life, with all his quirks, qualities and defects, all this could be construed as grossly excessive behaviour in the local context (and indeed too final a rupture in the case of execution). This was doubly true in that it was done with reference to counter-revolutionary conspiracy whose substance was not always self-evident. It was this sense of the inadmissibility of excess even in this land of vendetta that was voiced by an incautious bystander at Courthézon (Vaucluse) as a jacobin, back in office in the Year IV, arrested an opponent: 'n'as-tu pas honte d'amener ce jeune homme dans le corps de garde, après le malheur que vous avez occasionné à cette famille'.[110] Jacobins themselves were well enough aware of what was being held against them. François Baumet, former vice-president of the revolutionary tribunal of the Gard, argued in his defence that 'je me suis montré humain envers les détenus, honnête à l'égard de leurs parents. Je n'ai jamais porté préjudice à personne, je n'ai fait aucune dénonciation'.[111]

The severity of punishment corresponded to the degree to which the victim had infringed these rules. Thus, it was enough to make some ordinary jacobins pull up the Liberty Tree, but men prominent enough to organise the referendum on the 1793 Constitution and to become captains in the local *armée révolutionnaire* were subjected to a brutal *charivari*.[112] As for a departmental administrator of the Year II, responsible for the whole range of

110 A.D. Vaucluse 7 L 84, j.p. of Bédarrides to *accusateur pub.* of Vaucluse, 21 frim. IV.
111 F. Rouvière, *Histoire de la Révolution française dans le Gard* (4 vols., Nîmes, 1887–9), vol. 4, p. 175. Note the striking similarity between François Liberton's petition – 'il n'a jamais dénoncé personne, il n'a fait du mal à personne' (A.D. Bouches-du-Rhône L 3043, to Mun. of Aix, 6 mess. III), and the last words of poor Jay – 'je n'ai rien fait, ni rien dit contre personne' (A.N. BB18 690, evidence of Veuve Jay).
112 A.N. BB18 690, evidence of Capray Martin.

coercive government, he was seized, paraded round the town of Salon, forced to beg pardon in the locale of the old club (reopened for the purpose), and then brought out in front and hacked to death.[113] Women were not spared, though the number killed was small.[114] On the whole, *égorgeurs* were uncertain in their attitude to killing women. There were a lot of threats to deal with them after their menfolk, but when one killer at Tarascon suggested after a night's murdering 'à présent, allons aux femmes', the others said 'il y en a assez pour aujourd'hui'.[115] Another counter-jacobin restrained a colleague saying 'que voulez-vous faire aux femmes? Elles n'ont que la langue.'[116] Women could say more in traditional society because they had so few other weapons of defence. Nonetheless, the tongue could be extremely dangerous and the women killed were probably those who had gone too far with exceptionally damaging denunciations in the Year II. In general, the most reproved jacobin women were arrested and the others were publicly beaten or had their hair cut.[117] These were women who had played roles in the club or in public festivals or who had been particularly violent in their abuse of victims of the Terror.[118] They could be represented as having broken the rule that female *honnêteté* consisted in self-effacement and reserve without which a woman gave rise to scandal.[119] The accusation of sexual misconduct was the most serious one that could be levied conventionally against a woman as it went to the heart of ordered society. Reactionary officials in Marseille made the connection between female jacobinism and such scandal explicit when commenting upon the jacobin riot of 3 fructidor Year V/20 August 1797 in which participated women 'connues publiquement par leur immoralité et leurs principes sanguinaires'.[120] It was for this reason that they were usually called 'putain' rather than the angry but more familiar 'bougresse'. This was also why, in the Year III, the most disliked jacobin women were put in prison, which was where ancien regime prostitutes were put – 'c'est ici qu'on met les garces, les putains, les déesses'.[121] Similarly, all the

---

[113] A.N. BB[18] 176, *procès-verbal* of Mun. of Salon, 16 prair. III.

[114] Cobb is too generous in his assessment (*Police and People*, p. 146).

[115] A.D. Bouches-du-Rhône L 3051, evidence of fille Raoux, it is clear that he had killing in mind rather than anything else.

[116] A.N. BB[18] 690, evidence of femme Giraud. Cf. A.D. Var 2 L 956, enquiry of j.p. of Grasse, germ. III: a former member of the rev. committee says to a loquacious colleague in jail: 'Toi tu as une langue de putain, il faut que tu dises tout.'

[117] E.g. A.D. Vaucluse 1 L 138, Boursault to Dist. of Orange, 15 vend. IV.

[118] A clear example in A.D. Vaucluse 7 L 84, accusation against femme Sourdon and femme Colomé, 25 fruct. III.

[119] Cf. A.N. BB[18] 175, *Françoise Salvat … aux citoyens juges composant le tribunal criminel du département des Bouches-du-Rhône* (n.d.): 'je suis accusée du crime le plus grave; on impute à une femme faible, connue par des moeurs douces, d'avoir provoqué au meurtre et à l'assassinat'.

[120] A. Mun. Marseille 1 D 19, Canton du Centre, 5 fruct. V.

[121] A.N. BB[18] 690, evidence of femme Forest.

women locked up in the fort at Tarascon were eventually moved to Le Refuge, the ancien regime reformatory for women of easy virtue.[122]

The scale of violence exercised against an individual did not correspond merely with the official importance of a jacobin in the Terror, as the male examples in the previous paragraph might suggest. The reactionaries attributed two specific crimes to their enemies – theft and murder.[123] They viewed the multiple requisitions and forced sales of the Year II as a system of theft. The orders of the government had not validated them, since that government itself had been illegal either since the fall of the king or the expulsion of the Girondins according to one's point of view. However, counter-jacobins do not appear ever to have deliberately killed someone for these 'thefts', although people later died as a result of injuries received. Often the beatings were accompanied by demands for restitution of the stolen goods and, in the traditional manner, counter-jacobins could often be satisfied by the return of the goods or compensation. At the very most, the jacobin's own possessions were pillaged in an act of substitute restitution. At the same time, his goods or crops were frequently destroyed. The significance of the latter gesture was, however, precise. The reactionary sought certainly to undermine the financial position of his victim, to reduce him indeed to poverty. That was just punishment, even if it was the consequence of a man being so crippled that he could not work. The counter-jacobin did not, however, seek to extrude him from the community; none of these gestures amounted to one of expulsion.[124] Only where *égorgeurs* had tried but failed to kill someone can one see an act of expulsion taking place, as the intended victim's goods were put up for public auction in his absence.[125] Certainly, numbers of jacobins fled their localities. This does not necessarily mean that they were correct to assume that their lives were in danger or even that they would have suffered financially as much by staying on as they did by leaving. After all, Maurie not only stayed on throughout the Year III in Sainte-Cécile, that most tortured of villages, but also complained loudly about the goings-on without being molested.[126]

This nuance is important for it endows the murders with all their

---

[122] A.D. Bouches-du-Rhône L 3051, evidence of Veuve Monnier.

[123] Rather than cite multiple examples for the next two paragraphs, the reader is referred to the Tableaux des assassinats in A.N. BB[18] 183 which illustrate the whole range of examples for the Bouches-du-Rhône. Similar evidence, though in much more scattered form, exists for the departments of Var, Vaucluse, Drôme and Loire.

[124] Cf. Y. Castan, *Honnêteté et relations sociales*, p. 81, and N. Castan, *Criminels du Languedoc*, p. 219

[125] The case of Brachet, *portefaix* at Tarascon, is especially significant. The *portefaix* were notoriously anti-jacobin and Brachet was 'réduit à la mendicité par la méchancheté des portefaix qui l'ont chassé pendant trois ans' (Years III to VI) 'de son travail, l'ont empêché de gagner sa vie et de nourrir sa famille' (A.N. BB[18] 183, Tableaux des assassinats, Tarascon). But note that they neither killed him nor expelled him from the town.

[126] A.D. Vaucluse 7 L 85, enquiry of germ. IV, evidence of Maurie.

significance. Murder was the act of expulsion, the definitive extrusion of the individual from the community. Indeed, presumably in exceptionally severe cases, a degree of symbolic extrusion existed beyond death. In these cases bodies were mutilated, especially by destruction of those features that render a person distinctively individual – eyes, face, hands.[127] Bodies were dragged through the streets like dead animals and thrown onto the municipal refuse or else into the Rhône or the Durance or the sea which were the equivalent.[128] Sometimes, killers insisted upon the body being buried elsewhere than in the cemetery, in a field like a dead animal or else not buried at all.[129] In one case, they even came back to dig up the body and throw it into the river.[130] This kind of action, particularly mutilation, seems to have been predominantly the work of a crowd, especially of women, after the event. This was the atavistic brutality of peasant triumphs. It was particularly visible in urban and rural popular violence in the early years of the Revolution in the Midi and one might possibly read its incidence here as some evidence of a wider popular approval of these particular murders.[131]

The counter-jacobins saw murder as justice, a fit response to the Terror's tribunals which they saw as arbitrary and murdering. Before killing a man, one group cried 'veux-tu connaître le nom de tes juges?' and gave their names.[132] Of course, the obvious victims were members of revolutionary tribunals or those who had played prominent repressive roles in administrations or committees. Above all, however, the most hated person was the denunciator. Indeed, in the Year III, printed lists of denunciators were sometimes established from the papers of revolutionary committees in order to

---

[127] A.N. BB¹⁸ 175, denunciation by Decomis: women and a crowd 'se portèrent à mutiler et à défigurer avec tout ce qui tombait sous leurs mains les cadavres des deux assassinés'. A.N. BB¹⁸ 183, Tableaux des assassinats, Gémenos: 'assassinée en plein jour sur la place publique, on lui creva les yeux et la gorge'. Ibid., Rocquevaire: 'on leur coupa le nez et oreilles'.

[128] Fréron, *Mémoire historique*, p. 273, Virion of Montélimar 'dont le cadavre fut ignominieuse-ment jeté à la voierie'; A.D. Vaucluse 1 L 226 d. Sainte-Cécile; fugitive patriots to central admin., 26 niv. IV, 'd'autres morts . . . ont été traînés à la voierie par les pieds'; A.N. BB¹⁸ 179, enquiry by j.p. of 2ᵉ *arrond.* of Marseille, 15 mess. IV, evidence of Mallet; A.N. BB¹⁸ 183, Tableaux des assassinats, Les Baux, 'ils le traînèrent comme un chien mort par toutes les rues du village'; at Avignon, Nappier was torn apart by the crowd and the pieces thrown into the Rhône along with the bodies of the executed judges of the Commission d'Orange (Soullier, *Révolution d'Avignon*, vol. 2, pp. 284ff).

[129] A.D. Bouches-du-Rhône L 3054, evidence of Gennère, grave-digger, 'plusieurs voulurent qu'ils fussent enterrés sur la place' (i.e. 'sur place'); A.D. Bouches-du-Rhône L 3051, evidence of femme Michel, 'Allez-vous-en voir Balaquet qui a la baïonette dans le corps que les chiens dévorent'; A.D. Drôme L 1856, Veuve Tourangeau affair.

[130] A.N. BB¹⁸ 183, Tableaux des assassinats, Châteaurenard.

[131] N. Castan, *Criminels du Languedoc*, pp. 194–7; Lucas, 'Problem of the Midi', pp. 24–5.

[132] A.N. BB¹⁸ 433, Descombes to Min. Just., 22 fruct. IV. Similar incident in A.D. Drôme L 1869 d. Pelisse.

serve as counter-jacobin handbooks.[133] The three men from Mondragon chosen for assassination in the Pont-Saint-Esprit convoy were all known as major denunciators and witnesses at the Commission d'Orange.[134] The Thermidorean municipality of Courthézon made a particular effort to get Chauvin back from Montélimar because his evidence had caused the death of seventeen people.[135] The denunciator broke a fundamental rule of traditional social behaviour. He took upon himself to intervene without personal motive in the relations between another person and justice, knowing full well how deadly that could be. Traditionally, one could only reveal all one knew to justice in defined circumstances – above all, in cases of monstrous crime or if the church commanded it through *monitoires*.[136] Yet, most counter-revolutionary crimes were not monstrous by traditional standards (although the jacobins deliberately used this vocabulary about them) nor did the references to *patrie* and Republic in the jacobin public exhortations equivalent to the *monitoire* satisfy traditional perceptions. On the contrary, jacobin proclamations assaulted traditional values: the Commission Temporaire of Lyon called denunciation a virtue, pointed to the pecuniary rewards, and urged relatives to denounce each other and servants to inform upon masters.[137] The denunciator had not been justified in ignoring the traditional claims of discretion and group loyalty.[138] As one of the jacobins' victims said, 'si le déclarant avait commis le crime le plus horrible, on (ne) le traiterait pas plus inhumainement'.[139]

It is possible, therefore, to discern in a great deal of counter-jacobin violence a discourse upon jacobinism couched in terms of the traditional society. Counter-jacobins deliberately employed the forms and symbols of traditional behaviour; they sought to present themselves publicly to the community at large in terms of the community's traditional values. Even though their impatience may have caused them to outrun these constraints, they seem to have sought consciously to legitimise their behaviour within those same values. Their action proceeded from personal suffering presented as unreasonable; their action was therefore not unprovoked and arguably lay within the area of a person's obligation to his own reputation and interest. Their action was not random but measured retribution in a way in which arguably the Terror had not done. Their action was public and direct unlike

---

[133] *Liste générale des dénonciateurs et des dénoncés tant de la ville de Lyon que des communes voisines* (Lausanne, 1795).

[134] A.D. Vaucluse 1 L 225 d. Mondragon.

[135] A. Mun. Montélimar, *registre des delib.*, 6 mess. III.

[136] Y. Castan, *Honnêtete et relations sociales*, pp. 95–6.

[137] A.D. Loire L 188, proclamation of 7 frim. II.

[138] Note how, earlier in the Revolution, patriots had tried to rouse the population at Cabris against a man on the grounds that 'il avait déposé ce qu'il fallait tenir caché' (A.D. Var 2 L 855, enquiry of 12 pluv. III).

[139] A.D. Vaucluse 7 L 84, affair of the rev. committee of Malemort, enquiry of 14 brum. III.

the private denunciation or the evidence about a helpless man to a deadly tribunal. Unlike denunciators or revolutionary committees, they usually prefaced their acts with public threats which convention deemed the necessary warning before action. Above all, horrible crimes legitimised horrible retribution. Counter-jacobins could claim that what they did was no more horrible than what had been done to them or to their relatives. Summary execution in the street was no more or less than summary trial and execution under the guillotine. It was this idea that lay behind the conversation, so redolent of traditional assumptions about crime and retribution, that took place between a bystander and Marron, the father of the *veuve* Tourangeau's killer, at Saint-Paul-Trois-Châteaux when her body was found. Brunet said 'que le crime était horrible et qu'il serait à désirer qu'on en découvrit les auteurs, à quoi quelques personnes lui répliquèrent qu'il ne fallait rien dire'. Marron *père* agreed with Brunet's general sentiment but said 'que c'était pour punir cette foutue canaille de Payan qu'on ne reverrait plus dans le pays'.[140]

It is only by placing the violence of the Thermidorean and Directorial years in a longer perspective that one can begin to explain this pattern. Indeed, the reference of counter-jacobin reproach was not confined to the Terror but stretched back to behaviour in the earlier years of the Revolution. In the Year IV, the *agent municipal* of Pignas (Hérault) reported with alarm that those people who, in February 1792, 'ravagèrent notre commune et la firent dévaster par sept à huit cents hommes de Montpellier' were threatening to do it again.[141] The men arrested as *sabreurs* at Marseille gave significant dates when they termed their opponents 'les assassins de 1792, 1793 et 1794'.[142] There was indeed plenty of southern violence before the Terror to provide a catalogue of mutual reproach. The Bagarre de Nîmes (June 1790) and the Glacière Massacre (October 1791) foreshadowed the prison massacres of the Year III. The civil war between papalist and patriot parties in the Comtat opened up conflicts that were still being acted out after Thermidor. The *jacqueries* of 1792 in the Comtat, Haut Languedoc and Basse Provence fostered further aggressive action by local jacobins, whilst the growing crisis of the new Republic brought armed patriot expeditions, clashes and murder in early 1793, and finally the federalist civil war of that year. In the space available here, it is possible only to point to one or two themes relevant to the preceding analysis. These certainly do not constitute a full discussion of the pre-Terror violence.

The struggles after 9 thermidor must be seen as further steps in long-standing conflicts between rival groups. Indeed, the intensity and clarity of the Terror in the south-east owed a great deal to the existence of a well-defined group of victims for the repressive machine and a well-defined group

---

[140] A.D. Drôme L 1856, evidence of Louis.   [141] A.N. F7 7102, *procès-verbal* of 12 pluv. IV.
[142] A.N. BB18 174, petition to 500, 3 pluv. IV.

of victors to operate it. In local terms, the Terror constituted what appeared in late 1793 to be the definitive victory of the jacobins over their local enemies. The Year III reversed the situation and the continuity of names on either side of the divide thereafter points to the perpetuation of the group rivalries. There came into existence an alternating pattern of which the participants were very aware. There was more than bravado in the cry of Barthélémy Romieu at his arrest in Saint-Rémy (Bouches-du-Rhône) in the Year III: 'A dieu honnêtes gens, à dieu braves gens, mais nous reviendrons bientôt et nous apporterons une savonnée pour pendre...'[143] 'A ton tour, Drivon,' gaily cried one reactionary in the Loire as he thrust him into prison, 'en attendant la nôtre.'[144]

Whatever profound social forces were in conflict here in the earlier Revolution, they were clearly acted out primarily in terms of local issues and personalities. The *commissaires* of the electoral assembly of the Bouches-du-Rhône commented on troubles in the village of Eygalières in 1792 that 'la révolution n'y était pour rien, qu'elle ne servait que de prétexte aux deux partis pour s'accuser réciproquement d'incivisme'.[145] Even in the town of Arles, a relatively dispassionate analysis in the Year IV stated that

le peuple tout entier à lui-même et fort peu à la chose publique a contracté l'habitude de concentrer les grands intérêts de la nation dans ses passions et ses sentiments personnels. Pour lui, les crises révolutionnaires n'ont pas été l'époque de tels événements avantageux ou désastreux pour la liberté, mais un moyen de procurer à un parti la domination sur l'autre.[146]

The recurrence of the theme of 'deux partis' in this area throughout the revolutionary years is striking. It must be seen as a projection into the 1790s of what Maurice Agulhon termed, in the context of Basse Provence, 'cette aptitude à la division' in local life during the later decades of the century.[147] The acuity of the division before 1789 seems to have derived frequently from the rivalries and ambitions of a bourgeoisie of lawyers, *rentiers* and employers. They naturally stood at the centre of local affairs in small towns. In the rural context, although such men were possibly most widely implanted in the urbanised villages of Basse Provence, their presence (especially of lawyers) is widely attested throughout southern France.[148] These were the local *notables*,

---

[143] A.D. Bouches-du-Rhône L 3554.   [144] A.N. BB[18] 690, evidence of Drivon.

[145] A.D. Bouches-du-Rhône L 3036.

[146] A.N. F[7] 7090 d. 40, 'Mémoire sur la situation de la commune d'Arles en nivôse an quatrième'.

[147] M. Agulhon, *La Vie sociale en Provence intérieure au lendemain de la Révolution* (Paris, 1970), p. 231. Cf. W. Scott, *Terror and Repression in revolutionary Marseilles* (London, 1973), pp. 54–5.

[148] Agulhon, *Vie sociale*, pp. 103–22, 221–35, 264–84, offers a compelling analysis of this social group and of its political repercussions. See also two articles by P. M. Jones, 'The rural bourgeoisie of the southern Massif-Central', *Social History*, 4 (1979), 65–83, and 'Political commitment and rural society in the southern Massif-Central', *European Studies Review*, 10 (1980), 337–56. Also N. Castan, *Criminels du Languedoc*, pp. 113–45.

the *Messieurs*. However, their presence was not essential to such struggles in the villages; it was enough that two or three wealthy peasants should dominate the locality and conflict with each other for such rivalries to be active.

It is clear that the vitality of the southern *communauté des habitants* and of municipal institutions before the Revolution provided a context for confrontation. The Revolution inevitably aggravated these struggles. It entailed not only the eviction of an ancien regime power system of seigneurs and royal government, but also presented the opportunity to evict those *notables* who had consolidated their local power by their connections with that system, for example as seigneurial agents. Further, by erecting a whole new system of elective office, it opened up to competition all at once the whole structure of prestige, influence, and power. The commune of Moras (Drôme) offers a typical example of the importance of such office in a rural context.[149] Moras was dominated by the Quinieux family 'qui par sa fortune et son nombre couvre absolument le reste des habitants de Moras [et] qui avait toujours voulu tout tenir entre ses mains'. The family included the local *notaire* who, throughout the Revolution, either occupied the position of *juge de paix* or, when laws against multiple office-holding became too pressing, handed it over to his young cousin. He also made sure to get himself appointed the local *commissaire du Directoire* in the Year IV. The family clearly dominated local elections and its members controlled the municipality both as *maire* (or later *agent municipal*) and as *greffier*, an unstoppable combination in face of rural ignorance. The result was power in a very real sense: their weight 'paraît d'autant plus important qu'ils paraissent réunir toutes les autorités ce qui intimide le vulgaire jusqu'à imposer silence à ceux qu'ils fatiguent le plus'. They threatened anyone who opposed them; they fixed official records; and, as they dealt with all official business, 'nous ne savons jamais que ce qu'ils veulent bien nous apprendre'. The basis of the Quinieux family strength was undoubtedly a network of family and dependants held together by blood and marriage solidarity, by patronage, by employment, by debt and by deference. They and their creatures 'forment une masse qui en impose à la généralité des habitants'. Local office was essential for it allowed the family to serve its interests, to protect some of its members (in this case a refractory priest), and to look after 'une foule de parents et d'amis, d'où il resulte beaucoup d'abus pour la chose publique'.

The Quinieux family was relatively uncontested and there was no violence after Thermidor at Moras. Elsewhere such behaviour brought what amounted to protracted factional struggles. Events at Graveson were typical of many. The revolutionary history of the commune was dominated by the

---

[149] A.N. F7 7102, Villars to Directory, 1 pluv. IV. See also the example of Visan quoted above, note 108.

struggle between two *notaires*, Pierre Raoulx and Henri Mercurin.[150] The Raoulx family had been agents of the Marquis de Graveson but were strong enough to consolidate themselves in the early Revolution; the Mercurin family were victorious with the Terror. Both sides clearly controlled a number of families who represented their faction: 'si les Mercurin les abandonnaient', said one man, 'ils étaient perdus'.[151] Thus, with the Terror, the Raoulx family fled along with a number of their dependents and returned as 'émigrés' after the Terror. The Mercurin faction then became their victims, fifty-three of them being arrested in the Year III. In the Year IV, the Mercurin family returned at the head of their supporters, with one Mercurin as *commissaire du Directoire*, and exacted reprisals by arresting the head of the Raoulx clan, whilst billeting soldiers on the rest. In the Year V, once again the Mercurin family and supporters were beaten up and their property devastated.

On one level, therefore, the communal violence in villages and small towns after 9 thermidor appears very much as another episode in these struggles for local power. Family interests and networks of dependants were a central feature of local political struggles in the Midi after 1789, as they had been before. Such patterns existed on a regional as well as on a communal basis. The best-known examples are doubtless the jacobin clans of the Rovère and Payan families.[152] In counter-jacobinism, the prevalence of revenge for family reasons is one obvious symptom of this pattern and of the vendetta instinct that reinforced it. It is frequent to find groups of relatives among those identified as *égorgeurs*; in some places, members of one family directly assaulted members of another; elsewhere, one can identify a doubtless widespread pattern whereby a man holding local office had a son or close relative playing a leading role among the *égorgeurs*.[153] Indeed, the elite companies of

---

[150] A.N. BB[18] 178, director of jury of Tarascon to Min. Just., 2 flor. IV; BB[18] 183, Tableaux des assassinats, Graveson. This struggle provides an excellent example of the interlocking of communal and regional struggles. Pierre and Louis Raoulx were prominent in Federalism, but managed for a time to get the protection of Rovère and Poultier who denounced their Mercurin rival to the C.S.P. in brum. II; Pierre François Mercurin became an administrator of the department during the Year II and was the *commissaire du Directoire* later. Henri Mercurin died of natural causes before the Year III, but the struggle naturally went on.

[151] A.D. Bouches-du-Rhône L 3554, interrogation of Claude Chaix, germ. III.

[152] On these see P. Vaillandet, 'Le conventionnel Rovère et les Montagnards du Midi', *Mémoires de l'Institut historique de Provence*, 8 (1931), 39–62; ibid., 'La mission de Maignet en Vaucluse', *Ann. hist. Rév. fran.*, 3 (1926), 168–78, 240–63; ibid., 'Les débuts de la Terreur blanche en Vaucluse', *Ann. hist. Rév. fran.*, 5 (1928), 109–27; *Papiers inédits trouvés chez Robespierre . . supprimés ou omis par Courtois* (3 vols., Paris, 1828), vol. 2, pp. 405–31.

[153] On groups of relatives, e.g. A.N. BB[18] 186, enquiry by j.p. of Orgon, therm. VI, and A.D. Var 2 L 989 on the activity of Ollivier, his son and nephew at Le Castellet; on family attacks. e.g. Cobb, *Police and People*, p. 346, note Z, on murder of Martin family by Tronc family at Lambesc, and A.D. Var 1 L 282 d. Callian, on murder of Bellissen and his sons by the Rebuffet brothers; on officials–*égorgeurs* connection, e.g. A.N. BB[18] 175, denunciation by Decomis on the son of Pellicot, j.p. of Aix, and BB[18] 176, *Précis des cruautés exercées à Barbentane* on the son of the mayor.

'national guards' and the groups of militants in a locality were presumably recruited from the clientèle of the clan leaders, who might control them either by holding command rank in the 'National Guard' or else through relatives or dependants in such rank. It is this relationship that was reflected in the link between this 'National Guard' and the municipality. It was also reflected in the cases where the guardsmen appear to have been paid by local notables.[154] Finally, this situation also helps to explain the social diversity of the counter-jacobin group.

Of course, it would be absurd to reduce the revolutionary violence in the Midi to faction fighting. For one thing, the Revolution gave the poor and the weak a role that they had not had before. The conflicts between polarised groups indubitably articulated the whole complex structure of social tensions set in motion by the revolutionary crisis. Nonetheless, one can argue that where such tensions did not find expression through the rivalries of local notables, they were liable to remain inchoate and confined to the rural anarchy of délits champêtres and sporadic insurgency against châteaux and large property, to urban market riots and diffuse criminality. The detailed nature of tension and of the relationship of conflicting parties to it varied from area to area within this region in a complexity whose analysis is beyond the scope of this essay. In some places, parties had polarised over access to local resources, presumably well before the Revolution. At Graveson, the struggles between the two notaires masked conflicts over grazing rights.[155] The Raoulx family had doubtless used their position as seigneurial agents as a weapon before 1789. The composition of the Mercurin group (4 propriétaires, 10 cultivateurs, 7 agriculteurs and a small number of rural artisans) was entirely consistent with such a situation.[156] In areas of high protestant population, notably the Gard, Gwynne Lewis and James Hood have amply demonstrated that the struggles were grounded not only in confessional polarisations but also in the different economic structures associated with each.[157] In much of the Comtat it is clear that, whatever inter-communal and personal tensions were reinforced by the civil war, jacobin groups were essentially associated with the struggle of the large number of parcellaires in this area against the small number of large landowners.[158] In the villages and small towns of the

---

[154] E.g. A.D. Bouches-du-Rhône L 3049, evidence of Pignol: those who are said to pay at Aubagne are the ex-curé, a négociant, a notaire, a homme de loi, a bourgeois, a naval lieutenant, an aubergiste, a tanneur and a charron. The money was given to a cafetier to distribute, in a sense emphasising the dependent, 'retainer' character of the men.

[155] A.N. BB[18] 178, Etienne Lambert to director of jury, 28 flor. IV

[156] That is to say, those men arrested at Graveson in the Year III.

[157] Lewis, Second Vendée; J. N. Hood, 'Patterns of popular protest in the French Revolution: the conceptual contribution of the Gard', Journal of Modern History, 48 (1976), 259–93, and 'Revival and mutation of old rivalries in revolutionary France', Past and Present, 82 (1979), 82–115.

[158] Mlle Lombardi, 'Les Troubles agraires dans le Comtat Venaissin, les régions d'Apt et d'Orange

Var, jacobin groups frequently found their support among craftsmen and day labourers.[159]

It is striking how often the jacobins appear as the minority group in communal struggles. The patriot municipal administration of Salon echoed many such statements when it wrote that 'le nombre des bons républicains est fort petit ici dans notre commune'.[160] At Bédarrides (Vaucluse), they numbered about 30 out of a total population of 1,600 and at Seillans (Var) roughly the same number out of a population of 2,200.[161] At Le Buis (Drôme), they were 'une poignée de personnes' confronting 'une commune entière altérée par l'influence des scélérats'.[162] It is certain that the revolutionary discourse on rights and sovereignty, especially in its radical form, gave minority groups the means to harness to some degree the upsurge of popular grievance. At Cabris (Var), for instance, Maune *notaire* pursued his rivalry with Bounin *notaire* through banquets and by preaching that 'il y a une loi qui autorise de tuer les aristocrates' until, after several years of pillaging the property of Bounin and his clan, the onset of the Terror produced Bounin's arrest by the local revolutionary committee. Maune promptly seized his papers, thereby monopolising local legal business.[163] Such naked self-interest should not make us ignore in the motivations of many southern jacobins the element of conviction and the sense of the regeneration of the revolutionary nation. As Jean–Baptiste Mauric said, 'J'ai été membre de la société populaire de Sainte-Cécile; tant qu'elle a pu s'assembler, le peuple n'a pas été votre dupe, il a connu les loix, il a aimé la liberté que vous détestez; je suis membre de ce peuple'.[164] At the same time, it is true that in Mauric's home land of the Comtat the popular violence of the second half of 1792 did allow jacobin groups a temporary victory in their struggles dating back at least to the civil war. Delegates from their clubs met at Sainte-Cécile and helped to direct popular violence against châteaux and rich locals, raising swingeing financial contributions and participating in acts of serious violence against persons.[165] Indeed, 1792 appears a crucial year in much of the south-east, not simply in

en 1792' (unpublished *mémoire* of the University of Aix, 1970); see also the anti-rich statements by jacobins at Malemort report to the enquiry of brum. III (A.D. Vaucluse 7 L 84) and similar ones at Crest (A.D. Drôme L 1689, enquiry of niv. III).

[159] A.D. Var 1 L 282 d. Fayence, report by Girard cadet on the cantons of Fayence and Callians, 18 niv. VI; A.D. Var 2 L 955, evidence of Aragon, 'grand nombre d'artisans auraient traité une partie des citoyens d'aristocrates'; A.D. Var 2 L 291 suppl. 14, trial of Portal after Toulon rising, evidence from Le Beausset.

[160] Fréron, *Mémoire historique*, p. 88.

[161] Musée Calvet 2529 p. 46, *Les citoyens de Bédarrides . . . à la Convention nationale* (25 brum. III); A.D. Var 1 L 282 d. Fayence, inhabitants of Seillans to central admin. (Year V).

[162] A.D. Drôme L 202 d. Le Buis, letter from Blanchard, 18 pluv. V.

[163] A.D. Var 2 L 855, Cabris affair.

[164] A.N. BB[18] 888a, *Jean-Baptiste Mauric . . . au Directoire exécutif* (n.d.).

[165] A.D. Drôme L 196, especially 'Extrait du verbal des commissaires du département de la Drôme', 15 Jan. 1793.

terms of the undoubted escalation of jacobin-associated violence, but also in terms of jacobin inroads into the poorer element of the support that their opponents enjoyed.[166] Therefore, despite the social diversity of both jacobin and counter-jacobin groups after Thermidor and the frequent social resemblance of leading figures on either side, it is this pattern which allows us to endorse the view that, at this level as well as nationally, the Thermidorean Reaction was in an important sense a social reaction and to accept the social implications of the contemporary Thermidorean title of 'les honnêtes gens'.

Jacobins were not necessarily inherently more violent than their opponents before the Terror. It is true, however, that wherever they were in the minority they would be liable to call upon the support of like-minded groups outside. Similarly, they were likely to be attracted by the parallel and non-elective institutions of the club and the revolutionary committee. The great practical advantage of jacobinism was that it did provide a clear system of supporting alliances and the justification for them. It was for these reasons that jacobin behaviour before the Terror was so much more clearly identified with intercommunal expeditions than was that of their opponents. The purpose of such expeditions was nearly always to resolve municipal deadlocks or to reinforce local jacobin groups. Thus, at Valréas in mid-1792, the so-called *complot des notaires* involving three of the town's five *notaires* based on a 33-member *société patriotique* struggled in vain to evict the municipality until patriot National Guards were brought in from the neighbourhood. This is what was later held against the murdered Juge, one of the *notaires*.[167] At Le Barroux (Vaucluse), one faction in the municipality in July 1793 got an assembly of inhabitants to evict another faction because it had urged the population to march in support of Avignon against the Marseillais, a doubly unpopular proposal in that most people disliked marching anywhere and especially to help Avignon. Their opponents promptly brought in *commissaires* from the district with armed guards who reinstated them and made the commune pay through the nose.[168] These examples serve to illustrate a common phenomenon with many variants. In a real sense, the Terror represented the logical outcome of this pattern: unelected jacobins were installed in power by outside authority and were supported by a regular system of outside coercion. It was for this reason that communal violence went into abeyance in the Year II.

Jacobin violence before the Terror displayed some of the elements that we have identified in counter-jacobin behaviour. Jacobins also called upon the same repertoire of murder, arrest, assault, insult and damage to property.[169]

[166] Cf. Agulhon, *Vie sociale*, pp. 273–5.   [167] Lombardi, 'Troubles agraires', p. 90.
[168] A.D. Vaucluse 7 L 74.
[169] A.N. BB[18] 888a, *Adresse individuelle . . . du canton de Vauréas* provides a particularly clear account of jacobin use of the whole panoply of techniques. On *farandoles*, see also A.D.

They also danced the *farandole*. They also had recourse to skimmington, especially putting opponents on asses and parading them round town.[170] They also used forms of *bravade*, particularly on their return in the Year IV which was frequently a formal entry with armed dependants and a parade round the locality before going home.[171] They also formed rival 'National Guards' from time to time when they failed to get a proper share of it through elections; they too formed elite companies.[172] Above all, the jacobins also had their youth groups. This was particularly visible in the larger centres – a leading activist at Carpentras had the significant nickname of 'L'Abba' and one at Aix was called 'La Jeunesse'; indeed, in towns particular trade groups lent themselves to this, as with the jacobin *mousses* at Arles.[173] However, it was equally true of smaller communities. François Saurel, the dominant jacobin at Malemort, very clearly held the role of *abbé de jeunesse* in 'l'assemblée des jeunes gens de cette commune' in 1793.[174] This was a natural enough development. Already before 1789, the youth from different social backgrounds tended to clash and local notables had begun to use youth groups in their struggles.[175] In the Revolution, political alignments wove themselves into the fabric of youth behaviour, so that confrontations often became conflicts between patriot and reactionary youth. This was clearly what happened to the youth of Aubignan to whom this essay referred earlier; at Callian (Var), Pascal *aîné* 's'insinua adroitement à la tête d'un parti qui avait eu de disputes par une autre pour la danse, il alluma la discorde en faisant traiter l'autre parti de chouans et de royalistes'.[176] At Salon, one reactionary escaped harm in March 1793 on the grounds that 'il était trop

---

Drôme L 197, Bérard to Depart. of Drôme, Aug. 1792, and Rouvière, *Révolution dans le Gard*, vol. 4, p. 186.

[170] E.g. A.D. Vaucluse 7 L 84, enquiry into Malemort, brum. III, and A.D. Bouches-du-Rhône L 3038, evidence of Réveille.

[171] E.g. A.N. BB18, Lambert to director of jury, 28 flor. IV, and denunciation by some residents of Saint-Chamas, 22 flor. V; A.D. Drôme L 205 d. Saint-Paul-Trois-Châteaux, Mun. admin. to central admin., 18 germ. IV.

[172] E.g. A.N. BB18 175, Saint-Chamas affair; BB18 186, *mémoire* for Antoine Philibert Auriol; A.D. Drôme L 200, *procès-verbal* by Mun. of Saint-Paul-Trois-Châteaux, 6 (?) Apr. 1792; A.D. Bouches-du-Rhône L 3554, interrogation of Romieu of Saint-Rémy; H. Bellugou, *La Révolution dans le canton de Saint-Pargoire (Hérault)* (Montpellier, 1931), pp. 68–9.

[173] A.D. Var 2 L 981, trial of Maigre (Year V); A.D. Bouches-du-Rhône L 3043, *Pièces relatives à la fermeture des sections de la ville d'Aix* (Marseille, 1793); A.N. F7 7090 d. 40, Pomme, Grossy and Sabatier to j.p. of Arles, 5 niv. IV. Grasse is another clear case (A.D. Var 2 L 956, enquiry of 9 germ. III).

[174] A.D. Vaucluse 7 L 84, evidence of Jean, niv. III, recounting the *levée des 300.000* and the typical 'quête générale' organised by the young among the inhabitants as they would have done under the ancien regime. On the patriot Saurel family, see Cobb, *Police and People*, pp. 138, 350–1.

[175] N. Castan, *Criminels du Languedoc*, pp. 126 and 205.

[176] A.D. Var 1 L 282 d. Callian.

vieux pour être aristocrate'.[177] If the *levée des 300.000* provided excellent opportunities to remove some of the rival youth, the *première réquisition* presented jacobins with serious difficulties. Their political allegiances could not permit any great level of desertion or resistance among their youth. Yet, as a poor patriot from Tarascon was to write in the Year IV, 'les ginegence [jeunes gens] de premiere requisition patriote il sont partis, les aristocrat sont encore est [et] nous menace de coupt de paton'.[178] In the Year II, one suspects that this situation increased jacobin commitment to the Terror. Certainly, after 9 thermidor, elite company uniform and *l'habit national* formalised visually the antagonistic groups. *Volontaires* home on leave were prominent on the jacobin side and *l'habit national* was one of the commonest causes of apparently random *égorgeur* assaults.[179]

Nonetheless, whatever the similarities between the pattern of jacobin and counter-jacobin violence, the differences were more important.[180] In the first place, although jacobin violence was certainly not indiscriminate, it is difficult to discern in it the structure of punishment identifiable in counter-jacobin action. It seems aimed at all opponents and the gradation of violence appears related more to the wealth and influence of the victim than to specific conduct, as was much more the case with counter-jacobins. In the second place, the localism so characteristic of counter-jacobinism was rather less compelling with jacobins. The interference of outside forces was a consistent feature and, although local men were at the centre of such actions, they seem usually vastly outnumbered by outsiders who certainly did not deprive themselves of full participation in assaults. Indeed, the connection between persecutor and victim does not seem paramount in jacobin violence as it does in counter-jacobinism. Jacobins were prepared to assault and to kill people who were personally unknown to them and sought their justifications in the alleged counter-revolutionary character of their victims.[181] Moreover, jacobin violence changed its nature after 1793. Organised repression dominated the Year II. Under the Directory, although jacobins returned to ritual confrontations of threats, street chanting and *farandoles*, their assaults were relatively sporadic. They resorted once more to the intimidation of armed

---

177 A.N. BB¹⁸ 181, evidence of Pignard, 27 flor. III.
178 A.N. F⁷ 7106, Bopp(?) to Min. Pol. Gén., 13 pluv. IV.
179 E.g. A.D. Vaucluse 1 L 224 d. Caderousse, mun. admin. to central admin., 15 fruct. VI; A.D. Var 2 L 959, *procès-verbal* of 25 niv. V; A.N. BB¹⁸ 176, report of j.p. of Canton de la Paix, Marseille, 10 prair. III; Fréron, *Mémoire historique*, p. 85.
180 A clear overview for the Bouches-du-Rhône in Scott, *Terror in Marseilles*, pp. 40–59. See also G. Guibal, *Le Mouvement fédéraliste en Provence en 1793* (Paris, 1908). For troubles further north, consult in particular, A.D. Bouches-du-Rhône L 3036 and A.D. Drôme L 196.
181 Examples in A.D. Drôme L 196 (murder of Clop dit Camus and Tintin Clop at Malaucène); A.D. Bouches-du-Rhône L 3038 enquiries into murders at Tarascon (1792) and Maussanne (1793) and L 3043, enquiry into murders at Aix (1793); P. Vaillandet, 'Le premier complot du Marquis de Bésignan', *Mémoires de l'Académie de Vaucluse*, 2nd ser., 35 (1935), 1–40.

expeditions by National Guards or troops and tried to arrest and prosecute their enemies. Unlike before the Terror, jacobin murder was now rare.[182] Finally, after 1793, jacobins made only fragmentary use of traditional forms of reproach. Even before the Terror, it is difficult to perceive in jacobin behaviour anything more than a rather diffuse and unsystematic reference to traditional values and patterns of conduct in the local community.

Why, then, did counter-jacobin behaviour display such traditional features? In part, of course, institutions such as youth groups would instinctively articulate such values and behave in ways to which they had been accustomed before the Revolution. Yet, this does not explain the firmness of the reference in counter-jacobin action when compared with the mere echoes in patriot action before the Terror. Moreover, one should be careful not to assimilate youth action of either persuasion too completely to youth groups of the old society. Counter-jacobin youth groups in particular were decayed forms: this was no longer the youth that mostly sang and danced (though it certainly did that), it was the youth that mostly drank and killed. Stereotype, satire and ritual were paramount in the old society and contained the conflict within the confines of symbolism. Here, despite the recourse to fragments of symbolism, the supremacy of ritual had disappeared. Violence was paramount. In this, as in so much else, the Revolution seems to have accelerated a process already under way. Nicole Castan has argued that in the Languedoc (and we may apply this at least to some parts of the left bank of the Rhône) local societies found it increasingly difficult to control their turbulence and conflictual strains as the Revolution approached.[183] The communal violence of the revolutionary years in the Midi appears as the culmination of these tensions. The traditional modes of regulation degenerated from being a means of community self-regulation and self-defence into being a weapon of intra-community combat; the values that they had traditionally articulated became a vehicle for partisan reproach and a claim for support.

Indeed, if we are to envisage, on one level at least, the counter-jacobin offensive as part of a longer struggle for power, then the counter-jacobin appeal to traditional localism makes sense as a deliberate gesture. The localist stance was the natural one wherever reactionaries had in fact been those *notables* associated with late ancien regime local power; it was the natural recourse of those whose support had been bound up in habits of deference and ties of patronage constructed originally in the pre-revolutionary system. For such men, the appeal to traditional values was a means of legitimising their local victory in the Year III by emphasising the illegitimacy of their

---

[182] The worst violence seems to have taken place in large towns immediately on the return of the jacobins in the Year IV – e.g. Marseille (A.N. BB[18] 174, deputies of the Bouches-du-Rhône to Min. Just., 29 niv. IV), Aix (A.N. F7 7090, report by *conseil gen.* 10 brum. IV), Arles (A.N. BB[18] 174, President of *tribunal corr.* to Min. Just., 5 niv. IV).

[183] N. Castan, *Criminels du Languedoc*, especially p. 3.

opponents' victory in the Year II. More than that, this stance allowed them to encounter areas of support within the community that they might not previously have had, to recapture some that they had lost and to harness some of the more unruly or least integrated elements of the lower end. Particularly in villages, but not only there, the anti-seigneurial, anti-privilege, anti-big property upsurge of 1789 had contained a large element of an assertion of the local community, of its interests and of its traditional rights. Although the initial momentum of this protest brought much of it behind jacobin groups in 1792–3, by the Year III its essential localism must have strained its connection with jacobinism, by now identified with new demands and new forms of authority. The localist themes in counter-jacobin violence reflected a resurgence of the instinctive preference of southern communities for settling conflicts and tensions without reference to the outside.[184] The Year II revived this preference by giving renewed evidence that the intervention of outside authority was liable to be as injurious as it had been in the ancien regime.

Above all, the retreat into localism and tradition was in some senses the natural contradiction to the advance of the nation. Localism and its values were a much more sensible option for both bourgeois and popular elements in villages and smaller towns than the counter-revolution of the king with its dubious baggage of seigneurs and privilege. In this respect, counter-jacobinism resembles the support for the refractory priest, with which indeed it so often intertwined. It belonged to a pattern of rejection of the Revolution without a demand for the ancien regime by means of the reassertion of those local values and consciousness that were so alive in the Midi. In this sense, formal counter-revolution so apparently strong in this region was in fact the poor relation of this phenomenon whose clothes it sought to borrow. Furthermore, the contradiction between community and nation in the Midi had become, by the Year III, much more acute than it had appeared in the early revolutionary years. Religion, conscription and economic controls had allowed an unprecedented intrusion into the local community by imperious outside direction. Maurice Agulhon has emphasised that, however internally divided the southern community was in the late ancien regime, it was nonetheless united in its image of itself and in the face that it presented to the outside.[185] The ideal was that communal solidarity should contain within itself and preside over the struggles of its members. The jacobins, if only by their revolutionary affiliation, could be seen as the instruments of the erosion of the primacy of the local community. This was substantiated not just by their action in the struggles before the Terror, but above all by the completeness and the pervasiveness of their victory during the Terror. The case of Bédoin (Vaucluse), out of which the Thermidoreans made so much propaganda, could be used to show the logical conclusion of jacobin attitudes. The

---

[184] Ibid., p. 328, 'on préfère régler entre soi conflits et tensions'.
[185] Agulhon, *Vie sociale*, p. 223. Cf. Y. Castan, *Honnêteté et relations sociales*, p. 412.

village had been a trouble spot for several years and when, on 12 floréal Year II/1 May 1795, the Liberty Tree was cut down, the Terror authorities lost their temper: the village was burned to the ground, sixty-three people were executed and thirteen imprisoned, and the remaining population hid in the Mont Ventoux.[186] Ultimately, the only good jacobin was one who tempered the demands of the outside in the interests of the local community. Of course, there were such men in the Year II, just as there were men who restrained the full flood of reaction in the Year III.[187] But there were others who could not refuse the opportunities of power. And there were yet others for whom the nation was an inspiring ideal.

Seen in this light, the Years II and III appear as a major rupture in the Midi. In this land of polarised extremes, it became difficult for a long time to disentangle 'patriotism' from 'jacobinism'. In the short term at least, jacobin discourse implied the primacy of a man's obligations outside his locality, the supremacy of certain general values and a collective identity which assimilated his locality to a wider entity. This was true even if he saw these obligations and values primarily in terms of their benefits to his position inside his own locality and even if he envisaged the collective identity as no more than a network of factions similar to his own. At root, the jacobin justifications were incompatible with local values: one jacobin at Grasse said in the Year III that 'il savait qu'il était haï parce qu'il avait été membre du comité de surveillance mais qu'il avait toujours agi avec la loi à la main'.[188] It is here perhaps that lies the reason for the absence of any substantial murderous jacobin backlash in the Years IV and VI. By the time of the Directory, their own discourse had bound them to accept the supremacy of government directive and of the constitution of the sovereign people, and the primacy of the institutional process.[189] On the other hand, although traditional localism managed to contain the struggles of rival groups in the high country of the Massif Central during the Revolution, it was not so successful in the theatre of communal violence examined in this essay. Communal solidarity had already been much more under stress here before 1789. It was this that made some sections of the community so sensitive to the assault upon it, whereas others were prepared to go so far in jettisoning it. Moreover, unlike the Massif, these localities were exposed to the full and sustained blast of the Terror and could not hide from the demands of government and army as the Revolution progressed. The localism of the reactionaries was capable of sharp violence in the local context and of repelling outside authority; but it was unable by its very definition to transcend its own bounds and to present a

---

[186] A.D. Vaucluse 7 L 75.
[187] For the Year III, e.g. A.N. F7 7102, certificate for Etienne Sollier, 26 vent. IV, and A.D. Ardèche Fonds Mazan t. 19, report by *commissaires* at Largentière, mess. III.
[188] A.D. Var 2 L 956, enquiry by j.p. of Grasse, 20 germ. III.
[189] Cf. I. Woloch, *Jacobin Legacy* (Princeton, 1970).

constructive alternative to the Revolution. As a serious statement of opposition, the movement was destroyed by its own agents as much as by anything, as their behaviour degenerated into increasingly indiscriminate common-law violence thereby robbing their action of its significance by the end of the 1790s.

7

<hr>

Political brigandage and popular disaffection in the south-east of France, 1795–1804

GWYNNE LEWIS

On 1 March 1801, the Abbé Solier was executed in Le Vigan (Gard) for 'crimes committed against the Republic'. Solier, one of the most notorious 'political brigands' operating in the south of France during the period of the Directory, had commanded his *bande d'égorgeurs*, based along the borders of the departments of the Gard, the Hérault and the Ardèche, from 1795 to his death in 1801. He is by no means one of the forgotten heroes of catholic royalist resistance against the Revolution. The protestant writer, André Chamson, chose Solier as the hero of his latest 'roman dans l'Histoire'.[1] Philippe Senart has recently devoted two articles in the *Revue des deux-mondes* to an appreciation of Solier's contribution to the cause of catholic royalism, confronted in the Cévennes region by a powerful tradition of protestant republicanism.[2] Senart notes how, through the medium of the *veillées*, his grandmother would transmit accounts of the good *abbé* giving the first communion to catholic children in remote caves and woods; celebrating mass secretly during the worst bouts of persecution; dying a martyr for *le bon roi et les bons prêtres*. Through the works of Chamson and Senart, we are conducted along the tortuous paths of Cévenol folklore where *les étrangers*, then as now, are well advised to tread cautiously.

However, it was not only in the Cévennes – *la terre sainte* of protestantism – that the *égorgeurs* of the south-east operated. Radiating outwards from traditional areas of revolt and particularism, catholic royalist brigandage was to affect many regions within the former provinces of Languedoc and

<hr>

[1] *Sans Peur et les brigands aux visages noirs* (Paris, 1977). It was over fifty years ago that Chamson, one of the most celebrated of Cévenol writers, wrote his first 'roman dans l'histoire', *Roux le bandit*.

[2] P. Sénart, 'La Montagne blanche ou une Vendée cévenole', *Revue des Deux Mondes* (1979), pp. 103–12; 306–19.

Provence.³ Whether in tiny hamlets like Montréal (Ardèche), which Solier
knew well, or in Lyon, the second city of the realm, catholic royalist brigandage was to exploit the grievances of the *classes populaires* against a revolution which, in one decade, had done more to disrupt traditional customs and
relationships than a century of Bourbon rule. As Patrice Higonnet has noted
in his recent study of the French nobility during the Revolution, France, by
1799, had become 'a conglomerate of provinces, regions, or even towns,
often thrown on their own resources and removed from a government
whose principles and practices were hopelessly at odds'.⁴

We have used the term 'political brigandage' to emphasise the degree of
organisation and politicisation which characterised the catholic royalist
movement in south-eastern France after 1795. The activities of the brigands
were, for the most part, directed towards well-defined objectives, particularly from 1795 to 1797. This is not to say that many of the individual *bandes*
did not operate in accordance with some of the time-honoured conventions
of 'classical' or 'criminal' brigandage; that they did not, especially in their
own localities, exploit communal feuds and private vendettas. Guerrilla wars
often have their roots buried in such personalised conflicts. The *égorgeurs* did
indeed fight for the ideal of the 'good old' church and the 'good old' king:
from this standpoint, they may well be described as 'revolutionary tradi-
tionalists'.⁵ But unlike those of Hobsbawm's archetypal bandits, Solier's
actions were usually directed from above and were fundamentally shaped by
the exigencies of war and revolutionary politics. Of late, some historians have
placed too great an emphasis on *la longue durée*. Certainly, the 'past historic'
can, and will in this study, be used to provide us with important angles of
vision, but the *égorgeurs du Midi* were as much a product of the peculiar
circumstances of post-Thermidorean France as of traditional eighteenth-
century brigandage.

What is perfectly clear, as Marion pointed out almost half a century ago,
is that, during the late 1790s, all the conditions for the rapid development of
brigandage were present: 'démoralisation générale, mépris de la vie humaine,
trop enseigné par les événements de la Révolution, crise économique intense,
misère extrême, perte de l'habitude de travail, profonde division dans la
société, timidité et impuissance de la répression'.⁶ Undoubtedly, these factors
also help to explain the increase of criminal brigandage in many regions of
France, most dramatically in the case of the *bande d'Orgères* (Eure-et-Loir),⁷

³ This study will focus, in the main, on the catholic royalist movement in the departments of the
   Hérault, Gard, Ardèche, Drôme, Ain, Isère, Haute-Loire, Vaucluse, Bouches-du-Rhône,
   Basses-Alpes and the Var.
⁴ *Class, Ideology, and the Rights of Nobles during the French Revolution* (Oxford, 1981), p. 222.
⁵ E. Hobsbawm, *Bandits* (London, 1969), p. 22.
⁶ M. Marion, *Le Brigandage pendant la Révolution* (Paris, 1934), p. 77.
⁷ R. C. Cobb, *Reactions to the French Revolution* (Oxford, 1972), pp. 181–211.

and it would be idle to suggest that the south-east remained immune to the many viruses of crime incubated by the circumstances of the Revolution. Murder, robbery and rape, in their more traditional garb, stalked the high-ways and the *mas* and *bastides* of Languedoc and Provence as they had always done. There will, therefore, be many grey areas between the activities of the catholic royalist *égorgeurs* and those of the *chauffeurs* of old. Many of the latter clearly viewed the 'politicisation' of brigandage as, almost literally, a god-send; like the fifteen *scélérats* who broke into a farm in the village of Puyricard (Bouches-du-Rhône) demanding to know if the owners were hiding a refractory priest. When the door was, somewhat naively, unlocked, the brigands burst in announcing that 'they could forget about priests and hand over fifty *louis*'.[8] There were *fausses armées contre-révolutionnaires* during the Directory just as there had been *fausses armees révolutionnaires* during the Terror.

However, Maurice Agulhon, in his account of brigandage in the Var during our period, distinguishes quite clearly between 'political' and 'criminal' brigands,[9] whilst the distinction was certainly not lost on the authorities in the south-east of France at the time. In 1795, the municipal administration of Annonay referred to 'le brigandage de la pauvreté', adding that the number of brigands roaming the department was increasing owing to 'la rareté des subsistances et la stagnation des manufactures'.[10] The season was winter and the department, the Ardèche, one of the poorest in France, whose population had increased rapidly during the second half of the eighteenth century without any corresponding increase in food production.[11] The Ardèche proved to be a very 'royalist' department but, in the Ardèche, as in many other poor departments of France, the spectre of misery often wore the uniform of a 'royalist' brigand. The distinction between the 'political' and the 'criminal' brigand was indeed blurred. The *commissaire du gouvernement* in Marseille produced a most perceptive report during the winter of 1800 in which he stressed the significance of 'la misère et la suspen-sion de tout commerce et presque de toute industrie' in precipitating periodic and, above all, seasonal outbursts of brigandage, adding that the authorities in the city had done virtually nothing to deal with the basic causes of this kind of unrest, preferring to use it as a stick with which to beat the government in Paris. However, this kind of criminal activity, the *commissaire* con-cluded, produced 'un autre classe de brigand', not to be confused with the type of brigand fighting for throne and altar.[12]

---

[8] Archives Nationales (hereafter A.N.) BB[18] 177, municipality of Puyricard to Minister of Justice, fructidor Year VI.

[9] *La vie sociale en Provence intérieure* (Paris, 1970), p. 398.

[10] A.N. BB[18] 124, to Minister of Justice, 30 frimaire Year IV.

[11] A. Molinier, 'En Vivarais au XVIIIe siècle: une croissance démographique sans révolution agricole', *Annales du Midi*, vol. 92 (1980).

[12] A.N. BB[18] 188, *commissaire près le tribunal de première instance* to Minister of Justice, 14 frimaire Year IX.

The above report is particularly interesting given that it dates from December 1800 when the activities of the catholic royalist *égorgeurs* were, it is often alleged, becoming increasingly difficult to distinguish from those of the more traditional brigand. It is true that after five years (in some cases much longer) of unremitting warfare against the Republic, with no more money forthcoming from the English and the occasional prospect of a return to 'le bon vieux temps' dashed by yet another *coup d'état*, maintaining the original sense of purpose and idealism did pose acute problems. The internal dynamics of brigandage – the loneliness, the secrecy, the death of one's friends, the impulsion towards *le geste héroique* – all conspired to remould the *égorgeurs* into facsimiles of older forms of eighteenth-century protest. It was Victor Hugo, in *Quatre-Vingt-Treize*, who remarked: 'La guérilla ne conclut pas, ou conclut mal; on commence par attaquer une république et l'on finit par détrousser une diligence.' Catholic royalist brigandage could hardly expect to remain exempt from such a law.

However, an analysis of the early creation and subsequent organisation of the larger *compagnies*, as well as of the local *bandes*, reveals the existence of a reasonably sophisticated and concerted, if not cohesive, movement. Catholic royalism had its headquarters in Lyon and Lausanne, its *état-major* and its local leadership; it had its *compagnies* which moved from department to department, usually sub-dividing into smaller *bandes* to avoid confrontation with republican troops, its *commissaires* and recruiting-sergeants. It is too readily forgotten that the royalists did – as they had planned to do – win a very significant electoral victory in 1797 and that, after the *coup d'état* of 18 fructidor Year V/4 September 1797, they contributed, in no small measure, to the fiscal and administrative confusion which reigned in the south-east of France during the late 1790s. This is not to say that the fall of the Directory should be attributed to a catholic royalist plot: the movement was too fragmented, too localised, too intermittent to sustain such a thesis.[13] But to deny the degree of organisation which did exist and, particularly, to underestimate the widespread popular discontent which catholic royalism exploited is to obscure the nature and seriousness of the problems confronting the Directory or, as Martyn Lyons has phrased it: 'Studying the Revolution without considering the Counter-Revolution is like watching someone shadow-boxing.'[14] The Soliers did attract considerable support, and that support came, in part, from the many peasants and artisans who had welcomed (as in the Vendée) the early stages of the Revolution only to see hope gradually disappear as, after 1794, a free-market in land and a black-market in food threatened even the 'economy of makeshifts' which had sustained them before 1789. In the last analysis, the success of catholic royalism rested,

---

[13] See the discussion in P. Higonnet, *Class, Ideology*, pp. 225–6.
[14] *France under the Directory* (Cambridge, 1975), p. 37.

as we shall see, on the failure of the Revolution to satisfy the needs of the poor, who were also called upon to bear the brunt of the war effort.

It was the Thermidorean *représentant-en-mission* to the Midi who helped create the ethos for the allegedly 'spontaneous' White Terror of 1795.[15] Isnard, son of a rich merchant from the Var, was propelled into his evangelical attack upon the terrorists of the Year II, partly through the influence of his family background and the repercussions to the popular risings of Germinal and Prairial in Paris, and partly through the connivance of the local authorities, desperately keen to divert attention from their dismal failure to cope with the consequences of a free-market economy aggravated by the exceedingly harsh winter of 1794–5. What better way than to load upon the shoulders of 'les bêtes sauvages de l'an II' the miseries of the poor, the underfed and the unemployed. In Lyon, Marseille, Tarascon, Aix and Nîmes, hundreds of former supporters of the Terror were massacred, usually with the tacit approval of the local authorities, often in circumstances as brutal as those which characterised the September Massacres of 1792.[16] Many of the catholic royalist *compagnies* – often referred to as the *Compagnie de Jésus* in Lyon or the *Compagnie du Soleil* further south (there was also at least one *Compagnie de la Lune*)[17] – had been formed during the long, hot and bloody summer of 1795. The origins of some of the local *bandes*, such as those commanded by the Abbé Solier and by Dominique Allier, stemmed from the counter-revolutionary movements which had taken place in the Gard during the early years of the Revolution. However, the continued existence of the *compagnies* was obviously related to the developing programme of counter-revolution which, so far as the south-east was concerned, was being masterminded from Switzerland. The disastrous Quiberon expedition in the west,[18]

---

[15] Marion, *Le Brigandage*, p. 57, quoting the *représentant* Isnard, 'Si vous n'avez pas d'armes . . . déterrez les ossements de vos pères et servez-vous-en pour exterminer tous ces brigands [the terrorists of the Year II].' The *représentant* in the Gard, Olivier Gérente, declared that he was willing 'to perish a thousand times over rather than fall once again beneath the yoke of bloodthirsty and rapacious men'. G. Lewis, *The Second Vendée* (Oxford, 1978), p. 81. See also J. Godechot, *La Contre-Révolution* (Paris, 1961).

[16] See, for example, A.N. BB[18] 180, *extrait de l'état civil des citoyens de cette commune de Marseille*, 18 prairial Year III. The *juge de paix* found 'une infinité de cadavres défigurés et méconnaissables dans deux cachots où il paraissait qu'on avait mis le feu'. Half-burned bodies were mingled with a few survivors who were only just alive when the authorities arrived.

[17] 'Il y a dans les quartiers [around Pierrelatte] un rassemblement considérable de ces brigands qui ont formé entre eux une association connues sous le nom de *chevaliers de la lune*'. A.N. BB[18] 278, *commissaire près le tribunal criminel de la Vaucluse*, 25 prairial Year V. The report from the Minister of Police to the Minister of Justice on 12 messidor Year V noted that 'la compagnie du soleil, l'émulle [*sic*] de celui de Jésus de Lyon, est organisé [at Aix] et là-bas le soleil ne se cache pas'. Ibid., BB[18] 178.

[18] See M. Hutt, 'Quiberon: l'attaque du 16 juillet 1795', *Annales historiques de la Révolution française*, vol. 45 (1973).

which involved the execution of seven hundred men, allied to the subsequent failure of the royalist uprising of 13 vendémiaire Year IV/5 October 1795 in Paris, obviously strengthened the hand of those – like the Comte de Précy – who had consistently supported the cause of popular insurrection in the south-east.

The importance of foreign agents, particularly William Wickham, in financing the catholic royalist movement has been well documented:[19] their gullibility and failures have often been exaggerated. D'André's scheme to coordinate activities in Paris with those of the royalists in the provinces with the aim of gaining power, ostensibly at least, by constitutional means was, by most criteria, successful. There can also be little doubt that the *égorgeurs du Midi* made a most valuable contribution towards this success. Beginning in most cases with *ad hoc* associations of army veterans, deserters and the unemployed, the leadership of the royalist movement in the south-east, directed from Lyon and Switzerland, gradually created at least the framework of a well-armed and fairly well-disciplined striking-force. In the summer of 1796, the *commissaire du gouvernement* in Aix, for example, could inform the Directors in Paris that 'le projet de Vendeiser le midy n'est plus un mistère [*sic*]'.[20] A few months later, the Minister of Police warned the authorities in Lyon that 'des royalistes, dirigés par Précy, qui est en ce moment à Berne et que l'on regarde comme l'agent en chef de Louis XVIII dans le Midi, ont des projets sur Lyon et les départements voisins'.[21] By 1797, the royalist organisation was well known to the authorities in Lyon, 'its trunk being in this commune, the branches extending along the river Rhône to the sea'.[22] The republican *commissaire* in Chambéry (Mont-Blanc) succeeded in discovering the methods and the routes by which money, muskets and gunpowder were transported from Berne and Lausanne to Lyon.[23]

A study of the most important figures acting as intermediaries between the counter-revolution abroad and its sympathisers in the south-east will quickly dispel lingering doubts about the organised and politicised character of catholic royalist brigandage. What strikes one immediately is the long apprenticeship they had served in the craft of counter-revolution; how political brigandage during the Directory was linked to earlier catholic royalist movements in the south-east. It is also significant, as we shall discover later, that the leadership included a liberal sprinkling of former priests and petty nobles. Like the ex-priests, Urban Hippolyte Borel who, along with

[19] W. R. Fryer, *Republic or Restoration in France, 1794–97* (Manchester, 1965); H. Mitchell, *The Underground War against Revolutionary France* (Oxford, 1965).

[20] A.N. BB¹⁸ 179, 26 thermidor Year IV.

[21] Ibid., F⁷ 4231, to the *général de division* in Lyon, 15 ventôse Year V.

[22] Ibid., reports of 9 brumaire and 17 nivôse Year V to the Minister of Police.

[23] Ibid., to the Minister of Justice, 27 brumaire Year V.

his three brothers from the town of Mende (Lozère), became an important liaison agent between Précy and the local commanders of the *égorgeurs*. According to a confidential police report sent directly to Barras at the peak of the royalist offensive in the spring of 1797, Borel and his colleagues, 'ces agens de Pitt et de Vickam', were holding meetings three times a week in the café Berge in Lyon.[24] The Borel *frères* had been involved in the catholic royalist *camps de Jalès*, based along the borders of the Gard and the Ardèche which, from 1790 to 1792, laid the foundations for a popular counter-revolutionary movement in lower Languedoc. Described at the time of his arrest as a 'capitaine de l'armée royaliste', Borel was charged with being 'un des quatre frères Borel qui ont toujours joué un rôle principal dans les insurrections de ce département'.[25]

The Allier brothers, Claude and Dominique, had also received their political baptism during the *camps de Jalès* from 1790 to 1792. Claude Allier, a *curé* serving the villagers of Chambonas in the Ardèche, had been executed for his part in the Lyon insurrection of 1793. His brother, Dominique, was to become one of the most feared leaders of the *égorgeurs* as well as fulfilling the role of an active liaison agent. Forced into hiding during the Terror, the privations he had suffered appear to have exhausted, albeit temporarily, his unusually large reserves of energy, since, following his arrest, he was reported to have informed the *représentant-en-mission* who visited him in prison that 'il ne pouvait attendre que la mort que ses forfaits lui avaient meritée'. Dominique, in fact, was to summon up enough energy to serve the royalist cause until his eventual execution in 1798. Having worked as a *marchand de tabac* before the Revolution, Dominique had travelled extensively throughout the south of France, from Montpellier to Marseille and to Lyon, invaluable experience for his subsequent career. According to his own testimony, he had also spent some time in England, Switzerland and in Koblenz during the early years of the Revolution.[26] Released from prison, very significantly, during the spring of 1795,[27] Allier's *bande* was to be involved in some of the most successful raids launched by the catholic royalist *égorgeurs*, such as the attack on the army barracks in Barjac (Gard) in the spring of 1796. His men were also responsible for some of the worst atrocities committed in the south-

[24] Ibid., letter from Privas (Ardèche) sent by 'Lachamp', 8 ventôse Year V.

[25] A.N. BB¹⁸ 472, *commissaire près le tribunal criminel de la Lozère* to Minister of Justice, 16 germinal Year VI.

[26] A.N. F⁷ 4578, *rapport en vertu du décret de la Convention*, 6 ventôse Year III; F⁷ 4559, *commissaire près le tribunal du district d'Alais* to the Committee of General Security, 13 vendémiaire Year III.

[27] Yet another example of the remarkable activities of the *représentants en mission* in the Midi. Allier was unquestionably one of the most wanted counter-revolutionary leaders in the region. Three weeks after his release by the local *représentant*, the Committee of General Security – 'la religion du comité ayant été surprise' – made a determined effort to secure his recapture. A.N. F⁷ 4775, dossier Tondu (the latter was alleged to have sheltered Allier in his Parisian appartment).

east, like the 'massacre of Laudun' later on in the same year. Dominique –
following the example of his brother – was finally caught and executed in
Lyon in front of 'an immense crowd' on 28 brumaire Year VII/18 November
1798. His last words were reliably reputed to have been: 'Vive le Roi! Un
roi est un Dieu sur la terre.'[28] Surely, the dying words of a 'revolutionary
traditionalist'.

Arrested at the same time as Allier was his close friend and fellow-royalist
agent, the Marquis de Surville, from the commune of Viviers in the Ardèche.
Both men, along with two other royalists, had been discovered hiding in a
peasant's house in the small commune of Tiranges (Haute-Loire). When the
gendarmerie broke in during the early hours of the morning, they found the
four men hiding in a cellar which also contained all the necessary equipment
for counterfeiting French notes. Surville, an infantry captain before the
Revolution, was described as 'colonel-légionnaire et commissaire pour sa
majesté dans l'intérieur du royaume'. According to the local *commissaire du
gouvernement*, the Comte de Précy himself had been with Allier and Surville
the previous day.[29] The authorities quickly realised that they had captured
two of the most important royalist agents operating in the south-east of
France: no fewer than 150 men were posted to guard the building which
contained all the secret correspondance discovered on Surville and Allier. A
few hours before he was due to be shot, Surville asked the commanding
officer of the local garrison if it could be arranged for him to see Barras, since
he possessed extremely important information on royalist plans for the south-
east. The officer, fearing that this was simply a stratagem to delay his execution, told Surville to write down, in the presence of a senior officer, everything which could be of use to the government. Surville naturally refused,
and after writing a few farewell letters to friends in Switzerland, was shot at
eleven o'clock on the morning of 27 vendémiaire Year VII/18 October 1798
in Le Puy (Haute-Loire).[30] The Surville family was destined to play a very
significant role in the history of catholic royalism during the nineteenth
century.[31]

Apart from the experience of agents like Surville, the royalist *bandes* could
also exploit the knowledge acquired in the Bourbon army by royalists, like
the Chevalier de Lamothe who concentrated his activities mainly in and
around the departments of the Ardèche, the Lozère, the Haute-Loire and the
Vaucluse. Lamothe, another former artillery officer, was finally arrested in
the summer of 1798 as he was about to organise a big *rassemblement* on the

---

[28] A.N. BB[18] 440, *général de division* to Minister of Justice, 28 brumaire Year VII.

[29] Ibid., *l'administration centrale* of the Haute-Loire to Minister of Justice, 3ᵉ jour complémentaire
Year VI; *commissaire près le tribunal correctionnel d'Ambert* to Minister of Justice, 15 brumaire
Year VII.

[30] Ibid., *l'administration centrale* of the Haute-Loire to the Minister of Justice, 19 fructidor Year VI.

[31] See Brian Fitzpatrick, *Catholic Royalism in the Department of the Gard* (Cambridge, 1983).

borders of the Ardèche and the Haute-Loire.[32] On the right bank of the river Rhône, in the former enclave of the Comtat Venaissin – which had belonged to the Papacy until the Revolution – the Marquis de Bésignan and the Baron de Saint-Christol emerged as the leaders of the local *bandes*. Saint-Christol survived to relate his experiences in his memoirs which, although exaggerating the importance of the royalist movement during the Directory, as well as his own contribution to it, do stress the thread of continuity which characterises the history of catholic royalism in the Midi.[33] In the department of the Basses-Alpes, one of the leading *chefs de bande* was Jean-François Berard, prior to the Revolution 'un noble, chevalier, et lieutenant-général de la sénéchaussée de Forcalquier'. Berard had participated in most of the counter-revolutionary movements which had affected the Basses-Alpes, the Drôme and the Vaucluse, including the Monnier conspiracy, and had been arrested in 1792 as 'un agent des princes'. His brother was an 'émigré chanoine, un gros bénéficier'.[34] In Marseille, the royalist leader in the Year IV/September 1795–September 1796 was no less a figure than the commander of the eighth military division, General Willot, who had created a so-called 'compagnie de police secrète' (a time-honoured French tradition!) commanded by a soldier named Chabrier, 'dont la vigilance et la probité me sont connus', so Willot assured the government. The municipal authorities in Marseille, however, described Chabrier, who had only recently been released from the prisons of Aix, as an *égorgeur* who had definitely participated in the horrible 'massacre of the Fort Saint-Jean' during the White Terror of 1795.[35]

Agents like Surville, Borel, Lamothe and Saint-Christol recruited the leaders of the local *bandes*, communicated the orders of the Précys and the D'Andrés and channelled the necessary funds and arms to their men. The *abbé* de Solier was one of Allier's lieutenants. Born in 1732, the son of David Solier, seigneur de Lafabrègue, he had served for many years as *curé-prieur* of Colognac (Gard), deep in the protestant region of the Cévennes mountains. It appears, from his subsequent exploits, that he had a natural penchant for the military life, but that being the younger son of a seigneur he found himself inside a cassock rather than a *casque*. Thus it was that the mores of aristocratic society, combined with the accident of revolution, transformed

---

[32] Lamothe was never brought to trial. He was massacred in his cell on the night of 14/15 vendémiaire Year VI by the soldiers who were, allegedly, guarding the prison. A.N. BB[18] 439, *commissaire près le tribunal criminel* of the Haute-Loire to Minister of Justice, 16 vendémiaire Year VI.

[33] *Précis des mémoires* (Avignon, 1818); also, J. Barruol, *La contre-révolution en Provence et dans le Comtat Venaissin* (Cavaillon, 1928).

[34] A.N. BB[18] 108, petition of Jean-Français Berard to the Minister of Justice, floréal Year VI.

[35] A.N. F[7] 4268, Willot to Minister of Police, 16 fructidor Year IV. See also secret report to Minister of Police, 2 brumaire Year V: 'La faction royaliste, semblable à un peleton de neige, grossit tous les jours ... surtout depuis l'arrivée de M. Willot, général-divisionnaire qui s'y est annoncé un vrai dictateur.'

god-fearing *curés* into commanders of brigand *bandes*, particularly if they
hailed from the fiercely independent (and desperately poor) region of the
Vivarais and had been blooded in the *camps de Jalès* of 1790–2. It was during
these years that Solier had made the acquaintance of Dominique Allier.[36] Yet
another former priest, Fontanier, called *Jambe de Bois*, whom Allier elevated
to the rank of 'major', had fought alongside Solier and Allier in the last
insurrection of the *camps de Jalès* in 1792: hence, presumably, his false leg.[37]
Fontanier was to lead his *bande* in the departments of the Hérault, the Gard
and the Ardèche.

The methods by which the local leaders of the *bandes* were recruited are
exemplified in the case of a *chef de bande* named Cédage, 'fils d'un ci-devant
noble'. In the summer of 1801, Cédage and five of his men were cornered
by an army patrol near Le Puy (Haute-Loire) following the hold-up of a
coach carrying government funds. Cédage, after a violent struggle in the
course of which one of the patrol was killed, was sabred to death. Under
interrogation, one of his *bande* informed the authorities that Cédage had
recruited them to hold up 'la caisse publique pour servir le Prétendant'.
Cédage had apparently been appointed as *chef de bande* following a meeting
with a royalist agent in Clermont who instructed him to concentrate on the
seizure of taxes carried in government coaches. He was told that he could
keep half of the money seized to pay his followers, the other half being earmarked for the royalist central fund.[38]

Finally, the case of Xavier Bertrand from the canton of Valgorge (Ardèche),
provides us with a remarkable example of the way in which catholic royalist
brigandage exploited long-standing antagonisms between the local seigneur
and the wealthy *bourgeois*, particularly the lawyer and purchaser of national
lands, hated alike by the petty nobility and the impoverished peasantry, the
latter subjected increasingly to the strains and tensions of a nascent industrial
society. During the early 1780s, the Vivarais (Gard/Ardèche) region had
experienced a series of revolts known collectively as *les masques armés* in which
the major themes were the 'relations de créancier à débiteur, position clef
occupée dans ces relations par l'industrie de la soie, industrie à la fois rurale et
urbaine, et, surtout, tentatives de rapprochement de la noblesse locale avec
les classes paysannes'.[39] In April 1789, a *notaire* named Barrot had been
savagely attacked in the little village of Planchamp situated on the borders of

[36] A. Chamson, *Sans Peur*, pp. 55–7. During his apprenticeship as an *égorgeur*, 'il ne s'agissait que
d'abattre, au coin d'un bois ou au détour du chemin, un voyageur solitaire connu pour son
dévouement au nouveau régime'. A good example of the 'politicisation' of traditional brigandage.

[37] G. Lewis, *The Second Vendée*, pp. 94–7.

[38] A.N. BB[18] 441, *commissaire près le tribunal correctionnel du Puy* to Minister of Justice, 24 messidor
Year VIII.

[39] M. Sonenscher, 'La révolte des masques armés de 1783 en Vivarais', *Fédération historique du
Languedoc méditerranéen et du Roussillon*, XLIVe congrès (May, 1971).

the Lozère and the Ardèche. By this time, such attacks had become ritualised – the wearing of masks and white shirts; the seizure and burning of the notarial records.[40] Just over a decade later, the same *notaire*, now aged eighty, and whose son had been returned as a deputy for the Lozère department during the Directory, was the target for yet another attack by masked men who were, on this occasion, driven off leaving one of their number dead outside Barrot's house. A few weeks later, a *bande* of 120 brigands returned to exact their revenge. Barrot, who had consolidated his fortune during the Revolution and who had survived so many of the slings and arrows of outrageous royalism, was finally killed, along with – and how revealing this fact is – a constitutional priest who had been staying with the family. The leader of the 'trouppe de chouans' responsible for Barrot's death was alleged to have been Xavier Bertrand, eldest son of Claude Bertrand, 'ci-devant seigneur' of Valgorge, a parish which had figured in the *masques armés* revolts of 1783.[41]

Many of those arrested as emissaries for the royalist cause, travelling between their master's home and Lyon or Switzerland, prove to be valets of former seigneurs. Jean-Pierre Gutton, commenting upon the research of Nicole Castan, has remarked how 'Les valets forment . . . avec les fils de la famille des bandes armées qui peuvent se borner aux entrées bruyantes dans les cabarets et les lieux de danse, aux tapages, aux charivaris. Elles peuvent aussi aller jusqu'aux violences et aux vols et terroriser une région.'[42] A Polish servant, Philippe Souschinki, was arrested with his master, Xavier Bertrand. Vidal, one of Cédage's *bande*, was a *domestique à gages*. Antoine Hommage, a former wigmaker and subsequently valet to a noble called Vaugirard was arrested in the winter of 1797 carrying letters from Lyon for his master. Hommage, in the course of his service, had travelled – usually with Vaugirard – to England, Germany and Switzerland.[43] The Revolution did not transform *les moeurs féodales* overnight: indeed, it will be one of the arguments of this study that the opportunity of fighting for 'Church and King' during the Directory and Consulate often strengthened the old bonds between seigneurs, priests and those who depended upon them. Paternalism and patronage were the most effective recruiting-sergeants for the royalist cause. When Xavier Bertrand was finally sentenced to death as an *égorgeur*, dozens of villagers, from the shepherd's wife to the local blacksmith, signed petitions demanding a pardon. Bouche *fils* was the son of a former *procureur du roi de la sénéchaussée de Forcalquier* (Basses-Alpes). His closest friend, and

---

[40] A.N. BB[18] 441, *accusateur public* to Minister of Justice, 23 frimaire Year IV.

[41] A.N. BB[18] 473 contains a voluminous file on the Bertrand case including a letter from Barrot's son to the Minister of Justice, 15 floréal Year X, which stresses the theme of continuity in the history of catholic royalism in the former Vivarais region.

[42] J.-P. Gutton, *Domestiques et serviteurs dans la France de l'ancien régime* (Paris, 1981), p. 21.

[43] A.N. BB[18] 87, *administration centrale* of the Loire to Minister of Justice, 24 nivôse Year VI.

fellow *égorgeur*, was an émigré named Durand. Both were relatively young but, as the *commissaire du gouvernement* at Forcalquier explained to the Minister of Justice, they could hardly be excused as youngsters who had been led astray, since 'Ils ont eux-mêmes égarés les bastiers, les perruquiers . . .'[44]

It is noticeable that for most of the period under discussion the activities of the catholic royalist *compagnies*, the timing and objectives of their campaigns, were dictated as much by political and military factors as by the natural rhythm of the seasons. Following the failure of the 13 vendémiaire Year IV uprising in Paris, the *égorgeurs*, commanded by dedicated counter-revolutionaries like the Baron de Saint-Christol, unleashed a major reign of terror in the border regions of the Drôme, the Ardèche and the Vaucluse which was to continue, sporadically, throughout most of the autumn and winter months of the Year IV (1795-6). In December 1795, no fewer than 600 brigands were involved in the assassination of republican sympathisers, particularly those who had bought *biens nationaux*, around Montélimar (Drôme), Valréas and Bollène (Vaucluse).[45] In the Ardèche, purchasers of church and émigré property were also amongst the first victims of the *égorgeurs*.[46] It is true that, from 1795 to 1797, the activities of the *bandes* tended to reach a peak during the months of February, March and April, but this was not always because, in spring, a young brigand's fancy naturally turned to killing. Voting in the primary assemblies to choose local judicial and administrative officials, as well as the electors, responsible for the final choice of deputies to the councils in Paris, were usually held in March and April. Annual voting had been one of the less happy stipulations of the Constitution of 1795, providing opponents of the regime with a wonderful opportunity of raising the temperature of the political debate.

Terror, organised through the *bandes*, was one sure method of exercising real political influence, since the censitary system was geared entirely in favour of the wealthy and, what was more important, in favour of those wealthy Frenchmen who had not been outlawed by the legislation passed against priests and nobles. The catholic royalists in the department of the Gard had adopted terrorist tactics during the so-called *bagarre de Nîmes* in 1790 – a bloody (at least 300 catholics were killed) and abortive attempt to prevent the wealthy protestant community in the department from seizing political and administrative power for the first time in its history. The worst excesses of the White Terror of 1815 in the south-east of France were to occur during the election of deputies to the *chambre introuvable* in Paris.[47] If,

---

[44] A.N. BB¹⁸ 108, *commissaire près le tribunal criminel de Forcalquier* to Minister of Police, floréal Year VI.

[45] A.N. BB¹⁸ 227, *représentant-en-mission* to Minister of Justice, 17 nivôse Year IV.

[46] A.N. BB¹⁸ 124, *juge de paix* of Valréas to Minister of Justice, 1 prairial Year IV.

[47] G. Lewis, *The Second Vendée*, pp. 1–40, 208–11. Also J. Hood, 'Patterns of popular protest in the French Revolution: the conceptual contribution of the Gard', *Journal of Modern History*, vol. 48 (1976).

from 1795 to 1797, catholic royalist brigandage was to be, in the main, an urban phenomenon, this was partly in accordance with D'André's 'Grand Design' to influence the choice of deputies to be sent to Paris. In addition, and probably of greater significance, during the elections of 1796, the royalists had made a determined and, in many places, successful bid to seize the key posts of *juges de paix* and *directeurs du jury*. The National Guard and municipal administrations of many towns and villages had also fallen to the royalists. The national success of the royalists in the elections of 1797 was founded upon the solid achievements of their supporters during the local elections of the previous year. For example, the *commissaire près l'administration centrale des Bouches-du-Rhône* sadly informed the Minister of Justice in April 1796 that 'l'esprit de découragement est à un tel point ... que tous les commissaires des cantons, même ceux que vous avez confirmés, se sont présentés pour donner leur démission'.[48] If a minority of republicans braved the will of the political brigands of the Directory, their resolve must surely have been weakened by exemplary acts of brutality like the 'massacre of Laudun' by Allier's *bande*, in which twelve members of the same family, from infants to grandparents, had their throats cut from ear to ear.[49] The term, *égorgeur*, was not applied lightly in the Midi.

Denunciations of the brigands continued to reach the government throughout the winter of the Year V although, once again, it is not until the period immediately preceeding the vital elections of that year that the trickle of complaints becomes a torrent. On 3 ventôse/21 February 1797, the *commissaire du gouvernement* in Lyon informed the Minister of Police that 'La faction royaliste a abandonné sa tactique hypocrite. Elle a recommencé dès quelques jours ses attentats contre la sûreté individuelle. Assassinats, mandats d'arrêt, lettres de proscription, tout a été mis en oeuvre pour empêcher le peuple d'exercer sa souveraineté.' It was customary for the royalists in Lyon to provide advance warning to their prospective victims. Just before the elections were due to take place, a *patissier* named Buvel, a republican supporter, discovered the following daubed in red paint on the front door of his shop: 'Buvel, lis et trembles, si tu es buveur de sang.'[50] Similar tactics to prevent republican voters from attending the primary assemblies were adopted by the catholic royalists in Marseille;[51] whilst in the commune of Donzère, on the borders of the Drôme and the Vaucluse, a catholic royalist *bande*, accompanied by members of the municipality, who had previously organised a *farandole* through the streets (an increasingly popular method of adapting traditional patterns of behaviour to political ends), visited all the surrounding communes on voting-day in order to frighten republicans from

---

[48] A.N. BB¹⁸ 176, 26 germinal Year IV.   [49] G. Lewis, *The Second Vendée*, pp. 100–1.

[50] A.N. F7 4231, *rapport sur les délits qui ont immédiatement précédé et accompagné la tenue des assemblées primaires et électorales*, floréal Year V.

[51] A.N. BB¹⁸ 177, *commissaire près l'administration centrale* to Minister of Justice.

the polling-booths.[52] In reading these reports one has, of course, to be aware
of the natural tendency for republican officials to exaggerate the problems
confronting them, in the hope that the government might be forced to adopt
harsher tactics against the royalists. However, the multiplicity of reports
coming from so many varied sources in so many departments, as well as the
fact that it is difficult to exaggerate a dead body – and there were plenty of
these discovered during the elections of the Year V in the south-east – make
it impossible to dismiss the above purely as examples of republican hyperbole.

It is, therefore, hardly surprising that in 1797 the royalists should have
recorded important electoral victories in many regions of the south-east,
particularly in those most affected by political brigandage. The prize of
political power, however, was to be snatched from their grasp by the *coup
d'état* of 18 fructidor as elections were annulled in over half of the departments
in France. One year later, due in large measure to the widespread purges of
royalist officials, the republicans were to exact their revenge. When the
villagers turned up at the local church to cast their vote in the commune of
Piolenc (Vaucluse) in April 1798, for example, they discovered that their
entry had been barred by a detachment of National Guardsmen from the
town of Orange (a sufficient deterrent in itself, given the reputation of the
dreaded Commission d'Orange during the Terror). The brave, or foolhardy,
few who insisted on voting were clubbed aside with accompanying accusations of 'Tu es un chouan; tu es égorgeur'. Seven catholic royalist villagers
were killed in the ensuing violence.[53] Voting behaviour in many regions of
the south-east during the late 1790s should perhaps be analysed, not by the
use of 'swingometers', but by counting the number of sabres present inside
and outside the electoral assemblies; which is why criticisms levelled against
Barras and his colleagues for failing to 'modernise' the political process and
promote the emergence of opposition or centre parties, when viewed from
the steps of the local church in Piolenc, for example, would probably have
been compared to the accusation that a one-legged, blind man was not really
trying when he fell off a tight-tope.[54]

The *coup d'état* of 18 fructidor, the repercussions of which were to be felt
in every sphere of government, did at least give the Directory another two
years' grace. The reactivation of the harsh legislation against émigrés and
priests (particularly the laws of brumaire Year IV), the purges of the police
and the administration, drove most royalist *bandes* from the urban centres
into the countryside. It is significant that more frequent reports of the

---

[52] A.N. F7 4268, petition of 1,000 voters who had allegedly been too frightened to attend the
electoral assemblies.

[53] A.N. BB18 890, *adresse individuelle des malheureux habitans de la commune de Piolenc*, 20 germinal
Year VI.

[54] See, for example, L. Hunt, D. Lansky, P. Hanson, 'The failure of the liberal experiment in
France, 1795–1799: the road to Brumaire', *Journal of Modern History*, vol. 51 (1979).

activities of the brigands begin to appear from departments like the Isère, the Ain, the Haute-Loire, the Basses-Alpes and the Var. After 1797, the counter-revolution tended to spread outwards from the traditionally disturbed regions of the former Vivarais and the Comtat Venaissin, as well as from cities like Lyon and Marseille, as the newly installed republican authorities launched an all-out attack on royalist centres of power. From an electoral and urban standpoint, catholic royalist influence had been reduced by the *coup* of Fructidor; geographically, it had been increased. The feeling of anger and frustration which swept through the royalist camp as news of the *coup* reached the south-east exploded into what Maurice Agulhon, writing of brigandage in the Var, has called 'cet automne dramatique'.[55] Encouraged by the manoeuvres of royalist deputies from Provence like Rovère, as well as by D'André and General Willot, *chefs de bande* in the departments bordering the Rhône joined forces to launch a despairing assault upon the Republic. Saint-Christol – never a humble man – announced that he was now commanding 'The Army of the Corps Législatif', given that the elections of the Year V had in fact produced a royalist Council of 500, adding that, in his opinion, 'an infamous tyranny has established itself on the ruins of the Constitution [of 1795]'.[56] From the Bouches-du-Rhône, the *juge de paix* of Lambesc lamented the horrors perpetrated by the *égorgeurs*, explaining that 'la terreur pour les patriotes est plus grande que jamais'.[57] From the Basses-Alpes, the Minister of Justice received the news that the *bandes* were driving 'the department to the verge of anarchy'.[58] In brumaire Year VI/October 1797, the royalists took over Carpentras for two days before being defeated by a detachment of National Guardsmen from Orange.[59] In the Vaucluse, as in other departments of the south-east, traditional inter-communal rivalry had long since been institutionalised by the Revolution.

Some historians have posited a relationship between the increasing misery of the countryside after 1797 and the pattern of brigandage in the more rural and mountainous areas.[60] Certainly, the financial expedients adopted by the Directory, the continuing, and related, strain of war, as well as fewer good harvests, may well have pre-disposed many peasants and rural artisans towards the *égorgeurs*. However, in addition to the more general causes of popular dissatisfaction, which we shall discuss later in more detail, the geographic dispersion of brigandage, together with a reappraisal of its major

---

[55] M. Agulhon, *La vie sociale*, p. 371. [56] Saint-Christol, *Précis des mémoires*, pp. 72–3.

[57] A.N. BB¹⁸ 182, to Minister of Justice, 6 vendémiaire Year VI.

[58] A.N. BB¹⁸ 109, *commissaire près le tribunal criminel*, 20 brumaire Year VI. Royalist '*commissaires*' toured the countryside surrounding Forcalquier enrolling men for the *bandes*, offering as bait the cause of 'religion et le roi' and, probably of equal importance, regular pay.

[59] A.N. BB¹⁸ 890, *rapport du commandant de la garde nationale d'Orange*, 6 brumaire Year VI.

[60] See, for example, M. Agulhon commenting favourably upon the conclusions of R. Schnerb, 'De 1792 à l'an IV . . . c'est dans les villes que l'on souffrit de misère, de l'an IV à l'an X ce fut aux champs'. *La vie sociale*, p. 371.

objectives, were bound to affect its character. Attacks on leading republicans continued unabated, but these were increasingly accompanied by assassinations and robberies in isolated hamlets; government tax-collectors became prime targets as did the mail coaches travelling between Lyon and the major cities of the south-east. Appealing for assistance from the army, the *agent municipal* of Aix informed the Minister of Justice on 13 nivôse Year VII/2 January 1799 that 'hordes des brigands retranchés dans les bois et dans les campagnes sortent de leur retraite et détroussent les gens sur les grandes routes'.[61] Here again, however, the problem was not simply an economic or a seasonal one: military factors were playing an increasingly important role in the evolution of catholic royalist brigandage. The army was too busy preparing for the renewed fighting in Italy, as a result of the formation of the Second Coalition, to bother too much about brigandage in Aix; whilst those youngsters called to the colours as a result of the Jourdan conscription law of 19 fructidor Year VI/5 September 1798 had obviously chosen to stay in Aix rather than bother about the Italians! Military and political considerations were still influencing the course of catholic royalist brigandage despite the change of habitat forced upon it by the *coup* of 18 fructidor. Saint-Christol was still operating in and around his old haunt of Bollène in the spring of 1799, whilst the Abbé Solier was about to launch a series of raids in the Vivarais region, in the course of which government tax-collectors would find themselves relieved of 59,000 francs.[62] For the true 'political brigand', the objective was now to undermine the credibility of the regime by attacking its officials, robbing it of its taxes, as well as calling into question, through terror, the revolutionary land settlement. In the pursuit of this last objective, the *égorgeurs* would be eagerly aided and abetted by the returning émigré. We have seen how Cédage's *bande* was instructed to hold up government coaches. As late as 29 floréal Year VIII/19 May 1800, the Minister of Justice thought it advisable to warn the authorities in the Lozère that, according to information he had recently received, the *bandes* had obviously created 'un système de brigandage principalement dirigé contre les caisses et les voiture publiques'.[63] Just because the *égorgeurs* were now in the business of highway robbery in a big way, one should not automatically assume that all planning and purpose had been lost.

By this time, of course, Napoleon Bonaparte had begun his rise to supreme power. Whatever the merits of the historical myth of greatness, the Corsican was to work no miracles so far as brigandage was concerned: indeed, the new year of the new century saw the *égorgeurs* as strong (at least, numerically), if not stronger, than ever. Albert Soboul, amongst others, has emphasised the themes of continuity between the Directory and the Consulate: one of those themes would certainly be the history of political brigandage between 1795

---

[61] A.N. BB18 184, 13 nivôse Year VII.   [62] A. Chamson, *Sans Peur*, p. 126.
[63] A.N. BB18 473, to the *commissaire près le tribunal criminel*, 29 floréal Year VIII.

and 1804.[64] Many royalists viewed the *coup* of 18 brumaire Year VIII/10 October 1799 with some satisfaction; after all, had not a 'military dictatorship' in England preceded the return of the Stuarts in 1660? In February 1800, the municipal authorities in Nyons (Drôme) issued a frantic appeal for troops, explaining that 500 *égorgeurs* had sacked the commune of Richerenches and were now in command of the town of Valréas, which had long practised an open-door policy towards the brigands.[65] Similar reports were despatched from the Lozère and the Ardèche where, in ventôse, 300 well-armed brigands were encamped around Joyeuse, yet another favoured haunt for the *bandes*. Here again, republicans and purchasers of national lands were amongst the first victims.[66] The following winter, the government received the bleak news from Marseille that it had been three years since anyone had been able to travel safely in the countryside around the city;[67] whilst, in the Basses-Alpes, the first prefect of that department reported in September 1801: 'Nous sommes ici sur un volcan.'[68]

In departments like the Ardèche, the Vaucluse and the Bouches-du-Rhône, where violence appeared to be endemic, the situation did not improve markedly until the advent of the Napoleonic Empire and, even then, isolated bands of brigands continued to make it dangerous for travellers to stray too far from the main cities and highways without an escort. However, by this time, many of the leading royalists, whose careers link the early spasms of counter-revolutionary activity in the south-east with the political brigandage of the Directory, had been executed, usually by the military commissions which were prepared to deal more ruthlessly with brigands than the departmental *tribunals criminels*, too enmeshed in local affairs and personalities. Indeed, the latter, in most 'royalist' departments had been one of the most effective props supporting catholic royalist brigandage. Borel, Surville, Lamothe, Allier, the Abbé Solier had all been executed by 1801. The brief period of peace which France enjoyed; the gradual installation of a more efficient and impartial administration and judiciary, to say nothing of Napoleon's outstretched hand to the émigrés, obviously signalled the end of any coherent and effective royalist opposition. The Concordat with the Papacy took the 'catholic' out of the catholic royalist movement. After 1801, the *chauffeur* once again began to supplant the *chouan*, proving that, even on the highways, the Revolution had ended.[69]

---

[64] M. Lyons, *France under the Directory*, p. 237.

[65] A.N. BB¹⁸ 892, *commissaire près le tribunal criminel* of the Vaucluse to Minister of Justice, 12 germinal Year VIII.

[66] A.N. BB¹⁸ 127, *commissaire près le tribunal criminel* of the Ardèche to Minister of Justice, 24 ventôse Year VIII.

[67] A.N. BB¹⁸ 187, *juge de paix* to Minister of Justice, 3 frimaire Year VIII.

[68] A.N. BB¹⁸ 110, le jour complémentaire Year IX.

[69] A handful of feared brigands, like Pellissier from Aubagne (Bouches-du-Rhône) and Pepin from Saumane (Vaucluse), continued to infest the south-east well into the Empire. The former

It had all begun with such high hopes, even for the poor catholic royalists (and were not most Frenchmen in 1789 poor and, at least nominally, catholic and royalist?) for whom the much-vaunted attack on feudalism and privilege appeared to offer the hope of a brighter future. After 1794, the disadvantages had clearly begun to outweigh the advantages, just as a handful of priests and seigneurs had told them they would. During the Directory and Consulate, catholic royalist brigandage achieved the degree of success it did (and, as we have seen, this was far from negligible) because it was able to exploit the profound and growing sense of disaffection from the Revolution which characterised so many sections of the population in the former provinces of Languedoc and Provence which, as de Tocqueville pointed out over a century ago, had never fully been integrated into the Bourbon state. This disaffection was most positively expressed in the massive popular resistance to conscription, the rejection of the religious settlement of 1791 and, under-lying it all, the determination to defend traditional customs and rights against the hesitant, but increasingly pervasive, incursion of 'individualism'. If, as we have argued above, the White Terror of 1795 was rooted in the social and economic dislocation consequent upon the abolition of price controls, aggravated by the severe winter of 1794-5, subsequent legislation attacking the rights of the poor in the fields, forests and vineyards, accompanied by a social policy which, through indirect taxation, meant that by late 1796 the poorer sections of the community were being asked 'to pay their own relief',[70] all contributed to the widespread sense of dissatisfaction with the Revolution, hence providing the *bandes* with a potential reservoir of support. In all three areas of discussion, conscription, religion and 'communitarian' versus 'individualist' rights, we can trace the impact of the modern, lay, bureaucratic state upon provincial and particularist loyalties.

The success, in terms of recruitment, of political brigandage – indeed of all kinds of brigandage – during the Revolution owed more to the introduction of mass conscription than to any other single cause. After 1795, the rank and file of the royalist *compagnies* was drawn, in the main, from young men desperate not to get into the army as well as from deserters equally desperate to get out. The *milice* had, of course, been extremely unpopular during the ancien regime, but, compared with the thousands levied by that archaic institution, the mass levies of 1793 and in particular of 1798 imposed an intolerable strain upon people's loyalty to the fledgling national state. Charles Tilly, in his study of the Vendée, noted how the failure to implement the legislation on

was accustomed, like the bull-fighters of the region, to carry the ears of his victims in his pockets; the latter was given a passport for Spain by the French government in 1806 so that it might 'rid the department of this plague'. A.N. BB[18] 190, *commissaire de police* of Aubagne to Minister of Justice, 29 prairial Year X; BB[18] 898, prefect to Minister of Justice, 24 January 1806.
70 C. Lis and H. Soly, *Poverty and Capitalism in Pre-Industrial Europe* (Brighton, 1982), p. 210.

conscription fatally undermined the authority and appeal of the *patriote* party in the west.[71] Valid for the west in 1793, the thesis has even more credibility when applied to the south-east by the end of the 1790s, given the strains imposed by a decade of revolution and war. Thoroughly disillusioned with revolution and its concomitant problems, many communes decided to contract-out. Young men avoiding military service began to form so many bridges spanning the aggressive designs of the catholic royalist *bandes* and the defensive needs of the village community. Both may well have been 'backward-looking', but for the majority of the poor there was no other way to look.

We know from his memoirs that Saint-Christol's *compagnie* was composed mainly of deserters and young men avoiding military service. One of Dominique Allier's 'sergeants', Denis Sage, had joined Allier's *compagnie* 'pour n'avoir point voulu partir avec les citoyens de la levée en masse, craignant d'être puni pour avoir différé son départ'.[72] On 1 fructidor Year IV/18 August 1796, the president of the *tribunal criminel* of the Vaucluse informed the Minister of Police that about '8–10,000 réquisitionnaires et déserteurs... sont prêts à commencer la guerre civile au premier signal qu'on leur donnera'.[73] As the royalists became more confident during the spring of 1797, the problem became increasingly acute for local authorities: as the president of the *tribunal criminel* of the Drôme explained in a letter stressing the critical situation of his department: 'Les causes de ces calamités sont connues. La France est inondée de déserteurs.'[74] The *compagnie* of 600 brigands which launched a military-style offensive on the town of Pertuis (Vaucluse) – again just before the spring elections – had been recruited 'en majeure partie de déserteurs et réquisitionnaires'.[75] The Jourdan conscription law of 1798, described by Marion as 'the most unpopular law of the Revolution',[76] could only exacerbate the problem decreeing, as it did, the annual call-up of young men between the ages of twenty and twenty-five. Despite the fact that two of the key agents of Louis XVIII in the Midi, Allier and Surville, had been arrested a few weeks before the passing of the law, the *commissaire près l'administration* at Ambert noted that the royalists were not too down-hearted; indeed, 'on médite de grands coups en comptant sur le secours que la loi de la conscription doit leur fournir'.[77] The following spring, the Minister of War was forced to send troops to the Yssingeaux

---

[71] C. Tilly, *The Vendée* (London, 1964), p. 305.

[72] A.N. F7 4559, *interrogatoire de Denis Sage*, 22 fructidor Year III.

[73] A.N. BB18 888, 1 fructidor Year IV. Just over a year later, the mayor of Hermaux (Lozère) was shot on his doorstep by 'des déserteurs, agens du fanatisme et de la réaction'. BB18 471, 21 nivôse Year VI.

[74] A.N. BB18 277, to Minister of Justice, 18 pluviôse Year V.

[75] A.N. BB18 890, *commissaire du tribunal criminel* to Minister of Justice, 23 ventôse Year V.

[76] M. Marion, *Le Brigandage*, p. 124. Agulhon states that the law had a particularly adverse effect upon the Army of the Alps. *La vie sociale*, p. 125.

[77] A.N. BB18 440, to Minister of Justice, 15 brumaire Year VII.

region of the Haute-Loire, since, of the total number of young men 'qui devait se rendre aux armées, la majeure partie a déserté en route'.[78] A year later, similar comments were being made about deserters in brigand strongholds like Sainte-Cécile in the Vaucluse.[79]

During the Year VIII/September 1799–September 1800, the flight from the hell of belonging to an army which was rapidly decomposing provides a further explanation for the marked increase in brigandage which affected many departments of the south-east, particularly those on the right bank of the Rhône. In frimaire Year VIII/December 1799, 1,200 deserters seized control of the town of Draguignan (Var) for several days.[80] Reports from the authorities in the Basses-Alpes allow us to follow the dismal retreat of the deserters. Two hundred of them passed through Forcalquier at the end of November, cursing the terrible privations they had been called upon to endure, deprived of food and footwear, obliged to watch their superior officers pillage and plunder their way to personal fortunes. According to one official report, hundreds of men were 'dying like flies' from disease as they straggled along the Barcelonnette valley on their way back, hopefully, to their homes.[81] Maybe it was one of these *grognards*, recalling the horrors of the Italian campaigns, who was arrested two years later during 'un tableau fantasmagorique' in Valence (Drôme) for shouting at the top of his voice when an actor, dressed as the First Consul, appeared: 'C'est le . . . coquin de Bonaparte. Otez-moi ce coquin, ce voleur . . .'[82]

The massive resistance to conscription may legitimately be construed as the defense of the local community, in some cases of the local economy, against the rapid encroachment of the state. Only a few years previously, villagers had drawn lots to decide the fate of a handful of men destined for the army; now the sword of Jourdan hung over all the young bachelors of the village, apart from the sons of the rich, of course, who could afford to be bought out. Little wonder that entire communities, through the mediation of the pro-royalist (pro-village?) mayor, *juge de paix* or non-juring priest, should have devised such ingenious methods of defeating the predatory agents of the state. In many communes, due to the intransigence of the local curé and his influence over the community, births, deaths and marriages had not been recorded in the registers of the *état-civil* after 1792, with the result that many pages had been left blank. These same pages were filled in the late 1790s with marriages alleged to have taken place during the early years of the Revolution. In the winter of 1801, the first prefect of the Ardèche informed the

---

78 Ibid., to Minister of Justice, 29 floréal Year VII.
79 A.N. F⁷ 7695, *petition des citoyens paisibles de la commune de Sainte Cécile*, 17 thermidor Year VIII.
80 M. Agulhon, *La vie sociale*, p. 378.
81 A.N. F⁷ 7695, to Minister of Police, 11 and 16 frimaire Year VIII.
82 A.N. BB¹⁸ 86, *commissaire près le tribunal criminel* of the Drôme to Minister of Justice, 22 nivôse Year IX.

Minister of Justice that many of the registers in his department were worse than useless: 'Vous y verrez,' he explained, 'à quels abus on s'est porté pour échapper à la loi de la réquisition.' In Saint-Chamas, for example, a commune composed of just eight houses (whose inhabitants were all called Chamasson !), forty marriages had allegedly taken place during the early years of the Revolution, all within a few months, and all with strangers from the department of the Gard![83] Brides apparently crossed departmental boundaries during the late 1790s almost as frequently as brigands. In the Basses-Alpes, the canton of Méolans acquired the notoriety of a Gretna Green during the Directory, offering so many marriages 'que les réquisitionnaires des autres cantons s'y rendent pour obtenir des exemptions'.[84]

It was at harvest-time, and during the many village *fêtes*, that the relationship between local communities and the *bandes* tended to be reinforced. It was rather injudicious of the gendarmerie to arrive in the strongly royalist commune of Genas in the Ain to round up the usual 'conscrits et réquisitionnaires', for example, not only during a *fête*, but a day or two after the harvest had been gathered in. The inevitable result was a pitched battle involving 300 villagers and the subsequent humiliating flight of the gendarmerie.[85] Doubtless, there would have been a few drinks and many tales of bravado to shouts of 'Vive le Roi !' in the local *cabaret* that evening. The roots of 'royalism' were embedded in the culture and cohesion of such communities. Many of the poorer families, as well as those *propriétaires* who employed labour, could be seriously affected by the loss of one or more pairs of hands from the fields as, indeed, could the small industrial concerns just beginning to make an impact on the economy of the southeast. The following report comes, once again, from the region where the *bandes* of Allier and the Abbé Solier operated. The owner of a small coalmine in the *forêt* d'Abilon, near Alais in the Gard, writing at the time of the White Terror of 1795, informed the *Agence des Mines* in Paris that he could double his production of coal if only he could obtain the necessary powder for shot-firing and, in particular, more workers. He had lost fifteen young men over the previous two years, 'only one of whom, Jacques Gabourdès, has returned, the rest, presumably, having been killed or taken prisoner'.[86]

Many young men chose to maim themselves rather than serve in the army. In a revealing report, produced at the time of the Jourdan law, the *officier de santé* of the military hospital in Grenoble warned the Minister of War of the increasing number of youngsters who were either burning themselves, or claiming to be deaf or, most common of all, slicing off their index fingers or

[83] A.N. BB¹⁸ 125, to Minister of Justice, 22 nivôse Year IX.
[84] A.N. BB¹⁸ 109, Minister of Justice to Minister of Interior, 24 germinal Year VII.
[85] A.N. BB¹⁸ 396, Minister of Police to Minister of Justice, 11 brumaire Year IX.
[86] A.N. F¹⁴ 4240, *rapport de l'Agence des mines*, 21 ventôse Year III.

their thumbs. The authorities at the hospital had witnessed, 'au grand préjudice de l'agriculture et du trésor public, des hommes décidés incurable et incapable de servir' coming, usually with their relatives, from all over the Drôme, the Ardèche and the Ain to get medical exemption certificates. The complaint of one elderly mother was not, the *officier de santé* remarked, untypical: 'ma récolte périt, mes deux autres fils sont morts à la guerre, il ne me reste que celui-ci qui est malade et cependant les gendarmes sont logés dans ma maison jusqu'à ce que j'ai un ordre du commissaire pour les renvoyer'. A few days previously, a young man had died in the hospital from his self-inflicted wounds. The gift sent anonymously to the *commissaire du gouvernement* in the Isère – a bloody index finger in a cardboard box – was a grisly, but symbolic, reminder of the attitude of young people towards military service in the late 1790s.[87]

If mass conscription weakened the social and economic fabric of village life, the religious policies of the Revolution proved to be equally effective in alienating substantial segments of the catholic population. We have noted the relatively high proportion of priests leading the local *bandes*, many of them in the former Vivarais region of the Cévennes where religion tended to be taken rather seriously. It had not been in Montaillou alone that *les bonshommes* had beckoned credulous villagers towards the Cathar heresy during the Middle Ages.[88] It is not surprising, therefore, that it was in the Cévennes hills that 'warrior-priests', like Claude Allier, the Abbé Solier and Fontanier *jambe de bois* preferred to operate. They knew their fellow-priests and their isolated parishioners in the little hamlets and villages, some of which were cut off from the outside world for months on end. Instructive, too, that those priests who had accepted the Civil Constitution of the Clergy should have been dubbed '*les intrus*' in these claustrophobic communities. Even where anti-protestant sentiment did not exist, the role of the priest as the arbitrator between the village and the outside world was usually crucial. As in the Mauges region of western France, where the *curé* was 'unquestionably the moral, charitable, and intellectual chief', so in many rural cantons of the south-east priests were to exert a powerful influence over their parishioners during the 1790s. The following report is typical of many received by the government concerning the influence of the church:

Les acquéreurs des biens nationaux sont menacés et pillés . . . le fruit de leurs travaux leur est enlevé, sans qu'il soit possible de trouver des témoins qui veuillent rendre hommage à la verité par le Grand Empire que les prêtres non-soumis aux lois ont sur

---

[87] A.N. BB[18] 394, *mémoire au ministre de la Guerre*, 3 frimaire Year VII. The *officier de santé* asked the Minister to take a break from 'le tumulte des affaires . . . pour entrer avec moi dans l'humble chaumière du cultivateur'. These reports from the military hospital in Grenoble establish direct links between desertion and the strength of catholic royalism.

[88] A. Chamson, *Sans Peur*, p. 17.

les habitans des campagnes qu'ils menacent des peines les plus effrayantes dans ce monde et dans l'autre s'ils ne leur rendent leurs biens.[89]

Non-juring priests did indeed fan the flames of hell a little for anyone attending services conducted by the constitutional priest. *Colporteurs* continued to peddle devotional works, some of which exhorted the faithful to pray for the royal family and to continue paying the *dîme*.[90]

The *dîme* had never represented a very heavy burden for catholics in Provence and this, along with the need to protect the catholic tradition against the incursions of protestantism in some areas, may help to explain the relative popularity of priests.[91] In any case, by 1795, it was no longer the priest who was levying the *dîme*, but the wealthy, possibly republican, *fermier* who had consolidated it, where appropriate, into the rents exacted from his tenants. The catholic priest had, therefore, ceased to be much of a threat by 1795, if he had ever been regarded as such; rather, he was now a persecuted figure, epitomising much of what had been best in the old traditions. Scores of villages in the south-east refused to accept constitutional priests – *les intrus* – preferring the clandestine administrations of their former *curé*. Those constitutional priests who did take up their functions in rural areas against the will of the majority of the inhabitants invariably pursued an embattled and precarious existence, one which usually meant ministering to the republican minority and thus deepening social cleavages. The constitutional priests in Planchamp had been killed alongside the wealthy republican *notaire*, Barrot. Whatever decisions were made in the corridors of power in Paris or Rome, villagers normally solved their problems in accordance with the old traditions. Despite (or, perhaps, because of) the passing of the Concordat, purchasers of church property were still being attacked in the commune of Chasseradès (Lozère) as late as 1803 'par quelques personnes armées de fusils, habillées en femmes ou portant une chemise sur leurs habits'. The crowd had organised this traditional demonstration in order to secure the return of lands 'pour servir au paiement des ministres du culte auxquels ces biens appartenaient d'origine'.[92]

Many refractory priests had, of course, returned to their parishes between

---

[89] A.N. BB[18] 439, *commissaire près le tribunal criminel* of the Haute-Loire to Minister of Justice, I fructidor Year V.

[90] A.N. BB[18] 394, *directeur du jury de Grenoble* to Minister of Justice, 26 germinal Year VI. The *abrégé de la doctrine chrétienne* contained 59 pages whose 'poison', according to the *directeur du jury*, was circulating 'dans la commune et les environs de Grenoble et y cause les ravages les plus funestes'. The Minister appears to have been rather baffled, since he could not discover what the relevant punishment was to fit the crime.

[91] E. Leroy Ladurie, 'Révoltes et contestations rurales en France', *Annales E.S.C.*, vol. 29 (1974) stresses (as befits an *annaliste*) the long struggle against the *dîme* in parts of Languedoc. Agulhon, writing on Provence, does not emphasise anti-clerical sentiment, pointing out that priests were rarely well-off in this province. *La vie sociale*, pp. 71–3.

[92] A.N. BB[18] 474, *commissaire près le tribunal criminel* to Minister of Justice, 12 nivôse Year XII.

1795 and 1797, usually with the tacit approval of the local authorities. Objections from over-zealous republicans were usually dismissed during this period, not only by the local population, but also by the departmental tribunals. Four priests had returned to their parishes in the *arrondissement* of Bourg (Ain) during the White Terror of 1795, provoking the anger of the minority of 'bons républicains' in the region. On 30 brumaire/21 November 1795, the latter had organised a detachment of troops to arrest one of the four priests living in the commune of Coligny. Whilst the troops were still some distance from the commune, the villagers had rung the tocsin to warn their neighbours in the near-by hamlets and although, after a violent struggle, *curé* Decoeur had, in fact, been arrested and placed in what served as the village gaol, over a hundred villagers successfully released him the same evening. The *tribunal criminel* of the department subsequently discharged all those brought before the court for this serious challenge to the authorities.[93] And it was not only in isolated communes that 'les bons prêtres' attracted support. In the town of Belley, refractory priests participated in a civic ceremony only a fortnight before the *coup* of 18 fructidor, and then marched alongside the municipal authorities to reopen churches which had been closed since the Terror.[94] Not that all refractory priests had gone about their ecclesiastical business in peace – much depended upon the political balance within any given community and the proximity of the local army garrison. One refractory *curé* named Baumont, living near Aix (Bouches-du-Rhône) had been assaulted by soldiers during the spring of 1796. The aged priest had only narrowly escaped death, his sexual parts having been severely mutilated. As they left the house, the soldiers had shouted to a group of women who had gathered around the front door: 'You can do what you like with what's left of him,' a revealing comment on male anti-clericalism in revolutionary France.[95]

The anti-clerical reaction which followed the *coup* of 18 fructidor in the south-east was to be immediate and, in many departments, intense. On 17 vendémiaire Year VI/8 October 1797, the National Guard arrived in the village of Cordéac (Isère) at three o'clock in the morning to surprise the local priest, now reduced to holding services in the middle of the night to avoid arrest. The detachment was, at first, repulsed by the customary crowd of chanting, stone-throwing villagers whose leader, Manuel Royer, just happened to be hiding his eldest son from the clutches of the local army recruiting-officer. On this occasion, however, the *curé* was finally seized by the Guardsmen, destined to become one of the early victims of the post-Fructidorean reaction.[96] In Cordéac, as in many other villages, young men

---

93 A.N. BB[18] 88, *commissaire près le tribunal criminel* to Minister of Justice, 3 floréal Year IV.
94 A.N. BB[18] 86, *commissaire près l'arrondissement de Belley* to Minister of Justice, 9 fructidor Year V.
95 A.N. BB[18] 176, *directeur du jury d'Aix* to Minister of Justice, 27 prairial Year IV.
96 A.N. BB[18] 394, *administration municipale* to *administration centrale*, 18 vendémiaire Year VI.

had played an important role in protecting their priest, highlighting the new relationship which had been forged since 1791 between many of the clergy and the 'natural defenders' of eighteenth-century village society, its youth, whose unspiritual and often lubricious antics during the *fêtes* of the ancien regime had not always elicited the approval of the church.[97] On 9 pluviose Year V/29 January 1796, the gendarmerie had entered the village of Lalleyriat (Ain) in an unsuccessful bid to arrest a refractory priest named Bouvier. Five *réquisitionnaires* had formed the advance guard of the villagers who had so stoutly defended their *curé*. One of them, Henri Baudet, was alleged to have uttered some extremely tasteless remarks concerning the merits of the First French Republic as he and his friends celebrated over a bottle of wine that same evening. Unfortunately for the young man, some 'jeunes républicains' from a neighbouring commune were drinking in the same *cabaret*. Henri was challenged to a duel which culminated in a fatal sabre-thrust to his stomach. What is particularly interesting (though by no means unique) about this incident is the fact that the young man accused of Henri Baudet's death was a close relative – Gaspard Bertet Baudet – whose own brother had been attacked by Henri four years earlier![98]

Quarrels between families from neighbouring 'republican' and 'royalist' communes, the avoidance of military service, the defense of 'notre bon curé', this was the stuff of village politics well into the reign of Napoleon Bonaparte. Practically the entire youth of the village of Le Bacon (Lozère) descended upon the house of Pacoul *père et fils* during the spring of 1801, demanding that the former resign his position on the municipality and that the family should return the former *curé*'s house which the Pacouls had bought as *biens nationaux*. Whether one was 'republican' or 'royalist' often depended on an individual's relationship to public power and his private purse. The wealthy republican Pacoul was finally forced to concede defeat and, to celebrate the 'royalist' victory, Pacoul *fils* was forced to carry the refractory priest back to his old house on his shoulders.[99] Youth, after all had suffered most from the laws of conscription and the lack of employment possibilities. Little wonder, then, that young men should have placed at the service of 'throne and altar' the experience gained through many a *romérage* and *bravade*. The installation of a new municipality in the brigand strong-hold of Sainte-Cécile (Vaucluse) was celebrated in thermidor Year VIII/August 1800 with 'fireworks and *farandoles*', and blessed by three refractory priests who, during

[97] M. Vovelle, *Les métamorphoses de la fête en Provence de 1750 à 1820* (Paris, 1976).

[98] A.N. BB[18] 88, *procès-verbal du tribunal criminel*, 20 pluviôse Year IV. Henri had served two years in prison for the attack upon Gaspard's brother.

[99] A.N. BB[18] 473, *commissaire près le tribunal criminel* to Minister of Justice, 11 ventôse Year IX. It was often costly not to take the claims of *la jeunesse* seriously. On 6 ventôse Year XIII, the youth of a small village near Marvejols (Lozère) burned down the house of a couple who had been married that day, because the latter refused to pay out the traditional small gifts of money enabling the youngsters to purchase drink.

the *fête-Dieu*, actually rebaptised many of the youth of the village[100] – perhaps, an act of gratitude on the part of the clergy as much as one of rededication to the service of God.

During the early years of the Revolution, it had been the legislation concerning religion and conscription which had produced new allegiances within many communities or, perhaps, they had just politicised old ones. Certainly attitudes hardened increasingly against the *gens d'affaires*, the urban merchant or the *laboureur* 'avide de biens' as the chase for office and land saw the latter given, at least, a head start – tax qualifications for voting, national land sold to the highest bidder. However, it was not until after 1795 that political power was vested more fully into the hands of the really wealthy, and that *biens nationaux* could be bought for a song; it was only after Thermidor that the 'individualist' aspect of legislation on forest rights and access to the fields and the commons began to alienate wider sections of the community, generally, although not always, the *classes populaires*. Confused and uncoordinated as it was, the gradual emergence of a more capitalist and individualist ethic becomes obvious after 1795. As Higonnet concluded: 'The years of the Directory were the period in which the whole of the Revolutionary bourgeoisie, already won over to social conservatism, finally adapted its principles to its practice, albeit in a circuitous way . . .'[101] It would have been surprising if the leaders of the counter-revolution had not exploited the possibilities inherent in this situation. The fact that successive administrations, from Barras to Bonaparte, could introduce change along capitalist lines only gradually and in a confused manner was, in no small measure, due to the resistance of the mass of ordinary Frenchmen; resistance which, in parts of the south-east, the catholic royalist brigands articulated politically. For, in the last analysis, it was the disenchantment with the Revolution, the assault on traditional practices, which finally cemented the fragile bonds between an increasingly disaffected population in the south-east and the *égorgeurs*. Who else offered to protect them from the 'constitutional' priest, the recruiting-sergeant and the purchaser and encloser of lands which village communities had exploited 'de temps immémorial'?

Emphasis has quite rightly been placed on the importance of geography in explaining the incidence of brigandage. Forests and mountains, rivers, and major trade routes, small towns nestling on the borders of two or more departments, all provided the habitat of catholic royalist brigandage. For de Gaulle, France stopped at Lyon: for the *égorgeur du Midi*, the counter-revolution began there. The departments of the Ain and the Isère were to attract the brigands, partly because of their proximity to Lyon, and partly because they were situated along the Swiss border. The headquarters for many brigands operating in the Basses-Alpes was the *bois de Caderache*. In the

---

100 A.N. F⁷ 7695, *les citoyens paisibles* to Minister of Justice, 17 thermidor Year VIII.
101 P. Higonnet, *Class, Ideology*, p. 254.

Lozère – Haute-Loire region – one band was based in the late 1790s in the *forêt noire*, a typical brigand habitat with its old *château* in the middle and tiny hamlets like Bonneval and Le Croiset clustered around its edges.[102] Regions 'de bois épais, de montagnes presque inaccessibles, de gorges affreuses', provide the classic topography of brigandage, making it well-nigh impossible for regular troops to track the brigands down.[103] It was clearly advantageous, given the administrative problems involved in crossing departmental boundaries, particularly for the gendarmerie, if the forest were situated across, or near, two or more departments; even better if it lay in close proximity to the major routes of communication, like the forest used by the brigands near Pierrelatte in the Drôme.

Yet one should not be too obsessed by the obvious. It is true that each *bande* tended to operate most effectively within its own locality, but the movement, as a whole, was a dynamic rather than a static one. The catholic *égorgeurs* used forests and mountains as retreats, not as self-contained bases. What is far more interesting is the relationship between the *égorgeurs*, 'pastoral economies and areas of mountain and poor soil'.[104] The *bandes* moved out of the forests into the hamlets and villages with the occasional foray into the larger urban centres; they mingled with the local population in fairs, *fêtes* and inns, appealing to the disinherited of the Revolution from the shepherd to the seigneur. It is true, of course, that many a seigneur before the Revolution had been as keen a destroyer of 'traditional rights' as any idealised 'bourgeois'. It is also true that individualism – *pace* Marc Bloch – did not begin with the fall of the Bastille. But all this is really beside the point. By 1795, many seigneurs and priests could claim, like the poor, to have become the dispossessed of the Revolution, victims of the all-encroaching power of the state. The poor had often been used by seigneurs before the Revolution to help repulse the advance of the wealthy, educated *bourgeois*. This unholy alliance could operate even more effectively in the circumstances of post-Thermidorean France.

There is, in fact, a clear correlation between the activity of the *bandes* and resistance to the legislation passed after 1794 concerning traditional rights of access to the forests, *vaine pâture*, and the *droit de parcours*, resistance which increased perceptibly after the Terror given the government's concern over the widespread devastation of woodland, mines and roads. The success of catholic royalist brigandage in certain regions of the south-east was linked to

[102] A.N. BB¹⁸ 472, an extremely interesting and perceptive report prepared by the *aide-de-camp commandant le détachement envoyé dans la forêt noire*, 30 brumaire Year VII.

[103] This was obvious to the local authorities, who stressed that only by despatching *local* commissaires into the forests could precise information be gleaned from the women and children scattered about in hamlets 'qui peuvent voir dans le jour rôder dans les bois ces brigands; ils les appercoivent le soir lorsqu'ils sont réunis'. A.N. BB¹⁸ 472, *administration municipale* of Villefort to Minister of Justice, 27 floréal Year VI.

[104] E. Hobsbawm, *Bandits*, p. 25.

the offensive launched by the *journalier* with his *lopin de terre*, the *cultivateur* with his small flock of sheep or goats, the small *vigneron*, the *bûcheron* and the *charbonnier*, indeed, by all those who depended upon rights of access to the forests and the fields. Before the Revolution, it had been the custom for seigneurs in the south-east to respect, however grudgingly, traditional practices of 'pâturage, glandage, lignerage et bûcherage'.[105] At the end of the eighteenth century, as Alain Molinier has shown for the Vivarais – together with the Comtat Venaissin, the most troubled region in the south-east – population increase unaccompanied by any real sign of an agricultural revolution had produced an explosive situation in which traditional rights became vital for the survival of the poorer sections of society. The population of the Vivarais had increased from 224,769 inhabitants in 1759 to 273,598 by 1793.[106] Guy Lemarchand has placed particular emphasis on the increasing importance of common lands during the Revolution as the struggle for survival became more desperate.[107] In 1789, the poor had survived by means of an 'economy of make-shifts':[108] by 1799, even that meagre economy was under threat.

The link between political brigandage and social unrest was clearly evident in the report of the *commissaire près l'administration municipale* of Buis (Drôme) during the spring of the Year V, when the royalists were most confident of success: 'Les brigands sont partout ... les propriétés sont devastées, les fruits des champs sont la proie des voleurs. On s'introduit dans les clôtures, on viole l'asile des citoyens, les bergers conduisent leurs troupeaux dans les vignes, dans les verges, dans les prairies; on coupe les arbres, on dégrade les bois.'[109] And this was by no means an isolated case. We find repeated complaints from the authorities concerning the violent defense of traditional customs and practices from most departments where catholic royalist *bandes* operated. 'Les vols de bois sont les délits de tous les jours et de tous les instants', the *commissaire près le tribunal correctionnel* at Vienne reported on 22 floréal Year IV/11 May 1796.[110] Reports from the *arrondissement* of Bourg in the Ain refer to the massive spoliation of forests after 1789.[111] In the *forêt de Blaches* near Pierrelatte (Drôme), 2,380 trees had been felled and 1,400 virtually destroyed within a couple of years: 'On va jusqu'à dire dans ce canton qu'on ne doit pas acheter ce que l'on peut se procurer pour rien.'[112] It was this same forest which provided shelter for the *bandes* of Saint-Christol and the Chevalier de Lamothe. Before the Revolution, the *forêt de Blaches* had belonged to the

---

105 M. Agulhon, *La vie sociale*, pp. 26–7.   106 A. Molinier, 'En Vivarais au XVIIIᵉ siècle'.

107 G. Lemarchand, 'La féodalité et la Révolution: seigneurie et communauté paysanne', *Annales historiques de la Révolution française*, vol. 52 (1980).

108 O. Hufton, *The Poor in the Eighteenth Century* (Oxford, 1974), pp. 16–17.

109 A.N. BB¹⁸ 279, to Minister of Justice, 6 ventôse Year V.

110 A.N. BB¹⁸ 395, to Minister of Justice.

111 A.N. BB¹⁸ 88, *commissaire près le tribunal criminel de Bourg*, 22 prairial Year V.

112 A.N. BB¹⁸ 278, Minister of Finance to Minister of Justice, 28 fructidor Year VI.

Chartreuse Order, which had tolerated many of the traditional customs upon which the poor depended for their livelihood. Much the same applies to the *forêt de Saoû* (also a brigand base after 1795) which had been placed in lay hands in December 1772 'à la charge de laisser jouir les habitans de droits dont ils justifieraient'.[113] Forests in the badly affected *arrondissement* of Sisteron (Basses-Alpes), another key area of brigand activity, provided the background for constant disputes between the local authorities and village communities throughout our period. Commenting on the scale of the devastation which had taken place in woodland around the commune of Clemensane since 1795, the prefect of the Basses-Alpes reported that attacks on *gardes forestiers* were still continuing in the spring of 1804: in the most recent case, they had been conducted by 'une troupe dans laquelle il y avait plusieurs hommes habillés en femmes'.[114]

'Les demoiselles des Basses-Alpes' were very likely to have benefited from the support of the local authorities, particularly the *juge de paix*, elected during the Years III and IV. In the village of la Côte-Saint-André (Isère), three villagers accused of stealing wood were given the minimum possible fine by the local *juge de paix* despite the serious nature of their offence, a considerable number of trees having been transported from the wood in carts. The *juge de paix*, who had also served as the mayor of the village for a short time, was described by the municipal administration as 'a former jacobin turned royalist reactionary', a not untypical volte-face given the determination of some local officials to defend 'les petits contre les gros', which is what some jacobins said they were doing in 1794, and what most royalists said they wished to do in 1797.[115] The *juge de paix* of Langeac (Haute-Loire), defending seventeen *cultivateurs* hauled before the courts by a *propriétaire* named Gueffier, provides us with a similar example. Gueffier had shot at one of the *cultivateurs* 'qui lui criait de le laisser tranquil, qu'il n'avait fait aucun mal dans son bois, qu'il était occupé à lier un fagot de mauvais bois qu'il avait rammasser [sic]'. Dead or live wood, what Gueffier, and those like him, wanted was for no one to be allowed to enter his property. The *juge de paix*, however, not only refused to allow the case to go to a higher court, but actually decided to instruct Gueffier to return the ropes and axes he had confiscated from the *cultivateurs*![116]

The significant point to stress when dealing with the causes of popular disaffection in the south-east after 1795 is that, in practically every case involving a dispute between the community and individual landowners, the

---

[113] A.N. BB¹⁸ 279, sub-prefect of Die to Minister of Justice, 3 pluviôse Year XIII.
[114] A.N. BB¹⁸ 110, to Minister of Justice, 24 floréal Year XII.
[115] A.N. BB¹⁸ 394, *administration municipale* to Minister of Justice, 27 pluviôse Year VI. The *juge de paix* had actually attempted to arrest the gendarmes despatched by the municipality to arrest the villagers!
[116] A.N. BB¹⁸ 441, *copie du jugement préparatoire*, 20 frimaire Year V.

government came down unequivocally on the side of the latter, despite the fact that the Rural Code of 1791 contained many ambiguities. The *juge de paix* la Côte-Saint-André, for example, lost his job; whilst the *juge de paix* of Langeac was told by the Minister of Justice, in no uncertain terms, that if he did not allow the case to go forward to a higher court, he would also be looking for more suitable employment.[117] When, on 25 prairial Year IV/13 June 1796, the *commissaire près le tribunal correctionnel* at Saint-Marcellin (Isère) complained to the government about the number of trees being felled, to the long-term detriment of the community, by an individual who had recently purchased the wood as *biens nationaux*, the Minister replied: 'C'est avec raison, citoyen, que les particuliers invoquent le droit qu'ils ont de disposer librement des bois qui leur appartiennent.'[118] A similar case in the Drôme, concerning *citoyen* Pierre Buis, whose entrepreneurial activities had alienated the poor *cultivateurs* of a commune near Valance, elicited the response from the Minister that Buis had a perfect right to do precisely as he wished with his property, 'cette question ne présente pas le moindre doute'.[119] Finally, in 1799, the Minister of Finance, rejecting the defence put forward by poor villagers in the Ain that their practice of collecting dead wood from the local forest derived from 'les ci-devant Chartreuse de Seillan', suggested to the Minister of Justice that such pleas represented 'une tolérance infiniment dangereuse et qu'on ne saurait faire cesser trop tôt'. The Minister of Finance also pointed out that, since poor villagers were usually incapable of paying damages, the threat of imprisonment should be used more frequently.[120]

The same conflict can be traced in those wine-growing districts which evinced a sympathy for the catholic royalist cause after 1795. Here again, the legislation dealing with such thorny problems as the *ban de vendange* tended to be confusing, if not contradictory. The laws of 1791 permitted municipalities to maintain the *ban* – on unenclosed land – before the date agreed upon by the local community, so long as this had been the custom before the Revolution. The legislation was vague, however, on the exact penalties which local authorities could inflict upon offenders. On 5 fructidor Year IV/22 August 1796, the *juge de paix* of Ceyzériat (Ain) had written to the Minister of Justice: 'Je pense qu'il serait nécessaire de sollicter une loy qui deffendit aux citoyens d'enfreindre les bans fixer par les communes pour les récoltes des vignobles et des prairies',[121] adding that the real problem was the

---

117 The *juge de paix* of Côte-Saint-André made a valiant, though somewhat despairing effort to save himself, explaining to the Minister of Justice that, since so many disputes within his jurisdiction were settled by word of mouth, he did not keep precise written records and was, therefore, a bit vague concerning the case which provoked the Minister's anger! A.N. BB[18] 394, 11 thermidor Year VI.

118 A.N. BB[18] 395, 25 prairial Year IV.

119 A.N. BB[18] 278, *président du tribunal criminel* of the Drôme to Minister of Justice, 29 thermidor Year VI.

120 A.N. BB[81] 88, see correspondence of 21 nivôse and 18 floréal Year VII.   121 Ibid.

ludicrously inadequate punishments which were being invoked against those who ignored the *ban*. Similar problems arose in the Drôme for the municipality of Coteaux de l'Hermitage, the distinctive quality of its wine depending upon the precise degree of maturity reached by the grapes. In this commune, all the vineyards, belonging to different growers, were enclosed within a single walled area. There was, as the municipality pointed out, no point in fining those villagers who ignored the *ban* the equivalent of three days' wages, as the law prescribed, since this amounted to less than four francs. What the municipality wanted, and what it did not get from the Minister of Justice, was the right to fine offenders 'sous les peines utilisées dans les communes du canton depuis des tems immemorés [*sic*]'.[122]

Equally if not more contentious in some regions were disputes involving traditional rights of *vaine pâture*. On 25 thermidor Year III/12 August 1795, the Committee of Public Safety had published a decree confirming the rights which the *propriétaire* possessed over the entire produce of his harvest. The Committee was responding to petitions received from farmers seeking to exclude villagers from their fields after the first reaping of the crop, emphasising that this exclusion was based 'sur le droit sacré de propriété que les malveillants s'efforcent d'altérer sur different points de la République'. The refusal to allow villagers to benefit from what was left of the harvest after the first reaping – *le regain* – represented a very substantial loss, not only for the really poor, but for all those who depended upon the fodder and grazing rights associated with traditional practices. The government's new policy or, to be more precise, its redefinition of the old policy, was to be resisted all the more fiercely given that the Rural Code of 1791 had confirmed, where customary, rights of 'vaine pâture, parcours et glanage'.[123] The decree of 25 thermidor Year III had been circulated too late in the south-east to affect that year's harvest: it was only in the following year that popular reaction gained momentum. By 1797, local authorities and tribunals found themselves confronted with hundreds of disputes relating to the previous year's harvest. What is more, they appear to be very unsure of the laws pertaining to such disputes. Were traditional rights of grazing and gleaning legal or not? Was the decree of 25 thermidor Year III 'une loi d'exception', aimed simply at increasing supplies of fodder for the army? 'C'est dans cette diversité d'opinion qui s'élèvent des rixes qui donnent lieu à des plaintes' one *juge de paix* in the Haute-Loire wrote to the Minister of Justice in the spring of 1797. The Minister's reply went through four sets of corrections! Finally, it was established that, although the legislation of 1791 had confirmed the use of

---

[122] A.N. BB[18] 278, *administration municipale* to Minister of Justice, 12 thermidor Year VI. Similar cases can be found in the Isère: the mayor of la Chapelle de la Tour informed the Minister of Justice on 6 brumaire Year V that despite the ban fixed by the municipality the previous year individual growers were increasingly tending to harvest when it suited them.

[123] G. Lemarchand, 'La féodalité et la Révolution', pp. 553–4.

vaine pâture on unenclosed land, the decree of 25 thermidor Year III had, in fact, revoked this right 'jusqu'après la seconde faulx des prés non-clos'. The Minister emphasised that the decree should now be accepted as 'le dernier état de la jurisprudence sur la vaine pature'.[124]

The agrarian 'Thermidorean Reaction' was to provoke widespread resistance in many regions of the south-east, particularly, of course, where the use of *vaine pâture* had been customary, like the departments of the Lozère and the Haute-Loire. On 23 thermidor Year V/10 August 1797, the *commissaire près l'administration municipale* of Allègre (Haute-Loire) informed the government that the issue was provoking major unrest within his jurisdiction: *propriétaires*, paraphrasing the decree of 25 thermidor, were saying that 'le territoire français est libre comme les personnes qui l'habitent, et ils ne peuvent etre assujettis aux sacrifices que peut exiger le bien général, que sous les conditions d'une juste et préalable indemnité', a clear enough articulation of the philosophy of individualism. The poorer villagers, on the other hand, 'qui veulent et prétendent dépouiller le propriétaire de la seconde herbe des prés, opposent que de tout tems et ancienneté ils en ont joui'. Once again, the government came down unequivocally on the side of the *propriétaire*, confirming that the legislations of the Year III had granted 'l'usage de la vaine pature dans les prés non-clos, jusqu'à la seconde faulx et la levée des regains, au profit de la propriétaire'.[125] In prairial Year IV, the *président du tribunal criminel* of the Lozère reported that, in many communes, *journaliers* and *cultivateurs* were still invading pasture and forest land which certain individuals regarded as their private property, adding that, given the non-existence or loss during the Revolution of so many documents, he found it very difficult to decide upon legal entitlement.[126]

In the very royalist commune of Mazeyrat (Haute-Loire), a group of *propriétaires* took eight villagers to court in an attempt to deny them access to their fields – recently acquired as *biens nationaux* – immediately after the first harvest, a right which, as the villagers explained, 'ils ont exercé de tems immémorial'. The *propriétaires*, anxious to exploit anti-seigneurial sentiment (at least amongst the authorities), argued that this right only derived from an agreement between the villagers and the former seigneur, in fulfilment of which the villagers had been obliged to transport the lord's grain to his warehouse.[127] True or false, the villagers would surely have preferred the return of their seigneur, as well as the chore of carrying his grain, than to see themselves deprived of all access to fields which had provided them with an essential part of their livelihood. In the commune of Malzieu (Lozère), which gave considerable support to the *égorgeurs*, one of the biggest landowners had

124 A.N. BB[18] 439, correspondence of 16 prairial and 17 messidor Year V.
125 Ibid., correspondence of 23 thermidor and 7 fructidor Year V.
126 A.N. BB[18] 471, to Minister of Justice, 24 prairial Year IV.
127 A.N. BB[18] 439, Minister of Police to Minister of Justice, 20 vendémiaire Year VI.

begun to herd his cattle 'dans les paccages communs' to the exclusion of flocks belonging to his poorer neighbours. Citizen Brun happened to be one of those republican *juges de paix* who obviously cared little about communal rights, since he had long been accustomed to reject them in favour of the rights of the highest tax-payers in the commune. Brun acted and, what is more, sought the sanction of the Minister of Justice to go on acting, as many a seigneur had done before the Revolution – as judge and jury of their own cases.[128]

If further proof were needed of the link between political brigandage and popular disaffection one has only to examine the relationship between seigneurs, returning after 1794 to reclaim their land, and the catholic royalist brigands. Seigneurs like Alexandre Nicolas Esprit Fulque, formerly a noble living in Oraison in the Basses-Alpes, certainly one of the towns in that department most adversely affected by the activities of the *égorgeurs*. Fulque *père* was typical of many Provençal petty nobles. He had left Oraison during the Terror, but claimed that he had never stepped outside the department. It appears that Fulque – who estimated that his financial losses as a result of the Revolution amounted to 50,000 livres a year – had been a popular seigneur since, when he returned in 1797, 'la majeure partie des habitants furent à sa rencontre pour lui témoigner le plaisir qu'elle avait de l'avoir parmi eux'. One of Fulque's immediate aims had been to recover the property he had lost since 1789, either amicably through the courts or, less amicably, through pressure exerted upon the twelve individuals who had acquired his land. The struggle dragged on for many years, in the course of which time one of the twelve men involved was savagely murdered. Fulque's own son was accused of having been a member of the *bande* responsible for the crime. Not unnaturally, the murder of one of the purchasers of Fulque's land was said to have 'jeté l'alarme chez tous les acquéreurs de biens nationaux'. Whether the son was personally guilty or not, there can be little doubt that the family attracted considerable support from the poorer members of the community in and around Oraison, themselves the victims, perhaps, of the success of men like the former mayor, Guillaume, alleged to have been possessed 'd'une avidité excessive de biens', or Paul Hugues, a *ménager* who had loaned money to Fulque before the Revolution in order to help finance the seigneur's own land deals.[129] How many times was this scenario to be repeated in the south-east – the richer peasantry seizing seigneurial and church lands during the early years of the Revolution only to succumb, under the Directory and Consulate, to pressure from the returning lord, aided and abetted, at times, by the exemplary knife of the *égorgeur*.

[128] A.N. BB¹⁸ 474, the Minister of Justice informed Brun on 24 nivôse Year XII that in all cases which came before him, and in which he was personally involved, 'Je présume que vous serez assex sage de vous en abstenir'.

[129] A.N. BB¹⁸ 110, petition to Minister of Justice, s.d.; prefect to Minister of Justice, 3 fructidor Year XII.

Even more instructive, involving as it does so many of the points we have
discussed above, is the case of a seigneur named Emery, custodian of the
château de Guisan about forty miles from Valence (Drôme). On 28 brumaire
Year VI/18 November 1797, a detachment of gendarmes had gone to arrest
the seigneur's two sons, widely acknowledged to have joined one of the
catholic royalist *bandes*. The usual battle ensued between the villagers and the
gendarmes, as a result of which four of the former and three of the latter were
shot. The Emery *frères* had, in fact, been hiding, along with the refractory
priest, in the house of the seigneur's former agent, Magnan.[130] A few years
later we find Magnan, still acting on behalf of the *ci-devant* Emery, organising
a group of villagers to raid fields on the mountain-side of Couspeau, near the
commune of les Tonils, during which hundreds of sheaves of corn were
carted away (to the seigneur's warehouse?) and the rest of the harvest
destroyed. The land had belonged to Emery before the Revolution, although
he does not appear to have farmed it in any meaningful way. It had, however,
been a constant source of friction between the seigneur and the inhabitants
of the small communes around the mountain of Couspeau. During the
Revolution, a number of the more enterprising *cultivateurs* had enclosed part
of the land, thus affecting the traditional rights of access for the poorer
members of the community. Magnan had taken the case to court and, given
the pro-royalist sympathies of most tribunals, had successfully reclaimed the
land on 6 fructidor Year IX/24 August 1801, hence the raid on crops of the
cultivateurs of les Tonils. According to the latter, if Magnan and Emery were
not stopped, they would 'faire revivre chez nous le règne du despotisme
seigneurial', establishing in the process 'une autorité plus tyrannique qu'ils
n'avaient jadis'.[131] Why? Because, as we have pointed out earlier, the newly
forged relationship between former seigneurs and priests and the poorer
artisans and peasants – in their very different ways, all victims of an increasingly capitalist society – posed a very serious threat to the richer peasant, to
the urban lawyer or merchant who had made significant gains during the
Revolution, but whose grasp on power, particularly at the level of the state,
was still feeble. Hence the need for that type of dictator that Napoleon
Bonaparte was obliged to become.

It is fitting, perhaps, that we should finish with two examples taken from
the department of the Vaucluse, one of the most troubled, from the standpoint of political brigandage, throughout the Directory and the Consulate.
One case involves the considerable pressure exerted upon Michel Febvre by
the agent of a former seigneur named Maclar. Febvre, who had purchased

---

130 A.N. BB¹⁸ 278, *directeur du jury de Die* to Minister of Justice, 4 frimaire Year VI. The villagers
were to pay a heavy cost for their resistance (this was, after all, post- not pre-fructidor). A
week later, a considerable number of troops arrived and arrested forty 'suspects', some being
locked up for several days in the former *curé*'s house; others were imprisoned in Valence.
131 A.N. BB¹⁸ 280, *petition des habitans souverains de la commune de Tonils*, s.d.

some of Maclar's land as *biens nationaux*, was warned that 'il fallait rendre ces biens à monsieur Maclar parce qu'ils avait été acquis injustement et contre les lois, que ceux qui les rendraient auraient la protection de monsieur Maclar'. Just in case the paternalist carrot did not work, the *égorgeur* stick was waved as advance warning. If Febvre refused to cooperate, he was informed that 'monsieur de Maclar avait trois fils qui ne manqueraient pas d'en prendre vengeance'.[132] The final example, involving a seigneur named Cambis, comes from the commune of Jouques near Orange. The seigneur, accused by the prefect of the Vaucluse of having been 'coalisé avec les brigands' during the Directory, was fighting a rear-guard action against the wealthier *cultivateurs* of the commune who had divided up the common lands for their own use during the Revolution. Here again, the seigneur received support from the poorer members of the commune, like the *cultivateur* Ponchon, arrested for grazing his four goats on the common lands. Cambis's main enemy was yet another *acquéreur de biens nationaux*, the former mayor, Billoty.[133]

The form of brigandage which afflicted the south-east of France during the Directory and Consulate was not created by the failure of the administrative and judicial authorities to tie up the loose ends of the Revolution, important as this failure was. It was 'political' in that it was clearly linked to the work of the émigrés abroad as well as to events in Paris, particularly during the period 1795 to 1797 when a very determined and, so far as the election results were concerned, successful attempt was made to accomplish a 'constitutional revolution'. Nor did the 'political' or 'organised' dimension of the work of the catholic royalist brigands disappear with the *coup* of 18 fructidor Year V although, clearly, the methods and the objectives of their operations changed to suit altered circumstances. Republican officials and purchasers of national lands continued to attract the attention of the *égorgeurs* throughout our period. After 1797, however, as the movement became more 'rural', attacks on isolated farms and the increasing number of highway robberies moved the *chouan* ineluctably closer to the *chauffeur*. Nonetheless, two months after Bonaparte had seized power, the brigands responsible for the murder of a 73-year-old-man near Suzette (Vaucluse) were still wearing the white *cocarde* of the Bourbons: 'Ils disent, avec audace, qu'ils sont les chefs de l'armée royale et catalique [*sic*].'[134] It was probably a member of this same *bande* who was arrested not far from Suze a few days later with 'les mots compagnie de Jésus' tattooed on his forearm.[135]

Of course, sceptics could point to the naivety of accepting *cocardes* and

[132] A.N. BB[18] 889, *procès-verbal du directeur du jury de Carpentras*, 13 ventôse Year VI.

[133] A.N. BB[18] 897, prefect to Minister of Justice, 11 prairial Year XII.

[134] A.N. F[7] 7695, *commissaire du canton de Suze* to the *administration centrale* of the Vaucluse, 26 frimaire Year VIII.

[135] A.N. BB[18] 893, *juge au tribunal civil* of the Vaucluse to Minister of Justice, 1 nivôse Year III.

tattoos as evidence of political commitment. Were they not simply the fading symbols of the glory that had once been the *Compagnie de Jésus*? For some, probably so; for others, like the Abbé Solier, almost certainly not. The Soliers of the south-east, who had served the cause of counter-revolution from the early 1790s to their deaths, cannot possibly be dismissed as traditional brigands wearing but the masks of royalism. The republican deputy Barrot, whose 80-year-old father had been killed by Bertrand's *bande*, was under no illusions about the seriousness of the threat from the catholic royalist movement, pointing out to the government, as late as 15 floréal Year X/5 May 1802, that ever since the days of the *camps de Jalès* there had existed 'un germe de contre-révolution qui n'a jamais été extirpé'.[136] As late as the spring of 1800, several royalist *compagnies* had congregated at Villefort (Lozère) for a reunion and tactical briefing before going their separate ways, one *compagnie* moving into the Aveyron, one into the Haute-Loire, the other returning to the Ardèche. The *commissaire*, who had received first-hand accounts of the activities of these royalist *compagnies*, remarked that Villefort was the centre of a very active correspondance network linking several neighbouring departments as well as the key centre of Lyon.[137]

The degree of success achieved by the catholic royalist movement in the south-east, however, must also be explained by the massive resistance to the government's military, religious and economic policies. By stoning the recruiting-sergeant, the 'constitutional' priest and the 'individualist' landowner, poor villagers in particular were defending their local identity and traditions, not only against 'outsiders', but also against their wealthy neighbours who represented so many republican trojan horses within the village body politic. The wealthier peasantry may well have been satisfied by the agrarian reforms and the possibility of purchasing *biens nationaux*, but for the vast majority of *journaliers* and poor *cultivateurs* the Revolution had afforded them little relief by 1794 and, thereafter, with the clearer articulation of the individualist policies of the Thermidorean elites, they were to be deprived of what little they had. If, as Olwen Hufton has stated, the poor on the eve of the Revolution were only surviving in 'progressively difficult circumstances and with progressively less chance of success',[138] what were the odds on survival after 1795? There was, of course, always the army, *or* the catholic royalist *maquis*.

The importance of the assault on traditional rights at the end of the eighteenth century obviously extends far beyond the boundaries of Languedoc and Provence. It was to be very significant, for example, in the 'Church and King' insurrections in Italy. The *Santafede* movement in Calabria

---

[136] A.N. BB[18] 473, to Minister of Justice.
[137] A.N. BB[18] 125, *commissaire près le tribunal criminel* of the Lozère to Minister of Justice, 17 floréal Year VIII.
[138] O. Hufton, *The Poor*, p. 367.

attracted support in forest regions, like the Sila, from peasants 'deprived of their rights by those who have usurped the common lands and so of all means to procure their subsistance'.[139] Further light could be thrown upon the problem by comparing 'Church and King' movements in Spain, Italy and France during the 1790s and the 1800s. It is interesting that in France the increasing resistance to Napoleon after 1810 was to be fuelled, as it had been under the Directory, by local resistance to the government's military, religious and economic policies. Napoleon, like all dictators, had merely placed many of France's more pressing problems 'on ice'. The thaw when it came, after 1810, led to the recrudescence of catholic royalism in the same areas which had been affected by the *Compagnies de Jésus* in the later 1790s.

[139] Communicated by Dr John Davis of the University of Warwick, who also made several helpful observations during the preparation of this chapter.

8

◇◇

Rhine and Loire: Napoleonic elites and social order

GEOFFREY ELLIS

I

A few years ago, while preparing a review article on Marxist interpretations of the French Revolution,[1] I realised how lonely someone looking at that debate from the Napoleonic end, the 'other' end as it were, could feel. If the historiographical consensus which passed as the orthodox view of the Revolution from the 1930s to the 1950s could be called 'Marxist', granted a good deal of diversity within its fraternity, its main focus was on the revolutionary period itself, or on what were considered 'strategic' parts of it. Since the mounting attack on received Marxist lore, first in the Anglo-Saxon countries, and then in France itself, the limelight seems to have shifted from the years 1789–94 to the old regime, in other words to the 'causes' or 'origins' of the Revolution. That indeed is now the main area of pragmatic research on the subject.[2] Few historians, whether for or against the 'bourgeois revolution' of the Marxist paradigm, would now insist that the Year II was the strategic or exemplary year of the Revolution. If anything, it is seen as an aberration, as an atypical phase. Whatever else it has done, the debate on the Marxist interpretations has made us all much more aware of the empirical continuities of French social and economic history, and especially of the constancy of landed relationships.

Yet Marxists have never abandoned their fundamental concept of the French Revolution as a 'bourgeois revolution', even if some among them have redefined the term in the light of more recent factual evidence.[3] Nor

I should like to thank the British Academy for an allocation from its Small Grants Research Fund in the Humanities, which enabled me to collect most of the primary material used in this essay during a visit to France in 1979.

[1] 'The "Marxist interpretation" of the French Revolution', *English Historical Review*, 93 (1978), 353–76.

[2] On this, see the useful bibliographical survey in the introductory chapter of William Doyle's *Origins of the French Revolution* (Oxford, 1980).

[3] For one – it has been suggested 'Althusserian' – adaptation of older Marxist arguments, and

have they given up their idea that this 'bourgeois revolution' was consistent with the motives and aims of a thrusting 'capitalist' class before 1789, and that it somehow satisfied those aims. So, too, by concentrating on the often very mixed aims and propertied interests among well-to-do commoners and *privilégiés* towards the end of the old regime, and by thus calling any tidy 'class' model of the Revolution into question, critics of the Marxists have generally paid them the respect of arguing within the same time-scale. The old Marxist fortress had another important rampart, however and, presumptive though it was, it concerned the longer-term effects of the Revolution. Indeed, the causes, the development and the effects of that whole process were seen by this schema as inter-related and consistent parts of the same dialectical dynamic, which some have even thought of as historically inevitable. The empirical attack on this schema, again, has stressed how inconsistent and confused the Revolution's social and economic consequences were in 'class' terms, how they worked very differently within social and professional groups, and what great regional disparities they brought. But too often, unfortunately, the polemical issue has been assumed to run out of steam around 1799, and sometimes even earlier, when the revolutionary achievement is assumed to have been consolidated, or in part subverted, and when post-revolutionary society supposedly took stable form. It is not clear from many accounts, whether Marxist or otherwise, when the essential Revolution ended, or even if it ever did. One recent work on the French bureaucratic cadres speaks of 'post-revolutionary society' specifically in the context of the Directory.[4] Others might well prefer to draw the line at Brumaire, or at Napoleon's creation of the Legion of Honour in 1802, or possibly at the proclamation of the Empire in 1804 or perhaps as late as the institution of the imperial nobility on a formal basis in 1808.

Now, if the Revolution ruined or embarrassed as many magnates among the old merchant oligarchies as it enhanced the careers and wealth of other sorts of bourgeois, it is difficult to establish certain links with a triumphant merchant and industrial capitalism. Yet who would now doubt that such capitalist enterprise was seriously disrupted by the revolt of Santo Domingo, by the severance of French colonial trade, by forced taxes on the rich and by the disastrous inflation of the assignat? If, on the other hand, landed property and income remained the essential measure of wealth and of social pre-eminence in Napoleonic France, as before the revolutionary upheavals, then the 'bourgeois revolution' of the old paradigm needs a change of face. Its association with forward-looking capitalist functions would have to be redrawn in a much more clearly proprietary profile, or in other words

for criticism of it by the old guard, see the discussion on pp. 373–6 of my cited review article, where further bibliographical leads are given.
[4] C. H. Church, *Revolution and Red Tape: the French Ministerial Bureaucracy 1770–1850* (Oxford, 1981), p. 229 and *passim*.

defined in terms of landed property as the crucial capital asset, as the major
source of income and as the principal area for investment and reinvestment.
But in that case one might well ask whether it was very different from the
predominant proprietary capitalism of the old regime, of whose reality the
important writings of George V. Taylor leave us in no doubt.[5] It now seems
clear that the Revolution in some ways quickened trends in the French land
market already apparent before it. The speed of the process was determined
largely by sales of property confiscated from the church and from the
émigré nobility. It does not follow, however, that the revolutionary land
settlement brought any real democratisation of French proprietorship. Those
who were already the better-off proprietors of town and country were its
main beneficiaries, and the wealth of former nobles continued to count for
much. The émigrés themselves, we now know, had devised ruses to regain
title to their lands placed under orders of confiscation and sequestration
during the 1790s, or else did so under Napoleon, whether by restitution or,
more expensively, by repurchase.[6] As a result, the Revolution had left France
with a repaired and reconstituted conservative tradition to reconcile with its
more recent radical one. The Napoleonic elites, whether one studies them at
the upper end of the imperial nobility itself, or through the much wider and
therefore perhaps more typical catchment area of the '*notables*' all over
France, were among the earliest variants of that process of assimilation. We
remain poorly informed on the particular mutations within such propertied
groups, on their many regional variations and on how they came to reflect
social standing – 'notability' in fact – in the aftermath of revolution.

These are big issues, and they concern the continuities as well as the
changes in French social history. Within the space allowed, this essay
attempts to extract the main elements of a debate which, judged in terms of
English works, has had very little attention here. It gives a short bibliographical guide to the major secondary sources now available, and it then
discusses their central themes and controversies. Its third and most substantial part offers some preliminary findings of my own work on primary
material from two contrasting regional angles, the departments of the Bas-
Rhin and the Loire-Inférieure (now the Loire-Atlantique). The limited nature
of its scope and primary sources does not permit any comprehensive answers

---

[5] Notably 'Types of capitalism in eighteenth-century France', *English Historical Review*, 79
(1964), 478–97; and 'Noncapitalist wealth and the origins of the French Revolution', *American
Historical Review*, 72 (1967), 469–96.

[6] An *arrêté* of 20 October 1800 lifted the sequestration on the lands of émigrés whose names had
been eliminated from the prohibited list. This was confirmed by a senatus-consultum of 26
April 1802, with the exception of woodlands and forests already declared inalienable by the law
of 23 December 1795, for reasons of national defence, and of buildings already put to public
use. On the other hand, the *arrêté* of 18 July 1800 had declared as irrevocable all sales of *biens
nationaux* hitherto effected at the expense of émigrés, even if they had been or were about to be
excluded from the prohibited list.

to the question of who benefited most in material terms from the Revolution; but it does help us to see who, at least in the areas here studied, *mattered* most in the public life of Napoleonic France. This, then, is an attempt to define 'notability' by empirical enquiry and to comment on its place in the social order of the Consulate and Empire.

The historiography of the subject is much better served now than it was some twenty or thirty years ago, when Ernest Labrousse and Albert Soboul gave us a few crude brush-strokes on a largely blank canvas.[7] Since then, the debate on the French Revolution from the 'other' end, that of its social and closely related economic effects, has come into its own. What might be called the new social critique of Napoleonic France had its first major fillip in the later 1960s, especially at the Sorbonne conference in October 1969[8] which marked the bicentenary of Napoleon's birth. One whole section of the published proceedings here deals with social questions, and twelve scholars then communicated samples of their work. Most of these were confined to social and professional analyses of various departmental lists of *notables*, but others were more broadly aimed. Jean Tulard, for instance, in his useful overview, stresses the primacy of landed wealth within the Napoleonic elites from a number of angles.[9] Monika Senkowska-Gluck's contribution has been influential in showing how Napoleon's social policy, as evidenced in promotions to his imperial nobility and its endowment through land-gifts, was closely linked with his dynastic ambitions, particularly in his treatment of the subject states in Italy (as from 1806) and in Germany and Poland (as from 1807).[10] Tulard's interest in the subject was followed up a few years later in another general survey, this time more closely directed to the constituents and their relative value of the wealth and income of the imperial nobles.[11] No clear pattern of a class and least of all of a caste-like coherence emerges here. The common leaven is once again land, whether of old or more recent acquisition.

[7] E. Labrousse, 'Voies nouvelles vers une histoire de la bourgeoisie occidentale aux XVIIIe et XIXe siècles (1700–1850)', *X Congresso internazionale di scienze storiche: Roma 4–11 settembre 1955, Relazioni*, vol. IV, 365–96; A. Soboul, 'Bilan du monde en 1815: Esquisse d'un bilan social', *XIIe Congrès international des sciences historiques: Vienne, 29 août–5 septembre 1965, Rapports*, I, *Grands thèmes*, 517–45. Another early seminal essay, more particularly concerned with the old regime in France, is Marcel Reinhard, 'Elite et noblesse dans la seconde moitié du XVIIIe siècle', *Revue d'histoire moderne et contemporaine* (hereafter *RHMC*), 3 (1956), 5–37.

[8] The proceedings were published by the sponsoring body in a special number entitled 'La France à l'époque napoléonienne' of *RHMC*, 17 (1970). Most of the papers also appear in the *Annales historiques de la Révolution française*, 42 (1970).

[9] 'Problèmes sociaux de la France impériale', *RHMC*, 17 (1970), 639–63.

[10] 'Les donataires de Napoléon', ibid., 680–93.

[11] 'Les composants d'une fortune: le cas de la noblesse d'empire', *Revue historique*, 253 (1975), 119–38. See also the relevant parts of his *Paris et son administration 1800–1830* (Paris, 1976) and *Napoléon ou le mythe du sauveur* (2nd edn, Paris, 1977).

By the 1970s this topic had also attracted the attention of Guy Chaussinand-Nogaret, Louis Bergeron and Robert Forster, of whom the first- and last-named had worked hitherto mainly on the old regime. Their joint article[12] approaches the question at the height of the Empire in 1810 and is based on a computerised analysis of the lists of electoral colleges in five departments (the Haute-Garonne, Côte-d'Or, Yonne, Seine-Inférieure and Nord), with a total sample running to some thousands of *notables* in regions considered by the authors to be representative of the diversity of French society at that time. In the mid-seventies two important works appeared. One was Romuald Szramkiewicz's study of the high personnel of the Bank of France,[13] the other Bergeron's doctoral thesis on the Parisian banking, merchant and industrial elite.[14] At the same time Chaussinand-Nogaret published a volume of selected secondary writings covering the subject more generally and over a much longer period.[15] In more recent years these efforts have gone the way of so much modern historical research in France, and have been channelled into the sponsored programme of a central *équipe*. Under the auspices of the Centre National de la Recherche Scientifique, and under the general direction of Bergeron and Chaussinand-Nogaret, the departmental series of *Grands notables du premier empire* is now well launched.[16] Eight volumes have appeared to date,[17] and more are expected. While these are uneven in quality and concerned mainly with the *crème de la crème*, that is the sixty to ninety most distinguished *notables* (*personnes les plus marquantes*) rather than the highest taxpayers (*les plus imposés*) or members of the electoral colleges, who

---

[12] 'Les notables du «Grand Empire» en 1810', *Annales E.S.C.*, 26, no. 5 (1971), 1052–75.

[13] *Les régents et censeurs de la Banque de France nommés sous le consulat et l'empire* (Centre de recherches d'histoire et de philologie, E.P.H.E., IVᵉ Section, Paris, 1974).

[14] *Banquiers, négociants et manufacturiers parisiens du directoire à l'empire* (2 vols. in typographical photocopy, Paris, 1975; now available in a single volume in the Mouton edn, Ecole des hautes études en sciences sociales, Paris, 1978). A good digest of some of this material had appeared in Bergeron's textbook, *L'Episode napoléonien. Aspects intérieurs 1799–1815* (Nouvelle histoire de la France contemporaine, vol. IV, Paris, 1972), now also available in Robert Palmer's English translation, *France under Napoleon* (Princeton, N.J., 1981).

[15] *Une histoire des élites 1700–1848. Recueil de textes présentés et commentés* (Paris and The Hague, 1975).

[16] Ecole des hautes études en sciences sociales (Centre de recherches historiques), C.N.R.S., Paris.

[17] Vol. 1 (1978) on the Vaucluse (by Alain Maureau) and the Ardèche (by Germaine Peyron-Montagnon); vol. 2 (1978) on Mont-Blanc and Leman (by André Palluel-Guillard); vol. 3 (1978) on the Bas-Rhin (by Michel Richard) and on the Sarre, Mont-Tonnerre, Rhin-et-Moselle and Roër (by Roger Dufraisse); vol. 4 (1979) on the Jura, Haute-Saône and Doubs (by Claude-Isabelle Brelot); vol. 5 (1980) on the Gard (by Armand Cosson), Hérault (by Henri Michel) and Drôme (by Gérard-Albert Roch); vol. 6 (1980) on the Alpes-Maritimes and Corse (by Jean-Yves Coppolani), Aude (by Jean-Claude Gegot), Pyrénées-Orientales (by Geneviève Gavignaud) and Bouches-du-Rhône (by the Abbé Paul Gueyraud); vol. 7 (1981) on the Aube and Marne (by Georges Clause) and Haute-Marne (by Georges Viard); and vol. 8 (1982) on the Loir-et-Cher and Indre-et-Loire (by Jeanine Labussière) and Loire-Inférieure (by Béatrix Guillet).

did not always coincide, their biographical information in alphabetical format will be valuable to researchers in the field. In an even more ambitious programme, based on an analysis of the social, professional and financial details of members forming the departmental and *arrondissement* electoral colleges in 1810, Bergeron and Chaussinand-Nogaret have tried to construct a composite map of such *notables* in all the 131 departments of the formal Empire.[18] The feed-in to their computer extends to very sizeable samples of anything up to 70,000 individuals, but the 'identikit' imperial *notable* who finally emerges inevitably has vague features due to gaps and variations in the original information about his constituent parts. The exercise nevertheless offers important findings about the social and professional composition of the electoral colleges. Perhaps the most illuminating sections are those dealing with the partial evidence of stability within or mobility among the various professional groups. Jean Tulard has also added to our published manuals in the field, although his detailed alphabetical list of and accompanying commentary on the princes, dukes, counts, barons and chevaliers of the Empire cover only the upper reaches of official notability under Napoleon.[19]

Outside the formal unit of the Empire, where the effects of Napoleon's social policy take on a rather different aspect, particularly in Germany and Italy, published works are still thin on the ground. Helmut Berding's study of the kingdom of Westphalia is only a guide to some of the sources available for German social history across the Rhine during the Empire.[20] By comparison with writings in French, at least, and by comparison with their own major contributions to the social history of the old regime and of the Revolution, English-speaking historians have not paid much attention to Napoleonic elites hitherto. I cannot name a single work in English which could be called a serviceable general statement on the subject. All we have is an assortment of books and articles dealing with particular groups, like the relevant parts of T. D. Beck's quantitative analysis of the French legislative personnel from Napoleon to the July Monarchy,[21] Irene Collins' account of the membership and functions of the Napoleonic legislative body, tribunate and senate,[22] Clive Church's long-ranging survey of the bureaucratic cadres[23] and E. A. Whitcomb's studies of the prefectoral and diplomatic corps under

---

[18] *Les «masses de granit». Cent mille notables du premier empire* (Paris, 1979), a computerised analysis based on the 'programme Couturier' at the Centre de recherches historiques.

[19] *Napoléon et la noblesse d'empire, suivi de la liste complète des membres de la noblesse impériale* (Paris, 1979).

[20] *Napoleonische Herrschafts- und Gesellschaftspolitik im Königreich Westfalen 1807–1813* (Kritische Studien zur Geschichtswissenschaft, vol. VII (Göttingen, 1973).

[21] *French Legislators, 1800–1834. A study in Quantitative History* (University of California, Berkeley and Los Angeles, 1974).

[22] *Napoleon and his Parliaments 1800–1815* (London, 1979).

[23] *Revolution and Red Tape.*

Napoleon.[24] The *notables* of provincial France and the *hommes d'affaires* of the Empire are virtually unapproachable through recent English writings. So far, the whole debate has more or less passed us by.

II

It seems appropriate, then, to preface my own regional material here with an introductory digest of what has emerged in the debate up to now, what its central themes and controversies are, and what conclusions (if any) are generally agreed. The first variable is the terms to be used. In addition to its less precisely definable social and cultural senses, 'notability' under the Consulate and Empire had official meanings. At the start of the period, the *notables* tended to emerge from two main groups: incumbent officials in local administration, and men of the various legal professions, both public and private. As a reflection of those who mattered in French society, the earliest consular lists are something of a mirror-image, since the *notables* coming through the filtering-up process of primary, secondary and subsequent elections were often the people, or the sorts of people, responsible for compiling the lists. Economic magnates and former nobles, including the émigrés who were either returning or who were about to return under the Napoleonic amnesties of 1800 and 1802, were relatively under-represented in them. Tulard estimates, for instance, that the old nobility accounted for rather less than 3 per cent of the *notables* who first came through the complicated electoral process of the communal *arrondissements* and the subsequent departmental lists, as set out in the law of 13 ventôse Year IX/4 March 1801.[25] After the senatus-consultum of 4 August 1802 a much more specific and intimate link between notability and landownership was established. For by this measure the members of departmental electoral colleges now to be formed *had* to be chosen from among the 600 most highly taxed citizens of the respective departments, as identified from the official returns and under the authority of the Minister of Finances. This technical requirement survived all the later avatars of the Napoleonic system. From about 1810, however, it was supplemented by the demand for lists of the sixty or more – usually more – 'most distinguished' and 'most influential' persons in each department. This was to introduce a more qualitative criterion alongside, indeed above, the quantitative layers of the highest taxpayers, and it is a sign of Napoleon's growing wish to bring in and honour the old nobility, wherever possible. Further ministerial directives required similar lists of the most outstanding merchants and manufacturers in each department. These were taken into account when appointments were made to official bodies like the *jurys de*

[24] 'Napoleon's prefects', *Amer. Hist. Rev.*, 79 (1974), 1089–1118; and *Napoleon's Diplomatic Service* (Durham, N.C., 1979).
[25] *Noblesse d'empire*, 26 n.

commerce (operating within the trade tribunals since 1801), the central *Conseil général de commerce* (an advisory body operating since 1803) and the *Conseils de prud'hommes* (set up as from 1806 to hear and resolve industrial disputes).

Yet whatever its sense and whatever professional functions it denoted, notability under Napoleon had an essential base in landed property and its proceeds. The *plus imposés* themselves were identified according to the *foncière*, the basic land tax returns, not to the *mobilière*, which was assessed on industrial revenues and on dividends from stock (*rentes*), or to the *patente*, a much smaller tax on specifically commercial income. One distortion as a result was that commercial and industrial wealth and income, which could be expressed in terms other than revenue from land, were under-represented in the lists and sometimes excluded from them. Allowing for this, the *notables* who emerged under the Napoleonic ground rules, whether they were active in public life or not, were bound to be a plutocratic group. They were *possédants* by pre-requirement rather than, on the once fashionable analogy of the eighteenth-century *privilégiés*, an 'élite des Lumières'. Enlightenment, in the sense of encouragement for *les talents*, erudition and aesthetic refinement, may well have had its representatives and even its Maecenases among the Napoleonic *notables*, timid and reticent though some will have been; but none of those qualities was necessary for membership of the 600 *plus imposés* or of their political elite in the departmental electoral colleges. The economic catchment area of the latter was itself often modest. Many of the *plus imposés* in the lower reaches of their lists were men of small holdings, local magnates at most, and not uncommonly much less. Tulard again, in an attempt to find the lowest common factor for membership of the departmental electoral colleges, offers 3,000 francs of annual landed income, roughly corresponding to 60,000 francs of capital, as a crude measure.[26] In some departments a higher figure would have applied, but in many others there would have been a lower plateau. The vital qualification, however, is that well-to-do merchants, manufacturers and *rentiers* were often left off the lists, where their income from land was less than that from other assets, and where the economic routine of daily life required their full-time professional commitment.

If, then, it was practically impossible to be a *notable* without some property qualification or other, not all owners of landed property and other assets aspired to notability in the sense of seeking to rise in official service, and so to enhance their careers in public life. Many – very likely most – did not actively pursue such a career, and the great majority of the old nobility appear to have deliberately eschewed it. The latter on the whole took as little active part in the public affairs of the Empire as their social standing and economic weight made unavoidable. They, most of all, did not follow avidly in the entourage of the new master, and the returned émigrés were not only the most reticent of all, but were generally regarded with most suspicion by

[26] Tulard, 'Problèmes sociaux', 651, 663.

Napoleon and his officials. One could no doubt find examples in all departments of nobles who became *ralliés* and were active in the public life of the
Empire. The likes of Philippe Comte de Ségur, Albert Duc de Luynes, Louis
Comte de Narbonne, the Duc de Broglie (until his death in 1804), Talleyrand-
Périgord and the former *parlementaire* Mathieu-Louis Molé were only some
of the richer prizes. To them one should add many more whose families had
been only recently ennobled, or who had bought offices giving an expecta-
tion of ennoblement, by 1789: Marmont, Rémusat, Berthier and Roederer,
for instance. Appointments to the post of chamberlain within the imperial
household often drew on old noble families, such as d'Aubusson de la
Feuillade, Croy, Mercy-Argenteau, Choiseul-Praslin, Turenne and d'Haussonville; while the ménage of the empress similarly had names like Rochechouart-Mortemart and Bouillé. Most of those named, and others like them,
also received imperial titles and very often entailed properties (*majorats*) to go
with them. As the imperial nobility was itself more flamboyantly displayed
after its formal inauguration in 1808, so greater efforts were made to
strengthen the ranks of such *ralliés*, and so to enrich the whole coin of courtly
life and to make the house of Bonaparte more respectable.[27]

Nevertheless, such families formed only a small section of the old noble
community, and many more lived through the Consulate and Empire in
comparative obscurity, removed from official service and favours. They
could claim, after all, that they had their lands to tend to and old assets to
salvage. Although exact figures are not available, Tulard thinks that as many
as four-fifths of the old aristocracy may have been uncooperative towards the
Napoleonic regime or at any rate absent from the ranks of known *ralliés*.[28]
Their acquiescence in it is to be presumed only by their residence in France
and on the principle of *qui tacit consentit*. This reluctance to serve makes easy
generalisations about social fusion and the politics of reconciliation under
Napoleon all the more difficult, especially if one adds in magnates among the
merchant and industrial communities who also shunned or were lukewarm
towards official careers in the imperial service. One might also wonder how
and why it was that the old nobility were allowed to withdraw from the
public scene on such a scale. It is clear that they did so with the knowledge
and perhaps even at the wish of the prefects or of the emperor himself. They
were not exactly absentee *notables*, since their political inactivity did not mean
that they had ceased to matter in the economic life of their regions, but they
might perhaps be called the 'low-profile *notables*' of the Empire. Their
appearance on the lists of the electoral colleges was sparse and erratic. What
is more puzzling, they sometimes do not appear even on the lists of the 600

---

[27] I have drawn on Tulard, *Noblesse d'empire*, 102–4 and 153, for particular details of the foregoing
paragraph. I should also like to thank my colleague, Rory Browne, for his expert guidance
on the families in question.
[28] *Noblesse d'empire*, 104.

highest taxpayers of their departments, although they would surely have qualified as such. This particular form of opting out of public life and its rewards under Napoleon leaves us with unanswered questions about their real influence in local life, and of course it also casts doubt on the authenticity of the official lists themselves. It was probably the result of a tacit under-standing, a sort of unofficial selective amnesia, on the part of the prefects, with or without the emperor's knowledge or approval. The veil it throws over what notability could mean in regional terms during the Empire is both real and regrettable. One may even wonder whether these *non-dramatis personae* of Napoleonic France were all rejuvenated for political or other public service under the Bourbon Restoration.

It is clearly necessary, then, to distinguish between Napoleonic *notables* who were active in some way in the affairs of state or of the army, whether at central level or in the departmental or local context, and those who were not. Within the active group, a distinction could also be made between *notables* of the capital, whose domicile or work kept them in or near Paris and so within the orbit of the Imperial Court for much of the year, and those of the provinces who rarely went there. A distinction between civilian and military elites within the group of official *notables* is possible too, as it could determine the form and the value of the likely imperial rewards. Napoleon could make such a distinction without fuss or ceremony, combining as he did the supreme civilian and military functions of head of state and commander-in-chief of the Grand Army in his own person. He seems indeed to have encouraged a formal and hierarchical view of his system of honours. At the crest of the quasi-pyramid were the imperial titles and the outworks of the Imperial Court, with its satellite households. Several of these were based abroad, following Napoleon's dynastic placements of 1805 and 1806 in Italy, of 1806 in Holland, of 1805–7 in Germany and of 1808 in Spain. Then, on the civil side, came the ministries in Paris, each of which commanded little empires of recruitment. According to one recent estimate, the total staff of the central ministries was 3,650 strong by the end of the Empire, the Ministry of War alone accounting for 1,500.[29] The nucleii of family dynasties had time to form in some of them, as with the Masson, engineers in the Ponts et Chaussées, or with the Portalis in the council of state, or with the Parisot in the prefecture of police.[30] Broadly on a par with the ministers and the councillors of state came the senators, who enjoyed at least the illusion of venerability by virtue of their exclusive numbers, their stipends and the *sénatoreries* granted to the most favoured among them.[31]

---

[29] Church, *Revolution and Red Tape*, 374 n. 39, where further details are given.
[30] Tulard, 'Problèmes sociaux', 653.
[31] The constitution of the Year VIII provided for a senate of sixty members to start with, to be increased over the next ten years by two annually. It was the function of senators to choose the 300 members of the legislative body and the 100 members of the tribunate, formed by the

The Imperial decree of 1 March 1808 instituted the graded titles of prince, duke, count, baron and chevalier,[32] and at the same time appointed the ten 'Grand Dignatories' of the Empire.[33] The title of count was to be awarded to ministers, senators and councillors of state who merited such recognition. That of baron might similarly go, where appropriate, to the presidents and distinguished members of the departmental electoral colleges, to the presidents and *procureurs-généraux* of the principal courts of law, to archbishops and bishops (it was in fact also bestowed on members of the imperial chapter of Saint-Denis) and to mayors of large cities. The title of chevalier de l'Empire was considered appropriate for officers of the Legion of Honour, and in practice its favours were much more widely spread. The emperor had the discretion to award any of these titles to other subjects, whether in civil or military service, as seemed to him fit. In this way distinguished members of the legislative body and former tribunes – the tribunate was abolished on 19 August 1807 – might find a place somewhere on these layers of honour and reward, as might prefects and other local officials. Lower down the civil hierarchy the borderland between civil and military functionaries, and between administrative and judicial ones, was blurred and inter-running. It offered vast scope for public service and, through it, for instance at the level of the *grands commis* in the ministries and directions, opportunities for social elevation into the ranks of the official *notables*.

The Napoleonic military establishment was even more concretised in rank and graded in rewards. Immediately below the emperor stood the four

same constitutional provisions, from official lists of 'national notables', the pick of the departmental filtering-up process of elections. The senate kept this role after the system was changed by the senatus-consultum which on 4 August 1802 instituted the electoral colleges. Senators were to be appointed for life, to receive an annual stipend of 25,000 francs and they could not hold other official positions. In January 1803 Napoleon created the thirty-six *sénatoreries*, corresponding to the area of an assize court. Each beneficiary was to enjoy 25,000 francs in addition to his senatorial stipend, and in recognition of certain judicial and administrative functions in his jurisdiction, also received a stately residence there, to be made over from the residual stock of national lands. In the event, as Tulard has shown, the nominal value of the *sénatoreries* was not matched by actual returns, as frequent complaints by disappointed senators made clear. Tulard, *Noblesse d'empire*, 27–32.

[32] It is important to distinguish here between the chevaliers de l'Empire appointed as from 1808 and the chevaliers of the Legion of Honour, appointed as from 1802, who were much more numerous.

[33] That is, the grand-elector (Joseph Bonaparte, king of Naples and then of Spain); vice-elector (Talleyrand, prince of Benevento, formerly foreign minister and grand chamberlain); arch-chancellor (Cambacérès, duke of Parma); arch-chancellor of state (Eugène de Beauharnais, viceroy of Italy); arch-treasurer (Lebrun, duke of Emilia); high constable (Louis Bonaparte, king of Holland); vice-constable (Berthier, chief of staff, prince of Neuchâtel and later of Wagram); grand-admiral (Joachim Murat, grand duke of Berg and then king of Naples, the husband of Caroline Bonaparte); governor of the departments beyond the Alps (Camillo Borghese, the husband of Pauline Bonaparte); and governor of the Dutch departments (Lebrun again).

honorary and fourteen active marshals appointed by a decree of 19 May 1804. Eight others were added to this exclusive body, the peak of the high command, between 1807 and 1815. Close to them came the generals who also counted among the top brass of the Imperial Army. Most of the marshals and several of the leading generals received the title of duke, along with Imperial land-gifts (*dotations*) convertible into *majorats*. A few more favoured ones – Bernadotte, Berthier, Davout, Masséna and Ney – became princes. Other officers were fairly evenly distributed over the ranks of the counts, barons and chevaliers. The total number of Imperial nobles so rewarded between 1808 and 1815 varies according to the source, Émile Campardon putting it as low as 3,264, and Albert Rébérend as high as 4,016; but if the most recent statement is to be believed, the figure is at least 3,364, and probably rather more.[34] Tulard concedes here that there are omissions, where the archival records are missing or dubious, and his list also excludes members of Napoleon's family. But if such allowances are made, the distribution of titles in that list breaks down as follows: 34 princes and dukes, 459 counts, 1,552 barons and 1,319 chevaliers. If, too, this whole sample is analysed by professional category, the heavy preponderance of military men is immediately apparent. Some 59 per cent of the total were so employed, as against 22 per cent who were high civil functionaries (councillors of state, prefects, bishops, inspectors, magistrates), 17 per cent who are described as '*notables*' (senators, members of the departmental electoral colleges, and mayors), 1.5 per cent broadly grouped under the heading of '*talents*' (doctors, academics, members of the Institute, archivists, sculptors, composers and some others), which meant that the remaining category of trade and industry made up less than 1 per cent.[35]

The same military bias is more obvious still in the membership of the more lavishly bestowed Legion of Honour. By April 1814 its numbers exceeded 38,000, of whom 34,361 were chevaliers and the rest officers. By one estimate, Tulard puts the military component at 87 per cent,[36] by another at more than 90 per cent.[37] Military men also had the lion's share of the imperial land-gifts. Official estimates of the total number of such beneficiaries (*donataires*) vary, according to dates, from just over 4,000 to almost 6,000. The estimated value of their nominal endowments, made up of rents due from conquered lands in Germany and Italy, ranges similarly from some 20 to nearly 30 million francs in all annually. As Helmut Berding has shown, the Westphalian and

---

34 Emile Campardon, *Liste des membres de la noblesse impériale, dressée d'après les registres de lettres patentes conservés aux Archives nationales* (Paris, 1889); Albert Révérend, *Armorial du premier empire, titres, majorats et armoiries concédés par Napoléon Ier* (4 vols., Paris, 1894–7); Tulard, 'Les composants d'une fortune', 137, and his *Noblesse d'empire*, 93–8. Tulard's alphabetical list, under each title, is given on pp. 175–356 of the last-named source. *N.B.* Individuals who received more than one imperial title are counted once only, at the higher honour.

35 Tulard, 'Problèmes sociaux', 655; *Noblesse d'empire*, 94.

36 'Problèmes sociaux', 655.   37 *Noblesse d'empire*, 48–9.

Hanoverian lands had a crucial part to play here.[38] Together they accounted for over half the disposable stock, and they are a good illustration of the ways in which so many of the subject states were milked for the wherewithal to further Napoleon's developing social policy and dynastic ambition in France itself. And again, if most of the *dotations* enjoyed by military men were allocated at the modest level of 5,000 to 10,000 francs a year or less, many of the richest prizes at the other end of the scale went to favourites like Berthier, Davout, Masséna, Ney, Caulaincourt, Soult and Bessières. It is only fair to add, however, that in many cases the real value of the *dotations* fell far short of their nominal value, especially towards the end of the Empire, and this was itself due in part to the debilitating effects of the Imperial fiscal policies on the economies of the subject states.[39]

Whatever one's definition of official notability under the Empire, it would then have to accommodate that intrusive military ingredient. What of its bearing on social origins? Of Tulard's list of Imperial nobles whose backgrounds are known, a little more than a fifth (22 to 22.5 per cent) were from noble families of the old regime, and something around that mark (19.5 to 20 per cent) were from the popular classes, whose route into the imperial nobility had invariably been through the army. The central core of the group, some 58 per cent, was of 'bourgeois' stock.[40] From such evidence Tulard feels able to conclude that 'cette noblesse d'Empire préparait la fusion de la vieille noblesse et d'une élite bourgeoise'.[41] From it one might similarly infer that the old textbook clichés about 'careers open to talent', 'social fusion' and 'the politics of reconciliation' are indeed well-founded. In my view, however, this may be too 'official' and too top-heavy a view of notability under Napoleon. In provincial France, beyond the titles and rewards of the military and civil establishments, the social balance of pre-eminent subjects looks rather different. The membership of the departmental electoral colleges shows a smaller proportional representation of the old nobility, though the figure of roughly a fifth in the later imperial lists of *les personnes les plus marquantes* is much the same, and the military element is usually well short of 10 per cent. The latter was no doubt due in part to the absence of officers on active service, and as a result the proportion of men of popular origin in the lists of departmental *notables* is much lower than that which had been borne aloft by the motor of the army into the Imperial nobility itself. In the departmental context, at any rate, *notables* qualifying for membership of the 600 plus *imposés* were unlikely to have started their professional careers from poor backgrounds.

---

38 *Napoleonische Herrschafts- und Gesellschaftspolitik*, esp. 65–7 and 133–4 (notes). The statistical matter given in the appendixes on pp. 148 and 150 of the same work sets out the comparative position of the sources of the land-gifts and the groups of *donataires*.
39 Tulard, 'Les composants d'une fortune', 122–7; *Noblesse d'empire*, 111–17.
40 'Problèmes sociaux', 656; *Noblesse d'empire*, 97.   41 'Problèmes sociaux', 658.

Yet the biggest difference between the departmental *notables* and the Imperial nobility as such is the very low representation in the latter of *hommes d'affaires* and of those, *propriétaires* and *rentiers*, who might be described as living off independent means. Both these groups feature prominently in the lists of the *plus imposés* and of the departmental electoral colleges. The capital assets of the *hommes d'affaires*, by which generic term I here include bankers, merchants, manufacturers and those engaged in the various service trades, were not directly dependent on state employment and reward. It may well be that their low incidence in the Imperial nobility testifies to Napoleon's well-advertised dislike of their kind, but it would be a mistake to conclude from this that they had no important public functions and therefore no weight as *notables* in his regime. Some, we know, were influential economic advisers; others were high functionaries in the Bank and its provincial services; and others again were government contractors. At local level, such men might similarly be drawn into service in the advisory chambers of commerce set up by the *arrêté* of 24 December 1802 and in the consultative chambers for manufacture, arts and crafts created by the measures of 12 April and 29 July 1803. *Propriétaires*, in the sense of landowners deriving their income mainly from rents, and who are sometimes called '*non-actifs*' to distinguish them from working farmers described as '*propriétaires exploitants*' or '*cultivateurs*', account for anything up to a fifth or even a quarter of the departmental electoral college lists. If all these groups are taken together as the 'landed interest', so to speak, the proportion rises to a third, and often more. Louis Bergeron and Guy Chaussinand-Nogaret rightly claim that, under the Empire, 'le propriétaire, modèle social du notable, en est aussi le modèle économique'.[42] The *rentiers*, whose income came chiefly from dividends on government stock (*rentes sur l'état* of sundry issue), sometimes appear in number, sometimes not, depending on the preferences of prefectoral nomenclature. It is a fair guess that, as a group, they must have over'apped a good deal with the *propriétaires* and *hommes d'affaires* alike. Under whatever label they are grouped, their presence was real enough.

Such differences between the professional balance of *notables* in provincial France and those who formed the Imperial nobility itself are massively illustrated in the findings of Bergeron and Chaussinand-Nogaret. Using the electoral college lists for both departments and *arrondissements* over the whole Empire in 1810, their sample takes account of 66,735 *notables* whose professional status was then known. It breaks down into the following order of categories, with the respective percentages of the total in brackets after each: *propriétaires* (24.55), lower local administration (18.12), functionaries in civil administration (15.76), liberal professions (14.37), trade and handicrafts (10.79), *propriétaires exploitants* (8.23), military men (2.35), clergymen (1.23) and all others (4.57).[43] If this broad balance is acceptable at all, the sorts of

[42] Les «*masses de granit*», 62.   [43] Ibid. 43.

people who mattered in the departments present a rather different picture from the professional physiognomy of the Imperial nobility as such. In other words, we have at least *two* views of even *official* notability under the Empire. Since the provincial view was much the more common and populous, it should be seen as the more typical. When the superstructure of the Napoleonic state fell in 1814, honorific bearings and all, the *notables* of provincial France could and often did continue to matter in the social and economic life of their regions. The changes of 1814 and 1815 might then be seen as yet further adjustments, after a period of some stability, to the flux of new political realities. The constancy of landed wealth and of landed relationships was not fundamentally affected. At the end of the Empire, we are in this sense back where we started.

In sum, notability under Napoleon represented various social and professional mutations within the constant nexus of landownership. Its public or official quality was due to the role in which the emperor had himself cast his *notables*. They were a functioning elite, and a subservient one at that, since real political power was signally denied them. They were an elite graded in some way according to an official hierarchy, in which the element of Imperial choice and reward had an increasing part to play. They were nevertheless an elite open to men of talent, especially to determined careerists in the bureaucratic services, in the legal professions and in the army, which might be called the strategic channels for bourgeois social advancement. The functionaries and the lawyers were the great survivors of public life – *les perpétuels*, who in Tocqueville's famous image kept the body politic intact and active while its successive heads were being chopped off. Often the same people returned in a sort of institutionalised relay to resume public office where they had left off, or been forced to leave off, at an earlier stage of events since 1789. 'Des éternels conventionnels, délivrez-moi, Seigneur', wrote the *Diplomate* on 9 December 1799, at the start of the Consulate,[44] and the theme of '*plus ça change . . .*' continued after the 'purge' of 1802 and on into the years of the Empire. If Napoleon's predilection for old nobles became more evident as from 1807, at any rate in new appointments and new rewards, he did not disperse the incumbent personnel who linked him with the revolutionary past. His elites were the result of a process of social adaptation, rooted in property and honoured in service, from which cream might rise above the homogeneous milk. Their professional ingredients were no doubt old and familiar in many cases, but the Imperial blend – the social balance – was particular. As '*masses de granit*', as it were the plinths and columns of an aspiring edifice, they seem perhaps disappointingly matter-of-fact. The Napoleonic elites, like the revolutionary ones before them, represent a pragmatic social adjustment to the professional challenges and opportunities of on-going events.

---

44 Quoted in Collins, *Napoleon and his Parliaments*, 20.

III

The departments of the Bas-Rhin and the Loire-Inférieure, whose economic fortunes during the revolutionary and Napoleonic wars were rather different, at first glance suggest an interesting contrast in social and professional adaptation. What follows is a selective investigation of that supposition. It would be too fanciful to present this account as the story of two river valleys, Rhine and Loire, or even of two great entrepôt towns, Strasbourg and Nantes. But at least there is a basis for comparison here between the social and professional milieux of communities orientated, on the one hand, towards inland economic opportunities, and on the other towards maritime trade. It should be said at once that agriculture, with all its traditional structures and resistance to rapid change, remained the primary economic sector of both departments under Napoleon, as before. Not surprisingly, then, the 'landed interest' is prominently represented in their departmental electoral colleges, but as will be seen, its particular forms reveal interesting differences. The appearance of the fairly ubiquitous civil servants and local government officials, as well as of the many sorts of legal functionaries, is plain in each case too. Alongside the landed community and the administrative and judicial careerists, there were commercial and industrial magnates who either were still or had once been more dynamic in their economic development. Given the varying impact of the maritime wars and of the Continental Blockade on the two regions, one might expect to find such differences reflected in the composition of their official elites. This essay offers evidence for a critical assessment of that assumption.

By the time the Empire was proclaimed in 1804, the department of the Bas-Rhin, and the city of Strasbourg in particular, had recovered well from the economic hardships of the 1790s. During the Blockade of 1806–13, as the sea lanes were closed to French shipping, and as Imperial trade was reorientated towards inland markets, the department was at the hub of an active Rhenish traffic in imports and exports alike. Its population, which at the start of the Consulate was put at 448,480, had risen to 488,350 by 1806, and it continued to grow fast, passing the half-million mark by 1808 and rising to 532,488 by 1812.[45] The population of Strasbourg itself increased from 49,056 in August 1802 to 51,465 in 1806, and by 1812 (with the annexation to France of Kehl across the Rhine on 21 January 1808) had reached 54,820.[46] The harvests of the Consulate and Empire were generally good, and in spite of endless complaints and petitions about the ruinous effects of

---

[45] Official census returns for the Year VIII, A.N. F²⁰ 30; census of 1 January 1806, A.N. F²⁰ 31; *Annuaire du Bas-Rhin* for 1808, p. 56, and that for 1813, p. 187.

[46] Figures cited in the 'Arrêté no. 1964 contenant règlement pour l'exécution du senatus-consulte du 16 thermidor an X, relativement aux assemblées de canton, aux collèges électoraux, &c.' of 19 fructidor X (6 September 1802), *Bull. des lois*, no. 213; *Annuaire du Bas-Rhin* for 1807, p. 156; and that for 1813, p. 165.

official economic policy, the agricultural sectors of the Bas-Rhin enjoyed stability under Napoleon, at any rate until the military reverses of 1813–14. The commercial houses of Strasbourg, a strategically placed *lieu de passage* for the carrying trade of the upper Rhine, handled anything up to a third of the Empire's imports and exports at the height of the Blockade. Even if the endemic smuggling trade is excluded, and all commentators agree on its vast scale and value, the crude volume of recorded traffic through Strasbourg in 1808 and 1809 was four times greater than during the years immediately preceding 1806. The figure for that year, moreover, was itself two or three times higher than at any point in the 1790s for which comparable statistics are available.[47] Although the economic crisis of 1810–11 for a time stopped the expansionary momentum of 1807–10, the main commercial trend was upward, and several official sources show 1812 as the high-water mark of the city's entrepôt trade during the entire Napoleonic period. Though less spectacularly than its carrying trade, the industries of Strasbourg were carried along by the same expansionary rhythm. Alsatian merchants and manufacturers could later look back on the years of the Empire as something of a golden age – many actually did so under the Restoration – when Strasbourg, 'la ville des routes', had become 'le boulevard de la France'.[48]

Economic fortunes in the Loire-Inférieure during the same period were altogether less happy. At the start of the Napoleonic regime, in the Year VIII, the department had a population of 369,305, and six years later it had risen to 404,463.[49] These returns were down on the 419,669 inhabitants recorded at the earliest departmental count of 1790,[50] and no doubt they reflect in some way the declining economic vitality of the region over the period. Nantes itself, the second French port after Bordeaux for most of the eighteenth century, had fewer inhabitants (77,162) in 1806 than the 81,638 officially estimated in September 1802,[51] and in this respect had declined even by comparison with 1789.[52] Its commercial dislocation during the maritime wars shows in many measurable ways. Between 1719 and 1789 the value of colonial goods imported through Nantes had increased from 20 to 100

---

47 The figures for total regular traffic, as recorded by the chamber of commerce, were 80,942 metric quintals in 1806; 111,288 in 1807; 176,504 in 1808; 179,241 in 1809; 210,636 in 1810; 216,323 in 1811; 278,516 in 1812; but the 138,042 metric quintals in 1813 reflect the impact of the Allied advance across the Rhenish trade routes. The full statistical record for the years 1797–1813 is set out in appendix B of my *Napolean's Continental Blockade: the Case of Alsace* (Oxford, 1981), 276–7, and is discussed in detail in chaps. 4 and 6 of that study.

48 For an assessment of historiographical versions of Alsatian economic fortunes under Napoleon, see my *Blockade*, 149–55.

49 Official census returns for the Year VIII, A.N. F20 30; census of 1 January 1806, A.N. F20 31.

50 Léon Maître, *Source-dictionnaire des lieux habités de la Loire-Inférieure* (Nantes, 1909), vi.

51 Testu's *Almanach impérial* (Paris, 1806), 801; 'Arrêté no. 1964 . . .' of 19 fructidor Year X, *Bull. des lois*, no. 213.

52 A round figure of 80,000 in 1789 is cited in Paul Bois (dir.), *Histoire de Nantes* (vol. 39 in the series Histoire des villes, Univers de la France et des pays francophones, Toulouse, 1977), 241.

million livres a year, while its exports in the same period had risen from 10 to 300 million livres worth.[53] The total value of the city's traffic over those years (the coasting trade included) had expanded from 80 to 600 million livres in the case of imports, and from 90 to 550 million in that of exports; and in the years immediately preceding the Revolution it had handled between a fifth and a quarter of all French colonial imports, with sugar far and away the major item.[54] The trans-Atlantic trade of Nantes before the Revolution had been dominated by large-scale contractors operating a traffic usually described as *armement en aventurier*, in ships of large tonnage, which presupposed extensive capital assets for their equipment. The slave-trade (*la traite des noirs*) had been an important branch of that traffic, and the French Antilles so predominated within it that Santo Domingo alone had received 85 per cent of the ships from Nantes crossing the Atlantic and 90 per cent of their cargoes in the year 1784.[55] Ancillary industries like shipbuilding, sailcloth manufacture and rope-making, along with woollens and linens for colonial export, had grown up in the *hinterland* of the port and were dependent on its continuing prosperity. If such trade had been engrossed by an established merchant oligarchy, *négociants* and *armateurs*, and was in that sense 'bourgeois', it had also attracted a sizeable amount of capital from the old nobility and from *anoblis*. Indeed, the trade had provided the means to *anoblissement* for aspiring bourgeois.

The first serious shock to the Nantais had come with the revolt of Santo Domingo in 1791, and the maritime war with Britain had intensified their troubles in the following years. According to the local chamber of commerce, the city had had 145 long-distance vessels of its own in service in 1789, with crews then totalling 5,365 men and with a trade worth 47.5 million livres. If allowance is made for servicing costs of 26.2 million, profits from that traffic had been upwards of 21 million. But in 1803 only 12 ships with 192 men were still engaged in this trade. The value of their operations had sunk to 1.7 million livres (francs), and total profits had shrunk to 842,169 livres. As the chamber lamented, 'le commerce maritime était donc dans un triste état, par suite de la guerre continuelle et des dépressions honteuses et acharnées de l'Angleterre'.[56] The decline reflects in the figures for the volume of imports and exports: in 1792, the last of the good years, the former had been 118,114 and the latter 143,049 tons. The returns for 1793 were well down in each case; and *total* traffic had fallen to 79,887 tons by 1802, to 53,772 by 1806, and to 42,242 by 1807.[57] Signs of a brief respite coincided

[53] Ibid. 139.   [54] Ibid.   [55] Ibid. 142.

[56] 'Mémorandum par année des délibérations et des décisions les plus importantes de la chambre de commerce de Nantes (1803–1903)', A.D. Loire-Inférieure 5667 in-4° 22, pp. 12–13, entry for 1803.

[57] Paul Jeulin, *L'Evolution du port de Nantes. Organisation et trafic depuis les origines* (Paris, 1929), table no. 7, p. 346.

with the new trade licences of 1810–12, but full recovery, after a prolonged post-war slump, did not come until the mid-1820s.

Altogether, the economic background of the two regional communities here studied seems in stark contrast. What now follows is an analysis of and commentary on some of the social effects of this. The primary sources used here are the official lists of *notables* in both departments, and some preliminary comments on them are necessary. It would have been wholly misleading to confine this study to the Consulate, as that would have left the climacteric of the Blockade out of view. It would also have been too restrictive to jump straight into the arena of the Napoleonic *notables* as it appeared in 1810, *in medias res*, at the height of the imperial grandeur, as many earlier studies have done. And clearly one would wish for a more broadly based and representative sample of *notables* than the sixty to eighty '*personnes les plus marquantes*' who are the focus of the departmental series of *Grands notables du premier empire*. It seemed to me more satisfactory to range over successive regional samples, from the earliest lists to those compiled at points well into the Empire, when routine renewals had taken over from innovatory exercises, and when the map of official notability had more or less settled down. This, then, is to study the elites in the process of their formation and to make allowances for changing social trends within them. My essay therefore examines the *notables* of the Bas-Rhin and of the Loire-Inférieure at three points, not one, in the period. The first source used is the earliest consular lists of eligibility drawn up towards the end of 1801, according to the law of 4 March of that year.[58] The second is the electoral college lists of the departments as they were first composed in 1803, from the official lists of the 600 most highly taxed citizens, following the senatus-consultum of 4 August 1802.[59] The third samples are drawn from 1807 (departmental electoral college of the Bas-Rhin) and from 1809 (that of the Loire-Inférieure), after their first renewals. Supplementary use is also made of the published lists of grand *notables* for each department, based on later prefectoral returns.

It would be as well to anticipate the many objections which could be made against these primary sources. In the first place, the earliest consular lists over-stress the presence of *notables* who were then active in the administrative and judicial services, to the relative neglect of those who may have mattered more in the economic life of their regions. Moreover, since there was a delay between the adoption of the constitution of the Year VIII and the first elections under its provisions in 1801, executive appointments at the departmental, *arrondissement* and communal levels had already been made in most

---

[58] 'Loi concernant la formation et le renouvellement des listes d'éligibilité prescrites par la constitution', 13 ventôse IX, *Bull. des lois*, no. 549.

[59] 'Senatus-consulte organique de la constitution, 16 thermidor X ... Titre III, Des collèges électoraux', *Bull. des lois*, no. 1876.

areas by the time of the first electoral exercise. As it was, the lists were headed by anything up to a hundred names which necessarily appeared on them *ex officio*, as in the case of the chief departmental officials, the members of the general council of each department and the high functionaries of the law courts. There was thus a technical predisposition for those managing the whole process, career administrators and lawyers, to job themselves and people of their sort on to the lists. One result was that the social and economic importance of landowners (not least the old nobility), merchants and manufacturers had an erratic and unreliable representation in them. The varying and frequently unwieldy size of the primary electoral unit, the communal *arrondissement*, also discouraged rural dwellers from travelling long distances to vote. As the barrister Duchesne had foreseen, the consequence was that urban dwellers gained a disproportionate voice over country people in the primary elections, while those actually elected to go forward by one from each hundred to the next stage of the creaming process reflected this same bias all the way up.[60]

The lists of the departmental electoral colleges as from 1803 at least reformed this abuse, though they in turn over-emphasised *land*-taxable wealth to the relative neglect of other capital assets or income. Under the new system, the primary electoral unit was the canton, an area corresponding to the jurisdiction of a justice of the peace, which was numerically more manageable. The cantonal voters chose a specified number of candidates to form both the *arrondissement* and the departmental electoral college, the latter of which, but not necessarily the former, had to be chosen from among the 600 highest taxpayers.[61] Napoleon himself appears to have had respect for these electoral colleges, both as reservoirs of talent to draw on and as visible evidence of the propertied basis of his 'political' nation. By 1814, he had awarded the title of baron to 103 members and 7 presidents of the colleges, and another 12 members and 4 presidents had become counts.[62] The lists nevertheless left much to be desired. Incompleteness was a common fault. The ages, marital status and sometimes even the full names of *notables* can be unrecorded. Similar blanks appear under the area of domicile and in the columns for current and past professional occupations. Estimates of individual

---

[60] Collins, *Napoleon and his Parliaments*, 48–9. The whole of this author's chap. 4 on the earliest lists of *notables* is a good summary of their procedures and deficiencies. I have drawn on it for details of the foregoing paragraph.

[61] Article 74 of the 'Arrêté concernant règlement pour l'exécution du senatus-consulte du 16 thermidor [an X], relativement aux assemblées de canton, aux collèges électoraux, &c.' of 19 fructidor X/6 September 1802 stated that, in the first instance, the 600 should be reduced to 550 names, with the others to be added during the course of the Year XI. *Bull. des lois*, no. 1964.

[62] Collins, *Napoleon and his Parliaments*, 93–4. Here again, this author's chap. 8 on the electoral colleges offers a useful digest of their procedures. I have drawn on it for details of the present paragraph.

wealth (*fortune personnelle*) are sometimes given in capital sums, sometimes in income (*revenu*) and sometimes they are to be inferred from a tax entry, which of course under the *foncière* was not in practice a uniform assessment. Often there are no estimates at all, and the prefects were prone to shield the capacity of many of the leading magnates under such unhelpful descriptions as 'aisée', 'riche' and 'très riche'. In some cases we are told that particular *notables* had improved their condition through the purchase of *biens nationaux*, but in many more cases that fact goes unremarked.

Yet perhaps the main hazard of the lists is that we have to go by the prefectoral nomenclature in identifying the professional occupations of the *notables*. Often, one suspects, the description used was that which the *notable* in question himself preferred. Persons whose main gainful employment was in trade, for instance, often appear on the lists in their official capacities as prefectoral councillors or as members of the general council of the department. Rural *notables* whose livelihood depended on farming, or who lived from income whether as *propriétaires* or *rentiers*, are quite often cited on the lists as mayors or as members of their municipal councils. There is no consistency of terms even among the prefects themselves. Letourneur's '*rentiers*' of the Loire-Inférieure in 1803, or those of Baron Vischer de Celles in 1809 might well have included many of the kind their colleague Shée in the Bas-Rhin chose to call '*propriétaires*'.[63] In the face of such vagaries, I have preferred to adopt the prefects' descriptions in all cases. To have done otherwise, even where one certainly knows that a *notable*'s gainful employment was not in the occupation officially stated, would have involved worse distortions. For either one would become enmeshed in double-counting, or else one would be introducing information extraneous to the lists for some *notables* but not for others. The lists are therefore analysed as they are, not least because as such they went forward as the official record and were so used by the central government. In spite of all their faults, we have to make the best of them; the alternative is in effect to bite the hand—the only hand as it happens—that feeds us on this subject.

The range of professional descriptions used, though far from precise within each group, fortunately allows of some broad classification. It seems in order, for example, to take *propriétaires* and *rentiers* together as men living off independent means, though it is not always clear whether their assets were based in towns or in the countryside or, as seems equally likely, in both. *Cultivateurs*, *agriculteurs* and occasionally *laboureurs* can also be classed as men of property working their own lands in the rural context, and to them the sprinkling of millers (*meuniers*) may be assimilated. The line between administrative and judicial functions is very fine, however. On which side are the

---

63 The prefecture of Etienne Letourneur lasted from March 1800 to March 1804; that of Baron Antoine Vischer de Celles from December 1807 to December 1810. Henri Shée was prefect of the Bas-Rhin from September 1802 to February 1810.

commissaires du gouvernement près les tribunaux, or their *substituts,* to be placed, for instance? A similar blurring of the edges is common between functionaries who worked in civilian posts and those who, like the *commissaires des guerres,* had duties with obvious military implications. I have grouped the latter and the whole range of civil officials, including all revenue officers, under one heading. The entry for army and navy is confined to serving soldiers and sailors, of whatever rank, and to them are added all those *notables* retired from the armed services and those with police functions. The legal profession forms another distinguishable group, both in public service and private practice, and absorbs a variety of professional descriptions: presidents and judges of the civil and criminal courts, their deputies (*suppléants*), justices of the peace, advocates, solicitors and attorneys (*avoués*), notaries, clerks of the court (*greffiers*), court ushers (*huissiers*), distinguished jurists (*jurisconsultes*) and many others simply referred to as '*hommes de loi*'.

The remaining groups are variously spread out over the wholesale, retail and service trades and industries, the medical professions and the occupations which might be loosely called academic, intellectual, spiritual and aesthetic. Within the first and largest of these groups, the most common description used is '*négociant*', followed by '*marchand*', sometimes with a specified branch of trade attached to it. '*Financiers*', '*banquiers*' and '*spéculateurs*' are conspicuous by their almost total absence, although some of them will have been taken in under '*négociants*' and '*rentiers*'. Almost nobody, it appears, wished to be known for official purposes as a *notable* engaged in banking, moneylending or insurance. The '*marchands*' were a mixed lot, ranging from large-scale wine or wood merchants to small grocers, and there was a fair incidence of *notables* employed in the service trades, such as bakers, innkeepers and *cabaretiers.* The last two groups were more numerous in the Bas-Rhin, probably because of Strasbourg's importance as a *lieu de passage* for troops and commercial carters. Anyone likely to be a *notable* from the manufacturing industries was a skilled craftsman and is so grouped, along with others, usually their social superiors, who are called architects, surveyors or sometimes simply '*entrepreneurs*' in private trade. There remains the usual miscellaneous pool of medical men (doctors and surgeons, both more numerous in the lists for the Loire-Inférieure), academics, writers, interpreters, artists and sculptors. Clerics are also included under this heading of 'Others', but their numbers were so small as to be insignificant. Finally, the lists contain a small number, less than 1 per cent in all, of retired persons or those who are described as former incumbents, like *ex-législateurs, ex-receveurs d'enregistrement* or *officiers retraités.* All these are included in the respective categories of their former employment.

Table 1. *Notables of the Bas-Rhin, November 1801*

Professional group	No. of *notables*	Percentage of 940 stated professions
Civil service, central and local government, and functionaries with military duties	463	49.25
Legal profession (public and private)	189	20.10
Grand commerce, small trades, and industry	141	15.00
Army, police	69	7.34
Medical practitioners, academics, writers, clerics	41	4.36
Notables living from land cultivation or from viticulture	37	3.93
(Professions not given)	(19)	(1.98% of 959)

The lists of notables of the Year IX

Granted those criteria of professional classification, a more detailed analysis of the earliest consular lists can now be made. Table 1 states the position for the Bas-Rhin on 10 November 1801 and is based upon the official descriptions given under the heading 'Profession' for 940 *notables* (or 98 per cent) of the 959 named.[64] The heavy preponderance of official functionaries stands out immediately. They make up very nearly half the given sample, and if the closely related legal *notables* are added in, the fraction rises to almost 70 per cent. This, it seems to me, reflects the fundamental *un*representativity of the first consular lists. It may be assumed that incumbent officials and legal officers had ensured, for professional reasons, that their names would appear on the list. It also seems that the prefect chose wherever possible to give an official description of a *notable*'s occupation, for example as 'mayor' rather than '*cultivateur*' or '*propriétaire*', or as 'councillor' of some sort rather than 'merchant'. As a result, the numbers of landowners, whether *actifs* or *non-actifs*, and of merchants and manufacturers are underscored. The absence of *propriétaires* and *rentiers* from this list may be due to the same official bias, or possibly to Laumond's preferred nomenclature.[65] Of the 463 public functionaries named, 37 (some 8 per cent) appear on the list *ex officio*, while the 190 mayors and their 73 deputies (*adjoints*) together add up to well over half (56.80 per cent) of their professional group. If the criterion of primary gainful employment had been used for the professional classification of these

---

[64] 'Liste des notables du département du Bas-Rhin, formée d'après les dispositions de la loi du 13 ventôse an IX, concernant la formation et le renouvellement des listes d'éligibilité prescrites par la constitution', signed by the prefect Laumond and members of the *Conseil de préfecture* in Strasbourg on 19 brumaire Year X. A.N. F¹ᶜ III Rhin (Bas-) 1.

[65] The prefecture of Jean–Charles–Joseph Laumond lasted from March 1800 to September 1802.

Table 2. Notables *of the Loire-Inférieure, December 1801*

Professional group	No. of notables	Percentage of 744 stated professions
Civil service, central and local government, and functionaries with military or naval duties	280	37.63
Legal profession (public and private)	174	23.38
Grand commerce, small trades, and industry	118	15.86
Notables living off independent means (*propriétaires*)	73	9.81
Army, navy, police	41	5.51
Notables living by land cultivation or by milling	34	4.56
Medical practitioners, academics, writers, interpreters, painters, clerics	24	3.22
(Professions not given)	(49)	(6.17% of 793)

notables, many local officials would have featured under other headings, and the 'landed interest' and trade would have been better represented among them.

The Loire-Inférieure was a less populous department than the Bas-Rhin and, as such, under the system of upward-moving hundreds, its earliest list of *notables* contains fewer names than that for the Alsatian department. Table 2 incorporates my findings as at 2 December 1801 and is based on the descriptions given under the column headed 'Fonctions qu'ils [the *notables*] remplissent' for 744 (or 93.82 per cent) of the 793 *notables* named in the list.[66] Again, the two groups broadly identified as public functionaries and legal *notables* together made up nearly two-thirds (61.02 per cent) of the total sample. Within the first group, the 96 mayors and their 48 deputies together accounted for more than half (51.42 per cent); over a fifth (22.14 per cent) were revenue officers or other civil servants and the *ex officio notables* amounted to 13.92 per cent. All the varieties of legal description appear in the second grouping, and no less than 52 persons (29.88 per cent of their class) were on the list as legal *notables ex officio*. Of the rest, the 48 notaries, 31 justices of the peace and 20 '*hommes de loi*' were most numerous.

Among the group headed *grand commerce*, small trades and industry, 73 of the 118 (61.86 per cent) were called '*négociants*', and it is here that the most prominent survivors of the old merchant oligarchy of Nantes made their mark in the public life of the Consulate. One need mention the names of only

[66] 'Liste des notables du département de la Loire-Inférieure, formée d'après les dispositions de la loi du 13 ventôse an IX . . .', signed by the prefect Letourneur and members of the *Conseil de préfecture* in Nantes on 11 frimaire Year X. A.N. F1cIII (Loire-Inférieure) 1.

some on the list – Charles Bouteiller, Louis Drouin, F.-M.-B. Dufou, Pierre-Joseph Lincoln, Denis Colas, Benoît Bourcard, François Faucault, Richard-Pivredière, Espivent-Villeboisnet, Rozier *père* – to recall some of the former splendour of merchant life in Nantes. There are many cases in the Loire-Inférieure, too, where *notables* whose main remunerative employment was in trade were cited on the list as departmental or other councillors. The two most obvious cases were those of Danyel-Kervégan and Mosneron-Dupin, both members of the general council. Altogether, the commercial and industrial representation was proportionally very similar to that in the Bas-Rhin. Alongside the scions of the older merchant houses, one finds wealthy *négociants* whose rise in the world had been more recent, usually by astute opportunism during the Revolution, and especially by the purchase of *biens nationaux* and by government contracting. Félix Cossin, Jean-Marie Haudaudine and Claude-Sylvain Pâris (who was mayor of Nantes at the time the list was compiled and who counted as a superior functionary for official purposes) typify these *nouveaux riches*.

The other professional groups in the sample were all of less numerical importance, but the 73 *notables* described as '*propriétaires*' may well have been a body with overlapping members. This list, unlike the later ones, does not use the term '*rentier*', and it is probable that some of those who were later grouped under that description were included among the '*propriétaires*' and '*négociants*' of December 1801. That a good number of the 793 *notables* named on it would have had their main income from stock seems a fair assumption, and what is therefore at issue is not their strange absence at the start of the Napoleonic period but the vagaries of prefectoral nomenclature. The 34 *notables* living by land cultivation or by milling were marginally higher, as a proportion of the total, than their counterparts in the Bas-Rhin; but those in the armed services and the police force had a lower representation in the Loire-Inférieure. Of the miscellaneous group, doctors and surgeons were the most numerous. In the Loire-Inférieure they included such distinguished practitioners as Bodin-Desplantes, Cantin, Dufrexou, Fabré (who became an Imperial baron in 1810), Guillaume Laennec (whose more famous nephew, René-Théophile, invented the stethoscope) and the Richard brothers. Among the academics of the Bas-Rhin, perhaps the most famous was Professor Koch of Strasbourg. The total eclipse of church *notables* is clear from the fact that in this, the year of Napoleon's Concordat with the Pope, only two *ministres de culte* are named on the list for the Loire-Inférieure, while the Bas-Rhin's had five.

The electoral college lists of 1803 and of 1807/9

Moving on into the later Consulate and to the Empire itself, we come across a type of document which, in spite of its lapses in individual detail, offers a truer picture of social and economic notability in provincial France than the lop-sided lists of 1801. As the determining senatus-consultum of 4 August 1802 required the departmental electoral colleges to function every five years, according to the five departmental series so designated, we can trace their *notables* both at the start of that process and on into the height of the Empire. The later lists are more detailed indeed, and as such are a better guide to the *notables* in public service than the first incomplete returns of 1803. Now, it would have been more representative of *economic* pre-eminence to go straight to the plenary lists of the 600 highest taxpayers drawn up at the same time. This would have provided roughly twice as many *notables* for analysis and would have offered units rather more comparable with the plenary lists of 1801. But such an exercise posed serious obstacles. The lists of the *plus imposés* are in themselves no guide whatever to their social or political or 'official' influence. Many if not most of these men appear to have played little or no part in the public affairs of the Empire, and as has been stressed in another context, their presence among the 600 was a mark of landed wealth, not of financial, commercial or industrial assets. In many cases, furthermore, so little was known about them, particularly in outlying rural districts, that most of the columns intended for detailed information are left blank. The departmental electoral college lists are themselves often incomplete in these respects, but at least they provide some more coherent basis for social and professional analysis. Yet my main reason for preferring them to the lists of the highest taxpayers is that, as *both* necessarily consisted of such taxpayers anyway, the electoral colleges had the added ingredient of voters' confidence. In other words, they were an elite in the sense of choice, and this recognition by their cantonal electors gave them a notability which could not lie in crude fiscal liability alone.

Both the Bas-Rhin and the Loire-Inférieure had populations large enough to qualify for departmental electoral colleges of 300 *notables*. The available lists, however, fall well short of that number, which no doubt reflects the constant and much-advertised difficulties the prefects had in finding eligible persons willing to serve in the colleges. The list for the Bas-Rhin compiled in June 1803 names only 142 *notables*; that for November 1807 names 216, but has no other details on two.[67] The lists for the Loire-Inférieure name 156 *notables* in November 1803 and 250 (plus nine others by Imperial appointment) in November 1809.[68] My findings for the Bas-Rhin at both dates are

[67] 'Liste des membres qui composent le collège électoral du département du Bas-Rhin', signed by the prefect Shée and his general secretary (Metz) in Strasbourg on 15 prairial Year XI; and the 'Liste des membres qui composent le collège électoral du département du Bas-Rhin ... d'après le dépouillement des procès-verbaux des opérations des assemblées cantonales, et en exécution des articles 34, 35, 36 et 37 du règlement du 17 janvier 1806, et des articles 5 et 33 du règlement du 13 mai de la même année', signed by Shée in Strasbourg on 3 November 1807. Both at A.N. F$^{\text{Ie III}}$ Rhin (Bas-) 2.

[68] 'Liste des membres qui composent le collège électoral du département de la Loire-Inférieure', signed by Letourneur in Nantes on 27 brumaire Year XII, A.N. F$^{\text{Ie III}}$ (Loire-Inférieure) 1;

Table 3. *Professional composition of the electoral college of the Bas-Rhin in June 1803 and in November 1807*

Professional group	1803		1807	
	No. of *notables*	Percentage of 142 stated professions	No. of *notables*	Percentage of 214 stated professions
Civil service, local administration, and functionaries with military duties	40	28.16	60	28.03
Notables living by land cultivation and by milling (*cultivateurs, laboureurs, meuniers*)	39	27.46	54	25.23
Grand commerce, small trades, and industry	29	20.42	46	21.49
Legal profession (public and private)	18	12.67	23	10.74
Notables living off independent means (*propriétaires* and *rentiers*)	7	4.92	20	9.34
Army, police	6	4.22	8	3.73
Others (medical practitioners, academics, clerics)	3	2.11	3	1.40

given in table 3, which is based on the same rules of classification as those applied to the samples of 1801.

Granted these classifying rules, one sees here a much greater diversity of and a rather more even balance between the main economic functions represented in the departmental electoral college. The coincidence of several types of notability in the same persons is also made clear by this record. Thus, for instance, *cultivateurs* and *laboureurs* would also often serve as mayors or at least as municipal councillors. Innkeepers were usually *cultivateurs* or *propriétaires* as well, while the leading merchants, in addition to being often described as *propriétaires* at the same time, were always likely to be well represented in the general council of the department. The possibilities for criss-cross professional routes in the administrative and judicial services were endless. The Napoleonic system of public service lived off itself in this way, concentrating more and more duties on an identifiable core of substantial local magnates.

The results of the two samples given above show some interesting differ-

and the 'Liste des membres . . .' signed in the absence of the prefect by Haumont, a prefectoral councillor, in Nantes on 23 November 1809, A.N. F^{1c}III (Loire-Inférieure) 2.

ences from the plenary list of November 1801. The top-heavy block of civil servants and local government officials has shrunk noticeably from very nearly half the sample at the earlier date to something between a quarter and third at the later points. In the nature of the electoral exercises of 1803 and 1807, moreover, those who came through the count within this group tended to be functionaries of some importance – not least the prefect and sub-prefects, their chief assistants, mayors of the larger towns and the main officers in the revenue and military departments – rather than incumbent clerks and little-known place-seekers. The proportion of the various groups making up the legal profession is also well down, notably in the count of 1807, when it was a little over a tenth, on the figure of a fifth in 1801. And here, too, the *notables* who came through were the more experienced and more distinguished public lawyers of their localities. If these two interlocking groups are taken together, their overbearing proportion (nearly 70 per cent) of the total in 1801 has dropped to something around two-fifths, again a little higher in 1803 than in 1807.

The space is filled, as might be expected from an electoral process geared to produce candidates from among the richest taxpayers of the department, by landowners of various kinds and by commercial and industrial magnates. Compared with its very small incidence (under 4 per cent) in 1801, land cultivation has risen markedly to more than a quarter of the later samples, and indeed had by then become the second largest group. Most of the *notables* so classified were *cultivateurs* or *laboureurs*, along with a sprinkling of millers. The increase in the commercial and industrial group is less pronounced, up to around 20 per cent from 15; and the group of *propriétaires* living off the means which land rents produced has advanced to nearly 10 per cent by 1807. Altogether, if those engaged primarily in land cultivation, in the wholesale, the retail and the service trades, in productive industry, and those living mainly from *rentes* are taken as a single unit, then what might be called the 'economic *notables*' of the department make up 52.81 per cent of the total sample in 1803 and 56.07 per cent of that in 1807. Even allowing for the technical factors which had grossly underscored their presence in 1801, one may conclude that their subsequent emergence to official prominence testifies to a robust and expanding economy.

Other details of these *notables* of the Bas-Rhin also tell us something about their role as pillars of the local society. If the list for November 1807 is analysed, as the fuller of the two, the age structure of the *notables* reveals a fairly typical preponderance of men in the prime of life. Of the 212 whose ages are given, 74 were in their forties, 64 in their fifties and 35 in their sixties. Of the others, 28 were in their thirties, 5 younger still and only 6 were aged seventy or more. The average age of the 212 *notables* in question was 49.89 years. Marital status similarly points to a body of established family men. Of the 210 *notables* for whom such details are available, the great majority (152

or 72.38 per cent) were married men with one child or more – usually more –
and another 25 were widowers with offspring. Only 10 were bachelors,
while 20 married men had no children, as was the case with 2 widowers and
a solitary *divorcé*. Families were often very large, rising in some cases to nine,
ten or eleven children. The average number of children among the 177
married men and widowers was 4.32, and this too suggests fundamentally
robust means of domestic support. Of the 214 *notables* for whom a residential
index is recorded, 61 (or 28.50 per cent) are said to have been domiciled in
Strasbourg. Altogether, the average *notable* of the Bas-Rhin in 1807 was a
middle-aged married man with several children and had a better than one-in-
four chance of living in Strasbourg, the *chef-lieu*.

   What, finally, of the wealth of these *notables*? The official entries under
this heading are less than satisfactory, and sometimes, one imagines, they are
deliberately intended to reveal as little as possible. One might begin by
considering the position of former hereditary nobles and *anoblis* whose names
appear on the electoral college list of November 1807. Michel Richard
identified 13 nobles (seven of them of the *noblesse d'extraction* and six former
anoblis) in the 69 '*personnes les plus marquantes*' of the department on 4 August
1812.[69] This is equivalent to 18.84 per cent of that particular list, the *crème de
la crème* of the Bas-Rhin's *notables*. I have counted eight of them (some 3.70
per cent of the total, which is broadly in line with their incidence in other
imperial departments) on the electoral college list of November 1807. There
were, among the old hereditary nobility, Zorn de Bulach of Osthausen,
Landsperg *père* of Niedernai, General Schauenbourg of Gendertheim and
Turckheim *père* of Strasbourg; and, among the *anoblis* of pre-revolutionary
times, Bruneteau de Sainte-Suzanne of Strasbourg, Bernard de Montbrison
of Obernai, Dartein of Kolbsheim and Brackenhoffer, who later became
mayor of Strasbourg (1810–15). Three of these eight have definite figures in
capital against their names. Bernard de Montbrison, with 500,000 francs, was
the richest *notable* of the department on this evidence; while Landsperg and
Schauenbourg, with 300,000 and 200,000 francs respectively, were among the
dozen wealthiest. But the other details are frustratingly cryptic. Zorn de
Bulach is described as 'aisé', and Dartein's entry states only that he had 'deux
propriétés rurales et une maison à Strasbourg'. Bruneteau de Sainte-Suzanne
has his wealth described in terms of 7,000 to 8,000 francs of *rentes*, and
Brackenhoffer's is put at 12,000 francs by the same reckoning. Both would
have had much higher capital assets, as the entries refer to stock only, to the
exclusion of property. Yet the worst case of understatement must surely be
that of Turckheim *père*, a prominent merchant banker. According to the
prefect's entry, his wealth was 'proportionate to 1,095 francs of land tax'
which, allowing for a 5 per cent assessment and a margin of non-taxable
property, would be equivalent to personal landed income of between 20,000

and 30,000 francs a year. And this tells us nothing at all about Turckheim's commercial assets, which dominated his portfolio.

Such fractional evidence, whether precise or disguised, suggests that the former nobles who were members of the Bas-Rhin's electoral college in 1807 were wealthy men. They were not the only ones to appear under the specious façade of 'aisé' or 'riche'. If we exclude all such cases, as well as *notables* for whom no estimates of wealth are given, the list has usable entries for 170 persons. We can roughly estimate the capital of eight others from entries given in income, using the ratio of 1:20 or 1:10. The result shows that the great mass of *notables* (134, or 75.28 per cent of this particular sample) were below the level of 100,000 francs of capital, and 76 of them (42.69 per cent) had less than 50,000 francs. The average for the 178 *notables* was 70,174 francs, corresponding to an annual income of 3,508 francs at 5 per cent and of 7,017 francs at 10 per cent. The 46 residents of Strasbourg for whom entries are made had a higher average of 80,804 francs of capital, equivalent to 4,040 francs of annual income at 5 per cent and to 8,080 francs at 10 per cent. On this evidence, then, the Bas-Rhin was comfortably above Tulard's lower plateau of 3,000 francs of annual income as an Imperial standard for membership of the departmental electoral colleges. One must stress again that all estimates here refer to *landed* capital only. If the wealthy landowners for whom no statistical entries are made and the commercial and financial assets of others are taken into account, the average capital assets of the department's *notables* are likely to have been appreciably higher, especially among the Strasbourgeois. According to an official list of the leading commercial and industrial magnates of the city in August 1810, at least eleven houses had capital assets of more than 500,000 francs, and another fifteen ranged from that level down to 100,000 francs.[70] These were company assets, of course, not private ones, but it is a sign of the inadequacy of the official electoral college lists that most of these *hommes d'affaires* do not appear on them. Even so, it seems clear that non-landed wealth was regularly underscored or ignored in these lists, and that the real wealth of their *notables* would have been considerably higher than the sums formally recorded by the prefects.

In spite of their missing details, the lists of the members of the electoral college of the Loire-Inférieure in 1803 and 1809 can be analysed in the same way. Their occupational structure is stated in table 4. These figures are based on the 122 *notables* (out of 156 named) in 1803 and on the 218 (out of 250 named) in 1809 for whom entries are made under the heading 'Professions ou Fonctions'. Quite apart from the differences between these and the list for December 1801, there are several important changes within the electoral college at the two given dates. In 1801, the administrative and legal pro-

---

[70] 'Liste des négocians et commerçans les plus distingués . . .' (in five categories) of August 1810, A.D. Bas-Rhin XII M 29; published in part in Ellis, *Blockade*, 292–3.

Table 4. *Professional composition of the electoral college of the Loire-Inférieure in November 1803 and November 1809*

	1803		1809	
Professional group	No. of *notables*	Percentage of 122 stated professions	No. of *notables*	Percentage of 218 stated professions
Civil service, local administration, and functionaries with military or naval duties	37	30.32	48	22.01
Notables living off independent means (*propriétaires* and *rentiers*)	16	13.11	60	27.52
Grand commerce, small trades, and industry	23	18.85	38	17.43
Legal profession (public and private)	23	18.85	36	16.51
Army, navy, police	9	7.37	17 (+9)	7.79 (11.45% of 227)
Notables living by land cultivation (*cultivateurs* and *agriculteurs*)	10	8.19	10	4.58
Others (medical practitioners, artists)	4	3.27	9	4.12
(Professions not given)	(34)	(21.79% of 156)	(32)	(12.80% of 250)

fessions had accounted for over 60 per cent of the *notables*; by 1803 their combined number was already less than half the electoral college, and by 1809 it was less than 40 per cent and in fact proportionally almost exactly the same as the corresponding group in the Bas-Rhin in 1807. Though slightly up from 15.86 per cent in 1801 to 18.85 per cent in 1803, the commercial and industrial group had not advanced but actually fallen back slightly to 17.43 per cent of the sample in 1809. *Prima facie*, this suggests either some reluctance among the merchants and manufacturers of the Loire-Inférieure to be electors, or else that their economic stagnation, or worse, detracted in some way from their capacity to fulfil that role. In proportional terms, the *notables* living by land cultivation were at their height in 1803, but by 1809 had declined to under 5 per cent of the total. Army, navy and police had an improving representation over the three counts, and if one adds in the nine military and naval *notables* of 1809 who were on the electoral college list by imperial appointment, then their score rises to 11.45 per cent, which is very much higher than anything the Bas-Rhin had been able to achieve in this group. The miscellaneous group shows little change over the period.

The most obvious difference lies in the incidence of *notables* living off independent means. *Propriétaires* and *rentiers* had been under 10 per cent of their list in 1801, and had advanced in proportion to 13.11 per cent by 1803. Their increase over the next six years was such that, by the end of 1809, they not only accounted for 27.52 per cent of the electoral college but were then its largest single group. Whereas much of the space vacated by the administrative and legal cadres in the Bas-Rhin was taken up by working farmers and to a lesser extent by *propriétaires* and *rentiers*, the two latter were plainly the most numerous intruders on to the scene in the Loire-Inférieure. It is tempting to conclude that this reflects a reorientation of economic functions within the economic elite. As openings for investment in commercial and industrial ventures were closed during the maritime wars, more and more of the old mercantile community transferred their surviving capital into land and stock. Both – but especially land – were traditional havens for displaced or surplus capital. If I am right in supposing that the departmental electoral college of 1809 mirrors this important shift at a point well into the Blockade, it is interesting to note that Paul Butel has found evidence of a similar trend in Bordeaux. There, too, one discerns a shift of fugitive capital into land from the more lucrative but much riskier attractions of *armement en aventurier* or the *guerre de course*, and even from traditional wine shipments, which were embarrassed by the blockade.[71]

As the older and more established commercial houses thus retreated into land-based securities, so the market for more speculative ventures and of course for military and naval contracting was opened up to brasher newcomers. In her biographical sketches of the 87 most distinguished *notables* of the Loire-Inférieure at the height of the Empire, Béatrix Guillet can find barely a handful who were scions of the families which had dominated the golden age of Nantes before the Revolution.[72] These few – Bouteiller, Arnous-Rivière, Dufou, Danyel-Kervégan and Drouin – survived alongside a newer sort of merchant, like Pierre Albert and Félix Cossin, whose great wealth had been amassed by speculative ventures and by government contracts. There is something poignant about Louis Drouin, who at the age of 85 was presented to Napoleon in Nantes in 1808 'à la fois comme le doyen du négoce nantais et comme le symbole du déclin économique de Nantes'.[73]

---

[71] Butel, 'L'activité économique à Bordeaux', *RHMC* (1970), 557, where individual illustrations are given.

[72] *Grands notables du premier empire . . . Loire-Inférieure*, vol. 8 (1982), 164–5, 172–3, 187–8, 189–90, 199–200.

[73] Ibid. 188.

His was a different world from that of Pierre Albert, who rose from modest origins as a butcher to make his fortune as a naval supplier. From such proceeds he had been able to buy *biens nationaux*, not least the abbey of Buzay, and he became one of the department's richest merchants under Napoleon.[74]

The electoral college list of the Loire-Inférieure in 1809 tells us quite a bit more about its *notables*. As a group, they were a shade older than their colleagues in the Bas-Rhin in 1807. Of the 158 whose ages are recorded, Louis Drouin alone was in his eighties, but 14 others were in their seventies, 39 in their sixties and 51 in their fifties. At the younger end, 34 were in their forties, 14 in their thirties and 5 younger still. The average age of these 158 *notables* was 53.67 years. The marital status of 176 *notables* is also recorded. They included 11 bachelors, 24 married men, and 6 widowers, all without children; but the large majority (116, or 65.90 per cent) were married and had families, and 19 widowers had one child or more. The average size of family among the relevant *notables* was 3.37 children, roughly one child less than among the *notables* of the Bas-Rhin in 1807. In residential terms, the same predominant influence of Nantes over its environs which Arthur Young had remarked on before the Revolution was still apparent. The list gives the domicile of all 250 *notables* named, and of these 108 (43.20 per cent) were residents of the *chef-lieu*. As a proportion of the total, this was appreciably higher than that of Strasbourg in the Bas-Rhin, and it was even higher among the '*personnes les plus marquantes*' who were later identified. Guillet found that 79 of her 87 grand *notables* were residents of Nantes, while 3 others had a *pied-à-terre* there.[75]

The personal wealth of 155 *notables* is also estimated in the list of 1809. Alas, these figures are not directly comparable with those for the Bas-Rhin, since, they are given in terms of landed income, not capital. By that criterion, only 6 *notables* were placed in the bracket exceeding 20,000 francs, and none rose above 40,000. I have counted 3 more in the range from 15,001 to 20,000 and 17 others in that from 10,001 to 15,000 francs. At the other end of the scale, 15 *notables* had landed incomes of 1,500 francs or less, while 42 were in the range from 1,501 to 3,000 and 26 in that from 3,001 to 4,000 francs. The remaining 46 made up the middle income group, which rose from 4,001 to 10,000 francs. The average income of the 155 here identified was 6,546 francs a year; but the corresponding figure for the 72 Nantais for whom entries are made was predictably higher at 8,280 francs. It was the latter who also counted most among the richest *notables* of the department. Of the 6 whose income was estimated at between 25,000 and 40,000 francs, 4 were residents of Nantes: François-Louis Guillet-Labrosse (a *rentier* with the highest recorded income on the list), Bonaventure Dufou (a merchant), Julien Leroux (a *propriétaire*) and Jean-Baptiste Bertrand-Geslin. The last-named had risen

[74] Ibid. 164.   [75] Ibid. 149.

from an early military career by a fortunate marriage with the rich merchant family of Geslin, whose only male heir had been a victim of the *chouans*, and had inherited its vast fortune. Bertrand-Geslin turned his own talents as a Napoleonic *rallié* to administration, and he was mayor of Nantes from 1805 to 1813, for which distinguished service he was rewarded with the title of baron. Two of the other richest *notables*, the former noble Jacques Debruc de Montplaisir (20,000 francs) and Debercy (18,000) both retired army officers, were residents of Nantes. So indeed were 13 of the 17 men whose income ranged from 10,001 to 15,000 francs, and 7 more of the 10 who fell within the group from 9,001 to 10,000 francs.

What, finally, of the old nobility of the Loire-Inférieure? Béatrix Guillet put their number at 15 (17.24 per cent) of her list of 87 grand *notables*.[76] I have counted 14 of them on the electoral college list of 1809: Blanchard, Biré-Méveillère, Bruc de Montplaisir, Calvé-Soursac, Demonty Cour de Bouée, Dufou, Juchault des Jamonnières, Martel, Pineau du Pavillon, Rousseau de Saint-Aignan, Sioc'han de Kersabiec (Jean-Augustin-Joseph), Talhouet, Trévelec and Urvoy de Saint-Bedan. Six others in the electoral college had been *anoblis* at the time of the Revolution: Arnous-Rivière, Bouteiller, Cottin, Danyel-Kervégan, Drouin and Montaudouin. At least three other members of the electoral college (Ducambout *père*, Goyon de Marcé and Pantin-Laguerre) are not among Guillet's grand *notables*, but are described as former nobles in the list of the 600 highest taxpayers of the department on 6 December 1805, while Francheteau, who is also included here, had been an *anobli* of the robe.[77] If only the old hereditary nobles are counted, the 17 whose names appear among the 250 members of the departmental electoral college in 1809 amount to 6.80 per cent of its complement. If former *anoblis* are also taken into account, the total of 24 is no less than 9.60 per cent of the college. Either way, this was a higher incidence than among their counterparts in the Bas-Rhin, and it was well above the imperial average. Most but by no means all of these old nobles were also among the richest landowners of the department.

IV

In bringing these two regional *sondages* to a conclusion, I would argue that the primary sources used illustrate different yet integral features of notability during the Consulate and Empire. The earliest lists are most useful in identifying the sort of career administrators and lawyers who, risen from the opportunities of the Revolution, perpetuated their sort under Napoleon. They

---

[76] Ibid. 150.
[77] A.D. (Loire-Inférieure) I M 58. This list also names four nobles who are included neither in the electoral college list of 1809 nor among Guillet's 87 grand *notables*: Labretesche *fils aîné*, Robinson-Rochequery, Bec de Lièvre de la Seillays and Amaury Boux. Nine of the twelve former nobles here listed are described as '*rentiers*' in frimaire Year XIV.

were the professional technicians of the Napoleonic system in its civil outworks, and they provided a link with the past. The group of military careerists who had also risen from the opportunities of the Revolution were less obviously apparent at the departmental level than in the Imperial hierarchy as such. The later lists of the departmental electoral colleges are more helpful in identifying the men of material substance and in establishing a rough balance between economic functions – the land, the business world, the workshop, the bureau, the court–as the Empire was consolidated. Perhaps the most interesting feature of the lists in both departments, but especially in the Loire-Inférieure, was the tendency for membership to become more aristocratic as the Empire advanced. The lists of 1810 and beyond have lost much of the common touch of 1801. The scrambling democracy of republican careerists has given way, by the progression of the Imperial ambition itself, to a superficially more exclusive social elite.

And yet these developments must not be exaggerated. One is more struck by the absence from public life of most of the old aristocratic families of provincial France. If their surviving wealth and social pre-eminence meant that they could not altogether avoid public recognition, most seem to have preferred a token role in the official service, not least as mayors or occasional electors. There were degrees of *ralliement* among them, and those who might be described as out-and-out Napoleonic enthusiasts were very much in a minority. For the rest, public service was taken on out of a sense of duty. In relative terms, they never dominated the electoral colleges. On the contrary, the lists reveal a fairer balance between social and professional groups, with working farmers, merchants and manufacturers counting for much in the Bas-Rhin, and *propriétaires* and *rentiers* emerging as the major group in the Loire-Inférieure by 1809. Arguably, such social manifestations were a mirror of economic mutations.

Among the economic *notables*, there was space for new men – for the speculator, the military or naval contractor, the privateer and the smuggler. Jean-Georges Humann in Strasbourg, Félix Cossin in Nantes: these *brasseurs d'affaires* were of a new type, distinct from the older and more established merchant community, and also richer than most. They are the nearest analogy in Napoleonic history to the Schumpeterian entrepreneurs of our own century, risking fortune and reputation where others held back. They are not the most heroic standard-bearers of Napoleonic notability, but they remain, for all that, an important ingredient of the granite mass. On the Rhine, as on the Loire, the politics of social assimilation took the old with the new, the rough with the smooth, the good with the bad, and produced its own blend. Notability during the Empire was not an essence of honour, and less still a moral essence. It was above all a sign of public prominence, of material substance, of duty if not always partisan loyalty. In spite of a slowly strengthening aristocratic flavour over the period, the great mass of the *notables* could not and did not aspire to the airs and graces of the old nobility. The latter, whose roots with the past lay in land, had themselves had to adjust to new realities. Social and professional readaptation was the lot of Napoleon's *notables*, but also their opportunity. In that sense they were in quality as well as time an essentially *post*-revolutionary elite.

Index

Agence des Mines 215
Agulhon, Maurice 18, 170, 183, 192, 197, 209
Ain, dept. of 153, 196, 209, 216, 218, 219, 220, 222, 224
Ainvelle (Vosges) 100
Aisne, dept of 105
Aix-en-Provence 159, 160, 165, 166, 172, 189, 199, 200, 210, 218
Alais (Gard) 215
Albert, Pierre 263, 264
Allègre (Hte-Loire) 136, 226
Allier, Claude 201
Allier, Dominique 154, 161, 199, 201, 202, 204, 207, 211, 213, 215
Alsace 22, 44, 48, 50
Altier (Lozère) 146
Ambert (Puy-de-Dôme) 213
Amiens 43, 59, 115
Angers 86
Angot, François 40
Annonay (Ardèche) 197
Apothicairerie générale 88
Apt (Vaucluse) 161
Ardèche, dept of 126, 127, 132, 142, 150, 153, 195, 196, 197, 201, 202, 203, 204, 205, 206, 211, 214, 216, 230
Ardennes, dept of 49
Ariège, dept of 93, 96, 101, 109, 111, 113, 114, 117
Arles (B.-du-R.) 34, 164, 172, 183, 189
armées révolutionnaires 27, 33, 34, 42
army 58–9, 62, 72, 74, 92–120, 167, 210, 243, 253, 262
Arnous-Rivière 263, 265
Arras 80
Ars, Curé d' 24, 30, 51
Arsac (Gironde) 99
Arzenc-de-Randon (Lozère) 138

Asnières (S.-et-O.) 103
Aspet (Hte-Garonne) 96
Aubagne (B.-du-R.) 161, 162, 166, 186, 211
Aubignan (Vaucluse) 163, 189
Aubusson de la Feuillade family 240
Aulard, Alphonse 24
Aurillac (Cantal) 98, 109, 118, 123
Autreville (Vosges) 103
Autun (S.-et-L.) 34, 45
Auvergne 22, 41, 123, 137
Auxerre (Yonne) 43
Aveyron, dept of 126, 127, 129, 137, 141, 147, 148, 149, 230
Avignon 34, 156, 161, 163, 164, 170, 188

Bagarre de Nîmes 182, 206
Bagnols (Gard) 154, 161
Bains (Hte-Loire) 137
Balatre (Somme) 97
Barère, Bertrand 57
Barjac (Gard) 201
Bar-le-Duc (Meuse) 72, 74, 76, 78
Barras 80, 201, 202, 208
Barrot 205, 230
Barthélémy, Etienne 79
Bas-Rhin, dept of 234, 247, 250, 253, 254, 256–61, 263, 264, 266
Basses-Alpes, dept of 196, 203, 205, 209, 211, 214, 215, 220, 223
Baumes, Jacques 84
Baumet, François 167
Bayeux (Calvados) 34, 41, 44, 45, 46, 47, 80
Beaumes (Vaucluse) 163
Beaune (Côte-d'Or) 83
Beck, T. D. 237
Bédarrides (Vaucluse) 187
Bédoin (Vaucluse) 192
Belley (Ain) 45, 218
Bérard, Jean-François 203

Berding, Helmut 237, 243
Bergeron, Louis 236, 237, 245
Bernadotte, Marshal 243
Bernard de Montbrison 260
Berne 200
Berthier, Prince 240, 243, 244
Bertrand, Xavier 204, 205, 230
Bertrand-Geslin, J. B. 264
Bésignan, Marquis de 154, 155, 203
Bessières, Marshal 244
Béziers (Hérault) 69, 81
Bienfaisance Nationale, livre de 57, 59
Blessy (P.-de-C.) 109
Bloch, Marc 121, 124, 143, 221
Bo 57, 59
Bodin-Desplantes 256
Bollène (Vaucluse) 206, 210
Bordeaux 76, 100, 108, 118, 248
Bordeaux, Parlement of 2
Borel, Urbain 200, 211
Bouche *fils* 205
Bouches-du-Rhône, dept of 158, 159, 160,
    161, 175, 183, 196, 197, 207, 209, 211
Bouillé family 240
Boulogne (P.-de-C.) 80, 103
Bourcard, Benoît 256
Bourg (Ain) 153, 159, 218, 222
Bourganeuf (Creuse) 103
Bouteiller, Charles 256, 263, 265
Brackenhoffer 260
Braudel, Fernand 17
brigandage 95–111, 157, 195–213, 220–31
Brignolles (Var) 161
Brioude (Hte-Loire) 147
Brittany 22, 34, 44, 107, 119
Brive (Corrèze) 77
Broglie, Duc de 240
Brumaire, *coup* of 18 211, 233
Bruneteau de Ste-Suzanne 260
Burgundy 22, 48
Butel, Paul 263
Buzay, *abbaye de* 264

Cabanis 55, 62, 90
cabaret 42, 97, 118, 171
Cabris (Var) 187
Cadillac (Gironde) 110
Callian (Var) 189
Calvados, dept of 115
Campagnac (Aveyron) 147
Campardon, Emile 243
Canada 55
Cantal, dept of 93, 94, 101, 105, 109, 111,
    116, 133, 141, 149, 150
Cantin 256
Carpentras (Vaucluse) 162, 163, 189, 209
Cassis (B.-du-R.) 162

Castan, Nicole 191, 205
Castan, Yves 176
Castanet (T.-et-G.) 75
Castellane, de 154
Caulaincourt, General 244
Caux, Pays de 48
Cayres (Hte-Loire) 136
Cédage, *chef de bande* 204, 205, 210
Cellier-du-Luc (Ardèche) 138
Ceyzériat (Ain) 224
Chabrier, *égorgeur* 203
Chambéry 200
Chambonas (Ardèche) 201
Champagne 22
Chamson, André 195
Chanaleilles (Hte-Loire) 135, 145, 150
Chaptal, J. A. 81
Charenton (Seine) 84, 88
charity 53–91
Chartres (E.-et-L.) 34
Chasseredès (Lozère) 145, 148, 150, 217
Chaudes-Aigues (Cantal) 133, 137
Chaudeyrac (Lozère) 138, 139
Chauny (Ain) 105
Chaussinand-Nogaret, Guy 236, 237, 245
Chénier, André 11
Cher, dept of 80
Choiseul-Praslin family 240
Cholvy, Gérard 26–7
chouans 32, 106, 211, 265
church, constitutional 21–52, 205, 217
church, post-Concordat 29, 242, 253, 256
church, refractory 21–52, 79–86, 105, 153,
    192, 200–1, 204, 214, 216–19
Church, Clive 237
Clansayes (Drôme) 162, 171
Clemensane (Basses-Alpes) 223
clubs 35, 39, 40, 43, 80, 174, 177, 178, 187,
    188
Cobb, Richard 1–20, 25, 53, 92, 152, 174
Cobban, Alfred 1, 3, 4, 13
Colas, Denis 256
Coligny (Ain) 218
Collins, Irene 237
Collot-d'Herbois 57
Colognac (Gard) 203
colonnes mobiles 94, 112
Combret (Aveyron) 150
Comité de Mendicité 54, 56, 57, 64, 87, 90
Comité de Salut public 24, 32, 35, 37, 57, 58,
    62, 63, 150, 225
Comité des Secours publics 57, 58
Comité de Sûreté générale 201
commissaires du pouvoir exécutif 184, 185, 200,
    202, 206, 207, 213, 216, 222, 224, 226,
    253
Commission d'Orange 162, 164, 181, 208

Commission Temporaire 181
common lands and rights 121–51, 186, 221–9
Compagnies de Jésus 154, 170, 199, 230
Comtat Venaissin 163, 182, 186, 187, 203, 209, 222
Concordat 26, 42, 52, 81, 211, 217, 256
Condé-sur-Noireau (Calvados) 75
Condéac 74
Condorcet 55
confréries 51
conscription 24, 29, 92–120, 190, 192, 210, 212–16
Conseil des Anciens 64
Conceil d'État 135
Conseil des 500 59, 209
Conseil général de commerce 239
Conseil général des hospices 90
Conseils de prud'hommes 239
Constituent Assembly 54, 136
Continental Blockade 247, 250, 263
contraception 24
Convention 54, 57, 58, 59, 62, 64, 86, 88, 131, 138
Cordéac (Isère) 218
Cossin, Félix 256, 263, 266
Côte-d'Or, dept of 236
Côte-St-André (Isère) 223, 224
Côteaux de l'Hermitage (Drôme) 225
Cotentin 22, 44, 51
Côtes-du-Nord, dept of 74
counter-revolution 37, 106, 154, 155, 157, 177, 192, 195–231
Courthézon (Vaucluse) 95, 177, 181
Coutances (Manches) 34
Crest (Drôme) 153, 171
Creuse, dept of 64, 103, 116, 128
Croy family 240

D'André 200, 207, 209
Danyel-Kervégan 256, 263, 265
Dartein 260
Dauphiné 44
Davout, Marshal 243, 244
Debruc de Montplaisir, Jacques 265
dechristianisation 21–52, 79–86
Delecloy 59–61, 63, 64, 66, 73, 74, 78
Delessert, Paul 79
départements réunis 104
desertion 92–120, 154, 156, 157, 167, 169, 171, 200, 210, 212–16
Deux-Sèvres, dept of 109
Diderot 55
Die (Drôme) 102
Dijon 86
Dinan (C.-du-N.) 74
Directory 47, 65, 152, 198

doctors 53–91, 115, 215, 243, 253
Donzère (Drôme) 207
Dordogne, dept of 109
Douai, Parlement of 108
Doyle, William 2
Draguignan (Var) 214
Drôme, dept of 104, 105, 115, 153, 160, 161, 162, 163, 184, 187, 196, 203, 206, 207, 216, 221, 222, 224, 225, 228
Drouin, Louis 256, 263, 264, 265
Dubois-Crancé 107
Dufou, F.-M.-B. 256, 263, 264
Dufrexou 256
Dunkirk (Nord) 95
Dupont de Nemours 55
Durand-Maillane 64
Dyle, dept of 72

Ecoles de santé 63
education 25, 29, 56, 63
elections 206–8, 238–9, 245, 250–1, 257
Embrun (Htes-Alpes) 75, 80
Emery 228
émigrés 167, 171, 201, 203, 205, 206, 210, 211, 229, 234, 238, 239
England 33, 201, 205, 249
Enragés 35
Epinal (Vosges) 101, 113
Erôme (Drôme) 115
Espivent-Villeboisnet 256
Estables (Lozère) 133–4, 150
Eygalières (B.-du-R.) 183
Eyragues (B.-du-R.) 175

Fabré, Baron 256
fanatisme 21–52, 106, 119
Faucault, François 256
Fautrel, Pierre François 102
federalism 106, 167, 182, 185
Finistère, dept of 106, 119
Flament, Chanoine 27
Flanders 22, 23
Florac (Lozère) 148
Foix (Ariège) 111
Fontanier, called Jambe de Bois 204, 216
food supply 8, 35, 37, 61
Forcalquier (Basses-Alpes) 203, 205, 214
forest laws 96, 108, 124, 141, 142
Forster, Robert 236
Fournels (Lozère) 135
Franche-Comté 22, 30, 41, 44, 47, 48, 50, 51
fraud 114-120
Fréguier, Boniface 159
Fréguier, *père* and *fils* 166
Fréron 80, 167, 170
Fructidor, coup of 18 152, 155, 198, 208, 209, 218, 229

Fulque, A.-N.-E. 227
Furet, François 3, 15

Galgon (Gironde) 102
Gard, dept of 154, 158, 168, 177, 186, 195, 196, 199, 201, 203, 204, 206, 215
Gardanne (B.-du-R.) 162
gendarmerie 94, 100, 101, 106, 107, 109, 111, 112, 113, 117, 141, 143, 165, 202, 215, 221, 228
Genton de Barsac 154
Germany 33, 235, 237, 241, 243
Germinal Insurrection 199
Gers, dept of 114
Gévaudan 41
Girod de l'Ain 66
Gironde, dept of 94, 98, 99, 108, 110, 113, 115, 118
Glacière Massacre 182
Godechot, Jacques 1
Gonesse (S.-et-O.) 22, 34, 39
Grasse 153, 193
Graveson (B.-du-R.) 158, 184–5, 186
Grégoire, Abbé 23, 37, 40, 43, 44, 45, 46, 47, 48
Grenoble 69, 215, 217
Guillet, Béatrix 263, 264, 265
Guillet-Labrosse, F.-L. 264
Guingamp (C.-du-N.) 74
Gutton, Jean-Pierre 205
Guyenne 123

Haudaudine, J.-M. 256
Haussonville family 240
Haute-Garonne, dept of 93, 96, 236
Haute-Loire, dept of 27, 101, 126, 127, 128, 135, 136, 137, 142, 143, 147, 153, 155, 196, 202, 203, 204, 209, 214, 223, 225, 226, 230
Hautes-Pyrénées, dept of 128
Hébertisme 35
Hennebont (Morbihan) 106
Hérault, dept of 44, 64, 107, 153, 182, 195, 196, 204
Hermaux (Lozère) 213
Hesdin (P.-de-C.) 97
Higonnet, Patrice 196, 220
Holland 241
Hood, James 186
hospitals 53–91, 115
Hufton, Olwen 3, 230
Hugo, Victor 198
Hyères (Var) 162

Idéologues 90
invalides 59
Isère, dept of 45, 196, 209, 216, 218, 220, 222, 223, 224, 225

Isnard 199
Italy 33, 95, 230–1, 235, 237, 241, 243

jacobins 38, 46, 57, 58, 80, 134, 152–94
Jalès, camps de 201, 204
Jaurès, Jean 2
Jerphanion 135
jews 37
Jones, Peter 8
Jouques (Vaucluse) 229
Joyeuse (Ardèche) 211
Juge of Valréas 164, 176, 188
juges de paix 108, 110, 136, 184, 207, 209, 214, 223, 224, 225, 226, 251
Jura, dept of 45, 127

Koblenz 201
Koch, Professor 256

Labrousse, Ernest 235
La Cavalerie (Aveyron) 129, 149
La Cresse (Aveyron) 148
Lacuée 64
Laënnec brothers 256
La Fère (Aisne) 72
La Folie (Hte-Loire) 101
Laguiole (Aveyron) 137
Laharpe 156
Lain (Yonne) 42
Lalleyriat (Ain) 219
Lamballe (C.-du-N.) 74
Lambaut, Antoine 98
Lambert, Abbé 30
Lambesc (B.-du-R.) 209
Lamothe-Picquet, Marquis de 155, 202, 211, 222
Landrecies (Nord) 108
Landsperg *père* 260
Langeac (Hte-Loire) 223, 224
Languedoc 51, 106, 123, 182, 191, 195, 197, 201, 212, 230
Lannion (C.-du-N.) 74
Laplanche 80
Largentière (Ardèche) 153
Larnage (Drôme) 115
Larochefoucauld-Liancourt, Duc de 55, 90
Laroquebrou (Cantal) 105
Laudun (Gard) 168, 202, 207
Laumond, J.-C.-J. 254
Lausanne 198, 200
Lavalanet (Ariège) 96
La Villedieu (Lozère) 146, 150
Law, John 67, 73
Le Bacon (Lozère) 219
Le Barroux (Vaucluse) 188
Le Bon, Joseph 80

Le Buis (Drôme)   187, 222
Lefebvre, Georges   15, 16, 121, 122
Legion of Honour   233, 242, 243
Le Havre   81
Le Mans   79
Lemarchand, Guy   222
Le Plagnal (Ardèche)   138
Le Puy (Hte-Loire)   34, 38, 81, 202, 204
Le Recoux (Lozère)   147, 148
Leroux, Julien   264
Le Roy Ladurie, Emmanuel   7, 17–18
Lesparre (Gironde)   98
Les Rotours (Orne)   40
Lestang, de   154, 155, 161
Letourneur, Étienne   252
Levier (Doubs)   45
Le Vigan (Gard)   195
Lewis, Gwynne   186
Libourne (Gironde)   81, 102
Limoges   72, 73, 83
Limousin   22
Lincoln, P.-J.   256
Locminé (Morbihan)   106
Lodève (Hérault)   41, 42, 43, 75
Loire, dept of   153, 155, 160, 162, 164, 167,
   183
Loire-Inf., dept of   234, 247, 248, 250, 253,
   255–6, 257, 261–6
Loiret, dept of   80
Lons-le-Saunier (Jura)   153
Lorraine   22
Loubaresse (Ardèche)   142
Loudun (Vienne)   81
Louis XVIII   213
Lozère, dept of   93, 126, 128, 130, 132, 133,
   134, 135, 138, 139, 141, 144, 145, 146,
   147, 148, 149, 153, 201, 202, 205, 211,
   219, 226, 230
Luc (Lozère)   138, 145
Luynes, Duc de   240
Luzarches (S.-et-O.)   116
Lyon   6, 27, 44, 45, 147, 153, 154, 158, 160,
   181, 196, 198, 199, 200, 201, 202, 205,
   207, 209, 220, 230
Lyons, Martyn   198

Mâconnais   48
Magnieu-Haute-Rive (Loire)   162
Malemort (Vaucluse)   162, 187, 189
Malta, Order of   129
Malzieu (Lozère)   226
Manosque (Basses-Alpes)   159
Marbeuf, de   50
Marion, Marcel   196, 213
Marmont, Marshal   240
Marseille   147, 152, 158, 159, 160, 162, 164,
   178, 197, 199, 201, 203, 207, 209, 211

Marvejols (Lozère)   76, 135, 219
masques armés   204
Masséna, Marshal   243, 244
Masson   241
Mathiez, Albert   2, 16, 24
Maubeuge (Nord)   97, 109
Mauric, J.-B.   187
Mayenne, dept of   94
Mazauric, Claude   3
Mazeyrat (Hte-Loire)   226
Mende (Lozère)   34, 38, 39, 103, 201
Mennecy (S.-et-O.)   22, 34
Méolans (Basses-Alpes)   215
Mercoire, *abbaye de*   140
Mercurin, Henri   185
Mercy-Argenteau   240
Meurthe, dept of   75
Mézières (Ardennes)   80
Millau (Aveyron)   130
Ministry of Finance   224, 238
Ministry of General Police   200, 207, 213
Ministry of the Interior   69, 72, 81, 84, 90,
   100, 117, 134, 135
Ministry of Justice   206, 207, 209, 210, 215,
   217, 224, 225, 227
Ministry of War   114, 213, 215, 241
Mirabeau, J.-A. de Riqueti de   129
Molinier, Alian   222
Mondragon (Vaucluse)   161, 165, 175, 181
Monnier de la Quarrée   203
Mons   76, 97
Mont-Blanc, dept of   50, 200
Montbrison (Loire)   160, 162, 166, 171
Montélimar (Drôme)   161, 171, 172, 181,
   206
Montesquieu   55
Montpellier (Hérault)   42, 48, 63, 74, 76, 79,
   81, 83, 85, 86, 88, 164, 182, 201
Montréal (Ardèche)   196
Moras (Drôme)   184
Morbihan, dept of   106, 110
Morlaix (Finistère)   77, 81
Mosneron-Dupin   256
Mouliets (Gironde)   108
Murat (Cantal)   101, 111
murder   100–110, 156, 158–68, 170–1, 175,
   178, 179–81, 190, 191, 197, 199, 206, 207,
   229, 230

Nancy   103
Nantes   247, 248–9, 255–6, 263, 264, 265, 266
Napoleon   37, 132, 210, 214, 219, 228, 231,
   233, 234, 235, 237, 240, 241, 242, 245,
   246, 251, 263
Narbonne, comte de   240
National Guard   161, 169, 172, 176, 186,
   188, 189, 191, 207, 209, 218

national lands   62, 75, 105, 140, 156, 176,
    204, 206, 211, 216, 219, 220, 224, 226,
    227, 229, 252, 256, 264
Nemours (S.-et-M.)   69, 83
Ney, Marshal   243, 244
Nièvre, dept of   113
Nîmes (Gard)   165, 182, 199
Nomexy (Vosges)   101
Nord, dept of   45, 94, 98, 99, 104, 108, 113,
    118, 236
Normandy   32, 39, 44, 47
Nuits-St-Georges (Côte-d'Or)   75
nursing sisters   79–86
Nyons (Drôme)   104, 211

octrois   70
Oraison (Basses-Alpes)   227
Orange (Vaucluse)   161, 166, 170, 208, 209,
    229
Orgères, bande d'   196
Orgon (B.-du-R.)   160, 165
Orne, dept of   27
Ouanne (Yonne)   49

Pamiers (Ariège)   112
Panisset of Chambéry   44, 45
Pâris, C.-S.   256
Paris   27, 32, 47, 56, 63, 64, 69, 70, 71, 77,
    78, 79, 80, 88, 90, 94, 147, 199, 200, 206,
    241
Parisot   241
Pascal *aîné*   189
Pascal, Lascalet   165
Pas-de-Calais, dept of   45, 97, 104, 109
Paulhac (Hte-Loire)   147
Payan, J.-F.   160, 182, 185
Pelouse (Lozère)   138
Périgord   47
Pernes (Vaucluse)   162
Pertuis (Vaucluse)   213
Picardy   44, 108
Pierrelatte (Drôme)   221, 222
Pignas (Hérault)   182
pilgrimages   51, 119
Piolenc (Vaucluse)   208
Poitiers   76
Poitou   47, 79
Poland   235
Polier   156
Polignac family   140
Pons   82
Pontarlier (Doubs)   42
Pont-St-Esprit (Gard)   158, 161, 165, 166,
    168, 175, 181
poor relief   53–91
Portalis, J.-E.-M.   241
Poujols (Hérault)   107

Poulain-Grandpré   64
Pourrières (Var)   159
Pradelles (Hte-Loire)   136
Prades-d'Aubrac (Aveyron)   149
Prairial Insurrection   60, 199
Précy, Comte de   200, 202
prefects   240–1, 242, 252, 257
protestants   37, 157, 195, 203, 206
Provence   34, 182, 183, 196, 197, 209, 212,
    217, 230
Puy-de-Dôme, dept of   70, 94, 101, 132
Puyloubier (B.-du-R.)   159
Puyricard (B.-du-R.)   197
Pyrenees   32, 44, 93, 117, 127

Quiberon   199

Raoulx, Pierre   185
Rébérend, Albert   243
Remiremont (Vosges)   110
Rémusat, de   240
Rennes   32, 84
rentes   67, 69–70
représentants en mission   17, 32, 80, 169, 170,
    199, 201
Revolutionary committees   35, 187, 188
Ribérac (Dordogne)   41
Richard-Pivredière   256
Richerenches (Vaucluse)   211
Robespierre   37, 52, 57
Rochechouart-Mortemart family   240
Rochefort, Comte de   136
Roederer, P.-L.   240
Romieu, Barthelemy   183
Rouen   34, 43, 48, 53, 116
Rouergue   41, 59
Rovère   185, 209
royalism   51, 106, 134, 152, 155, 157, 167,
    195–231
Roye (Somme)   97
Rozier *père*   256
Rudé, George   1, 2, 10, 14
Rural Code (1791)   130, 224, 225

Saillans (Drôme)   102
St-Brieuc (C.-du-N.)   74
Ste-Cécile (Vaucluse)   163, 179, 187, 214,
    219
St-Chamas (B.-du-R.)   159
St-Chély-d'Aubrac (Aveyron)   149
St-Christol, Baron de   154, 155, 203, 206,
    209, 210, 213, 222
St-Cyr-les-Colons (Yonne)   49
St-Etienne (Loire)   147, 160, 165, 166, 175
St-Etienne-de-Lugdarès (Ardèche)   138
St-Flour (Cantal)   98
St-Galmier (Loire)   164

St-Gaudens (Hte-Garonne) 96
St-Geniez (Aveyron) 149
St-Girons (Ariège) 111, 112, 117
St-Jean-la-Fouillouse (Lozère) 138
Saint Just 57
St-Laurent-en-Médoc (Gironde) 118
St-Marcellin (Isère) 224
Saint Martin 60
St-Maximin (Var) 159
St-Paul-Trois-Châteaux (Drôme) 154, 160, 161, 163, 182
St-Pons (Hérault) 63
St-Privat-d'Allier (Hte-Loire) 129
St-Quintin (Ariège) 101
St-Rémy (B.-du-R.) 175, 183
St-Restitut (Drôme) 163
Salembrier, Bande de 104
Salon (B.-du-R.) 159, 178, 187, 189
Santo Domingo 233, 249
Sarthe, dept of 27, 71, 107
Saumane (Vaucluse) 211
Saurel, François 189
Savoie, dept of 45
Schauenbourg, General 260
Sée, Henri 121
Ségala (Aveyron) 127
Ségur, Comte de 240
seigneurs 50, 129, 130, 131, 134, 139, 184, 192, 203, 204, 205, 212, 221, 226-8
Seillans (Var) 187
Seine, dept of 70
Seine-Inférieure, dept of 116, 236
Seine-et-Oise, dept of 113, 116
Senart, Philippe 195
Senkowska-Gluck, Monika 235
September Massacres 199
Sévérac (Aveyron) 129, 147
Shée, Henri 252
Sisteron (Basses-Alpes) 223
smuggling 96-7, 266
Soboul, Albert 2, 4, 14, 15, 121, 122, 124, 143, 210, 235
sociability 18, 25, 42, 170-4, 176-9, 181, 188-90, 191, 219
Société de Charité Maternelle 88
Société philanthropique 88
Solier, Abbé 195, 196, 199, 203, 204, 210, 211, 215, 230
Solliès (Var) 162, 163
Somme, dept of 59, 97, 115
sorcery 118-19
Soult, Marshal 244
Sourds-muets 88
Spain 94, 96, 211, 231, 241
Strasbourg 63, 85, 88, 247, 248, 253, 256, 260, 261, 264, 266
Suc (Ariège) 96

Sulniac (Morbihan) 110
Surville, Marquis de 155, 202, 211, 213
Suzette (Vaucluse) 229
Switzerland 33, 44, 199, 200, 201, 202, 205, 220
Szramkiewicz, Romuald 236

Talleyrand-Périgord 240
Tarascon (B.-du-R.) 158, 159, 160, 165, 167, 168, 175, 178, 179, 190, 199
Taulignan (Ariège) 105
taxes 38, 71, 210, 239
Taylor, George V. 234
Terror 37, 54, 62, 91, 131, 167
theft 98-111, 179, 197, 210
théophiles 37
Thermidoreans 36-7, 60, 131, 150, 168, 192
Tilly, Charles 212
Tiranges (Hte-Loire) 202
tithes 217
Titz, Gottlob 58
Tocqueville, Alexis de 212, 246
Toulon (Var) 95, 160, 164, 168, 170
Toulouse 34, 38, 136
Tourangeau, *veuve* 160, 171, 182
Tournai 86
Tourves (Var) 168
Tréguier (C.-du-N.) 74
Tulard, Jean 235, 237, 238, 239, 240, 243, 244, 261
Tulette (Drôme) 163
Tulle (Corrèze) 77, 109
Turckheim *père* 260
Turenne family 240

Uzès (Gard) 165

Vacqueyras (Vaucluse) 163
Valence (Drôme) 102, 214, 224, 228
Valgorge (Ardèche) 204
Valréas (Vaucluse) 164, 176, 188, 206, 211
Vannes (Morbihan) 107
Var, dept of 64, 153, 161, 168, 187, 189 196, 199, 209, 214
Vaucluse, dept of 158, 161, 162, 163, 164, 177, 187, 192, 196, 202, 203, 206, 207, 209, 211, 213, 214, 219, 228
Velay 32, 41, 127, 136
Vendée 22, 31, 198, 212
Vendémiaire Insurrection 200, 206
Ventenges (Hte-Loire) 143, 146
Versailles 93
Vicdessos (Ariège) 114
Vienne (Isère) 222
Vilaine 86

Villefort (Lozère)   230
Vinsobres (Drôme)   163
Vire (C.-du-N.)   69, 79
Visan (Vaucluse)   163
Vischer de Celles, Baron   252
Vivarais   45, 204, 209, 210, 222
Viviers (Ardèche)   202
Voltaire   55
Vosges, dept of   100, 103, 110, 113, 127
Vouneuil-sur-Vienne   40, 41
Vovelle, Michel   26, 34

wet-nurses   69, 76
Whitcomb, E. A.   237

White Terror   36, 48, 51, 152, 199, 206, 212,
   215, 218
Wickham, William   154, 200
Willot, General   203, 209
women   23–4, 28, 32, 34–7, 39–42, 45, 46,
   48, 174, 178, 180

Yonne, dept of   113, 236
Young, Arthur   264
youth groups   163, 169–73, 189, 191, 219
Yssingeaux (Hte-Loire)   213

Zeldin, Theodore   2
Zorn de Bulach   260